KV-611-823

Trafficking Cocaine

Colombian Drug Entrepreneurs
in the Netherlands

by

Damián Zaitch

KLUWER LAW INTERNATIONAL
THE HAGUE / LONDON / NEW YORK

A C.I.P. Catalogue record for this book is available from the Library of Congress.

ISBN 90-411-1882-9
ISBN 90-411-1884-5

Published by Kluwer Law International,
P.O. Box 85889, 2508 CN The Hague, The Netherlands.

Sold and distributed in North, Central and South America
by Kluwer Law International,
101 Philip Drive, Norwell, MA 02061, U.S.A.
kluwerlaw@wkap.com

In all other countries, sold and distributed
by Kluwer Law International, Distribution Centre,
P.O. Box 322, 3300 AH Dordrecht, The Netherlands.

UNIVERSITIES AT MEDWAY
21 FEB 2014
DRILL HALL LIBRARY

Printed on acid-free paper

1-0503-250 ts
First published in 2002

All Rights Reserved
© 2002 Kluwer Law International
Kluwer Law International incorporates
the imprint of Martinus Nijhoff Publishers.

No part of this work may be reproduced, stored in a retrieval system, or transmitted
in any form or by any means, electronic, mechanical, photocopying, microfilming, recording
or otherwise, without written permission from the Publisher, with the exception
of any material supplied specifically for the purpose of being entered
and executed on a computer system, for exclusive use by the purchaser of the work.

Printed in the Netherlands.

Trafficking Cocaine

WITHDRAWN
FROM
UNIVERSITIES
AT
MEDWAY
LIBRARY

DRILL HALL LIBRARY
MEDWAY

HC55
1300
4569

STUDIES OF ORGANIZED CRIME

Volume 1

Series Editors:

Alan A. Block, *Crime, Law & Justice Program, Department of Sociology,*
   The Pennsylvania State University
Frank Bovenkerk, *University of Utrecht, Willem Pompe Institute, The Netherlands*

Editorial Board:

Maria Los, *University of Ottawa, Canada*
Letizia Paoli, *Max Planck Institut, Freiburg, Germany*
Francisco Thoumi, *Senior Visiting Scholar at the Latin American and Carribean Center,*
   Florida International University, U.S.A.
Xiabo Lu, *Colombia University, NY, U.S.A.*

Para Eva, Oscar,
Martín y Gudrun

CONTENTS

LIST OF TABLES AND FIGURES

Tables

Figures

ACKNOWLEDGEMENTS

I am indebted to many people who helped me in this enterprise in all possible ways. First and foremost, I would like to thank Frank Bovenkerk, who enthusiastically supported me through the whole research process. He convinced me to undergo the ethnographic experience and always had confidence in me, improving my skills and boosting my self-confidence. He helped me in practical matters, taught me some 'tricks' and carefully read all my texts. More importantly, he encouraged my intellectual freedom and critical spirit.

The Amsterdam School for Social Science Research offered the ideal environment to carry out this research. I would like to thank all participants of the Anthropologists' Club for sharing their 'field' experiences with me. I express my gratitude also to the members of the VOC Club on classical readings. The managerial staff of the School was always ready to help me: my thanks to Anneke, Annelies, Hans, José, Miriam and Teun.

Further, I profited from the careful comments and critical remarks made by several people along the writing process. I am grateful to Alan Block, Anton Blok, Tim Boekhout van Solinge, Peter Boomgaard, Matthijs van den Bos, Remco Ensel, Frank van Gemert, Roy Gigengack Johan Heilbron, Ferdinand de Jong, Marc van der Meer, Mattijs van de Port, Marion van San, Kees Schuyt, Dina Siegel, Margaret Sleeboom, Francisco Thoumi, Oskar Verkaaik and Yücel Yeşilgöz for their notes, observations and intellectual companionship. I especially want to thank Reinhilde König and René van Swaaningen for their friendship and their essential support during my PhD defence.

In the Netherlands, many people close to the topic encouraged me greatly and generously helped me to find my way during fieldwork. My thanks go especially to Janine Janssen, Dirk Korf, Liduine Zumpolle and Martin Jelsma. I am deeply grateful to 'Padre Theo' from Casa Migrante, whose militancy for the Latino community in Amsterdam is an example. He helped me in several ways, but more importantly, he encouraged me to break the boundaries between scholar aspirations and social action. Furthermore, I thank Toos, Jesús and Anita for their support: they made my involvement in Casa Migrante an enjoyable experience. As I also volunteered in the Colombia Komitee Nederland, I wish to express my gratitude to Ans, Joaquín, Pilar and Rommel.

This research could not have been possible without the help of many Colombians and their families who told me their stories and shared with me many public secrets. For those who became good friends in the Netherlands (they know who they are), I express my commitment to our friendship. I will never forget the amount of hospitality and generosity I experienced during my visits to Colombia. Friends and colleagues offered me accommodation, food, protection, guidance and advice. They eagerly told me most of what I know about their country, opened the doors of their institutions and organised all sorts of things for me. Moreover, they repeatedly invited me to share with them, formally or informally, my own work. My special gratitude goes to Maribel Lagos and her family from Cali, and to Germán Silva from Bogotá:

they were my main pillars in both cities. Furthermore, I wish to heartily thank Germán Burgos, Jaime Escobar, Ana María Perez Gómez and her family, Marcela Márquez and the people from *Enlace*, Alexander Montoya, Angela Narváez, Miguel Rujana, Alonso Salazar, Jaime Valencia and his family, Gildardo Vanegas, Alejando Vargas, and the families Reyes and Rodríguez for their friendship and support.

From other places in Europe, many people influenced me enormously. Teachers, friends and colleagues, especially in Spain and England, read and corrected my texts, invited me to conferences and gave me their expertise and friendship. In this regard, I am indebted to Xavier Arana, Francesc Barata, Roberto Bergalli, Phil Carney, Valerie Jones, Pierre Kopp, John Lea, Iñaki Rivera, Oriol Romaní, Amadeu Recasens, Vincenzo Ruggiero, Ramiro Sagarduy and Jock Young.

I would like to express my gratitude to Henk van de Bunt, who gave me his crucial support during the final stage of writing the manuscript. More recently, colleagues and students of the departments of Criminology at the Erasmus University Rotterdam and the Vrije Universiteit Amsterdam gave me the necessary feed-back to keep researching the topic. Some people preciously helped me in correcting my *Spanglish* and putting words into image: my thanks to Joanna Swabe, Martín Zaitch, Ana Audivert and Nikolai Wolff. For her efficient and open-harted editorial work, I am grateful to Wieneke Matthijsse of the Willem Pompe Institute. Gudrun has supported me stoically throughout the heaviest period of writing. Her love gave me serenity and strength. Finally, I owe my parents my passion for knowledge and my striving for free thought.

Damián Zaitch

*Lecturer and Researcher in the Department
of Criminal Law and Criminology at the
Erasmus University Rotterdam, The Netherlands*

CHAPTER I

INTRODUCTION

"Although you mustn't pretend to be 'one of them', it is equally important that you don't stick out like a sore thumb in the criminal's natural environment"

Ned Polsky, *Hustlers, Beats, and Others.*

Traqueto is an interesting notion difficult to translate. For the past two decades, it has been the most familiar name used by Colombians to refer to a particular sort of drug entrepreneurs. Next to the *jíbaro* (street dealer), the *mula* (air smuggler) or the *patrón* (boss), Colombians have reserved that onomatopoeic name for some self-made, ambitious Colombian migrant-traffickers. Their sudden emergence in the Colombian society of the early 1970s is described by Arango (1988) with some romanticism:

> "Since the early beginnings of cocaine export to the American market, an individual emerged who was to play a key role in drug trafficking: the *traqueto*. In need of having some representative in the United States, the first Colombian narco-traffickers sent people to move from place to place, in search of new markets. Maybe in this way the name derives from the verb *traquetear,* 'to move' or 'to shake up' in one of its meanings.[1] (...) The *traqueto* is a courageous, imaginative and skilful individual who in order to leave a difficult economic situation, fearlessly takes the risk to travel to the United States with the responsibility of organising and controlling the mechanisms to receive the drug, to stash it in a safe place (*encaletarla*), to sell it to the wholesale distributors and to cash the money. In other words, he is a marketing and distribution head for the drug entrepreneur based in Colombia. From there, his strategic role in the chain between production and consumption. (...) After some time in the United States, the *traqueto* returns to Medellín with his own liquid capital and new manners and consumerist practices..." (Arango 1988: 24-25, my translation).

Many of these *traquetos* later became large cocaine exporters in Colombia; others were killed, went to prison or simply lost their fortunes. Still others managed to turn into legitimate entrepreneurs. Some of them truly represented, and still do, strong social models amongst many young Colombians across various social classes and countries. As it is often the case with other illegal entrepreneurs or social bandits, people tend to project on them the most contradicting values, feelings and expectations one can imagine. They are national heroes against American laws and truly emissaries of the American Dream; successful immigrants and ill-reputed parasites, arrogant and generous, sexist men and gentle, violent and funny, loyal with

---

1 Salazar et al. (1992: 46) suggest a second possible origin as *traquetear* also means 'to rattle' or 'to bang', in clear reference to the noise of their automatic weapons (DZ).

bosses and ready to betray everyone, good organisers and better improvisers, dangerous criminals and social benefactors, fair employers and, of course, faithful Catholics.

Nowadays, the *traqueto* label has gone beyond the sole notion of 'envoy' to be extended to any (male) Colombian cocaine exporter, importer and distributor operating in Colombia and overseas, Europe included. While the term *traquetos* used by themselves and their subordinates usually has a positive connotation, it can be negatively loaded if applied by, for example, other Colombian immigrants not involved in the business.

This book is about Colombian *traquetos* in the Netherlands and the people working for them. More specifically, it raises questions about their social, labour and organisational relations amongst themselves, with Colombia and with other social groups. It explores their legal and illegal arrangements, their relationship with other Colombian immigrants and some of their cultural repertoires.

1.1 THE PROBLEM AND THE ARGUMENT

Criminal organisations, secret drug networks, Latin American *mafia* and, of course, Colombian cocaine 'cartels'. These are the names and concepts widely used to describe both the Colombian cocaine industry and its many participants, from entrepreneurs to employees. The use of these notions is not fortuitous, but the direct result of considering Colombian cocaine exporters as members of highly structured groups, as concealed from mainstream society, as powerful political brokers or as running monopolist enterprises. These assumptions are particularly traceable in most accounts on the renowned cocaine organisations of Medellín and Cali.

The idea of a cartel, even if metaphorically invoked, suggests that drug producers and exporters are organised in economic-bureaucratic structures that secretly conspire to control prices and output in a monopolist fashion. The cartel model further emphasises a highly structured co-ordination, central operational control, strict labour division and sophisticated organisational skills. Almost uncontested during the 1980s and the 1990s, the notion of cartel has shown a remarkable resistance as new areas or groups have taken over the cocaine business in Colombia. For example, it has been repeatedly argued that the dismantling of the Cali cartel has only meant the rise of the ubiquitous Northern Cauca Valley cartel. Others prefer to talk about the emergence of new '*cartelitos*' (small cartels).

However, as the notion of *traqueto* suggests, cocaine cartels seem to go beyond regional or national borders to form transnational criminal organisations (Williams 1995). In fact, from their very origins they have worked internationally, integrating complex operations through various countries following the routes of international trade. First in the US and later in Europe, Colombian cocaine organisations have tried to secure some of the huge profits around cocaine import and wholesale distribution in consumer markets. Of course, and for reasons that I will explain in this book, they have been more successful in particular regions or markets than in others.

In the Netherlands, most observers, enforcement agencies and official reports have flirted with this idea of transnational Colombian cartels (Van Duyne et al 1990; Fijnaut et al. 1996; Prisma Team 2000). They are portrayed as hierarchically organised in secret, extremely violent 'cells' or overseas 'branches', which would 'belong' to a particular group in Colombia.

A strong 'ethnic' component is finally added to the picture: these criminal organisations are presumed to follow the routes of migration and heavily rely on overseas expatriate communities to operate (Bovenkerk 2001). Colombian cartels would predominantly use relatives, friends and vulnerable immigrants abroad as partners or employees, while host countries regard cocaine trade as an ethnic phenomenon and entire Colombian communities are faced with a spoiled reputation.

A first and more general aim of this study is to examine the nature of Colombian cocaine enterprises. To what extent are the different conceptual frameworks and methods used to approach Colombian drug traffickers adequate in revealing their social practices and relations? Are they organised along ethnic or kinship lines? Do they run their businesses as legal entrepreneurs? What sort of interdependencies do they establish amongst themselves and with larger social structures? In this way, the present book seeks to contribute to current discussions on contemporary forms of organised crime undertaken by anthropologists, economists and criminologists.

My itinerary starts in Colombia, a country often depicted as controlled by all-powerful drug organisations whose activities are said to be beneficial to many people, from peasants to bankers. In order to understand *traqueto*'s social practices, I need to begin by asking whether that has indeed been the case.

Chapter II will trace the historical origins of the cocaine business in Colombia and will examine the competitive advantages of that country for the development of a leading position. The economic dimension of the business will be briefly discussed, in order to present export volumes, prices and transaction costs. Since most Colombian involvement in the Netherlands is directly linked to business developments at source, I will further show how the groups producing and exporting cocaine are organised. By examining their social origins, regional differences and internal relationships, I will argue that those groups are smaller and more flexible and independent than the notion of cartel suggests. Finally, I will focus on their collusion with broader social and political structures, describing the sources and limits for social legitimation. I will compare Colombian cocaine organisations with Italian or Italo-American *mafia*-style groups and argue that they present major social and political differences.

Colombia, which produces and exports 75% of all cocaine consumed worldwide, has readily been identified as the source (and scope) of all the problems around the international cocaine trade. In this way, the role of 'receiving' regions such as the US or Europe has often been either played down or reduced to develop defensive strategies from external threats.[2] However, particular areas in consumer countries

---

2   The recent *Plan Colombia* is just another example of such a pure defensive strategy on supply sources. As stated by W. Ledwith, Chief of International Operations of the DEA: "We in DEA believe that the international trafficking organisations based in Colombia who smuggle their illegal drugs into our country pose a formidable challenge to the national security of the United States." (DEA Congressional Testimony before the Senate, 25-2-2000).

seem to function as main players in the global cocaine market chain. After Spain, the Netherlands has played, for example, the main role in the import and wholesale distribution of South American cocaine into Europe for the last decade.

A further aim of the present book is then to examine such a role, again to make sense of the *traqueto*'s activities in Europe. What does the European cocaine market look like in terms of demand and supply, and what is the Netherlands specific position in it? And more importantly, how do Colombian drug traffickers perceive such a position?

Chapter III will first argue that when cocaine was legal and produced in Europe (1860-1930), the Netherlands played a prominent role as coca importer and cocaine producer. In order to understand such a role today, I will then present some general indicators regarding current cocaine demand in Europe: prevalence trends, estimated volumes consumed, prices and purities. In the same fashion, the dynamics of European cocaine supply will be tackled. I will briefly explain what sort of groups are engaged in cocaine import and distribution within the European space. An attempt will be made to 'read' available cocaine seizure data. Further to this, I will trace the major cocaine lines and provide a cartography of cocaine trafficking into Europe. Why is the Netherlands so attractive for cocaine exporters and importers? The final section of chapter III will present the *traqueto's* points of views and perceptions of the Dutch business environment. They will discuss about the economic activity, logistic infrastructure, potential contacts and partners, and enforcement risks.

Colombian drug organisations have also been defined as transnational crime syndicates that use overseas immigrant networks to organise their business. By providing loyalty, contacts and infrastructure in export-import operations, Colombian immigrants in the US or Europe also secure some of the lion's share of profits made at import, wholesale and retail levels. In this way, whether they come from one end or the other, the *traquetos* could be seen as connecting cocaine exporters with distant immigrant diasporas.

However, and in order to explore such assumptions, one should first examine the Colombian immigrant groups in question: it might well be the case that they are not in a position to get involved with or help cocaine exporters. So the question arises: who are these Colombian immigrants living in the Netherlands? Although they are the largest and increasingly growing Latin American group, Colombians in the Netherlands remain an invisible and under-researched community.

Chapter IV will thus provide data on their migrant patterns, their demographic and social profiles, and their economic modes of incorporation. It will also describe the major obstacles they perceive or experience, and how they set the limits for ethnic solidarity and organisation. I will argue that the lack of (legal) Colombian entrepreneurs and enterprises on the one hand, and the weak patterns of ethnic solidarity on the other, inhibit defining this group as a middlemen minority or an ethnic enclave.

Even if the immigrant group lacks the social and economic characteristics to fully participate in the illegal business, some involvement still seems to be the case. Indeed, I found many *traquetos* and a heterogeneous group of migrants engaged in various levels of the local cocaine business. Therefore, a central question of this book tackles this involvement: what has been the specific role of Colombian nationals in transport, import, wholesale distribution and retail selling of cocaine in/into the Netherlands during the past 10 years? What sort of (legal and illegal) arrangements do *traquetos* make to conduct their operations? What are their social backgrounds and their chances of success and failure?

While chapter V presents my findings regarding their participation in cocaine smuggling and import, chapter VI will focus on wholesale distribution and retail selling. In each case, I will show their social backgrounds and their legal and illegal business arrangements, identifying the conditions that restrict or enlarge their opportunities as cocaine entrepreneurs and employees. I shall discuss their chances for success and failure, their relationship with local Colombian immigrants and their overall place in the Dutch cocaine market.

Amongst Colombian immigrants, two quantitative important groups have also been either criminalised or socially censured: prostitutes and illegal immigrants. Both vulnerable groups have often been easily associated with the cocaine business, at least as potential participants. The areas with *Latino* prostitution are said to integrate the whole spectrum: Colombian cocaine dealers, prostitutes, pimps and illegal immigrants. However, how the *traquetos* actually relate with them?

Chapter VII will thus describe the main characteristics of Colombian prostitutes and illegal immigrants. It will further analyse the relation of these specific groups in the cocaine business, examining their chances of getting involved in it, and their reasons for distancing themselves from cocaine dealers.

Colombian cocaine enterprises active in the Netherlands have also been portrayed as branches, cells or agents of Colombian cartels, as closed family businesses, or as flexible though homogeneous criminal networks. Yet, what is wrong with these approaches? If, as I will argue, a more dynamic picture of cocaine enterprises and *traqueto* performances can be given by studying their internal economic relations through ethnographic research, the obvious question is just what are the labour and business relations that Colombian *traquetos* establish amongst themselves?

Chapter VIII will be devoted to an analysis of these relations. A heterogeneous number of business and labour modalities will be identified, mainly providing critical evidence against the aforementioned models. I will argue that Colombian cocaine enterprises found in Europe resemble post-Fordist, 'just-in-time' enterprises. While arrangements are even more flexible due to the illegal nature of the business, flexibility is also essential for the interaction between legal and illegal entrepreneurs and enterprises.

Finally, when referring to the internal and external dynamics of cocaine trafficking groups, most observers have also pointed out the key role of violence, secrecy and trust for the shaping of social and business relations. Colombian *traquetos* are presented as being extremely violent, living in a secret world, and only relying on trusted equals. However, these resources have often been taken for granted. What is therefore the role of violence, secrecy and trust for Colombian *traquetos*? How are these resources used or manipulated?

Chapter IX will demonstrate how these social devices are both essential tools and serious obstacles in the daily performances of Colombian cocaine entrepreneurs in the

Netherlands. I will argue that *traquetos* have tried to administrate those resources by using them, avoiding them or acting them out. Chapter X will finally try to extract the main empirical and theoretical conclusions of this book.

This study on Colombian drug entrepreneurs – and their employees – in the Netherlands does not primarily aim to find enforcement recipes and solutions, which would imply a definition problem from the sole perspective of control agencies. I regard drug enforcement – and certainly the strategies followed against cocaine trafficking and traffickers for the last 20 years – as fertile ground for this phenomenon to flourish. Instead, the above questions try to address problems as defined by the various groups and individuals encountered prior to and during the research.

Drug enforcers, especially some Dutch and German police officials, claimed that this involvement was a never ending puzzle and a source of continuous headaches. Some admitted their difficulties in getting information about this group: informants are scarce, co-operation with Colombia is problematic, and occasional Colombian experts amongst police officers are often not keen to share sensitive data with their colleagues. Although most of their efforts are directed to simply finding out who is who in particular cocaine operations, some acknowledged the need for research beyond mere *misdaadanalyse* (crime analysis).

Also criminologists and drug experts pointed out that the issue of overseas participation of Colombians in the cocaine business was a knowledge gap and deserved attention:

> "Finally, there is no information about the involvement of Colombians in marketing cocaine in Europe, although it is accepted that this involvement is not likely to be large." (Thoumi 1995: 183).

Most Colombian immigrants I spoke with, not only justified the concern but also helped actively in my enquires. They usually claimed, especially the men, to be unfairly stigmatised by everybody – from their own relatives in Colombia and the Dutch authorities, to local shopkeepers and the media – as potential *traquetos*. This research, some people hoped, would establish the limits between *sanos* (healthy) and *untados* (involved), and would help to put things in place. Some informants in Colombia experienced the problem of overseas *traquetos* as a costly burden for Colombia. For example, Ernesto from Cali claimed:

> "Everybody here knows somebody who is working abroad [in the drug business]. It used to be open but now even their own families often don't know. They suspect, but they shut up because they will get a new car, a *finca* and many expensive gifts. They only worry when they are killed or imprisoned. See, their values have touched everybody. Even honest people now dress and think like *traquetos*. They bring *platica* [money], but it's poisoned money."

Others welcomed the research as a means to denounce and publicise their personal dramas. This was the case, for example, of imprisoned couriers and their families in Colombia. In sum, all sort of voices seemed to suggest the need for deeper research.

1.2 RESEARCH METHODS AND FIELDWORK ACTIVITIES

In 1994, a police scandal involving uncontrolled 'controlled deliveries' of cocaine from South America by corrupt officials shook the Dutch political scene (Middelburg and Van Es 1994). The case reached the newspapers and opened a broad debate on the nature of organised crime in the Netherlands and the police methods employed to control it. Both issues were extensively tackled by the parliamentary *Van Traa* commission, which produced a report (Fijnaut et al. 1996) that did not end the debate or the political turmoil created by the matter.[3] Two different but complementary research agendas opened in the years to follow. The first one, mainly based on the knowledge accumulated by the criminal justice agencies, aimed to assess the nature of particular illegal markets and activities – whether in the realm of white-collar, corporate or organised crime – in order to find more effective criminal or administrative policies.[4]

A second line of research developed from the question of the local involvement of specific ethnic or national groups in serious, organised crime. The issue had been posed before in terms of 'ethnic minorities and crime' (for example, Bovenkerk 1992, 1995c; de Haan and Bovenkerk 1993). However, the *Van Traa* report (Fijnaut et al. 1996) went a step further by systematically focusing on many groups and illegal activities, by breaking the taboos around this delicate subject and opening a debate on the extent, nature, impact and causes of what has been broadly known in America as 'ethnic organised crime'.

This research project was born out of this second impulse. Understandably, local criminal justice agencies and crime analysts know much more about mainstream groups, illegal markets, financial circuits or law enforcement strategies and performances, than they do about immigrant and ethnic minority groups, far away realities, or foreign drug dealers. Limited knowledge has also been complemented by all sorts of distorted images and mythologies fuelled by media entertainment and enforcement agendas. Police dossiers or judicial records have certainly proved insufficient to understand the social context, the cultural meanings and the economic constraints and opportunities of the people and groups to be studied. In order to grasp the social and economic relations at stake, and the ambivalence of practices and discourses around their illegal activities, this research agenda implies a commitment to qualitative field research as advocated by various traditions in anthropology and the sociology of deviance.

---

3   See for the academic debate Bovenkerk (ed.) (1996) and Franke et al. (eds) (1996). For a condensed English version of that report, see: Fijnaut et al. (1998) *Organised Crime in the Netherlands*. Den Haag: Kluwer Law International.

4   While these studies cover a broad scope and often depart from different theoretical frameworks, they all tend to share similar methodological strategies and to collect data from sources and individuals framed within respectful institutions. See on criminal organisations and enforcement strategies, Klerks (1996); Kleemans et al. (1998); Kleemans and Kruissink (1999); on criminal entrepreneurs and their enterprises, Van Duyne (1995); on white-collar and corporate crime, de Doelder and Hoogenboom (eds) (1997); Huisman and Niemeijer (1998); on money laundering and financial investigation, Hoogenboom et al. (1995); Nelen and Sabee (1998).

This study is mainly based on various sorts of qualitative data gathered in the Netherlands and Colombia from 1996 to 1999. Core fieldwork activities during that period included two sorts of personal interaction with Colombians who were directly, indirectly and uninvolved in the cocaine business in the Netherlands.

Firstly, I engaged in participant observation[5] within and around several *Latino* settings and circuits in the Netherlands: salsa bars, Latin American restaurants, migrant organisations, prostitution areas, churches, social and cultural events, telephone cells and private parties. In these settings – essentially restricted to the cities of Amsterdam, The Hague and Rotterdam – I met and established long term personal relationships with community leaders and Colombian immigrants both involved and uninvolved in the cocaine business. Building on trust and confidentiality, I managed to develop a personal network of more than 190 individuals who became key informants, intermediary contacts, acquaintances or friends during the research process.[6] While I gathered some biographical data from several people – concerning their social and economic background, their families, their past experiences, their criminal careers and so on – I did not aim to re-construct and present particular *life stories* or biographies: most people talked about recent or present events, and in many cases about others.[7] Instead, I concentrated on their specific views and practices regarding the cocaine business, and the particular social relations they establish as illegal entrepreneurs and employees.

I tried to 'move around' through various settings, talking with as much and different people as I could. In this sense, I did not focus on any particular family, neighbourhood, corner, gender or type of dealer, but I tried to cover the whole spectrum of Colombians involved in the cocaine business in the Netherlands. However, for reasons that I will later explain, I placed particular interest on active, free traffickers and their surrounding helpers.

Secondly, and concomitant with the long-term interaction with Colombian immigrants, I conducted open interviews or held informal talks – from serial, in-depth interviews to once-off, brief encounters – with several key informants. Some of these

---

5   For further detail about my roles as participant, observer or interviewer, see section 1.2.3.

6   See in the Appendix for an overview of all informants formally and informally interviewed in the Netherlands and Colombia.

7   *Life stories* of drug dealers or *mafiosi* are a scarce, useful source of knowledge about their illegal activities and relations. However, while they are maybe the most entertaining sources, they often suffer from serious biases. Ordinary people, events and relations are often forgotten or neglected. Active dealers and main bosses are reluctant to tell their whole stories. Secondary characters, always after retirement, conviction or collaboration with justice, tend to present themselves as they want to be portrayed (Bovenkerk 1995b: 33), usually as central and knowledgeable figures. Moreover, researchers and journalists are ready to accept or even push forward their sensational versions: important gangsters as interviewees guarantee professional prestige and commercial success. Finally, it is doubtful that one or two informants can reveal the complex and contradicting nature of drug or mafia organisations See for example Mermelstein (1990); Arlacchi (1993, 1994), Haenen and Buddingh' (1994); Haenen (1999) and Middelburg (1992, 2000). In my opinion, techniques incorporating direct observation and different degrees of interviewing with less pretentious figures – which imply more fieldwork commitments, time, critical distance and a willingness to protect informants – can reveal more complex and contradicting aspects of organised crime.

informants were approached through my participation or contacts in *Latino* settings: Latin Americans detained in the Netherlands for drug trafficking and Colombians involved in the illegal business with whom I did not develop any personal relation. Other key informants interviewed were contacted separately: police and liaison officers, drug experts in Europe and Colombia, human right activists, cocaine related lawyers, judicial interpreters, specialised journalists and diplomatic authorities.

The various settings visited, events observed, people encountered and interviewed during fieldwork in the Netherlands can hardly be quantified. Moreover, every interaction varied a great deal in terms of intensity, and despite my efforts to plan activities, control situations and cultivate relations, I was often guided by common sense, chance, luck and obvious fieldwork restrictions.[8] With some informants, I either lived for a while or even went on holidays with. With others, I only talked for 5 minutes, and I could hardly hear what they said. Some informants disappeared or reappeared unexpectedly. To some places, I came back repeatedly. Bars and restaurants opened and closed down during my fieldwork and I had to keep with rapid changes. In a way, my fieldwork in the Netherlands was so fluid and amorphous as it was my object of study.

However, roughly considered, I frequented 2 Spanish speaking churches in Amsterdam and Rotterdam, visited people in 4 Dutch prisons (Haarlem, Over-Amstel, Esserheem and Breda) and hung around in the *Latino* prostitution areas including 2 hotels in Rotterdam, 3 streets in The Hague (Poeldijksestraat, Doubletstraat and Geleenstraat) and 4 areas in Amsterdam (Oudezijds Achterburgwal, Spui, Ruysdaelkade and Sloterdijk). I also frequented 4 budget telephone centres used by drug entrepreneurs (legal and illegal, 3 in Amsterdam and 1 in The Hague), visited 5 formal Colombian restaurants and 3 informal ones. Regular visits were paid to some 15 Colombian related salsa discotheques, 10 bars and coffee-shops, around 30 private and public Colombian parties, more than 15 Colombian birthday parties, and several dozen of Colombian events including concerts, dinners, demonstrations, lectures and bingo sessions. I visited the port of Rotterdam, attended 6 important hearings in Dutch courtrooms and accompanied Colombians to the Chamber of Commerce of Rotterdam. Finally, on three occasions, I managed to visit active *traquetos* in their own apartments.

All observations, experiences and interviews were immediately recorded in the form of fieldwork notes. The resulting material constitutes the empirical base for section 3.2 (chapter III) and chapters IV to IX.

In addition, I also gathered and analysed journalistic accounts of cocaine related cases (1989-1999, mainly from Dutch and Spanish newspapers, specialised magazines, documentaries and internet databanks). Next to the relevant literature on organised crime, cocaine markets and immigrant economies, I collected many Dutch and European reports that specifically focused on cocaine trafficking (and consumption) in Europe. This secondary data, although scattered throughout the whole book, form the basis for section 3.1 (chapter III) on the European cocaine market.

---

8   For these limitations, see section 1.2.4.

Some statistics on Colombian immigrants in the Netherlands were put together from city councils, migrant organisations and statistical offices. These numbers and estimations are presented in chapter IV.

Further to this, I made two fieldwork visits to Colombia in 1996 and 1997, where I stayed for a total period of five months mainly in Bogotá and Cali. With the major logistic support from the Universidad Externado de Colombia (Bogotá), Universidad Libre (Bogotá) and Universidad del Valle (Cali) I conducted dozens of interviews with drug experts, journalists, criminal lawyers of large cocaine exporters, a Dutch police liaison-officer, relatives of Colombian immigrants in the Netherlands, one MP, local community leaders, human rights activists, and some friends, relatives or ex-employees of small cocaine exporters. Again, interaction ranged from planned interviews and visits to casual encounters. In contrast with fieldwork activities in the Netherlands, and especially due to time and security restrictions, I kept a very low profile in Colombia, avoiding for example direct open interaction as social researcher with cocaine exporters. However, either as a simple tourist or as a friend's friend, in few occasions I was by chance confronted with drug exporters: in buses, restaurants, discotheques and even at their own birthday parties. While references to their illegal activities were often marginal or absent, I nevertheless learned a lot by observing. I also visited some of the key settings where cocaine exporters and their employees live, come from, socialise, have fun, kill each other, invest, study or use for their export operations. They included slums, upper-class neighbourhoods and *fincas* (country houses) around Bogotá, Cali, Medellín and Pereira; the harbours of Barranquilla, Santa Marta and Buenaventura; salsa discotheques around Cali; elite universities; *ollas* (drug dealing spots); prisons and tourist resources. In most of these places, I was guided or accompanied by 'insiders': researchers, community leaders, lawyers, local dwellers or friends. It was, however, both too dangerous and too far removed from my main topic to visit rural areas devoted to coca cultivation. Again, all interviews, visits and observations were recorded daily in fieldwork notebooks. Archives and reports from several Colombian institutions were also examined or made available.[9] Finally, in Colombia I collected most of the bibliographic, archival and journalistic material used in chapter II.

Although I eventually interviewed or informally talked with Colombian, Dutch, Spanish and German police officers, attended public hearings in Dutch courts and collected documents and reports produced by drug enforcement agencies, I neither tried to get access to closed police dossiers or judicial records, nor to use any institutional channel (for example prison authorities) to contact my informants. From the very beginning, some reasons prompted me to avoid using police and judicial sources.

Firstly, I assumed that these sources would be selective. Looking only in prisons and Court rooms would have implied restricting my study to 'failed' participants,

---

9   These institutions are: CISALVA and CIDSE (Universidad del Valle), ILSA (Instituto Latino-americano de Servicios Sociales Alternativos), DNE (Dirección Nacional de Estupefacientes), Dutch Embassy, Enlace Project (Ministry of Communications), Ministry of Justice, Foro Nacional por Colombia (Cali) and the Colombian Parliament (Foreign Affaires Comission).

usually vulnerable drug couriers and risk-taking importers and distributors, leaving aside successful or active entrepreneurs and employees as well as peripheral actors not targeted by police priorities and agendas.

A second problem related to the amount and the nature of the information officially available: data on Colombian *traquetos* from Dutch authorities was very scarce, highly secretive, or had already been made public after the *IRT affaire* and the *Van Traa* report (Fijnaut et al. 1996). Moreover, judicial and police files mainly concern names and operational details of the cases in question, but they usually have very little to tell about the backgrounds, expectations and careers of the people involved. Statements are often manipulated or cut to fit accusation and defence strategies. For example, earlier successful involvements in illegal activities or accounts about Colombia are hard to find in these criminal records. Grey areas, non-criminal aspects of drug dealer's lives and behaviours, and social relations with legitimate actors and institutions are neglected in this type of source. Full confessions are rare, Colombian *pentiti* in the Netherlands are absent, and convicted non-Colombian collaborators tend to hide or romanticise their ties with Colombian traffickers.[10]

Thirdly and most importantly, there was a problem of incompatibility. Since I decided to talk with drug dealers while participating and observing in their social environment, a simultaneous systematic contact with the criminal justice system would have been dangerous, unethical and inefficient (Bovenkerk 1998). I could have been either harmed or monitored by the police, I could not have guaranteed acceptable levels of confidentiality, and I would have closed many doors due to paranoiac distrust.

Finally, I must confess that it was more exiting and challenging to conduct ethnographic research amongst Colombian immigrants living in the Netherlands than to study dossiers of criminal justice agencies. Not only was most of the research on the topic conducted in the latter way, but also other people were better qualified to do it.

Regarding my fieldwork in the Netherlands, I am not going here to reproduce the well-known tool-kit of methodological dictums, tips and conclusions repeated by street ethnographers on drug dealers for the past 30 years.[11] I followed much of their advice and I often found the same problems and situations reported by them.

However, I will briefly point out some important aspects about the choices I made and the ways in which fieldwork activities proceeded.

---

10 As I will later explain, none of these problems (selectivity, fragmentary data, manipulation) are absent in their accounts to independent, trusted social researchers. However, the latter are confronted with other selectivity problems (access), other fragments of reality, and other forms of manipulation and different lies (exaggeration and so on).

11 See, for example, the impressive American tradition in street ethnography on drug users and dealers: Becker (1963), Polsky (1969), Ianni (1972), Agar (1973), Weppner (1977), Taylor (1984), Adler (1985), Adler and Adler (1987), Williams (1990), Williams et al (1992) and Bourgois (1995).

1.2.1 Access

From the very outset, I avoided any sort of cover research. Even when I played various roles, openness about my status as researcher proved essential in every situation. With key informants, I also spent a great deal of time discussing the general or specific aims of my study, provisional results, or my point of view on a wide range of topics: illegal immigration, the war on drugs, the Colombian situation, and so on. I even discarded an early attempt – in initial few cases – to delay the disclosure of core aspects of my research agenda such as the cocaine business. It turned to be unnecessary and could have been counterproductive.

Of course, not every single person encountered during fieldwork came to know what I was doing. Especially in crowd events such as parties and salsa discotheques, I was usually introduced by friends or informants to other Colombians simply as a friend. While I was never explicitly told to 'shut up', I remained rather discreet at first – and sometimes single – encounters with people. The same happened while hanging out in what I considered to be very sensitive places, for example budget telephone centres or prostitution streets. In several situations I remained an anonymous observer and listener for many people, while in other cases I made myself known to informants targeted for interviewing.

In fact, I had to make little initial self-presentation. I was usually either introduced or referred, so many people knew who I was when I met them for the first time. A 'snowball' technique was useful to meet new informants from the same level or setting (other prisoners, other illegal immigrants, other mixed couples) but did not serve to 'climb down or up' to contact Colombians involved in different sections of the cocaine business. I thus tried to open as many doors as I could in different settings. Further, I was not helped by any formal or informal research assistant.

Although my research population was spatially and socially dispersed, there were a relatively small number of institutions, places and events where Colombian immigrants interacted with each other. Some of them, such as churches, restaurants, discotheques or parties, congregated all sorts of Colombians and were well known to a wide range of migrants.

Central to the access was my participation as volunteer or social worker in three *Latino* organisations in Rotterdam and Amsterdam, where I had the chance to interact with many Colombians.[12] While these experiences were very important to meet all sorts of people for my research, my involvement there went beyond a purely academic interest. I was always explicit about my study with the leaders, 'clients' or informants I met through these institutions. My status as researcher was regarded positively as

---

12 In 1994, I worked for a year in the *Fundación Latinoamericana (Funla)* in Rotterdam West, when my research was still at an embryonic stage. I organised bingo meetings and parties, I edited a newsletter, and I helped illegal immigrants and prostitutes as social worker. I later volunteered for one year in *Casa Migrante* in Amsterdam (1996-1997), working as prison visitor for the *Bezoekersgroep Spaanssprekende Gedetineerden* (Visitors for Spanish-speaking prisoners). Finally, I collaborated for another year with the *Colombia Komitee Nederland* in Amsterdam (1997), where I organised parties and cultural events and maintained the news archive.

long as I was prepared to share and discuss my findings, provisional results or open questions. I eventually did it in the form of informal talks or lectures. I had the chance to interview social workers, priests, ex-guerrilla members and community leaders, and to learn a lot about the many immigrants agglomerated or helped by these institutions. Through several key informants met in these organisations I eventually came to know other people directly or indirectly involved in the cocaine business.

1.2.2 Building trust

Not only openness but also 'credentials' were very important to gain trust from people. For example, I met key informants during a public session at a conference on Colombia organised in Amsterdam. In some cases, I showed informants my room at the university and my publications. In others, I lent books from my private library or I stressed my links with prestigious Colombian scholars or universities. I made great efforts to explain and show the differences between my work and that of a police officer or a journalist, emphasising the public and scientific nature of my research.

I also tried to show the limitations of my inquires: I always insisted that I was not interested in knowing real names or what I considered to be dangerous information. This had nevertheless a limited effect: some informants were cautious about disclosing dangerous data anyway, while others did so despite my reservations.

In all cases, I guaranteed confidentiality and discretion. I changed all names of direct informants, and I sometimes blurred some traces of particular places and events to avoid recognition.

Nevertheless, some people acknowledged, either to me or to others, their initial suspicions. I was often asked about my 'interest' or about 'who pays for my research'. In four occasions, it was suspected that I worked for the *vreemdelingenpolitie* (aliens' police), the DEA, and a drug organisation.

I also feel that my situation of being an Argentinean living in the Netherlands helped to establish a good rapport with Colombian immigrants. Neither Dutch nor Colombian myself, I often felt fortunate to be in the intermediate position of a 'quasi-native' researcher. On the one hand, I was not considered part of the local, mainstream Dutch social environment. I joined hundreds of conversations in which 'the Dutch' were the object of open or backstage criticism, and I felt at ease in *Latino* settings and events. On the other hand, as a non-Colombian, it was easier to overcome internal suspicion and to stay outside of regional, social or political differences and conflicts amongst informants. Not only I did feel that I could distance myself if necessary, but I could also feign an ignorant status if required. In fact, I had everything to learn about Colombia and Colombians, and they enjoyed helping me in that process. I owe them, for example, my basic *salsa* dance skills, a key form of communication that brought me close to many Colombian men and women.

Acceptance from 'gatekeepers' was also important for building trust with informants. In a few cases, I was only recommended. In other occasions, I was introduced as a 'friend who is writing a PhD thesis on Colombians in the Netherlands', so I was left to tell the rest. I usually asked intermediaries to be or remain present during my first encounters with a newly introduced informant. It gave everyone a sense of security. Finally, I also relied on social sponsorship from powerful or respected individuals in particular settings like priests, lawyers or drug entrepreneurs.

1.2.3 Why do drug traffickers talk about their business?: roles and expectations

The reasons people had for sharing their knowledge and experiences around the cocaine business with me were manifold and sometimes puzzling. In one way or another, people liked to talk about the issue, whether it was on Colombia, on cases or people they knew, on their own views about the problem, or on their own involvement.

As I will explain in chapter IX, there are many public secrets around the lives of *traquetos* and their employees. Codes of silence and paranoid attitudes in the cocaine business are common, but so are conflicts, deception, betrayal, changing loyalties, public exposure, seek of recognition and prestige, show-off tendencies, or even the need to situate many illegal practices amongst law-abiding citizens and legal institutions. The cocaine business is not performed and discussed in obscure, remote underworlds, but in the same restaurants, churches, coffee-shops, bars and discotheques where people eat, pray, smoke, drink and dance. Cocaine couriers sit next to ordinary travellers, cocaine freights are unloaded and warehoused by legal stevedores, and dirty cash is handled by any bank or remittance agency. While these facts call for secrecy, they also encourage all sorts of information fluxes including gossip, lies, exaggerations, defamations and self-excuses. During fieldwork, I discovered that drug traffickers – and the people around them – keep fewer secrets than they pretend to do, while their activities involve a great deal of manipulation, public relations and image management.

This ambivalence does not explain more specific motives, but I think it formed the background for the conscious and subconscious reasons for why people had to talk to or show me around. Many informants spoke out of bitterness, stressing their position of underdogs, scapegoats or victims. They wanted me to record their sad story: wrong personal choices, unscrupulous *traquetos* preying on them, misfortunes in Colombia, undeserved sentences, inhumane migration laws or hypocritical drug policies. Others, on the contrary, talked to me and with others out of self-aggrandisement. They claimed to be more successful, wise and skilful than others and explained how stupid others were. They claimed to know a lot, to be fearless or to have risks under control. Other key informants still sympathised with my intellectual enterprise and claimed they wanted to 'help' me. Three informants, all with university degrees, felt themselves to be above the materialistic world of surrounding *traquetos* and even commented upon an early version of a chapter. For others I was an inoffensive student they could help in his final thesis. Others liked more the fact that I was going to be a 'doctor' very soon, and kept asking about the graduation ceremony and party.

However, it would be naïve to believe that informants talked disinterestedly even when they trusted me. In general, informants (involved and uninvolved in illegal activities) expected something from me in return. These expectations varied per person and their fulfilment usually marked the road to a more personal involvement and active role with informants. People talked to me because they considered me a friend, because I volunteered in their institutions or because they expected I was going to improve their public reputation. They asked me all sorts of favours and things: juridical advice, translation of documents, housing, money, books, email and mail addresses to receive post, or jobs. I was also expected to learn salsa and to drink or smoke with them.

I did most of these things and some more. I carried letters and gifts to their relatives in Colombia, I accompanied them to the aliens' police or to the hospital, and I brought them clothes and money in prison. I put people in touch with others, I organised Colombian parties at home, and I even housed them for some time. One informant, for example, constantly claimed that I was his 'psychologist' and I was forced to take that role.

Only in very few cases, did targeted potential informants refuse or evade a meeting. The excuses were busy schedules (a criminal lawyer), embarrassment (a prostitute) and fear (two detained drug couriers), but in these cases I either did not insist, I lost track of the people, or I failed to present myself as a trustworthy researcher.

1.2.4 Fieldwork limitations, dangerous mistakes and ethical boundaries

Contrary to regular claims of 'jailhouse' criminologists,[13] access was not the most problematic aspect of my fieldwork. Since I refrained from participating in core activities related to drug trafficking, I assumed peripheral roles (Adler and Adler 1987: 36) that only allowed me to socialise and talk with *traquetos* and their social set avoiding direct contact with operational illegal arrangements.

However, I was indeed confronted with several problems. Firstly, I had to listen to many lies, gossips and exaggerations: that A spent € 1,000 in one night, that the B bar was laundering money, or that C owed D some € 100,000. Moreover, in some peripheral roles I heard the same stories over and over again. Since I was also interested in accurate facts and general trends, I tried to observe a lot, to ask about others (cross-checking whenever possible) and to contrast the stories with information I gleaned from close outsiders and newspapers.

Secondly, I faced practical limitations. Informants often appeared and disappeared when I least expected it. After an initial failed attempt, I never used a tape recorder to record conversations, nor did I openly write notes during personal encounters. Key meetings and observations were reconstructed – either voice recorded or written in small notebooks – immediately after they took place. I also kept a daily diary for more general notes. In some situations, especially when I wanted to keep a low profile, I had to refrain from posing questions at all.

---

13 See for a critique Becker (1963); Polsky (1969); Chambliss (1975); Weppner (1977) and Adler and Adler (1987). Many organised crime researchers, often unwilling to put aside academic and everyday life roles, quickly discard ethnographic fieldwork as impossible and undesirable. See also section 1.3.4.

A third problem relates to the risks of over-involvement. As I explained before, the danger of 'going native' was partly restricted by my being a non-Colombian and partly by being open about the research. However, I had to make explicit that I should remain peripheral, far from cocaine loads and thousand guilder bills, and ignorant of dangerous details. I stressed this all the time, especially in those cases in which informants became friends. It generally helped: only by mistake did I come to listen a couple of business phone calls, to have lunch in a stash house and to observe how an informant deposited cash at a remittance agency. In these cases, I immediately withdrew from the setting and I told informants that it was dangerous and unethical to bring me that far even as a passive observer.

Several researchers have pointed out the personal risks involved in dangerous fieldwork (Sluka 1990; Williams et al. 1992; Lee 1995; Ferrell and Hamm 1998). While I took many basic security measures, especially in Colombia, in only very few occasions did I feel that I was in real danger. However, none of these cases were personal problems related to my status as researcher: I was never threatened, blackmailed or injured in any way. They all concerned potential situations that any outsider or insider could face in salsa discotheques, the streets of Bogotá or the slums of Cali. I received all sorts of tips and warnings from informants on how to avoid problems, often framed in paranoid attitudes that I also tried to control and manoeuvre. Nevertheless, I believe that a more active role around drug traffickers, a closer focus on violence or even more ethnographic research in Colombia on the issue would have certainly been a dangerous enterprise that I was not prepared to undertake.

Finally, I had to face ethical questions. In this type of research, a tension can exist between the need to protect the research population (from violent retaliation, capture, defamation or privacy intrusion), and the need to inform about harmful or criminal offences (to other informants or to the police) that come to be known by the researcher. However, despite its frequent mention, the latter problem is usually underplayed by ethnographers with 'dirty hands' for whom the consequences of blowing the whistle could be catastrophic.

My case was no exception. I always gave priority to protecting informants as long as I was not directly confronted with serious violent crimes or lives at risk. In those situations, I would have gone first to discuss the issue with my supervisor and colleagues, and with some *Latino* community leaders. However, that never occurred. What I considered serious crimes came to my knowledge long after they happened, after they were known by the police, or were too vague and second-hand to do something about them. Neither did I consider drug trafficking offences, illegal residence or unverified gossip of any sort as sufficient reason to break the neutrality promised to my informants.

The protection of informants was indeed the primary issue at stake. During fieldwork, I tried to restrict potential negative consequences for my informants in several ways. I usually discussed the topic with them to know and make them aware of boundaries and possible problems. I avoided gossiping and leaking information, and I respected every security rule proposed by informants during the research process. I already changed all real names in my field notes. For publication, I only named some informants, many others remaining anonymous due to explicit requirement or insufficient data to present them as characters. Some details and stories have been either excluded or used as background information to elaborate statements, while others are presented out of their real context. Some place names have also been changed.

1.3 THINKING ON *TRAQUETOS*: ETHNICITY, ENTREPRENEURSHIP AND DRUG DEALING

While I tried to study *traquetos* by sharing their social world for a while in the way that ethnographers do, I certainly addressed questions posed and discussed on the subject by criminologists, social scientists and economists.

The arguments in this book are influenced by findings and ideas developed from several fronts. They either belong to complementary disciplines or to competing paradigms, and they all focus upon one specific aspect of my research object. I favoured some, neglected others and still, in some cases, tried to integrate them by showing their limits and merits. However, I did not attempt to develop or rest under the shadow of any grand theory, at least not explicitly. I used notions and theories in a very instrumental way as long as they helped me to understand and explain social processes and relations.

1.3.1 Bad guys and culture: anthropologists on drug dealers

Whether they focus on cultural repertoires, marginalisation processes or internal social structures, a number of researchers, particularly anthropologists, have gone to the field to study drug dealers and smugglers in their daily routines.

Based on long-term participant observation, some American ethnographers managed to conduct research on drug dealers during the 1980s and the 1990s. These studies followed the growing focus upon street drug – especially marihuana and heroin – addicts during the previous two decades (Becker 1963; Agar 1973; Weppner 1977). In a pioneering study, Adler (1985) revealed the internal dynamics of an upper-level drug dealing and smuggling community in Southwest County, California. With the drug business still taking-off in America, she mainly found marihuana and cocaine international smugglers who financed their own consumption and who moved their trade in the context of a cottage industry. Not surprisingly, she explained their behaviour in terms of hedonistic ethos, freewheeling lifestyles and non-instrumental, irrational disenchantment.

On the opposite coast, Terry Williams (1990) really grasped the voices of some teenagers selling and using cocaine in New York City. Bourgois (1995) also conducted long-term ethnographic research on crack addicts and dealers in El Barrio (East Harlem). He tape-recorded crack-house conversations and produced a detailed description of street ghetto culture, exploring the links between structural oppression and individual action (Bourgois 1995: 12). Although more focused on cocaine users and crack smokers, other field researchers also conducted landmark studies of cocaine dealers 'from the native's point of view' (Waldorf et al. 1991; Inciardi et al. 1993; Sterk 1999).

In the Netherlands, a number of studies have followed the same path. These works highlight cultural and economic dimensions of street heroin addicts and dealers (Verbraeck 1985; Grapendaal et al. 1995), or behavioural and relational aspects of street networks of users and dealers in Amsterdam (Van Gemert 1988). They place an interesting emphasis on the interaction between drug dealing and local policy interventions. Focusing on upper levels, the research of Korf and Verbraeck (1993) on the dynamics between drug markets and law enforcement exposed a complete picture of the cocaine market in Amsterdam. Although it is not based on participant observation – they combined all sorts of qualitative sources – they privileged in-depth interviews with drug dealers. Their major contribution is, in my opinion, that they succeed in providing a dynamic, heterogeneous image of different organisational forms within the business. Janssen's ethnographic study (1994) of female Latin American imprisoned drug couriers exposed interesting data about their social background and their experiences in prison.

Other researchers in Europe also underwent the task of getting close to drug dealers (Taylor 1994), detained couriers (Green 1969; Green 1991, 1996) or so called 'professional criminals' (Hobbs 1995).

Especially important for my research has been the work of some Colombian social scientists around the figure of the *traqueto* in Colombia (Arango 1988; Molano 1987, 1997; Salazar 1990, 1993; Salazar and Jaramillo 1992; and Hernandez 1997). Beyond clear differences in rigor and style – they range from essayistic pamphlets and short stories to more conventional in-depth interview-based research – they all explore the social backgrounds and cultural performances of *traquetos* and some key actors around them: coca peasants and colonists, *sicarios* (hired killer) and drug couriers. Most interesting in these works is that the *traqueto* – a term explicitly used – is not merely presented as a criminal but as a powerful and dynamic social actor whose cultural impact has been enormous in Colombia.

These empirical studies have influenced my work in three ways. Firstly, they served as methodological models to follow. Secondly, they encouraged me to make sense of drug dealers' performances and meanings from their own perspectives, some of which are often in contradiction with those of mainstream society and criminal justice agencies. Finally, they offered me empirical results with which I could contrast my own findings.

However, my research group goes beyond these street and localised drug dealing networks. Colombian *traquetos* are on the one hand involved in international complex operations that involve several transactions, webs of organised groups, links with the legal economy, violence, corruption and money laundering. On the other, they are a particular national group with a privileged position in the world cocaine business. These two elements guarantee them a place in all criminological textbooks as another case of an ethnic or national group engaged in organised crime.

1.3.2 Criminologists and the arranged marriage between ethnicity and organised crime

Since the days in which organised crime in America was defined as an alien conspiracy (Cressey 1969) run by minorities and immigrants, criminologists and officials have only enlarged the list of ethnic minority groups with a prominent role in local or international organised crime: Sicilian *mafia*, Colombian and Mexican *cartels*, Chinese *tongs* and *triads*, Japanese *yakuza*, Vietnamese gangs, Jamaican *posses*, Nigerian and Turkish groups or, more recently, *Red mafia* gangs. The amount of research or books that purely attest the illegal activities of these groups is immense (for example, Ianni 1972; Abadinsky 1990; Williams ed. 1997) and all sorts of official reports periodically update that connection (Fijnaut et al. 1996; BKA 1998). Only in the field of drug trafficking in West Europe, the role of ethnic minorities or foreign groups has been repeatedly emphasised (Ruggiero and South 1995; OGD 1996a; Bovenkerk and Yeşilgöz 1998).

Bovenkerk (2001) has recently argued that the link between ethnic minorities and organised crime deserves further research. He finds the connection empirically grounded, socially relevant and ethically acceptable to study. By reviewing several theories and factors that could explain the link, he finally concludes that there are enough reasons to base a connection.

Firstly, geo-political factors such as weak states, political conflicts, smuggling traditions, geographic isolation, or the existence of trading minorities can certainly facilitate the involvement of peripheral groups in organised crime.

Secondly, Bovenkerk shows that the most accepted criminological theories explaining the aetiology of organised crime lead directly or indirectly to ethnic minorities. The strain between shared goals of economic success and denied institutional means to achieve them (Merton 1938) is expected to be stronger amongst the poor, the relative deprived, and so amongst some ethnic or national minorities. The theory of ethnic succession – new immigrant groups replace older ones that move out from organised crime through social mobility (Ianni 1974) – claims that organised crime is arranged along ethnic lines. Further, Chicagoan theories on social disorganisation and cultural deviance argue that groups in the margins can more easily engage in organised crime due to their social and cultural distance with mainstream society (Shaw and McKay 1972; Whyte 1943). These groups are also ready to deploy techniques of neutralisation (Sykes and Matza 1957) to eliminate the moral objections against criminal behaviour. Finally, ethnic minorities that enjoy an objective opportunity to earn money illegally will take it if enough resources are available and social controls failed (Cohen and Felson 1979). While these social theories are often at odds, they all tend to revolve around the idea of 'deficit' and structural exclusion.

Finally, a cultural approach also seems to back up a link. Family or ethnic ties are declared 'functional' to organised crime for their ability to control information flows, keep solidarity and secrecy, create trust and loyalty, construct symbols and exercise violence if required. These ideas permeate the thoughts of a wide range of criminologists, from subcultural theorists (Cohen 1955; Cloward and Ohlin 1960) to all sorts of *mafia* researchers.

To a certain extent, my own study seems to follow this itinerary. After all, I will here try to identify the factors that make Colombia the major cocaine exporter in the world and the reasons that Colombians get involved in the cocaine business.

However, things are not quite so straightforward. Bovenkerk himself warns about some pitfalls that should be avoided:

"The idea of a link has been discredited by a stereotyped treatment of policymakers and enforcers who have focused on the exotic aspects of ethnicity or subculture. History has been turned into legends and traditions were supposed to explain rigid group structures and initiation ceremonies. According to Mahan (1998:52) investigators fell into "the ethnicity trap" by analysing organised crime as a self-contained cultural environment. Instead, the sociologically relevant question should be whether ethnicity and organised crime overlap and if it is ethnicity that explains anything. Perhaps such link is only spurious because (a) the term ethnic minority is inherently problematic and the product of a racially biased social construction or (b) the term organised crime is questionable and its definition inevitably leads to the stipulation of minorities as the culprits or (c) organised crime as an economic phenomenon merely follows the logic of the market regardless of the ethnic descent of the people engaging in it." (Bovenkerk 2001).

These three latter arguments are, in my opinion, more than hypothetical: they are real problems in the attempt to find a meaningful connection.[14] Moreover, perhaps some of the factors and aetiological explanations of organised crime briefly sketched above deserve critical reassessment and do not lead so directly to poor, deprived ethnic minorities.[15]

---

14 Firstly, the idea of a biased social construction of ethnic minorities and migrants – as deviant others, external or internal social threats, scapegoats, and so on – has been repeatedly illustrated by many scholars (De Haan and Bovenkerk 1993; Young 1999; Taylor 1999). Secondly, state-sanctioned definitions of organised crime (Ruggiero 1996) stressing internal characteristics (cohesion, structure), illegal methods (corruption, personal violence) and social illegitimacy (offenders with no respectability or social status) almost tautologically tend to target excluded ethnic minorities. In fact, as long as Western native groups successfully define organised crime as a 'transnational' threat to Western states, democracies and economies, there are good chances that organised crime groups will be mainly 'found' in poor countries, peripheral regions or non-Western societies. Extensively, they will be singled out amongst immigrants from those areas. On the contrary, relational definitions that stress collusion with power structures (Blok 1974: 228), blur thin lines between legal and illegal profits (Passas and Nelken 1993), or consider social damage beyond the prestige or the nature of the perpetrators, may also find native, powerful and legitimate groups. This becomes evident if, for example, conventional organised and corporate crime are jointly analysed (Ruggiero 1996). Finally, the primarily economic nature of organised crime is uncontested and will be discussed in section 1.3.4.

15 Ruggiero (1993: 135, 1996: 30) rightly argues that notions of 'deficit' – social and material deprivation, tradition and absence of state, lack of socialisation, social control deficit, and so on – are persistently used to explain organised crime. These notions fail to reveal why certain deviances become 'organised', and why certain 'deficits' do not lead to deviance or clearly block the chances to succeed as a criminal. For example, geo-political factors are crucial for a group or region to succeed in illegal activities, less as social problems (backwardness, poverty, wars) than in terms of social advantages (good natural resources, modern economic infrastructure, know-how, good connections, and so on). In fact, organised crime can only reproduce itself if it develops external relationships with street crime, collective clienteles, power structures, the legal economy and the society at large (1996: 33). Ruggiero points out that: "Organised crime thereby could be interpreted as an outcome of

While I will keep my focus upon the already broad topic of drug trafficking, some findings in this book are indeed framed within more general discussions on the nature of contemporary organised crime. In that debate, some views are less interested in ethnicity, and more in social networks and economy.

1.3.3 Managers and network analysts: the art of fighting fluidity

Mainly reacting against the most static and bureaucratic definitions of organised crime – groups with pyramidal and hierarchical structure, fixed labour division, internal sanctions, and so on – criminologists have flirted with the notion of social network as developed by Boissevain (1974). He opposed structural-functional views on social groups by arguing that:

> "Instead of looking at man as a member of groups and institutional complexes passively obedient to their norms and pressures, it is important to try to see him as an entrepreneur who tries to manipulate norms and relationships for his own social and psychological benefit." (Boissevain 1974: 7).

In the hands of crime analysts, this approach focuses on the social dynamics of 'criminal networks'. It tries to identify actors, to see how they are connected to each other, and to understand and evaluate the nature and intensity of criminal ties. Despite these promising aims, the approach has been reduced to a (potential) law enforcement instrument: how to hit on vulnerable spots in a criminal network and how to 'remove' a significant actor. It is therefore no wonder that most sympathisers of this view are police investigators, policymakers, crime managers or consultants, and ministerial researchers (Van Doorn 1993; Jackson et al. 1996; Klerks 1996; Kleemans et al. 1998; Kleemans and Kruissink 1999).

The problems with this approach applied to organised crime are obvious. It is unlikely, in my opinion, that the dynamic and complex nature of social relations can be grasped analysing police and judicial dossiers. They might tell something about group structures – in one particular moment, about detected criminals – and identify some global aspects about the social relations involved. Not even ethnographic methods can produce the detailed, systematic data on social relations (including names, events and mutual meanings) typical of social network analyses.[16]

As a result, the approach is often misused. Firstly, while some crime managers

---

unfettered production, generated less by a deficit than a hypertrophy of opportunities. It could be seen as the effect of the gigantic and uncontrolled proliferation of ways in which status can be achieved; as an outcome of development rather than the consequence of underdevelopment" (Ruggiero 1993: 135). This might well explain, for example, why some of the wealthiest drug dealers in the world are ethnic Dutchmen. Finally, cultural perspectives are often crowded with reifying, taken for granted notions. Ethnicity and culture are presented as explanations for crime, when they should be in fact the very meanings and practices to be explained (Siegel and Bovenkerk 2001). Concepts like trust, solidarity, loyalty or secrecy are presented as being unproblematic, both as attributes of ethnic groups and as resources in organised crime.

16 See Wasserman and Faust (1994) and Powell and Smith-Doerr (1995) for an overview of applications and achievements of social network analysis.

sacrifice relevant social questions about relations, they place all their emphasis on charting networks to present them as aesthetic devices in research appendixes or as tools in computer programs.

Secondly, a tendency exists to view networks-as-things-in-themselves, and to refer to criminal networks as mere synonyms of criminal groups or organisations (coalitions, for network analysts). In these cases, the bureaucratic approach to organised crime is not challenged: flexibility is incorporated into the 'criminal organisation' paradigm as just another attribute of the structure. Social relations do not form the base of networks: they *are* the networks.

Network analysts recognise the flexible, loose and changing nature of illegal arrangements and transactions, for example amongst people involved in international drug trafficking. However, since their point of departure is crime and not sociology or economics, flexible relations inside these networks mean flexible *criminal* relations. All other dimensions of social linkages (familial, commercial, ethnic, labour, class, religious, gendered, geographical, political, legitimate, and so on) are only considered as context, as facilitators, as risk factors, but are isolated from what really matters: the criminal suspect and its criminal network.[17] This view ignores that what is basically flexible around drug traffickers is the way in which money is made (flexible accumulation), the interaction between different types of legal and illegal economic units (businesses, enterprises, single entrepreneurs, brokers and financiers) and the way in which many sorts of employees work and divide tasks, risks and responsibilities (flexible specialisation).

1.3.4 The economic rationale: illegal entrepreneurs, businesses and markets

According to many authors, organised crime is based upon the same principles of legitimate business and should be primarily defined and studied as an economic phenomenon. Illegal enterprises produce, sell or distribute illegal goods or services to customers who know that the goods or services are illegal (Haller 1990). The illegal nature of their trade gives shape to business arrangements and social behaviours, for example regarding secret procedures, corruption, the use of violence or the profit investments. However, choices and patterns mainly follow a general economic rationale – profit-making in lucrative markets – which can, for example, explain who succeeds, who fails, and what social relations tend to develop around illegal enterprises. From this perspective, Colombian drug dealers can be regarded as drug (Langer 1977), illegal (Haller 1990; Block 1991), illicit (Smith 1975), criminal (Van Duyne et al. 1990) or *mafia* entrepreneurs (Arlacchi 1986).

Drawing on Weber and Schumpeter, Arlacchi (1986) contrasts the type of traditional *mafioso* with present-day *mafia* entrepreneurs and enterprises. They are neither old-style men of honour and pure power brokers nor speculators and venture capitalists, but true innovative entrepreneurs with distinct markets, specific goods and new dynamic methods of production and distribution. In this way, Colombian

---

17 See for example Kleemans et al. (1998) and Klerks (1996).

traquetos share with other legal businessmen the three aspects of the Schumpeterian entrepreneur: an innovative quality in their economic operations; an element of rational calculation – evident for example in the management of risk and their investment strategies – and; an irrational, aggressive aspect which finds expression in the 'animal spirit' involved in the accumulation of wealth (Arlacchi 1986: xv).

The focus on economic actors and action also allows for the study of the structure and dynamics of illegal markets. Fruitful research has been conducted on the ways in which drug enforcement policies affect drug markets at all levels (Dorn and South 1990; Dorn et al. 1992; Dorn et al. 1998; Reuter 1983; Reuter and Kleiman 1986; Reuter et al. 1990; Wagstaff 1989; Lewis 1989; Kennedy et al. 1993; Kopp 1995, 1997; Ruggiero and South 1995; Santino and La Fiura 1993; Santino 1994; Savona et al. 1993; Wilson and Zambrano 1994).

In Colombia, several researchers have analysed the structure of the cocaine industry and its impact on the regional and national economies (Camacho Guizado 1994; Gómez 1990; Hernandez and Tellez 1990; Kalmanovitz 1990, 1994; Krauthausen and Sarmiento 1991; Rocha 1997, 2000; Sarmiento 1990; Steiner 1997; Thoumi 1995, 1997; Uribe 1997). In fact, it is not criminologists but rather economists and political scientists who seem to play a key role in Colombian academic debates on the issue. In the Netherlands, the entrepreneurial approach has mainly been endorsed by Van Duyne (1993b, 1995) who studied different business crime enterprises.

Some economic approaches on drug markets place a strong emphasis on geo-political factors and the ways in which politics and the illegal economy intertwine (Chambliss 1978, 1988; Labrousse 1993, 1996; Lee III 1989, 1991; Clawson and Lee 1996; Potter 1994).

In my opinion, there are two risks attached to economic views. Firstly, there is a tendency to 'over-represent' illegal enterprises in organisational or bureaucratic terms. Drug producers, exporters, smugglers and importers are often regarded as belonging to 'transnational corporations' (Zabludoff 1997). Their cross-border transactions are presumed to be sophisticated, well planned and integrated. Structures and connections are taken for granted with the deployment of *grand* economic categories,[18] while more modest, conflictive or paradoxical developments are discarded. Business and labour relations, if addressed, are completely deprived from context and locality, and blended with a sense of extra-territorial unity (for a critique, see Hobbs and Dunnighan 1998).

One should not think of cocaine enterprises as modern, bureaucratic structures. There are enough examples of 'entrepreneurs without enterprises' (Geertz 1979) or forms of entrepreneurship based on personal transactions that can be "more advanced in certain respects than the usual impersonal models, in that it makes use of naturally occurring social capital, a low-cost strategy" (Granovetter 1995: 140). Drug enter-

---

18 It is not surprising that, used by drug enforcement agencies, these economic notions usually refer to large business arrangements (*cartels, firms, syndicates, branches, subsidiaries*) or to functions (*vice-presidents, representatives,* and so on). Less impressive categories referring to small business, rotating tasks, informal transactions, work conditions or capital-labour relations are simply ignored and clearly absent from the jargon.

prises tend to be more dynamic, de-centralised, flexible, disorganised and smaller than often thought.[19]

The second risk is to take for granted that illegal entrepreneurs are very different from legal ones. Arlacchi (1986), for example makes a clear distinction between good and bad innovators:

> "In the case of the mafia capitalist, his pursuit of rational goals interacts very differently with the extra-economic and irrational sphere of his entrepreneurial activity. Far from progressively enlarging the sway of values and conduct of a rational-capitalist type, the entrepreneurial practices of the *mafiosi* extend the domain governed by archaic and predatory attitudes. Mafia capital accumulation is encouraging the recrudescence of a whole range of a primitive behaviour patterns." (Arlacchi 1986: xvi).

Supporters of a neat distinction between respectable businessmen and illegal entrepreneurs tend to see the latter as differently socialised (Sutherland 1949), as violent (Catanzaro 1992), or as negative entrepreneurs – unfair competition, bad effect on economic development, excessive financial resources, low wages, and so on – (Arlacchi 1986: 89-100).

However, many authors have argued that such a division sounds like a moralistic artefact (Ruggiero 1993: 140), and have provided empirical evidence that blur the boundaries between illegitimate and legitimate business (Block and Chambliss 1981; Smith 1982; Van Duyne 1991; Ruggiero 1993, 1996; Passas and Nelken 1993; Santino 1994; Savona 1999; Taylor 1999). They show how legal business originates from illegal proceeds, how legal and illegal businesses mutually provide services to each other, and how they exchange behavioural models. Moreover, Naylor (1997) convincingly argues that actions and not actors should be at the centre of the debate:

> "The illegal dumping of toxic waste does the same environmental and public health damage whether the culprit is an Armani-suited political party bagman or a cigar-chomping gorilla with a heavy Sicilian accent." (Naylor 1997: 39)

This book will explore not only different types of cocaine enterprises and entrepreneurs, but also their ability to articulate legal and illegal businesses or arrangements.

Once defined as (illegal) entrepreneurs, an interesting input can also be offered by theories dealing with economy, ethnicity and immigration. The basic idea is that overseas immigrants can form middleman minorities (Bonacich 1973; Bonacich and Modell 1980) or ethnic enclaves (Wilson and Portes 1980; Portes and Jensen 1987;

---

19 See for instance Reuter (1983), Haller (1990), Dorn et al. (1992), Korf and Verbraeck (1993), Bovenkerk (1995b), Ruggiero (1995, 1996), Kleemans et al. (1998), and Dorn et al. (1998). Their empirical material reveals, despite the different perspectives, agendas, or conflicting arguments of the authors, the flexible interconnections between cocaine entrepreneurs and their employees, the changing nature of the transactions, and, of course, the different risks attached to various types of business and labour arrangements involved.

Portes 1995), which can facilitate the drug trade by providing social capital (Waldinger 1995), specific labour markets (Bailey and Waldinger 1991), trust (Granovetter 1995), infrastructure, and a social environment where to embed economic transactions (Portes and Sensenbrenner 1993). Ethnic economies (Light and Karageorgis 1995) consist of the self-employed, employers, their co-ethnic employees, and their unpaid family workers, showing various degrees of entrepreneurial capacity. Research in the US has revealed, for example, that the ethnic economies of *Latino* immigrants – Cubans, Mexicans and Puerto Ricans – differ significantly from each other (Portes and Rumbaut 1990). Some groups tend to develop ethnic enclaves (Wilson and Portes 1980; Wilson and Martin 1982) while others remain with low paid jobs in the mainstream economy (Portes and Bach 1985). Some can colonise particular occupational niches, while others deploy all sorts of informal strategies to survive in the host society (Lewis 1964, 1968; Sansone 1992). International markets also offer legal and illegal investment opportunities to entrepreneurs from ethnic diasporas (Siegel 2001).

1.3.5 Sociology of work: labour relations in the cocaine business

A final illuminating approach – certainly one I want to explore in this book – pushes the economic argument even further. Not only are criminal entrepreneurs or drug markets to be analysed in their relation with larger constellations, as illegal businesses, investors, service providers and so on. Organised crime, and particularly drug trafficking, should be also examined in relation to its specific labour market (Ruggiero 1993: 141).

The idea that concepts from labour sociology such as specialisation, professionalism, job satisfaction, de-skilling or flexibility[20] can contribute to the understanding of drug trafficking is reflected in a growing body of research (McIntosh 1975; Adler 1985; Jonhson and Williams 1986; Reuter et al. 1990; Dorn et al. 1992; Hobbs 1995; Ruggiero 1995, 1996). At some stage, these researchers analyse crime or drug dealing as an occupation, as a job, as a task to perform for money.

This 'crime-as-work' approach is relevant since most actors in the drug business are some sort of employees, holding various skills, running different risks, some with career and promotion expectations. Adler (1985) argues that:

"Drug dealing, as an occupation, thus bears great similarity to the world of work. (...) Although the parallels between deviant and respectable work are limited, deviant occupations can be characterized by many of the same work problems, motivations, rewards, and experiences found in the legitimate world. (...) Drug dealers organised, planned, and executed their ventures in similar ways to other businessmen. They relied on an occupational body of knowledge which new recruits had to learn. A modicum of business acumen was required for success. It was also important to have contacts and networks of associates. Finally, dealers' occupational involvement took the form of a

---

20 See Wood (ed.) (1989), Amin (1994) and Tilly and Tilly (1995).

career, with the same entry, socialization, and retirement stages found among all workers, albeit manifested rather differently." (Adler 1985: 147-148).

The analysis of labour relations within drug enterprises can reveal many things about the logic, the shape and the dynamic of such enterprises. It can also illustrate how actors are (and were before) connected with other labour markets or other (legal) employers, and how people are recruited, trained, paid or discarded. Finally, it might even reveal something about conflicting interests and personal profiles.

Thus far the notions and approaches favoured in the present study. Colombian *traquetos* will be now presented as drug dealers, *Latino* immigrants, and illegal entrepreneurs and labourers.

CHAPTER II

THE DOMAIN OF COCAINE

Emergence, Impact and Organisation of Drug Entrepreneurs in Colombia

> "Left to themselves and the principles of Adam Smith, the consortia of Medellín investors would no more see themselves as criminals than did the Dutch or English venturers into the Indies trade (including opium), who organised their speculative cargoes in much the same way."
>
> E. Hobsbawm, *Murderous Colombia.*

INTRODUCTION

This chapter will be devoted to the analysis of the illegal cocaine industry in Colombia and its emergence, the nature of cocaine entrepreneurs and enterprises, and their social and political impact. The questions posed – and answered – here are essential for understanding further and more central chapters of the book.

In the first place, it may be asked just how and why did Colombia come to occupy such a prominent place within the cocaine market, becoming the leading world producer and exporter of the drug. Therefore, I will describe the emergence of the illegal business in Colombia and the factors that contributed to creating and maintaining its competitive advantage in relation to other countries in the region.

A second section will describe the processes of coca and cocaine production, and will provide some macroeconomic information about volumes exported, prices and cocaine income.

Thirdly, I will tackle the crucial problem of the business actors. In showing how the groups producing and exporting cocaine are organised, what social, labour and organisational relationships are developed, and what their social origins and regional differences are, I will introduce the theoretical notions essential to understand the activities of these groups or individuals in the European context. However, in thinking about illegal entrepreneurs moving at times in rather oligopolist market sections, does it necessarily mean that they have formed cocaine 'cartels'?

The illegal nature of this business implies some particular relationships between these entrepreneurs and the Colombian society and institutions. Thus, I will further analyse how this link is constructed and the sources of the social legitimation of the illegal entrepreneurs. Is it possible to speak about a Colombian cocaine *mafia*, analogous to the Sicilian or Italian-American ones? What is the social and political impact for Colombia, as these groups enter into collusion with the state or with guerrilla and paramilitary groups? I will demonstrate how the illegal business contributes to the amplification of other violence as well as to the construction of new social bonds and alliances. The problem of collusion with state and society is important to my argument, since issues such as legitimation strategies or the impact on non-involved groups, and questions on corruption and violence will also be tackled when describing the situation in Europe.

In no way do these aspects exhaust the treatment of the cocaine domain in Colombia. Important issues such as the economic impact,[1] domestic consumption,[2] coca cultivation[3] and the 'war on cocaine'[4] have been left aside.

---

1   Several top Colombian economists have extensively researched on the size and the macroeconomic impact of cocaine industry in Colombia. See Kalmanovitz (1990, 1994); Sarmiento (1990); Gómez (1988, 1990); Gómez and Santa María (1994); Urrutia (1990); Thoumi (1995, 1997); Rocha (1997, 2000); Uribe (1997) and Steiner (1997). Although there are some discrepancies in calculations, a wide consensus exists on the fact that negative effects of the cocaine business for the Colombian economy surpass the positive ones: 'Dutch disease', more informal economy, short-term and speculative mentality, agrarian counter-reform, unsustained growth and employment, and so on.

2   Domestic cocaine consumption exists though to a lesser extent than in the American or European context. In 1992, the consumption annual prevalence – people from 12 to 60 years old who tried at least once during the last year – was 3,0 per 1000 for cocaine and 1,3 per 1000 for *basuco* (cocaine base smoked with tobacco) in Colombia. In the United States, for the same year and consumption prevalence, these proportions rise up to 17 per 1000 for cocaine and 6 per 1000 for *crack* (smoked cocaine freebase). That difference might be even stronger if frequent consumption (addicts) rates are considered. In Colombia, other substances such as inhalant solvents show higher consumption rates. (Rodríguez Ospina et al. 1992; and National Institute on Drug Abuse 1994).

3   Neither will I go deeper into the specific issue of coca leaf cultivators, which constitutes an important topic given the enormous growth of domestic cultivated hectares in recent years.

4   Another dimension omitted in this chapter is the one of repression, that is, of the national and international policies applied in Colombia to combat the cocaine industry. Obviously, the illegal nature of this business and the state actions to fight against it are constitutive elements of everything that follows below, from the organisational forms of cocaine entrepreneurs to their social and political impact, from the relationships within the market to the place of violence and secrecy in it. Almost 20 years of the American war on cocaine and of the so called 'narco-diplomacy' in Colombia, have even determined the international relations of this country with the rest of the world. However, two reasons motivate me to avoid digging into this topic. Firstly, it is far removed from my central object of analysis. It makes no sense to deal with it, if it is not to take it again to study the criminal policies in the Netherlands and to engage in the discussion on alternative approaches – normalisation or legalisation policies –, matters that I do not intend to tackle in this book. The second reason is that most of what has been written on cocaine in Colombia, both in Spanish and in English, focuses on this problem of penal control policies, and maybe little more remains to be said. Many criminologists, jurists, political scientists and journalists, in Latin America as well as in the United States, have produced a huge range of serious writings on this topic during the last fifteen years. See Ambos (1997); Arrieta et al. (1990); Bagley (1990); Clawson and Lee III (1996); del Olmo (1992, 1996); Jelsma (2000); Labrousse (1993, 2000); Lee III (1989); McCoy and Block (1992); Tokatlian (1990, 1995, 2000); Uprimny (1994a, 1994b) and Vargas Meza (1999a, 1999b).

2.1 COCAINE IN COLOMBIA

2.1.1 Getting into business: from the 'bonanza marimbera'[5] to the Miami cocaine wars

Though in historical terms the emergence of Colombia as the main cocaine producer and exporter country in the world still remains rather astonishing in terms of its speed, the business 'explosion' and the consolidation of exporter groups in the early 1980s is the product of a formation process of some 20 years that goes back to the first half of the 1960s. Initially was a somewhat slow development, strongly accelerating from 1978 onwards, that evokes with no doubt the idea of short cycle export economies – i.e. a boom around one particular exportable product – widespread in Latin America in the nineteenth and twentieth century (Tovar Pinzón 1994: 92). Yet neither tobacco, nor quinine, indigo, rubber, coffee or marihuana left so dramatic and pervasive fingerprints in Colombia as those made by the boom of the 'white gold'. In trying to understand how initially the business developed, I will identify those settings and activities that invigorated the process. I shall then focus in greater detail on those factors that explain why Colombia – and the Colombians – managed to control production, export and wholesale distribution of cocaine into the United States.

Rise and fall of Colombian marihuana
The cocaine boom in Colombia was preceded by an immediately previous one: that of marihuana. Domestic production of marihuana had already developed in the 1960s, as a response to the growth of local demand, particularly from the cosmopolitan elite. However, its production and traffic remained insignificant until the early 1970s. Its expansion and boom, that lasted from 1971 to 1979, originated in the search for a new source of supply for the growing American market. Mexican marihuana had supplied that market until the end of the 1960s, but eradication programmes with the dangerous herbicide *Paraquat* reduced both the availability and the demand for this variety, opening the door to Colombia (Thoumi 1995: 126; Tokatlian 1990: 300).

All sources agree that the first local marihuana traffickers, both in the Atlantic Coast and in the Antioquian Urabá, were old smugglers of home appliances, cigarettes, whisky and textiles, traditional activities in both regions, who were very familiar with the routes and hideaways in the Antilles and the Caribbean (Betancourt and García 1994: 48-49; Salazar and Jaramillo 1992: 39; Arango 1990: 250-251). Around 1968-1970, these smugglers from Maicao, Santa Marta, Barranquilla, Turbo and Medellín (see Appendix I), while buying their merchandise in the International Free Port of Colón, in Panama, made their contacts with American buyers and dealers for sending the first shipments of marihuana.

---

5   *Marimba* is one of the Colombian names for marihuana, and *marimberos* the marihuana entrepreneurs. The *bonanza marimbera* is the marihuana prosperity boom that took place in Colombia during the 1970s.

Once the Colombian variety[6] became well-known and accepted in United States, many American traffickers – from independent adventurers, in some cases Vietnam veterans, to official envoys of American *mafia* organisations – began to arrive to the *Sierra Nevada de Santa Marta*, on the Colombian Atlantic Coast, providing peasants with seeds, cultivation instructions, financing and technical assistance.

In contrast with what would happened later with cocaine, these *marimberos* only produced and exported the weed, whereas the Americans always controlled its import and distribution in the United States. The Americans bought the marihuana at the port of shipment, loading the planes and the ships on the clandestine air strips or on the Colombian coasts. Although not structured in large organisations, they controlled enough resources to avoid a stronger Colombian business share. This is an important element, which to a great extent explains the fact that no stable and powerful Colombian groups emerged around the export of marihuana (Betancourt and García 1994: 67). The ephemeral character of the prosperity – for Colombians – and the propensity of the *marimberos costeños* to spend everything they earned also help to explain their decline.

Marihuana was cultivated in the provinces of La Guajira, Cesar, Magdalena and Bolivar, and was later extended to the zone of the Eastern Prairies. According to Camacho Guizado, in its heyday it managed to represent two-thirds of the supply for the American market (Camacho Guizado 1988: 103). Although cultivation and export continued during the following two decades,[7] the *bonanza marimbera* was over by 1980. Three circumstances converged to lead to this decline. First of all, the introduction of a new stronger variety, known as *sin semilla* (seedless), popularised and cultivated in California substituted the weed brought from Colombia.[8] In other words, there was a relocation of production. Secondly, United States strongly pressed the Colombian government to engage in the eradication of illicit crops. That was finally undertaken in 1978 by the elected president Turbay, in part due to accusations of suspected links with traffickers. With a huge military deployment and avoiding the use of herbicides, the operation was recognised as a 'success' by the American government. However, the real impact of the eradication (regularly accomplished later with other illicit crops) may well be put between brackets, and perhaps diminished a supply whose days were already numbered. Finally, some *marimberos*, a small group mainly from the areas of Turbo and Medellín, had already found a more profitable product, easier to transport, and with more promising prospects.

---

6   It is a soft variety that came to be widely known as *Santa Marta Gold*, and was very popular amongst consumers.
7   Domestic marihuana production had a brief revival in 1987-1988, declined, then made a come-back from 1993 onwards. However, its 'productive cycle' and its relative small volume compared with cocaine or heroin never recovered (Thoumi 1995: 128; Steiner 1997: 46).
8   Although this idea is broadly accepted by Colombian researchers, Reuter (1992) claims that in fact the strong variety *sin semilla* did not replace the milder Colombian weed, but consumption of the Colombian variety just dropped.

Cuba and Panama: the first contacts

Beyond any doubt, both the American *mafia* organisations as well as many other more or less independent adventurers also from the States, played a central role in the establishment of cocaine traffic from Colombia to the United States. This link had already been revealed in the case of marihuana. Two clear locations can be identified through which the first contacts were made.

It is well known that in the 1950s Havana had already been transformed into an important centre for illegal activities. The American *Cosa Nostra* regarded Cuba as an ideal place through which the illegal drug traffic could be organised to the United States.[9] Cuban groups were thus made into middlemen between the American market and the potential suppliers of illegal drugs, since they were not produced in the island itself. Though interest was mainly centred on heroin and morphine, cocaine was already commanding some attention. By the mid 1950s, several Antioquian smugglers operating in the Caribbean made contacts in Havana and opened the first 'lines'. In 1959, the FBI and the Colombian authorities had already dismantled a laboratory in Medellín, considered important for the time, where cocaine, heroin and morphine were refined and sent to Cuba for their distribution.[10] With the revolution and the massive Cuban emigration to Miami and New York, Cuban networks involved in drug trafficking were reorganised there. They took in their hands a big share of the yet incipient cocaine business on the East Coast, cocaine being used to a large extent as a luxury drug by the elite of the recently migrated. Additionally, American organisations such as *Cosa Nostra* left cocaine in Cuban hands, and were more concentrated on the heroin and morphine traffic. Little more is known about this early link between the Colombians and Cubans, partly due to the low level of demand, and partly to the lack of interest from American governmental agendas.[11] What is certainly clear is that, from the outset, the most important supply source of Cuban illegal entrepreneurs were Colombians (MacDonald 1988: 28).

Many testimonies indicate that years later, as in the case of marihuana, contacts established in Panama between Colombian smugglers and American dealers and intermediates provided another incentive to enter the business. Around the first half of the 1970s, and with a market in expansion, many of these dealers began to request cocaine, offering high prices, to smugglers that until then had been devoted to the supply of marihuana (Arango and Child 1984: 183). Some of these Antioquian smugglers decided then to specialise in cocaine, encouraged by the following circumstances: a) the *bonanza marimbera* had already declined in the Urabá region by 1974, moving up to the Atlantic Coast; b) there were contacts already established with Cuban organisations in Miami and New York; c) those contacts were energised with the huge migration of Antioquians to the United States, very strong from 1965; and d) they could refine cocaine with local input.

---

9   Lucky Luciano, who lived in the island for three years, and Meyer Lansky, played a central role in the establishment and organisation of Cuban groups within the incipient illegal drug business.
10 *El Espectador*, 22-5-59, cit. by Arango and Child (1984: 166-167).
11 Arango and Child (1984) and Henman (1981) even claim that the CIA covered Cuban traffickers, who mainly assumed anti-Castro positions.

In fact, the first shipments were made, according to one of those pioneers, with cocaine acquired by the Health Ministry or in official medical centres through false prescriptions and bribes to public personnel.[12] At this initial stage, cocaine was also refined in small laboratories with coca cultivated in the Cauca province. When demand began to expand, these entrepreneurs started to import coca paste and cocaine base from Bolivia and Peru, countries that were producing almost all the existing coca leaf.

A fundamental difference with previous marihuana contraband, and certainly a key factor for the success of these Antioquian cocaine entrepreneurs, was the immediate vertical integration achieved. From the beginning they controlled coca import, cocaine processing and subsequent shipment to the United States. In that way, they were able to neutralise possible competition development, for example from Peruvians or Chileans, or from other smaller Colombian groups that were struggling for a share in the market.[13] By integrating different steps and enlarging benefits, they knew they would also be better positioned in the supply market.

Although the social origins of these and other cocaine entrepreneurs will be analysed in more detail later, it is now important to stress that these Antioquian 'pioneers' are not those who would eventually make Medellín a world famous city. This first generation of illegal entrepreneurs began the cocaine business and dominated it until the mid or late 1970s. Even though they were old smugglers engaged in other activities as well such as clandestine gambling or foreign currency exchange, they not only had a certain social recognition but also saw themselves as being merchants with higher status and ethics than those who would come later. This explains the relative peacefulness that prevailed in Medellín until the end of that decade.

The young newcomers that would then replace them, came from middle rural or low urban classes, many with experience in theft, bank robbery, fraud or auxiliary positions with the old smugglers, all of them attracted by the new and profitable business. Still in 1976, Colombian police were describing Pablo Escobar as a "worthless mule", Carlos Lehder was dreaming in a prison while serving time for car contraband, and Jorge Ochoa was distributing the few kilos that his uncle managed to send him in Miami. All three of them were 27 years old and they would become, within a three or four years, leaders of their organisations and multi-millionaires.

Flourishing demand: from the 'mule' to the plane
Around the early and mid 1970s, there were clear signs of demand expansion. Cocaine re-emergence in the United States, after 40 years of silence, was the result of

---

12 Cit. by Arango and Child (1984: 184).
13 Gugliotta and Leen (1990: 22), claim that before 1973 Chileans were the main cocaine refiners, importing coca paste from Bolivia and Peru, and exporting it to the United States through Colombian smugglers. Pinochet's *coup d'état* would have finished the business in one year, leaving the market to the Antioquian entrepreneurs. This statement is rather striking since no single Colombian source backs up such a statement. Moreover, Latin American military dictatorships were not exactly devoted to hunt drug traffickers.

different factors: growing methadone programmes for heroin addicts who added cocaine to their addiction, restrictions on amphetamines as the most widespread stimulant, demographic developments – with the post-war baby boom – enlarging the group of young potential new users, and political and social turmoil, expanding the likelihood of experimentation. Cocaine was slowly leaving the exclusive and hidden American circles to reach a more public status and a broader audience, mainly amongst well-off youngsters who had experienced marihuana. (Courtwright 1995: 215-216). Still it was not an epidemic or stigmatised in the way it would be in the next decade, it became a fashionable habit for those who could afford it, whereas it was openly advertised and embodied with *glamour* by the mass media, show business and rock circles. A trendy fashion of the young and famous, also in line with more mainstream American values around work efficiency, sexual prowess and conspicuous consumption.

In 1970, American customs seized 100 kg cocaine coming from Colombia and in 1973, 96 foreigners had already been detained in Bogotá with different quantities of the alkaloid. In 1975, a small plane with 600 kg was discovered by the police at Cali airport, very rare for the times and a record that would stand for years (Gugliotta and Leen 1990: 23).

Most of the shipments were sent through 'mules' carrying several kilos hidden in suitcases or clothes, on regular commercial planes. Some of the future illegal entrepreneurs began making those trips themselves. For larger quantities, Colombian export products such bananas or flowers were used. Salazar and Jaramillo (1992) affirm that hundreds of crewmen of banana ships were dismissed between 1971 and 1974 under suspicion of being involved in drug trafficking (Salazar and Jaramillo 1992: 42-43).

Increasing control in regular entry ports on the one hand, and the enormous growth of demand on the other compelled cocaine exporters to seek new ways to move much greater cocaine volumes. It was then, toward the late 1970s, that the first regular 'pipelines' were established through the use of private small planes. Aided by experienced American pilots, they were able to transport 300 kg of cocaine or more in a matter of four to six hours. Also undetected speedboats entered the scene. This technological change is very important since marks the end of the craft stage of cocaine business and seals the immediate consolidation of emerging illegal entrepreneurs as Pablo Escobar or Carlos Lehder.[14]

The Miami wars
Although by 1978 Colombians were already controlling cocaine export to the United States, they did not yet hold wholesale distribution in the consumption centres. They were supplying, but the lion's share of the cocaine business, the distribution, was still in the hands of other groups[15]: Cuban-Americans in Miami, Puertoricans and Cubans

---

14 Carlos Lehder was one of the architects of this main step, buying an island in the Bahamas to use it as a bridge between *Medellin* and Florida.
15 See Table I, showing the cocaine price increase from production to retail selling.

in New York, and a huge number of independent or intermediary dealers, local or otherwise, in some cases linked to the urban 'mobs'. Over the course of four years, by 1982, the local Colombian networks had managed to control, though not in a peaceful way, cocaine wholesale – and in some cases also retail – distribution in the American market.

In Miami, the long standing alliance with Cuban networks broke down in 1979. The so called 'cocaine wars' reached their climax in 1981, with 101 drug related homicides reported (Bagley 1990: 183). The same year, even the Colombian consul in Miami complained about the massive arrival of 'undesirable' Colombians, admitting that:

> "The problem exists. I can not tell you about quantities, because that information do not go through the consulate (...) It is a problem that has invaded this country, because earlier everything went through local *mafias*. But it seems today that the Colombian *mafias* want to control all the market. That is what the press says. Poor Colombians living in this city are more and more distrusted. Because to say Colombian and *mafia*, drugs and death, is already the same thing."[16]

It has become a common place, particularly amongst police and DEA officers in their powerlessness to solve what they call 'Latin Drug Related Homicides', to explain the savagery of the cocaine wars in Miami and New York by blaming the Colombians exclusively. Again and again, their testimonies resort to a supposed national characteristic that would permit them to murder without remorse or consideration for age, sex or innocence of their victims. Some federal agents complained that they had a strong tendency to also kill the relatives and friends of their victims, claiming on the contrary that American *mafiosi*

> "performed their assassinations with decency, never injuring the family of the victim and sent flowers to the funeral" (sic) (Eddy et al. 1992: 67).

Such a *cliché*, more familiar to cinematography scripts, is not even corroborated by the three journalistic books written on the cocaine wars that more closely resemble *Scarface* or *Miami Vice*.[17] However, most serious researchers acknowledge that the willingness to exercise extreme violence was important for the consolidation of some Colombian groups.

Hostilities between Colombian groups in Queens or Miami would regularly continue through the following decade as long as new organisations in Colombia were emerging and collapsing. However, those cocaine wars of 1979-1982 were radical in a double sense. On the one hand, they led as a result to the Colombian control on wholesale distribution. On the other, these wars were also a necessary condition for

---

16 *El Mundo*, Medellín, 15-7-79, p. 8., cit. by Salazár and Jaramillo (1992: 45-46).
17 Eddy et al (1992); Mermelstein (1990) and Gugliotta and Leen (1990). These three books, with low literary value and even less scientific merits, base their stories on accounts from 'repentants' and the miscellaneous versions of American anti-drug enforcers.

the successful generation replacement that was taking place, at the same time, in Medellín. They meant the reduction and concentration of the control on supply and distribution to five or ten organisations, displacing the old pioneers that could never send more than tens or hundreds kilos to the United States.[18]

In sum, several facts reveal how, by 1981, a small group of Colombian illegal entrepreneurs based mostly in the Antioquia region managed to control cocaine production, exportation and also wholesale distribution in the United States:

a   The existence of a pioneer smugglers generation with early contacts in the consumer market and with a long experience in illegal import-export and smuggling.

b   The early control of the 'craft' supply and strong links with Cuban groups distributing cocaine in the United States.

c   The explosive expansion of demand for cocaine and the American incentive – first from *mafia* groups and later from Cuban or local distributors – to organise export on a large scale.

d   A large Colombian migration enclave, especially Antioquian, in Miami and New York, willing to participate in the illegal business.

e   High levels of violence, in Colombia as well as in the United States, that guaranteed the elimination of non-Colombian distributors and the generation replacement, concentrating supply in few hands.

f   A great ability to prematurely integrate several levels of the business and to quickly adapt production and transportation means to market requirements.

2.1.2 Why (in) Colombia?

Even though these facts partially explain the early control of the cocaine business achieved by Colombians, they are not yet sufficient to understand why it was in Colombia, and not another country such as Bolivia, Peru, Brazil or Mexico, that cocaine producing centres were installed. After all, cocaine can be produced in many places, Colombia had to import some of the raw material, such as coca leaves or chemical precursor products, and the Colombian internal market for cocaine was almost non-existent (Thoumi 1995: 167).

As Thoumi correctly points out, being an illegal industry in which high profitability is based on the high risks involved in production and traffic, it is in fact important to identify those factors that reduced or minimised the risks of cocaine business in Colombia. The 'competitive advantage' of Colombia is based on a combination of various factors.

---

18   A good example is Griselda Blanco de Trujillo 'The Black Widow', Colombian pioneer in cocaine distribution in New York and Miami. She enjoyed a lot of power in the early 1970s, and was a main character of the Miami wars, when she was overshadowed by the new big scale exporters.

Political factors

An illegal industry has better chances to flourish where the state is either weak or presents power structures that facilitate and encourage its development through some sort of collusion. The Colombian state combines both characteristics. Already before the period known as *La Violencia* (1949-1969) there were unequivocal signs of the growing de-legitimation of institutions and a clear weakening of state power presence.

The Colombian state is considered to be historically weak, almost absent for some social groupings such as rural peasants or illegal urban dwellers, and even unable to control large parts of its territory. In contrast with other more centralised models that emerged in Latin America after the civil wars of the nineteenth century, Colombia preserved unresolved the struggle between local or regional powers, perpetuating open or hidden war situations until today.[19]

Additionally, beside weakness, permanent struggle and relative autonomic regions, a political culture based on clientelism and patronage has shaped local and central power relationships (Leal and Dávila 1991). Within a context of rapid economic expansion and development experienced by Colombia for the last fifty years, these features encouraged both irresponsible and inefficient administrative bureaucracies. Indeed, the spread of various forms of corruption at all levels as a fundamental regulation instrument of social life has been a natural outcome. This triple character of a weak centralised state and autonomous political powers open to engage in corruption was very important for cocaine entrepreneurs to achieve the necessary indifference, protection or collaboration from local authorities. Marisol, a criminal lawyer and university teacher of Cali, explains:

> "Here in the *Valle*, not only in Cali, drug traffickers found support by buying people, especially the police, the public ministry, some judges, and many local and regional councils. And I don't mean three or four. Bogotá is far away and the *Valle* has always taken care of its own affairs."

At the same time, the growing institutional de-legitimation by generalised corruption, systematic judicial and police inefficiency – impunity – and the increasing indifference for solving serious social problems, only expanded the gap between *de facto* and *de jure* socially acceptable behaviours. A broad climate of distrust in the dead letter of legal frameworks – palpable not only with the expansion of guerrilla and paramilitary groups but also with the increase of many other private forms of conflict resolution such as theft or homicide – was an extremely fertile ground for the cocaine industry (Dombois 1990: 113).

These problems of political de-legitimation are not exclusive to Colombia. Nearly

---

19 See Umaña et al. (1962); Pecaut (1987, 1996); Betancourt and García (1990); Martin (1996); Deas and Gaitán (1995); Sánchez and Meertens (1983) and Bergquist et al. (eds) (1992). They show how both the disruption and continuity of many sorts of 'violences' in the history of Colombia can only be understood by the dynamism of local powers and their constant clashes. See Bayona and Vanegas (1995) for the links between local actors, power conflicts and the specific 'violences' in the Cauca Valley region.

all Latin American countries are familiar with clientelist relationships and experience corruption problems. Countries such as Peru or Mexico display an even higher degree of collusion between their national army or government and the illegal entrepreneurs. However, three facts made Colombia a special case: a) the processes began several decades earlier than in other Andean countries; b) they were more radical and long-lived; and c) they were accompanied by an extremely high level of violence (Thoumi 1995: 172).

Mixing economic modelling with criminological control theories, Thoumi (1998) has recently argued that the illegal drugs industry requires an environment characterised by institutions that do not impose behavioural controls and that tolerate and condone deviant behaviours (Thoumi 1998: 33). In his view, the role of social institutions is central and overshadows more simplistic explanatory models based either in individual (moral values) or structural (poverty, crises) elements.

Geographical factors
MacDonald (1988) and Whynes (1992) have put special emphasis on the geographical location of Colombia as decisive for its competitive advantage. Both stress its excellent strategic position between coca producing countries – Bolivia and Peru – and the American market. It has a flight range without stopovers, and good sea lines through the Caribbean. Such a position would be consolidated by two long coasts on both oceans, excellent river systems and vast forest and mountainous areas with scarce communication infrastructure, that makes them ideal for hiding cultivation fields, laboratories, and landing strips.

In fact, the mere geographical position is not that important for the location of an illicit industry in which production and transportation costs are small compared to the profits. This factor is more important for the location of cocaine transshipment centres, such as Mexico, which in fact enjoys an even better position – closer to the American market – than Colombia, but did not develop cocaine production (Thoumi 1995: 169). Other countries such as Brazil or Peru also have huge jungle extensions or large coasts and river systems, but only entered cocaine production in the 1990s, when stronger economic and political factors had transformed business conditions.

However, Colombian geography helped to maintain a rather big country split into regions – even some densely populated as Antioquia or the Cauca Valley – quite isolated and self-sufficient.

Economic factors
Next to the internal political factors already described, other economic considerations help to understand the Colombian competitive advantage.

In the first place, as explained above, the emergent cocaine boom had been associated with other smuggling activities. Colombia shares with other Latin American countries a long tradition in contraband, but it is one of the few with a vast experience in export contraband (Thoumi 1995: 173). Coffee, sugar, emerald or marihuana contraband clearly provided an extensive know-how for the development of foreign contacts, marketing routes and transportation techniques. It even furnished it, as in the case of emerald exploitation, with organisational models at the level of production as well as with experience with international black markets and money laundering. The cases of some emerald and marihuana smugglers are well known, who knew to step into the promissory cocaine business at the right moment. Furthermore, years and years of contraband generated certain social legitimacy and broke traditional social stigmas related to this activity.

Secondly, it is important to emphasise that Colombian capitalism always operated with the expectation of high short-term profits. This persistent speculative mentality around the boom of the moment, was never seriously transformed by more stable and long-term activities or investments. Although some attempts were made in that direction after World War II, many entrepreneurs continued with a rent-seeking traditional behaviour. The capital market liberalisation during the 1970s and the coffee boom of 1975-1978 contributed to reinforce speculative financial behaviours (Thoumi 1995: 174). An active black foreign exchange market, linked to contraband activities, served to finance capital flight, tourism and import contraband. During the administration of López Michelsen (1974-1978), the so-called *Ventanilla Siniestra* (sinister window) of the Bank of the Republic provided a great support to, first marihuana, and later cocaine illegal entrepreneurs. It made it rather easy for them to launder illegal profits.

Thirdly, Arango (1988) attempts to explain the success of Antioquian entrepreneurs in the illegal business referring to some immanent cultural features. He claims that the *paisa*[20] mentality is based on entrepreneurial values, with good skills for business, but with a strong tendency to measure social worth by personal material wealth, regardless of the means of attaining it.[21] This ethnocentric idea seems to ignore the fact that many of those early illegal entrepreneurs (even some of the Medellín groups) were not even *paisas,* and that for example the *valluno* groups (see section 2.3.2) showed better abilities to succeed in the cocaine business.

Another economic factor mentioned by Arango (1988), and Betancourt and García (1994) is the crisis of regional economies, deep on its way at the time of the cocaine boom: cotton in the Atlantic Coast, textile in Antioquia, sugar in the Cauca Valley, and emeralds in the central region of Boyacá and Cundinamarca. The crisis of these areas and their traditional elites provided fertile ground, or at least a triggering factor (Thoumi 1998: 34), for the emergence of new cocaine entrepreneurs.

Finally, as has already been mentioned, a fundamental factor was the large legal and illegal Colombian migration to the United States that supplied channels and clandestine networks for illegal export and distribution. Such migration, essentially *paisa*, had particularly large dimensions between 1965 and 1980 (Urrea Giraldo 1993). It preceded the one of other Andean countries by almost twenty years. From the approximately one million Colombians living in the United States, more than 200.000 are concentrated in Miami. Other more numerous groups as Cubans,

---

20 *Paisas* are the people from the Antioquia region. Descending from old Spanish colonists, they mixed to a certain extent with indigenous population but hardly with black communities. They were later colonists themselves in other Colombian regions. They are depicted as the 'white', 'entrepreneurial' Colombia.

21 Arango (1988) seems to confer them, in Weberian terms, a capitalist spirit without a protestant ethic.

Puertoricans or Mexicans were early displaced by them from business. It is clear that their ability to control wholesale distribution gave Colombians a premature privileged position. Although following chapters will analyse the characteristics of Colombian enclaves in United States and Europe, and their participation in the cocaine market, for the time being it should be said that this involvement of Colombian migrants in the United States sharply contrasted with the situation in Europe.

All sources emphasise that these networks did not hesitate to use high levels of physical violence to control this share of the market. Although Thoumi (1995) and Bagley (1990) are right in stressing the Miami wars as a central factor for the success of Colombians in the United States (Thoumi 1995: 172; Bagley 1990: 183), this ability to conquer wholesale distribution seems to be rooted in a broader set of opportunities. A large migrant enclave, legal and illegal, relatively concentrated, with its own local infrastructure though with few loyalties to the United States, with unbeatable conditions (contacts) and skills to access to supply sources, and disposed to enter the business at any price.

Control on wholesale distribution was central for the consolidation of illegal entrepreneurs in Colombia. They not only multiplied profits, but also considerably reduced detection risks by suppressing many Cuban informants who had links with the CIA and other police agencies in the United States. Some of those profits were immediately reinvested in the business, and allowed them to enlarge and energise production in Colombia, modernising and expanding transportation and communication technologies.

2.2 THE NUMBERS OF COCAINE

2.2.1 From coca to the 'kitchen'

The processes employed to produce cocaine are widely known and relatively simple. From 250 existing varieties of coca plants, about 200 are exclusively from South America, though only very few of them are used to extract the alkaloid. Traditionally, coca has been cultivated from Chile to Colombia and its ritual consumption was very extensive in pre-Columbian Andean communities, especially from Bolivia to the south of Colombia, as well as in the Amazon basin. Peru and Bolivia, countries in which its use has been socially and legally accepted for large portions of their peasant and indigenous population, used to be respectively the first and second coca leaf world producers in the 1980s, to be surpassed by Colombia at the end of the 1990s. Its cultivation requires only simple field clearing (slash and burn), seedbed preparation, seedling transplanting, and field maintenance. Harvesting is manual, after which the leaves are dried in sunlight (Thoumi, 1995: 130). Although alkaloid concentration can be up to 2,25% of the leaf weight, the actual yield is much smaller and extremely variable depending on several factors: the type and the quality of chemicals used, the variety and the age of coca plants, the proportions of chemicals

and coca leaves, the elapsed time since leaves have been cut, and the 'cook's' –
chemist – skills and experience.[22]

Coca in Colombia

Historically speaking, the coca cycle in Colombia has three visible phases. The first
one began with the coca boom at the end of the 1970s and lasted until 1982-1983. As
explained before, the first cocaine shipments were accomplished with small scale
local cultivation, which was very quickly surpassed by an increase in demand. The
result was an explosive growth of coca cultivation in the remote areas of *Amazonia*
and the Eastern Prairies, zones partly occupied by indigenous communities and partly
by old and new rural settlers. If, in 1980, Colombian coca production represented
around 2% of the total, for 1983 such participation had been increased to almost 10%.
However, coca prosperity came to an end in 1982, due to the drastic fall of prices and
the poor quality of illegal crops. The demand increase on the one hand, and a stronger
position on the other, forced Colombian illegal entrepreneurs to look to Bolivia and
Peru for a continuous coca supply.

The second phase of the coca cycle ran from 1983 to 1993, and was characterised
by the massive import of Bolivian and Peruvian base. Local cultivation continued
expanding, but remained at around the 10% of total coca production. For this period,
it is estimated that Peru only refined 5% of its own leaf production, and Bolivia
between 35% and 40% (Steiner 1997: 29). Colombian cocaine producers were buying
the base in both countries, to later transport it in small planes through the Amazon
region or the Ecuadorian border.

Finally, a new open phase since 1993 shows an increasing local vertical
integration, meaning the end of the rigid specialisation that dominated the scene
during the 1980s. Colombian coca cultivation experienced a new and accelerated
growth, with improved coca varieties and productivity, and the expansion of the so-
called 'commercial cultivation' (owned or financed by cocaine producers). These
commercial fields have much better yields than the old peasant productions from the
coca boom. At the same time, Peru and Bolivia increased domestic cocaine
production and base export to other countries such as Brazil.

Some reasons can be found for such increase in Colombian coca crops: the
relative recovery of cocaine base prices in 1993 (Uribe 1997: 62); the strengthening
of guerrilla and paramilitary organisations in cultivation areas (Thoumi 2001),
especially in the provinces of Caquetá, Guaviare, Putumayo and Meta (see Appendix
I); the growing international repression in the area at traffic level – for example with
anti-aircraft radar's in Peru or the crack-down of large illegal entrepreneurs in
Colombia – that encouraged traffickers to 'localise' their strategies, either by taking

---

22 This conversion factor (kg of coca leaves to produce 1 kg cocaine) is very important to calculate the
    amount of produced cocaine. Almost every study accept the factors proposed by the INCSR (Interna-
    tional Narcotics Control Strategy Report) which by 1996 were: Peru: 334:1, Bolivia 373:1 and
    Colombia 500:1. However, recent studies show that due to technological improvements, the productiv-
    ity of Colombian coca leaf per hectare duplicated in the second half of the 1990s, achieving the
    regional average (Rocha 2000: 66).

laboratories out of Colombia or by stimulating the local production of raw material, and finally; the important fall, in 1993, of Peruvian coca leaf production caused by a parasite that devastated cultivation in the Upper-Huallaga Valley in 1992. Rocha (2000: 46-56) points out that the recent expansion was favoured by trafficker's behaviour changes and social marginalisation in cultivation areas, while González-Arias (1998) refers to the labour availability by increasing internal migrations.

With most coca fields concentrated in the provinces of Caquetá, Putumayo and Guaviare, Colombia has managed to become the first world coca leaf producer with a share of 50%-60% of the total coca production (Uribe 1997; Rocha 2000; Thoumi 2001), becoming totally self-sufficient of cocaine base as well. This was accompanied by a substantial decline in cultivated areas in Peru and most notably in Bolivia, where a drastic reduction of 30,000 hectares seems to have marginalized the role of that country in the drug industry.[23]

The kitchen[24]

The processes for refining cocaine are quite crafty and require little infrastructure. In the first place, dry coca leaves are mixed with sodium bicarbonate, to release the alkaloid. This is done in simple improvised containers made of wood trunks and a plastic sheet. Then, sulphuric acid and kerosene dissolved in water are added. After some hours, the watery mixture is press or filtered, and it is air dried to obtain what is known as 'coca paste'. Besides chemicals, some toilet paper and filters, and a maceration pit are needed.

The second step, which is a bit more complex, consists of transforming coca paste into 'cocaine base'. The chemicals now used are sulphuric acid, potassium permanganate and ammonia. For filtration and drying, some garbage cans, electric generators, filters and ventilators are necessary. Despite the many impurities and toxicity it still has, cocaine base can already be smoked and represents the Colombian equivalent of American *crack* or Dutch *gekookte coke*. Mixed with tobacco, it is known in Colombia as *basuco*.

The last phase used to obtain 'cocaine hydrochloride' (HCL) is somewhat more complicated. More chemicals, electricity, filters, heat lamps, ventilators, microwave ovens, hydraulic or manual presses, chemical recycling facilities, packaging materials, washing machines and garbage cans are required. Cocaine base is treated with either acetone, ethyl ether, MEK (methyl ethyl ketone) or toluene, and with a solution of hydrochloric acid and alcohol. A precipitate is then obtained. After crystallisation has been completed after three or four days, it is filtered and dried, and cocaine is finally obtained. This final part of the process requires some cooking, and ether's flammability makes work in these kitchens extremely dangerous.

The kitchen's location clearly follows the logic of risk reduction. Coca paste and cocaine base processors, simpler and with less qualified work, are always found

---

23 This reduction in Bolivia is now presented as a successful story of forced eradication in the frame of the *Plan Dignidad* 1998-2002 (UNDCP 2001). However, this process could not have taken place without the new Colombian coca boom (interview with Eduardo Gamarra, 16-16-2001).

24 *Cocina* (kitchen) is the cocaine refining laboratory. Chemists working there are known as *cooks*.

around cultivation fields given the difficulty involved in transporting large volumes of leaves. They are generally portable and frequently moved to avoid detection. Cocaine kitchens, to the contrary, are usually found either in rural areas with some infrastructure or in urban centres. Larger and more stable kitchens are located in country estates or ranches owned by illegal entrepreneurs, with landing strips, militarised security systems and modern communications technology. In cities or towns, smaller kitchens are hidden under business front-stores in buildings or storehouses.

It is important to point out that these production processes are quite appropriate for a less-developed country: they are relatively simple chemical and agricultural processes, which are not capital intensive, without large economies of scale, with many domestic raw materials or easily importable, with scarce labour skills and with relatively common chemical products (Thoumi 1995: 131-132).

Chemical precursor products

From the chemical input, only ethyl ether and acetone, and to a less extent hydrochloric acid, thinner, MEK and potassium permanganate, have to be imported. Acetone has other uses in Colombia, but ethyl ether has very few and it is produced by a dozen of multinational companies. Until the strengthening of international controls for the trade of these products in the late 1980s,[25] nearly all the legally imported ethyl ether in Colombia ended up in the hands of cocaine producers (Thoumi 1995: 132). In fact, there are more than 40 chemical products that can be used to refine cocaine, well far beyond the 7 'scheduled' cocaine precursor substances listed in Table II of the 1988 Convention.[26] Illegal entrepreneurs constantly look for and introduce 'substitute' chemicals when more well-known products attract the attention of custom and trade controls.

Financed by the UNDCP, a detailed study of the Colombian DNE (National Drugs Bureau) analyses routes, origins and quantities of the 7 more used chemical precursors (Omaña 1995). To produce 1 kg of cocaine, approximately 590 litres of gasoline or kerosene and 16 to 25 litres of the main 7 chemicals are necessary (INCB 1998b). Trade in chemicals seems to be a business in itself, considering the huge volumes involved. Inversely to what happens with the final product, a gallon (3,8 l) of ethyl ether priced in 1985 at US$ 5,5 in the American free market, was to be valued at US$ 87 in the Colombian black market (Krauthausen and Sarmiento 1991: 190). Steiner (1997: 39) estimates that the cost of the chemicals to produce one kilo of cocaine is about US$ 200.

---

25 United Nations Convention against Illicit Trafficking of Narcotic Drugs and Psychotropic Substances of 1988, Vienna, 20 December 1988, which Colombia ratified in 1993.
26 These are acetone, ethyl ether, hydrochloric acid, methyl ethyl ketone, potassium permanganate, sulphuric acid and toluene. Amongst substitutes for scheduled substances, many solvents are used, the most popular being the methyl isobutyl ketone (MIBK). Recent data provided by the US indicate the increased use of ethyl acetate and n-propyl acetate, and substances such as potassium dichromate and sodium hypochlorite are reported to have been successfully used instead of potassium permanganate (INCB 1998b).

A report presented to the Congress of the United States 'complained' about the increasing European share in the market. Meanwhile, American exports of these chemicals to Colombia were reduced between 1989 and 1990 to a less than a half, imports originating from European countries had increased 340%, as well as the trade of the large laboratories with Venezuela, Brazil, Ecuador and Peru, from where chemicals entered Colombia by land, with fewer risks (Krauthausen and Sarmiento 1991: 177). Following some strengthening of European chemical controls, some chemicals often shipped through Europe to Colombia – especially MEK and potassium permanganate – started to originate directly from source countries, for example South Africa and China.[27]

The main entrance points are the ports of Barranquilla, Cartagena, Buenaventura and Santa Marta. The list of supplying companies during the 1980s and 1990s includes Shell, Exxon, Wesco, Kores, Baz-Rezin, Holland Chemical International, Nestlé, Merck, Cicolac, Dupont, Union Carbide, Sidney R., Maicena and many other multinational corporations. In fact, the products do not arrive only from the United States: Germany and the Netherlands play a central role in the supply of several chemicals. After them, in descending order of importance, Great Britain, Switzerland, Brazil, Mexico, China, Venezuela, Peru and Chile follow.

There are different channels for the import and distribution of chemicals. On the one hand, the 'diversion' of legal imports is a common method. Although increasingly difficult due to intensified controls, there have been more than 50 forms detected to defeat them: adulterated invoices; fictitious loans, transactions, returns or losses; duplicated licenses or permits, or ones already expired; double accounting; import with other denominations; use of false clients or suppliers; and of course, very difficult to control, authorised import by trade names linked to cocaine producers, with valid permits. Moreover, most chemical precursors can be substituted, making it extremely difficult for controls to work. As a general rule, these methods imply very little or no risk for the supplying companies. They are able to delimit civil or penal responsibility if anomalies arise. On the other hand, chemical precursors find their way in through the same clandestine networks of import contraband, networks that in some cases are integrated with those of cocaine export. This is the particular case of shipments from border countries: trucks that arrive to the laboratories by land without being detected.

2.2.2 How much is exported?

An estimation of annual cocaine volumes exported by Colombia is essential to determine both the cocaine income and the general size of cocaine business in

---

27 Originating from South Africa, MEK has often been shipped through Europe. Between December 1997 and March 1998, the US seized six shipments of potassium permanganate from China, about 80 tons that were en route to Colombia (INCB 1998b).

Colombia. Calculations vary substantially according to each source or author.[28] Discrepancies are mainly related to two things: disagreements in quantities and proportions of imported cocaine base from Peru and Bolivia, and differences in yield calculations.

The most moderate scenario has been proposed by Gómez (1988, 1990) and Gómez and Santa María (1994), who calculated an annual cocaine export average, between 1981 and 1988, of about 80 metric tons. For the same period, Sarmiento (1990) established minimal and maximal annual quantities in 41 and 100 metric tons, while Kalmanovitz (1990) calculated an average of 136 metric tons a year. Over a longer period that also cover the 1990s, Rocha (1997) arrived to very extreme minimal and maximal totals, with export averages of 68 and 574 tons. Uribe (1997) calculated cocaine production for 1994 in between 513 and 625 tons, while Steiner (1997) proposed new production calculations for the period 1980-1995, placing the annual average in some 338 tons. Rocha (2000: 72-73) has produced new calculations for the period 1985-1998 in which he follows Steiner's estimations. Despite the differences, nearly all sources show a drop between 1983 and 1985 – when prices crashed after a boom that clearly led to overproduction – and other important decreases after the record year of 1992 – due to the massive loss of coca crops in Peru.

Colombian cocaine export volumes must bear a relationship with other three calculations, all of them mutually consistent: with the quantity of world-wide produced cocaine – calculated between 1990 and 1995 in an annual average of 627 tons –, with the total cocaine seizures – averaged for the same period in 277 tons[29] –, and with the total volume of cocaine consumed – around 380 tons[30] annually. Taking into account these tentative indicators, the estimations recently proposed by Steiner (1997) and Rocha (2000) are definitely the most reliable ones for several reasons: a) they remain within the range proposed by all other serious studies; b) they propose quite acceptable hypothetical scenes, with well built and explicit methodologies and sources, c) they are the most recent and with longer series, and d) they are consistent with those other indicators.

Figure I presents the evolution of volumes of cocaine produced, exported and sold by Colombia from 1980 to 1998. It is presumed that Colombia refined half of the available cocaine until 1982, and from 1983 a 75% of the total supply. It is important to distinguish between the potential cocaine production – all refined cocaine base –,

---

28 They typically combine data from various official reports of American drug control agencies such as the *International Narcotics Control Strategy Report* (INCSR) and the *National Narcotics Intelligence Consumers Committee* (NNICC) with local statistics from the DNE, the DANE and regional field studies.

29 Data from DEA and the Federal Drug Seizure System.

30 Steiner (1997) calculates around 300 tons using data for the United States from Rhodes et al. (1994). As it will be illustrated in the next chapter, the hypothesis that the American market represents 90% of the total (what might have been true for the first half of the 1980s) certainly underestimates cocaine volumes consumed in other markets since 1989, especially in Europe and Latin America. A more realistic estimation of 65% results in a total annual consumption average of 380/400 tons. See also Rocha (2000: 179).

the amount of cocaine exported – production minus internal consumption and seizures – and the quantities actually sold in the market – exports minus 75% of non Colombian seizures, supposing that all cocaine is seized before being sold by exporters.

While cocaine exports steadily increased until 1987, from then on they experience relative stability, especially after 1993. The gap between production and export shows the discovery in 1984 of the huge complex of laboratories *Tranquilandia* and some of the 'hits' against large *Medellin* organisations (1990-1992). Despite ups and downs, Colombian cocaine sales seem to be rather stabilised during the 1990s at around 260-280 tons per year.

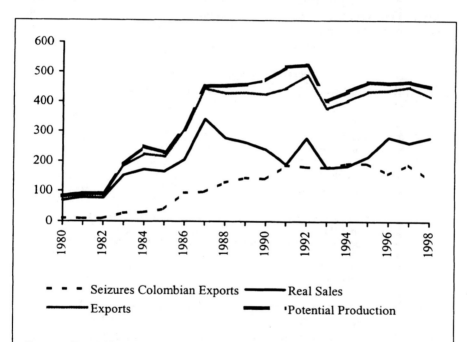

Source: For 1980-1995, Steiner (1997) and Rocha (1997), with data from INCSR, NNICC, DEA, the Federal Drug Seizure System and the DNE (National Drugs Bureau, Colombia). For 1996-1998, Rocha (2000). For the seizures of Colombian exports, 50% until 1982 and 75% since 1983 on world cocaine seizures (outside Colombia) + 100 % of seizures in Colombia.

Figure 1 Production, Exports and Sales of Colombian Cocaine 1980-1998 (Metric Tons)

2.2.3 Prices and costs

A central characteristic of the cocaine industry is that added value in each stage is not proportional to the implicated costs, but it is directly related to the risks involved in each phase of production and marketing (Thoumi 1995; Reuter et al. 1990). Thus, profit maximisation strategies do not try so much to reduce costs but essentially to minimise operational risks. This strong relationship between illegality (risks) and profits explains why, as Table I attests, while added price increases very little in the leaf cultivation and cocaine processing phases, the lion's share of the profit is made in subsequent transportation, wholesale and distribution stages. In contrast to what happens in other legal markets, cocaine producers and exporters are primarily interested in upward vertical business integration. Downward integration, palpable in recent years due to the increase of coca cultivation in Colombia, is aimed at securing a continual supply rather than increasing profits.

Table I Cocaine Price 1995 (US$)

Level	Price x kg	Percentage on final price
Cocaine base[a]	800	1,00
Kilo HCL in Colombia[b]	2.000	2,50
Kilo in Miami[c]	17.500	21,87
Kilo in the Netherlands, 98%[d]	25.000	31,25
Retail in the Netherlands, 60%[d]	80.000	100,00

a   Price of cocaine base needed to produce 1 kg of HCL. Source: Steiner (1997).
b   Source: Uribe (1997).
c   Average between minimum and maximum. Source: DEA, Illegal Drug Price/Purity Report, 1995.
d   Own calculation: US$ 48.- per cut gram (60%), US$ 80.- per pure gram, x 1000 = US$ 80.000,- per kilo.

However, prices do not only vary according to risks involved in each stage at the same time. At the same time, illegality produces a great market segmentation, rendering the business very competitive but remarkably non-transparent.[31] Kennedy et al. (1993) and Kopp (1995, 1997) correctly point out that wholesale and retail prices are far from the product of agreements between 'cartels' that 'control' the market. Prices are determined, on the one hand, by the strong competition between large organisations of cocaine entrepreneurs, organised to reduce risks and competing against many small groups or actors attracted by the huge profits. On the other hand,

---

31 Illegality imposes risks that reduce marketing options for buyers and sellers, for example regarding advertisement, supply, agreements, communication or investments. Actors and transactions tend to react to local conditions and personal circumstances, with visible price fluctuations in the short run. For the interaction between law enforcement, risk and prices, see Reuter and Kleiman (1986); Dorn et al. (1992); Thoumi (1995) and Caulkins and Reuter (1997).

it is widely accepted that the cocaine market is strongly demand-driven, and supply trends frequently follow than induce demand patterns. However, as the market is so opaque – since illegality prevents clear information flows – prices are very dependent on the access and the contacts of each buyer and seller to marketing and distribution networks (Reuter 1983). This explains the great price variation over place and time.

The costs of doing business

Although, as indicated before, the costs of putting a kilo of cocaine in the consumer markets are low in comparison with the net profits, they are not at all insignificant in absolute terms. They are important for calculating both the business income for Colombia, as well as the impact that the cocaine business – and especially exporters activities – has had on other actors involved either directly or indirectly.

Table II Costs for delivery at wholesale distribution in consumer markets, per kilo cocaine, during the 1990s

Cost	US$	Destination
Raw Material[a]	600-800	Colombian, Peruvian and Bolivian coca growers and labourers.
Transport to Laboratories[a]	100	Carriers (Colombians).
Chemical Precursors[a]	200	Local and multinational chemical industry.
Refining Costs[b]	200-300	Colombian cooks and labourers.
Transport to Consumer Markets[a]	3200	Carriers (Colombians) or other organisations (Mexicans).
Vigilance, Security and Bribes[a]	500	Weapon dealers, Colombian security employees, Colombian politicians, national and foreign customs and police officers.
Money Laundering[a]	1700-3400	Intermediaries, financial advisers, banks.
Other[c]	200	Lawyers, rents, etc.
TOTAL	6600-8700	

a Source: Steiner (1997) and Rocha (1997), both partially based on Zabludoff (1997).
b Source: Uribe (1997).
c Own calculation. It can be argued that seizures should also be included in this list as costs, what would increase the total by around 30%. However, seizures, captures and injuries can also be conceived as the risks behind price increases.

Table II shows the different costs[32] incurred by a typical large cocaine exporter, per kilo cocaine during the 1990s, a decade during which wholesale prices remained rather stable. Estimating for this decade an average price of US$ 17,000 to US$ 18,000,[33] these costs from about US$ 6,700 to US$ 8,700 represent between 38% and

---

32 This, of course, accepts the fact, shared by all sources, that Colombian cocaine exporters sell all cocaine at a wholesale level in destination points.
33 Steiner (1997: 35 and 39). His average wholesale prices for all the 1980-1995 serial are the most acceptable. They are based on many DEA reports that also consider the progressive Colombian penetration, between 1980 and 1985, in the American wholesale level and, from 1989, the higher prices of the European market.

50% of the wholesale price. It is interesting to note that the main part of these costs represent 'not Colombian' income: Bolivian and Peruvian coca producers, European or American chemical laboratories, foreign drug trafficking organisations such as the Mexican ones, the international financial circuit, and also foreign lawyers, corrupt policemen, or custom officials. When calculating Colombian cocaine income, Steiner (1997) reasonably indicates that 39% of the exporters gross revenues actually leaves Colombia at the costs described.

2.2.4 Colombian cocaine income: a 'narco-economy'?

Bearing in mind the cocaine volumes actually sold, wholesale prices, and production and transportation costs, it is already possible to determine just how much money enters Colombia every year for cocaine production and export. Net revenues oscillate between US$ 1 and US$ 3 billion per year, with an average of US$ 1,7 billion for the period 1987-1995.[34] Though in the number's game each economist arrives at different results, Steiner's (1997) estimations are similar to those of Sarmiento (1990), are located in the middle point of the range proposed by Rocha (1997), and, especially from 1987, in an intermediate place between the higher calculations of Kalmanovitz (1990, 1994) and the more moderate results of Gómez (1988, 1990) and Gómez and Santa María (1994). Rocha (2000) estimates for the 1990s an average of US$ 2 billion a year as cocaine income.

Adding the net income from heroin – about US$ 750 millions a year since 1991 – and marihuana exports – about US$ 300 millions a year from 1993 on –, it does not seem difficult to estimate that during the 1990s, the illegal drug industry has generated earnings for US$ 2,5-3 billion per year for Colombia.

All authors acknowledge that these figures have not passed unnoticed through the Colombian economy. The economic impact of illegal drug industry in Colombia has been huge and penetrating. However, they far from confirm apocalyptic statements that Colombia constitutes a 'narco-economy', as some sources and authors have repeatedly indicated.[35] There are no doubts about the fact that cocaine exports have represented about 70% of the Colombian exports during the first half of the 1980s, and since 1986 such percentage has been reduced and stabilised at 30% – mainly due to the dramatic drop in cocaine prices. Cocaine income has represented, following the same trend, an average of 7% of the Colombian GDP, decreasing to the relatively small percentage of 2% – 3% (Steiner 1997, Rocha 2000).

Two problems still remain with difficult empirical verification, which make one consider those US$ 2,5 billions a year to be an overestimation. In the first place, it is obvious to imagine that at least part of the capital earned by Colombian illegal

---

34   With a maximum of US$ 2,5 billion for 1989 and a minimum of US$ 1,1 billion for 1994 (Steiner 1997: 40-42).

35   Powerful mass media as CNN, *The Economist, Semana* or *Cambio 16* (Colombia), or authors such as MacDonald (1988: 45) do not have any problem in quoting sources or authors who without any foundation refer to annual profits of US$ 18 and 25 billions. American law enforcers also love these overestimates, but usually prefer to compromise with some US$ 7 billions.

entrepreneurs never enters Colombia, for it is likely kept, once laundered, in the international financial circuit.[36] Secondly, all testimonies and sources emphasise the growing role of Mexican cocaine entrepreneurs in recent years (Rocha 2000, Thoumi 2001). With 70% of American cocaine entering via Mexico and with increasingly common modalities of paying transportation costs with cocaine, Mexican organisations have increasingly become the actual exporters (and distributors) of Colombian cocaine to the US, going far beyond their traditional role as mere transporters.

2.3 COCAINE ENTREPRENEURS IN COLOMBIA: THE BUSINESS SOCIAL STRUCTURE

2.3.1 Social origins of illegal entrepreneurs

A central question in understanding the dynamics of the cocaine business in Colombia and the relation of illegal entrepreneurs to broader social and political arrangements is understanding their social origins. Where do cocaine entrepreneurs come from? Can any clear pattern be discerned?

Opportunities to become a successful drug entrepreneur in Colombia have remained, of course, unequally distributed. Except for the readiness to use personal violence and the ability to shield oneself from it, other social or individual constrictions and qualities do not seem to differ that much from those encountered in successful legal businessmen: sex, age, personal or family contacts, entrepreneurial skills of all sorts, personal attributes such as creativity, alertness or charisma, skills to both exercise power and deal with existing power pressures, and luck.

However, access to the entrepreneurial levels of cocaine business has been remarkably open to a wide and heterogeneous range of people. The social origins of cocaine entrepreneurs can not be traced to one social, economic or ethnically specific group. Although some backgrounds and patterns can be observed according to regional differences and historical events, they far from constitute general trends.

As indicated earlier, many of the first pioneer cocaine entrepreneurs were old marihuana, emerald, textile or home appliance smugglers who moved on to deal in this new profitable product. They usually already had some degree of social recognition and prestige, being either successful entrepreneurs with many contacts and accumulated experience, or powerful figures in their home regions of Antioquia or the Atlantic Coast.

Verónica Rivera, the so-called 'queen of cocaine' of the 1970s, began her career selling smuggled house appliances. She used her commercial networks to later export cocaine to New York and Miami. Another interesting example is Gonzalo Rodríguez-

---

36 However, the most serious studies on illegal import smuggling and money inflows to Colombia assess that the majority of money revenues generated by cocaine exports would have been repatriated to Colombia (see Steiner 1997: 88).

Gacha 'The Mexican', who had extensive experience in the illegal emerald business (Cortés 1993). Some well known *marimberos* also entered the cocaine business. José 'Mono' Abello, son of one of the most respected families of Santa Marta, started in the 1970s as a marihuana exporter and later became the most important cocaine entrepreneur of Santa Marta, also exporting to the American East Coast. Joaquín Gallo 'Mr. Big', once a marihuana distributor in Miami, was extradited in 1990 to the United States due to his cocaine import activities (Krauthausen and Sarmiento 1991: 147-148).

It should be noticed that even amongst these old illegal entrepreneurs and smugglers, the variety of people is enormous. They range from rather urban upper-class individuals from Medellín or Santa Marta, to more rural and violent entrepreneurs from the region of the Magdalena Medio.

The younger generation of Medellín traffickers, which broke through around 1979, was again very heterogeneous. Most of them had some sort of criminal career background and were not as well established as the former group. However, their individual backgrounds differed considerably. Pablo Escobar 'The Boss' was an urban low-middle class youngster who started out by stealing headstones from local graveyards, scratching off the inscriptions and reselling them at bargain prices. He later became a car thief and an auxiliary helper in a small cocaine organisation. Carlos Ledher, in contrast, was a well educated middle-class migrant, fluent in English and German, who started in the United States as marihuana retailer, car thief and smuggler. Yet different still is the situation of the Ochoa brothers, the other main examples of that Medellín trafficking generation. They belonged to a well-off rural Antioquian family, dedicated to cattle and horse raising, which also had a restaurant in Medellín. They started distributing cocaine in Miami setting up an export-import firm with their uncle. They enjoyed local protection and acceptance, which facilitated their legal economic activities and their relationship with authorities.

Also in the southern region of the Cauca Valley, it is possible to find a variety of social origins amongst drug entrepreneurs. Usually from urban origins and even belonging to middle-class families, some already had a criminal background. Gilberto Rodríguez Orejuela 'The Chess Player' and José Santacruz Londoño 'The Student', both well-known cocaine entrepreneurs from Cali, operated a kidnapping gang in the late 1970s. Furthermore, some members of former guerrilla groups converted into cocaine entrepreneurs. Yet many others did or do not have any past linked to illegal activities. Some were prosperous self-made local entrepreneurs linked to industrial or export activities, other were financially desperate merchants in need of quick financial resources. It is also possible to identify unemployed young professionals, ex-policemen or local politicians. As Arango and Child pointed out, there were some interesting production and export strategies, favoured by cocaine entrepreneurs to strengthen relations with civil and political society, which

> "...opened the doors for professionals, politicians, bank robbers, military officials, fraud perpetrators, policemen, broken merchants, unemployed, prostitutes, intellectuals, bankers, artists, cattle dealers, farmers, and so on." (Arango and Child 1984: 185).

The heterogeneous origins of cocaine entrepreneurs can be explained by three characteristics of the cocaine business in Colombia. First of all, it is not possible to link it with a particular set of political actors, and it does not express a particular social conflict between clear social groups. It has been both an urban and rural phenomenon, and indeed a rather 'open' and dynamic activity. Secondly, its huge prospects for quick social mobility raised expectations in all sorts of people, both excluded from and included in legal activities. In the third place, cocaine production and export in Colombia has had, certainly prior to 1995, rather low levels of negative social stigma attached to it. Many law abiding citizens would easily tolerate or even respect some drug entrepreneurs. They would become role models not only for the 'underdogs' but also for more or less successful and established individuals, sometimes even powerful, who would just wait for their opportunity to enter the business.

2.3.2 The many traditions of drug organisations: the cocaine centres

This heterogeneity is also evident when Colombian cocaine enterprises are collectively analysed. Regional differences, with their own social dynamics, political environment and cultural markers, have shaped many cocaine 'centres' or focuses, each one with its own importance and momentum.

Betancourt and García (1994) have identified five different centres. I will add here a sixth one, which became particularly noticeable during the late 1990s.

The Atlantic Coast focus

Historically, this is the first centre. Especially in the province of La Guajira and around the cities of Barranquilla, Cartagena and Santa Marta; this is where the marihuana boom (1972-1979) took place. During that period, La Guajira bore witness to high levels of violence. This was particularly noticeable where the newly wealthy marihuana producers did not belong to the traditional local elite. As explained before, these groups controlling marihuana production failed to develop more stable and powerful organisations, mainly due to the fact that they did not control the more profitable stages – import into United States –, the ephemeral nature of the marihuana prosperity, and their propensity to quickly spend the profits. Although some of the earlier marihuana smugglers in this region changed to cocaine in the late 1970s, they also failed to develop strong organisations and were clearly overshadowed by the Antioquian entrepreneurs.

In fact, their relative survival has to do with the importance of this area for exporters from other regions. Barranquilla, as the main Colombian port, has been particularly important for the shipment of big quantities of cocaine to overseas markets. With its traditional smuggling tradition, the area has also been an important cross-road for the illegal import of all sorts of goods. This includes islands such as San Andrés, in the Caribbean Sea, which also serve as a money laundering resource. Many failed illegal entrepreneurs of the Atlantic Coast later went to work for stronger organisations, for example as helpers or figureheads.

The Antioquian focus

The region of Antioquia, with its capital Medellín, was the first successful centre for the early control of the cocaine business. Also with a long tradition in smuggling, a first generation of old marihuana exporters and smugglers began cocaine production and export, which was rapidly integrated with base import and wholesale distribution in the United States. Most of the Colombian migrants living there came from this region. A generation change at the end of the 1970s marked the consolidation of a relative small number of illegal entrepreneurs, who managed to enlarge and solidify strong organisations.

With some exceptions, most of the members of these groups came from social circles that had few or no connections with the old Antioquian elite. Coming from middle rural or low urban classes, they had to strive hard for social recognition. Violence has played a particular role in their strategies for maintaining control of the business. They have been confrontational with the establishment, and have been accused of most of the assassinations of government officials, judges and rival competitors that took place during the 1980s (Thoumi 1995: 157). Their military strategies included the massive use of youngsters from the popular neighbourhoods of Medellín as hired-killers, the so-called *sicarios*, for whom these new cocaine entrepreneurs represented clear role models and the chance for upward mobility (Salazar 1990).

Violence was not the only resource available to these groups. Some of the Medellín traffickers tried to become, with very limited success, power brokers between urban marginalised groups and broader political arrangements. Escobar himself had a brief and unsuccessful passage in the Colombian parliament. He also tried to expand his social arena by granting favours or engaging in social beneficence, even developing social housing projects.

Arango (1988) has suggested that *paisa* entrepreneurial skills have been at the root of their business success.[37] Although Antioquia has been one of the more entrepreneurial regions of Colombia, *paisa* elite and society are amongst the more conservative and traditional in the country. Strong rural values are still dominant, and well-developed industries (textile, food, and so on) or modern cities seem to exist side by side with powerful traditional markers such as religious devotion, family bonds – especially revolving around the mother –, clientelist relations, and other symbols such as rural music, clothing or vehicles, horses and the land. This tension seems to be reproduced by cocaine entrepreneurs' behaviour. Although these groups displayed good entrepreneurial skills, their social, cultural and political behaviour have been strongly influenced by them and have at the same time reshaped many aspects of Antioquian social life.

The power accumulated by people such as Pablo Escobar, his wide organisation allegedly closed, highly structured and hierarchical, his extravagant ways as well as his clientelist and political strategies, and of course his extremely violent reputation,

---

37 However, some of the well-known members of the Medellín groups such as Lehder were not *paisas*, and in fact other groups demonstrated even better skills to succeed.

has converted him in the 'typical-ideal' Colombian drug entrepreneur. The fact that the Antioquian groups were highly devoted to organising themselves and co-operating in both military and political terms, has led to these organisations being portrayed either as a truly unified 'cartel' (Castillo 1987, 1991, 1996) or as a domestic version of the Italo-American *mafia* (Betancourt and García 1994). I shall later argue that both concepts have been misused in the analysis of Colombian cocaine organisations.

The Antioquian focus had its heyday during the 1980s, and was finally overshadowed by the *Valluno* centre in the early 1990s, after the imprisonment or death of their main illegal entrepreneurs.

The Central focus

Although closely tied to the emergence and development of the Antioquian focus, this central region of Boyacá and Cundinamarca had its own separate nature. This focus emerged around the illegal exploitation of emerald mines.

Due to a long-lasting state monopoly control on them, for many years emeralds had been illegally exploited by the *planteros* (emerald traders). An illegal extraction system (*planteo*) developed around these traders: the *plantero* supplied some miners with the basic mining equipment, arms for their own protection, house and food for their families. The miners, in return, were compelled to sell to them any emeralds they could mine. Breaking the agreement resulted in death. The *planteros* protected their miners by organising armed groups, and they became regional leaders capable of claiming control on a certain area. This system based on dependency relationships produced strong loyalties, closed organisations and high levels of violence in the region (Thoumi 1995: 139; Krauthausen and Sarmiento 1991: 143-145).

Some of these emerald traders moved on to the cocaine business. The *planteo* system could be applied to cocaine production, but only during the early stages of coca cultivation and cocaine refining. There are well-known cases of old emerald traders who years later appeared in the coca cultivation region of Guaviare, transformed into cocaine entrepreneurs (Molano 1987: 65). Others, such as Gonzalo Rodríguez Gacha 'The Mexican', became independent cocaine exporters.

This centre is the most rural of all, and has been characterised by the strong clientelist relationships, the tendency of illegal entrepreneurs to buy and defend land, and their subsequent support and use of paramilitary rural bands to fight guerrilla organisations and some popular movements. Betancourt and García (1994) have depicted this focus as the closest to the Sicilian *mafia* model. Although there are some clear analogies with the social systems described by Blok (1974) for rural Sicily, it should be emphasised that the roots for such *mafiosi* social arrangements are to be found in the emerald mining system and the problem of land-ownership *per se*, rather that in the cocaine business as such.

The East focus

With centres in Cucuta and Bucaramanga, this region next to the Venezuelan border also bore witness to the development of specific cocaine organisations. It grew unnoticed partially due to their low profile and the wars against and between the Medellín and Cali organisations. It was also formed around the active contraband in the area, mainly by Santanderian middle classes and *paisa* migrants. It has also displayed a rather dynamic nature, especially noticeable in the construction and trade branches.

The Valluno focus

Formed around the smuggling axis between the Pacific harbour of Buenaventura and Panama, the southern region of the Cauca Valley was already active in the cocaine business from the very beginning. With its centre in the industrial city of Cali, the Cauca Valley was strongly dependent on sugar cane production until the 1970s.

The involvement in the cocaine business was marked by the early control of the Amazon corridor, both a region for coca cultivation as well as a point of entrance for imported cocaine base. They were also specialised in chemical precursors import, and though in a smaller scale than the Antioquian entrepreneurs, they had their own well-established distribution networks in the United States (especially in New York).

Valluno groups expanded silently, and until 1984 all conflicts with the Medellín traffickers were solved in one way or another. However, status quo was definitively broken after Pablo Escobar declared open war against the state. Cocaine entrepreneurs from Cali profited from this conflict, and even collaborated with state agencies in the tracking down of Medellín groups.

In contrast, most of the *Valluno* illegal entrepreneurs had an urban, middle-class origin. More integrated into their local environment, they avoided open confrontation with government officials, politicians or the local traditional elite. Cali did not have the levels of violence that characterised other cities like Medellín. With a low-key approach, they used their wealth to gain the favour of politicians, clerics, military leaders and legal businessmen, mainly through corruption. Although some of them, such as the brothers Rodríguez Orejuela, had large and well organised illegal enterprises, a lot of smaller and rather independent groups flourished in cities such as Cali, Jamundí, Tuluá, Roldanillo or Cartago.

In fact, their clear success after the Medellín group started to collapse in 1991 was due to the fact that they were, simultaneously, investing in a legal business empire, cultivating political influence, and, more important, adjusting and improving their business methods: reducing risk, achieving economies of scale, just-in-time supply, developing new products – heroin – and markets – Europe and Japan – and introducing new technologies.[38]

The Northern Cauca Valley focus

Based around small cities like Tuluá, Roldanillo, Trujillo, El Dobio, Cartago and Pereira, this area has gained particular importance since the imprisonment of the big Cali cocaine entrepreneurs in the mid 1990s. In fact, organisations and entrepreneurs active in this region were always included within the focus with centre in Cali. Some of the former Cali entrepreneurs such as Henry Loaiza or the Urdinola family, in fact belong to this region.

---

38 'Colombia's Drug Business. The wages of prohibition', *The Economist*, 24 Dec. 1994 – 6 Jan. 1995.

Given that this area has been at the epicentre of the cocaine business in Colombia since 1995, three important characteristics should be mentioned about these groups. First of all, they have remained rather small and independent, and some of their illegal entrepreneurs belong to a younger generation. Secondly, they managed to adapt themselves to new risk minimising strategies, such as reallocation of resources, new agreements with foreign – Mexican – organisations, and so forth. And finally, these groups have engaged in successful product diversification: they control heroin production and export, which generated additional profits for about 700 million dollars a year (Steiner 1997).

Although this categorisation of different focal points has a socio-historical interest, it does not necessarily imply that they have functioned as independent and homogeneous centres. The relation between them is sometimes complex and has changed over time. There are, for instance, several organisations, located in specific regions, cities or towns, which were once linked and later became autonomous, and vice versa. Castillo provides a detailed description of organisations and drug traffickers based in Bogotá, Cundinamarca, Armenia, Pereira, Ibagué, Villavicencio, Leticia, Ciénaga, Santa Marta, Córdoba, Valledupar and Cartagena (Castillo, 1987: 41 and ss.). Only in the Cauca Valley region, did each town have two or more important drug entrepreneurs who operated more or less independently. The number of organisations is unknown. During the 'hot' year of 1989, the U.S. Senate reported that the Medellín organisation consisted of "approximately 200 individual trafficking groups".[39] In 1991, the U.S. Department of State claimed that there were between 150 and 200 organisations in total.[40]

Finally, another interesting difference between Colombian drug entrepreneurs is a generational one. The old generation of cocaine entrepreneurs, those that were successful and famous during the 1980s and early 1990s, have clearly had their day. They are either dead, imprisoned or retired, and their affairs and assets have been seized, laundered or inherited. That generation, incarnated basically by the Medellín and to certain extent the Cali groups, achieved some provisional 'central' powers and managed to produce 'big names'. However, in the beginning of the 1990s the dynamics of both the international cocaine market and the policies to combat it suggested that a new way to organise the business was necessary: flexibility, internationalisation, management and risk reduction were all central to the success of a younger generation. In 1994, Rodríguez Orejuela himself explained this shift:

> "There is a generation change in narcotics trafficking today. Most of the new generation are under 30 (years) and have no criminal record. They are not known by Colombian authorities, much less by the DEA...".[41]

---

39 U.S. Senate, Permanent Subcommittee on Investigations, Structure of International Drug Cartels. Hearings: Staff Statement, p.19.
40 United States Department of State (1991), Bureau of International Narcotics Matters. INCSR (International Narcotics Control Strategy Report). March 1991.
41 A Drug Deal?, *Time*, November 7, 1994, p. 14-15.

This new generation incarnated by minor bosses and generally unknown names, which accumulated profits faster and more safely than the old one, marks the end of 'fordist' factory production in the cocaine business. They have spread to new regions, even outside Colombia, relocating production processes, transport and distribution lines, and becoming the new small, flexible, anonymous and international cocaine entrepreneurs.

2.3.3 Flexible co-operation: entrepreneurs without 'cartel'

Types of enterprises
As was the case with the people and regions involved, cocaine enterprises are also heterogeneous. This illegal market should in fact be understood by the articulation of many kinds of legal and illegal enterprises, through the various market stages or sectors.

Regarding cocaine production, many sorts of enterprises can be identified. Some could take the form of the aforementioned *planteo* system, in which a single entrepreneur establishes close and client based ties with coca producers. However, most of the refiners produce cocaine simply by buying the raw material, employing people, and selling it to the exporters. These units vary from small laboratories owned by one person – common until the early 1980s but still surviving – to rather large refineries owned by many business partners, who at the same time are also engaged in cocaine export.

Export enterprises, on the contrary, tend to be larger. Illegality makes cocaine export a very complex market operation. Successful exporters combine economic, military and political resources (Krauthausen and Sarmiento 1991: 60). They need to have enough capital to cover costs and investments, subcontract services and pay-off law enforcers. They require at least a minimum security apparatus that is ready to use violence, can avoid theft, enforce agreements, neutralise law enforcement and discourage competitors. They finally need the proper connections, again to neutralise detection and to sell the product in the consumer markets. These requirements are hard to meet for independent, individual exporters. This market stage seems to be the most oligopolist of all. However, independent or individual exporters do exist. In fact, a proper combination of capital, violence and contacts is all that is needed to enter the business, at least for some time or for smaller quantities of cocaine. There are many cases in which former employees, even bodyguards, of large exporters became, after the death or imprisonment of their employers, new independent exporters.
Large export enterprises do not imply 'large' in a literal sense. They are large with respect to their availability of resources, the volumes exported and the profits made. As I shall further argue, illegality does not favour 'large', stable enterprises. The Rodríguez Orejuela brother's group, for example, worked through a very complex system of contracting and subcontracting with many external actors, enterprises and organisations.

Many modalities of cocaine transportation enterprises have also been encountered. Some illegal exporters have their own means of transportation. This is the case of the rather small ones – by paying people to carry small quantities – or the first entrepreneurs who were using their own small planes. However, as larger volumes and more distant markets appeared, specialised and separated transportation enterprises developed. Cocaine exporters usually contract their services, depending on the specific characteristics of each operation. Some are small, for example, one or two pilots with a couple of special planes. There are also illegal shipping companies, with their own personnel and speed boats. Transportation has also been subcontracted to foreign organisations, as it in the case of cocaine entering to the United States via Mexico. And, of course, as in the case of large volume exports to the European market, legal enterprises are used to transport cocaine. From airlines and shipping companies to import-export firms, from carrier to removal enterprises: all have been used to smuggle cocaine, either by paying-off some employees or by engaging more managerial staff.

There are also enterprises that specialise in money laundering. Although some exporters may have somebody to perform this task – for example when they also own financial institutions – this expensive service seems to be more often subcontracted to special people: financiers, stockbrokers or investor experts. The more obstacles there are to 'cleaning' their capital, the more they are forced to rely on the services of these companies.

With respect to military and security resources, most cocaine exporters do have permanent employees to perform some of these tasks – basically bodyguards and 'score settlers'. Yet again, cocaine exporters have frequently relied on external apparatuses, such as private security firms, independent hired-killers, or paramilitary armed groups. Other 'peripheral' companies offering their services to many cocaine entrepreneurs are also very common: law firms, real estate agents, architectural offices, and so on. Almost all of them deal also with legal clients and enterprises.

It is clear that many kinds of enterprises are interconnected at this level of the cocaine business, performing multiple tasks, having different organisational forms, and offering diverse professional expertise. However, a strict and rigid labour division is not always the case. Small producers can export now and then, large exporters can also settle scores personally, bodyguards may supervise transportation, or carriers may also be arranging up- and unload. Frequently, each entrepreneurial unit perform many tasks, changing and modifying them according to the dynamics imposed by illegality.

Finally, this flexibility is also reflected in the durability of cocaine enterprises. Some endure, but in the cocaine market many sporadic enterprises are rather frequent. It is common that two or more traffickers become partners for a single operation. At the level of production, throw-away kitchens are not rare.

On patrones,[42] deputies and labourers

The cocaine industry in Colombia offers both a precarious and stable occupation to a range of groups and individuals. A short list includes unskilled labourers, chemists, technicians, rural workers, peasants, carriers, boat and aircraft pilots, car and track chauffeurs, representatives, couriers, individual smugglers, bodyguards and escort personnel, racketeers, hired-killers, lawyers, accountants, finance consultants and investors, custom and police officials, intellectuals and merchants.

It should not be necessary to stress the heterogeneous nature of this labour force. It ranges from urban to rural, from unskilled to high-qualified, from subsistence wages to well-paid salaries, from collective to individual, from part-time to full-time, from very risky and violent to rather safe and mundane. They include poor residents from urban slums as well as upper-class individuals.

Although this can change from one organisation to the other, four typically different roles or tasks can be identified in large cocaine exporter enterprises: the *patrón* (leader or chief), the close assistants, the professionals and the mass unskilled workers. All cocaine enterprises have a *patrón* who co-ordinates all transactions. This role can also be shared by two or more people, usually when the entrepreneurs are close friends or relatives and equally active in the business: the Ochoa or Rodríguez Orejuela brothers, for example. Some like Pablo Escobar would maintain personal control on even small details, others would simply delegate more.

The assistants or *lugartenientes*[43] (deputies) are people close to the *patrón* to whom the practical development of operational matters is entrusted. They combine, in a rather eclectic way, the tasks conferred to private secretaries and managers in legal business. Close friends or relatives of the *patrón* often hold these positions. Next to them, some 'second grade' *lugartenientes* may also exist in large organisations. They take more specific responsibilities, such as the acquisition of cocaine base, transportation, wholesale distribution or the co-ordination of military and security resources (Krauthausen and Sarmiento 1991: 45).

Individual professionals for specialised functions are employed by the entrepreneurs. Chemical engineers, experienced pilots, security experts – often retired policemen or military officials, economists, lawyers and a wide range of professionals for the administration of their legal businesses: hotel and business managers, and so on. Except for the latter, they all receive higher salaries than the average they would obtain in the legal workplace market.

Finally, cocaine entrepreneurs employ many people with almost no labour qualifications. They are absolutely essential for business development, and perform one or several tasks in a very flexible way: bodyguards, kitchen workers and watchmen, raw material and cocaine up- and unloaders, chauffeurs, couriers or

---

42 *Patrón* (boss, chief) is the usual name used by employees when they refer to the cocaine entrepreneur. Despite the fact that derives from the same root than *padre* (father), the word means in Spanish both 'protector' and labour employer (boss), the later stressing more a factual (not moral) authority over the labourer. This second meaning is the one used by cocaine employees.

43 This word, of a clear military and administrative nature, is not often used by cocaine actors themselves. It implies a bureaucratic institutionalisation that these enterprises do not have.

encaletadores (cocaine load-keepers). Naturally, not all of them require the same skills and they do not have the same occupational prestige. This can vary, for example, from the low ranked *lavaperro*[44] to the rather professional courier. However, it is interesting to point out that most of these flexible workers either perform more than one of those tasks at the same time, or have been 'promoted' from one to the other. Although some of them have high expectations of eventually becoming entrepreneurs, for the majority it means a regular, irregular or even an extra job.

Colombian cartels?

When analysing Colombia's drug organisations and entrepreneurs, the first, major obstacle is the enormous popularity and durability of the term 'cartel' in almost any account about these phenomena and groups. Since the DEA first applied it to the Medellín traffickers in the early 1980s, this term, borrowed from economics, has been widely and uncritically used by policy-makers, politicians and journalists of all kinds. However, this is more than a semantic problem. Within the context of a war on cocaine, it has no doubt been and still is politically useful for many groups to call cocaine export organisations 'cartels'. As a convincing metaphor, it implies: a) a very powerful and highly organised enemy, easily identifiable, b) the image of a conspiracy against the consumers through secret agreements on prices and output, c) oligopolist raw market exploitation; d) a threat to the 'fair' economy and entrepreneurs; and e) a legitimation for continuous requests for more resources and powers to fight it.

Academics and researchers have appreciated the concept variously. Most of the studies have rejected or criticised it,[45] but the term still persists. Some scholars, mostly from America and Europe, dedicate a footnote or a paragraph to explain their reservations, only to continue talking about cartels without further notice.[46]

In economic terms, a cartel is a formal agreement between firms in an oligopolist market to co-operate with regard to agreed procedures on such variables as price and output. The result is diminished competition and increased co-operation over objectives such as, for example, joint profit maximisation or avoidance of new entry.

Several problems crop up when looking at the reality. The first surprise is that both media and official government sources continually make references to several cocaine cartels – generally associated with some city or region – which by definition refutes the very existence of a cartel. Secondly, the illegality of the cocaine business renders the formation of a workable cartel difficult. The risk minimising strategies that must be followed to make an illegal operation successful encourage a loose

---

44 Literally 'dog cleaner', this is the common pejorative word for those engaged in the more unskilled jobs in the cocaine business, for example, teenagers who clean the *patrón*'s car.

45 Most notably Thoumi (1995); del Olmo (1992, 1996); Camacho Guizado (1988, 1994); Betancourt and García (1994); Kopp (1995); Krauthausen and Sarmiento (1991); Krauthausen (1994, 1998); Naylor (1997); Silva García (1997); Tovar Pinzón (1994) and Uprimny (1994b). Others like Arango (1988); Arango and Child (1984); Salazar (1990); Castillo (1987, 1991, 1996) or Gugliotta and Leen (1990), vary in a rather eclectic way between terms such as 'cartel', '*mafia*' and 'narco-traffic'.

46 See as examples Labrousse (1993); Lee III (1989, 1991); Clawson and Lee III (1996); Smith (1992); Santino and La Fiura (1993); Bovenkerk (1995b) and Van Duyne (1995).

structure, in which it is not possible to plan production levels, to achieve economic agreements and to give orders to be carried out through several layers of production and distribution (Thoumi 1995: 143). The groups have no control over production volumes, including even coca production. On the other hand, prices at the retail end vary a great deal from place to place, depending on the access of each buyer and seller to distribution and marketing networks. Neither stability nor changes in prices are at all related to any kind of agreement between producers and exporters.

In organisational terms, relations between different actors – coca peasants, paste manufacturers, carriers, cocaine refiners, exporters, distributors, and so on – tend to be fluid and flexible: cocaine business structure quickly adapts itself to changes in the business environment brought about by the activities of law enforcement agencies and other factors (Thoumi 1995: 143). Although things like, for example, insurance mechanisms against loses appear to be well-organised, many of these relations are short-lived, and participation in shipments or transactions mutates constantly. The fact that cocaine trafficking requires a range of interconnected and specialised personnel – buyers of paste or base, chemists, engineers, pilots, wholesalers, money launderers, accountants, lawyers, professional assassins, and so forth – does not imply *per se* a very highly organised structure.

There is empirical evidence challenging the popular view that drug trafficking is dominated by pyramidal structures with 'Mr. Big' at the top in control of everything. To reject the image of Colombian cocaine groups as powerful and centralised corporations with boards of directors and vice-presidents for every different branch, is not to deny that Colombian cocaine entrepreneurs do organise themselves in tasks such as co-insuring cocaine shipments, engaging in joint smuggling or production ventures, or exchanging loads. Nor does it mean that they have not reached specific agreements – hardly ever economic ones, and more often of political and military nature regarding assassinations and counter-intelligence. Neither does it mean that they do not control some of the phases of the process in an oligopolist way – for example exportation to American and European markets – nor that they operate without economic rationality.

The cocaine business can best be seen as a complex articulation of very differentiated networks in which relational ties – basically dyadic ones – function in various ways. They range from typical peasant production relations, to face-to-face interactions characteristic of the dealer-consumer relation, to more business-like ties such as in large-scale production and exportation. Even within these 'entrepreneurial' stages, one finds with a range of small independent exporters, varying from individual adventurers smuggling a few grams with high risk, to small groups controlling specific markets. The dyadic character of the relations is related to the illegal nature of the business. In general, participants in the business only know about their own role and the immediate level below them, but they hardly know anything about the levels above, and they completely lack a general picture of the business (Thoumi 1995: 141-142).

In fact, the relatively decentralised and amorphous nature of such groups and coalitions, and the frequent use of relatives, friends and neighbours for different tasks and functions, has also been a key pattern for protection and success. As put by Arango and Child:

> "...Every *capo* is the maximum authority of his organisation. It is very difficult to destroy the organisation simply because it does not exist. If somebody falls down or for any reason loses his markets, his position is immediately taken over by another" (Arango and Child 1984: 186, my translation).

Furthermore, the institutional organisation of cocaine entrepreneurs is rather precarious, and it precludes anything resembling a bureaucracy in Weberian terms, especially one that would survive after the replacement of its leaders (Krauthausen and Sarmiento 1991: 36).

Far from decreased competition, as a cartel implies, frequent violent clashes seem to be common between various groups, which attests to the difficulty that any group has in exercising strict control over the business and over their organisations. Even successful vertical integration of processes – from coca leaf production to market distribution – by a certain group or individual has been precarious, variable and always subject to conflict and mutation. The cocaine business is in fact remarkably open to newcomers, including those who take the place of former entrepreneurs as well as those who exploit new markets and new routes. This dynamism, caused by the spread of persons who want to enter a business that offers great opportunities, virtually enables anyone with the money, the supplier and the ability to avoid being caught or ripped off, entrance at any level (Block and Chambliss 1981: 56).

Between co-operation and savage competition
In sum, the cocaine market can be conceived as a sandglass (see Figure II) regarding the number of participants, with the two extremes highly competitive and a central oligopolist sector (cocaine exporters). Although they have a strong negotiating capacity between coca producers and cocaine consumers, they do not constitute a 'cartel' since the dynamic of the upper competitive sector (for example with price formation or production volumes) prevails. Illegality and risk minimising strategies have a double impact in the oligopolist sector: they make any organisational arrangement or entrepreneurial structure sporadic, flexible and changeable; and they create a *sui generis* link between small and large export enterprises based in a combination of co-operation and savage competition.

Co-operation between large enterprises hardly takes place in economic terms. Despite some ephemeral – supposed – agreements in the early 1980s about territorial distribution of the American market (Castillo 1987: 114-115), co-ordinated actions have a military nature: assassinations, death squads and counter-intelligence usually against common enemies such as state officials of guerrilla groups. Business co-operation between large and small or individual entrepreneurs, on the contrary, does exist. There are three known systems created by large enterprises to allow and encourage independent or individual exporters to keep active in the market.

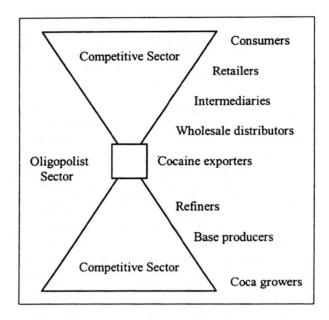

Figure II Structure of Cocaine Market

The first mechanism is called *apuntada* (join up) and consists of a joint export venture offered by large exporters to people outside their organisations. They participate, according to their own financial resources and their relation with the exporter, either with money or with cocaine. Since the total amounts of cocaine are large, they are sent in various shipments lowering the overall risk. In fact, not only small organisations can participate with their modest quantities, but any capital investor can become a cocaine exporter. This system is used not only to distribute risks but also to compensate favours from friends, politicians and civil servants, extending the business into society (Krauthausen and Sarmiento 1991: 32; Thoumi 1995: 145). It is also usual that large entrepreneurs allow smaller ones to send cocaine loads through their own networks, just charging for the service. A third way of co-operation is evidenced by the transportation insurance mechanisms also granted by large entrepreneurs. In this case, they offer to the small exporter not only the line, but 100% refund if the load is seized. If it is not, then the insurer gets a percentage. Large entrepreneurs can offer this insurance service due to their ability to reduce risks.

However, next to these co-operation mechanisms, savage competition – i.e. without rules – seems to be a principle within this oligopolist sector. Most evident between large entrepreneurs, this competition has taken various forms: from direct open war (physical elimination, thefts or attacks) to collaboration with law enforcers tipping them off about other entrepreneur's movements and operations. In fact, a great deal of the cocaine seizures and big 'hits' by law enforcers rely on these tips. Savage competition is even visible within organisations themselves: many large entrepreneurs killed or imprisoned have been betrayed by people of their own organisations, who have used violence or have broken their silence.

2.4 THE SOCIAL IMPACT OF COCAINE ENTREPRENEURS

This particular business social structure has indeed had a strong impact on Colombian society and institutions. The same social conditions that favoured the development of the cocaine business in Colombia for the last 25 years, have at the same time been, in the majority of the cases, reinforced by business expansion. If in economic terms the existence of the cocaine industry has been fairly negative, in social and political terms it has been a disaster for Colombia and one that may be added to the already many existing problems in the country. I will analyse this impact in the final part of this chapter.

Yet the cocaine business is not the 'source of all evils', as it has often been portrayed. The impact of cocaine entrepreneurs has been heterogeneous, changing from place and time. The cocaine business has definitely contributed to state de-legitimation, growing corruption, increased feelings of impunity and to all sort of problems regarding Colombian foreign relations. It has also contributed to the increase of the long-suffered internal armed conflicts, and the amplification of other social violence. All these social phenomena were there long before the cocaine business appeared, and will probably survive if the business disappeared tomorrow. Some questions about the political nature of cocaine organisations will also illustrate the readiness of many observers to seek omnipresent explanations for complex social problems around drug enterprises and entrepreneurs

2.4.1 Social legitimation: strategies and encapsulation

Whatever their origin, cocaine entrepreneurs as the *nouveaux riches* tend to develop medium or long term strategies for reducing the local opposition of traditional dominant groups. The possibility for these new entrepreneurs to gain recognition and acceptance varies with the socio-cultural and economic conditions of each region and depends on several other variables as well. These include the land-owning situation; the local patterns of capital accumulation and the ways in which capital is laundered or reinvested; the presence or absence of guerrilla or paramilitary activity; the nature of political leadership and local community organisation; the forms of state repression; the strength or weakness of local social organisations; and so forth (Camacho Guizado 1994: 168). Whether the entrepreneur has a rural or a urban background also influences their behaviour and acceptance.

As enriched peasants transformed in land-owners, some reproduce and reinforce the values of the local community through philanthropic action and clientelist relations within the rural areas. Next to the development of patron-client relations, they would be primarily directed to consolidate themselves as new land-owners. The social acceptance of this group has been rather weak, since they have resorted to extreme violence against the state, other competitors, old land-owners and guerrilla organisations.

Not very different has been the case of cocaine entrepreneurs coming from poor urban strata. They encountered social resistance from the traditional elite, and had to strive hard for social recognition. They combined open violence against the state and competitors, social investments – from jobs to some infrastructure – to gain the support of popular groups and some attempts to support financiers, industrialists, merchants or politicians in need or decline with credits or capital investment. A paradigmatic case here is Pablo Escobar.

However, other illegal entrepreneurs did better, for example those who already had good connections with middle and upper urban classes. As mentioned earlier with respect to *valluno* cocaine entrepreneurs, their strategies combined very selective violence, local economic investments and the cultivation of local and national loyalties through massive corruption. With a lower profile, their 'social investments' were not direct but mediated through political and social institutions: churches, municipalities, football clubs, existing political parties, and so on. Yet not all of them managed to be accepted. Many middle-class professionals or other individuals who got rich quick did not enjoy local recognition. However, clashes with local elite were avoided and their pretensions for social acceptance were reduced to ensure the future acceptance of their children as members of the intellectual or economic local establishment (Hernández and Téllez 1990).

2.4.2 Colombian mafia?

Though not as much as economic agents, Colombian cocaine entrepreneurs have also been seen as powerful political and social actors. Large social power accumulated through illegal activities, interweave and conflict with state and local agencies through corruption or violence, clientelist relations and family business, all things that quickly allow many observers to portray drug entrepreneurs as true *mafiosi*. Again and again, media and law enforcers around the world have been tempted to use the word *mafia*[47] as a synonym for Colombian cocaine organisations.

Even respected Colombian researchers as Betancourt and García (1994) or Arango (1988) apply and elaborate on the concept to 'adapt' it to the Colombian context.[48]

---

47 Despite differences and changes, with *mafia* I refer to the specific Italian phenomenon, particularly the Sicilian *Mafia*, the Calabrian '*Ndrangheta* and the Campanian *Camorra*.

48 In their well-researched book, maybe one of the best and more serious works in this field, Betancourt and García (1994) devote many efforts to reconstruct and present several typologies of *mafia* organisations (Sicilian, Italo-American, European) to apply later the models to the many regional centres identified in Colombia. However, this attempt is not at all convincing. They face a vast range of organisational features and socio-political arrangements that in a rather a-historical way are forced under the umbrella-concept of *mafia*. As a result, they end up with vague conceptualisations such as "...for the Colombian case, we understand '*mafia*' as those groups identified with economic, political, social or cultural interests, which assume an illegal attitude to the state and its juridical norms. They do not resort to judges or the state agencies to solve their conflicts, but on the contrary they use their own

The information they provide, however, is good enough to avoid easy analogies with the Italian case.

For Krauthausen (1994, 1998), Colombian drug organisations and the Italian *mafia* are two different forms of what has been broadly defined as 'organised crime'. Their point of departure follows a different logic and even their everyday activities diverge to a certain extent. They differ very much concerning historical origins, organisational models and their relations with civil society.

In the first place, Colombian drug entrepreneurs are primarily guided by a 'logic of market', opposed to the 'logic of power' that primarily characterises *mafiosi* groups (Krauthausen 1994: 119). What is important for *mafia* groups is the exercise of social, political and especially economic control, through protection and extortion, within certain territorial limits (Gambetta, 1996). As territorial control is a primary feature, the creation of monopolistic niches and the diversification in several legal and illegal activities often occurs. Blok (1974) has highlighted this dimension of local power brokers:

> "*Mafiosi* depend very much on personal relations with a local clientele – their 'home farm' so to speak – whose growth takes time. Their power domains are locally phrased, and it is precisely their control over a distinct locality that enables them to influence higher levels of society as power brokers.' (Blok 1974: 225-226).

The evolution from a 'traditional' to a more modern 'entrepreneurial' or 'financial' *mafia* (Arlacchi 1986) does not contradict this centrality of the 'logic of power'. There is no reason to believe that these groups will limit themselves to the field of protection and extortion, if other classical legal and illegal economic activities (for example construction or drug trafficking) would be even more beneficial in the end. They will definitively profit, as economic agents, from their advantaged position – networks, loyalties, political control, and so on – over other actors: for them, power becomes a bridgehead for market performance.

For Colombian drug organisations, on the contrary, territorial control only plays a secondary role. They have grown and live from and for a market that is international. Although Colombia in general and some of its regions in particular – due to social, economic or geographic competitive advantages – constitute something like a 'home farm', it only derives meaning from the dynamics of the drug market. Their monopolistic ambitions – which, as I mentioned before, are more a dream than a reality – relate to the several phases of the international cocaine market. Their influence in higher levels of society (or even politics) is not based in their capacity to

---

hired-killer organisations, *created with the aim of appear themselves as local agents able to impose respect and acceptation.*" Betancourt and García (1994: 139, translation and italics are mine). Beside the fact that, as local agents, the most respected and accepted groups are in no way those using high levels of violence, this definition oppose '*mafia*' to the 'state' in open contradiction with the historical typologies presented and all sources quoted. Moreover, when they do frame *mafia* in more precise terms (power interweave with state, mediation between clients and power holders, migration enclaves, family organisations, and so on) they simplify reality, overstate some aspects, and clearly neglect others.

negotiate or mediate the collective interests of others. Very few have engaged in politics, and even when they had the power to appoint local authorities their only concern has been to protect their business and integrity.

In Colombia, where the state has been weak and never actually achieved a legitimate claim on the monopoly of violence, there are of course many local – violent – powers that either 'parallel' the state or act as mediators between clients and power holders. However, in general, these local powers do not mainly coincide with the Colombian drug organisations. Again, as in the case of *mafiosi* groups, one logic does not exclude the other. The logic of power also plays a role amongst drug organisations, that also exercise protection, extortion, grant favours to friends, and so on. Yet the considerable social, economic, political and military control that some traffickers exercise within their zones of residence, is a direct result of their success as illegal entrepreneurs. In part, this control is essential to protect an illegal business. On the other hand, this control is a consequence of capital accumulation in the drug market, and their strategies – through many forms of philanthropy, sponsorship and social investments – to become accepted as new local dominant classes (Camacho Guizado 1994: 163). The market becomes, in this case, an excellent bridgehead for power.

Moreover, *mafiosi* groups and Colombian drug organisations have different historical origins. The emergence of Italian organisations, going all the way back to the second half of the nineteenth century, runs rather parallel to and is interconnected with the process of state formation.[49] Since their very dawn to existence, state and *mafiosi* groups have competed and co-operated with regard to shared properties such as territorial control, protection, extortion, violence and power.[50] Colombian drug organisations, on the other hand, have emerged and developed, in the short period of 20 years, from the exploitation of one specific economic illegal activity. Competition or co-operation with state institutions – and their functions – has been more of an outcome of business success or failure than an original attribute. From a historical point of view, Italian *mafiosi* organisations are better comparable with the diverse local factions before, during and after the period of *La Violencia* (1946-1966), with the groups controlling the emerald mines in the centre of the country, and of course with paramilitary and guerrilla groups.

Contrary to the secret and family-oriented character of *mafia* groups (Blok 2000), Colombian organisations are well known for their public and 'open' nature. Blok (2000: 89) has argued that Sicilian 'families' are coalitions mainly based on agnatic, affinal or ritual kinship. Kinship would not only solve the problem of trust deficit inside these illegal groups, but it would also provide strong symbolic bonds around blood metaphors.

It is also very common to find brothers, brothers-in-law, couples or friends working together in Colombian cocaine organisations. However, kinship and

---

49 "...the rise and development of Sicilian *mafia* must be understood as an aspect of the long-term processes of centralisation and national integration of Italian society." Blok (1974: 213).

50 Charles Tilly (1985) has shown how protection and extortion have been basic practices in the formation of modern European states.

friendship relations inside these groups are more subordinated to economic considerations (risk minimising) than they are intrinsic features of cocaine enterprises. For example, many people in the cocaine business actually want to keep their own relatives out of it, not only for fear or shame, but also as a way to safely transform illegal profits into legal family assets. Even when many relatives are involved, they do not do it as 'members' of any structure: they tend to defend their immediate individual interests, sometimes keeping separate 'lines' or joining different networks. Moreover, cocaine enterprises are too flexible and short-lived to be 'inherited'. There are some cases in which brothers or wives take over after bosses are imprisoned or killed. However, it is more often the case that subordinates or competitors replace failed entrepreneurs by stealing contacts, lines and employees, thus fragmenting and reorganising former groups.

Colombian cocaine enterprises function with a very loose, changing internal sets of rules. Their pragmatic practices contrast with stricter codes of conduct of *mafia* organisations. The lesser tendency for the hierarchical imposition of authority and the lack of initiation or recruitment rituals are also distinctive features in Colombian drug organisations.

Finally, these differences also imply divergent relations with civil society. Even being illegal entrepreneurs, first of all *mafia* groups will be seen by other social groups as more or less legitimate power brokers. Their intrinsic 'para-intra-state' nature remains the key feature in their relation with society. Colombian drug traffickers, on the contrary, will be judged by surrounding social groups primarily as more or less legitimate entrepreneurs. Even when they exercise violence or provide protection, they will tend to be accepted or opposed as economic actors.

2.4.3 Social and political impact

Cocaine entrepreneurs and the state

The cocaine business has had a wide impact on the political and administrative system in Colombia, accelerating the de-legitimation processes already taking place before the rise of cocaine industry (Hartlyn 1993). This de-legitimation regards several institutions such as the police, the judicial and legal system, state bureaucracies in general, etc. The process has taken place through different means.

A first resource has been corruption. The widespread use of different forms of 'contributions' – regular or special payments, donations, favours, and so on – from the very local level to the top, has ranged across institutions connected or not with the state: political parties, judiciary, public ministry, police, military, parliament, city councils, universities and legal enterprises. Although the illicit drug industry amplified corruption, already existing traditional clientelist and closed political relations provide a very fertile soil for collusion. Some state institutions have suffered more than others: police, judicial system and the legislative power have lost, both in reality and under the eyes of public opinion, more credibility than, for example, local or national executive power. Buying off journalists has also damaged information rights.

A second way of weakening the state has been the open use of violence and intimidation. In cases such as Escobar's war in the late 1980s, it included assassinations, car or other bomb attacks, kidnapping, systematic murder of police forces and judges, the spread of intimidation and threats, and so on. Although the state has reacted in some cases, also with violence and spectacular operations, most of this violence has remained unpunished and has helped to 'normalise' societal feelings about impunity, injustice and powerlessness.

Illegal entrepreneurs have also entered into competition with the state. Although, as I shall further argue, they do not primarily seek territorial control through various forms of political and social control, they have in fact profited from state deficit. Social programmes sponsored by Medellín traffickers in urban slums clearly indicated that local and national authorities were unconcerned about these social groups and problems. Successful paramilitary actions against guerrillas, also sponsored by drug entrepreneurs, have shown the powerlessness of the regular army. The private security boom or social cleansing groups supported by Cali traffickers have also exposed a deep crisis in public law and order.

Another threat has come from abroad. The existence of the cocaine business allowed the international community, lead by American foreign policy for Colombia, to strongly interfere in domestic politics, through diplomatic pressure, economic and political sanctions, and all sort of conditioning for help and co-operation, weakening national sovereignty and turning international relations into an undesirable 'narco-diplomacy' (Tokatlian 1995). Until now, American anti-drug policies for Colombia have neither aimed to amend the endemic state democratic deficit, nor have contributed to build a democratic civil society. The illegal industry is merely seen by foreign states and enforcement agencies as a matter of 'national security'.

Finally, the illegal drug industry has been pervasive in amplifying the 'dishonesty trap' into more general relations within civil society and with the state (Thoumi 1995: 236). The real or imaginary individual success of illegal entrepreneurs has had a negative impact for the democratisation of society. As moral entrepreneurs, they do not stress values around solidarity, but often those on individualism, materialism, violent solution of conflicts or respect for the hierarchies, enforcing widespread disrespect for any laws and the rights of other citizens, and the idea that state institutions are almost an obstacle for personal success. Widespread impunity has also contributed to such a situation.

Cocaine entrepreneurs, guerrilla and paramilitary groups
Twenty years of the cocaine business in Colombia has also introduced new developments within the military conflict between the state and guerrilla groups, with an outcome of increased violence, principally para-state and private violence.

The guerrilla groups, in particular the *FARC*,[51] have found in coca and opium growers a social base, who reciprocally have found in them some protection − not

---

51 Revolutionary Armed Forces of Colombia (FARC). This group appeared in the mid 1960s and linked to the Communist Party, it is one of the oldest guerrilla groups in Latin America. For the relation between coca producers and guerrilla movements, see Jaramillo et al. (1986) and Vargas (1999a and 1999b).

always agreed – against state repression. This relationship took and takes the form of a compulsory taxation (*gramaje*) for defending the illegal crops, the kitchens and the air-strips against state intervention. Beyond any doubt this has been, next to kidnapping and the 'revolutionary' taxation on land-owners and legal enterprises (*vacuna*), a key income source for the *FARC*. This has not only limited the government's opportunities for building alliances with coca peasants but has turned them into priority targets of their military actions against guerrilla groups. The repression of coca peasants and coca fields, without any alternative help for rural employment or crop substitution, has only reinforced the military power and the social legitimation of guerrilla organisations (Vargas Meza 1999a).

In the early 1980s, guerrilla groups also found a provisional alliance with large cocaine producers, providing protection of large cocaine refineries. A *narco-guerrilla* connection was politically used by United States, linking its anti-drug policies with anti-Communist policies in the region (Thoumi 1995: 159).[52] This 'killing two birds with one stone' policy has been recently resurrected by the Colombian military, since they got involved in anti-drug policies and both coca cultivation and guerrilla activity expanded.[53]

However, as early as 1982, guerrilla organisations and cocaine entrepreneurs clearly started going down opposite roads, since guerrilla organisations such as the M-19 tried to demand the *vacunas* imposed on traditional landowners, and targeted them as a source of financing, mainly through kidnapping and extortion. As a result, drug entrepreneurs organised themselves to defend their property and people, supporting and arming paramilitary groups to fight off guerrillas and anyone who sympathised with social reform. The social alliance between drug entrepreneurs and paramilitary groups has been particularly strong in the Magdalena Medio Valley and more recently in the Urabá and Córdoba regions, all areas where drug entrepreneurs have become the new landowners.[54] Cali witnessed in 1985 social cleansing and illegal executions not only against M-19 members but also against homosexuals, prostitutes, drug addicts, homeless and other so called *desechables* (disposables). These actions were supported by cocaine entrepreneurs. Also in the Northern Cauca Valley region many of these drug financed death squads conducted massacres against people accused of sympathising with guerrilla groups.

Paramilitary groups were not invented by cocaine entrepreneurs, but drug money improved equipment, training and resources. By supporting such paramilitary activities, cocaine entrepreneurs cemented their ties with two established groups in Colombian society: the land-owning classes and right-wing military factions.

---

52 In the same way that they have done with other illegal drug producing countries such as Burma and Afghanistan.
53 See the official version of the *narco-guerrilla* connection in Villamarin (1996). Most observers agree, however, that the *FARC* is refining and exporting cocaine to neighbouring countries, as well as it is supplying other cocaine entrepreneurs with raw materials (a.o. Clawson and Lee III 1996; Uribe 1997; Rocha 2000 and Thoumi 2001).
54 For the relation between cocaine entrepreneurs and paramilitary groups see Palacio (ed.) (1990); Reyes Posada (1990, 1991, 1997); Romero (1995), Martin (1996) and Medina (1990, 1993).

Cocaine entrepreneurs and social violence

The cocaine business has also contributed to the amplification of other diffused and social violent conflicts in Colombia. However, it should be pointed out that both Colombian government and the international opinion have tended to over-emphasise the centrality of cocaine business in the overall amount of violence and conflicts in Colombia.

In the case of Colombian authorities, this was to clearly underplay state and parastate related violence, and to shape social chaos into delimited conflicts with clear 'enemies'. In the case of international community, it was to fairly support the American led 'war on drugs' in Colombia. Violence in Colombia is a very complex phenomenon, but it has displayed particular continuities and discontinuities, with different historical and social roots.[55]

During the 1980s, the drug business was directly responsible for approximately 16 of the 100 homicides committed each day in Colombia.[56] The other 84% were both political and social violent deaths with no connection with the cocaine business. Those 'drug related deaths' included scores settled between drug traffickers, social cleansing sponsored by drug organisations, massacres of indigenous and rural community leaders by paramilitary groups financed by drug traffickers acting as new landowners, and private ways of justice by individuals, *sicarios* or other people paid by drug entrepreneurs. To this number, many deaths related to the drug business, such as 'cooks' or couriers killed in 'labour accidents', should be added.

Next to the already mentioned paramilitary violence, the cocaine business promoted the development of the *sicario* industry by generating a demand for individuals willing to use violence. Again, the widespread use of hired killers has gone far beyond the cocaine business, expanding into political or interpersonal conflicts.[57]

It can be argued that cocaine business development also increased fire-arm possession, accounting indirectly for many more deaths. However, the spread of fire-arms in urban areas is more related with broader feelings of fear and insecurity in a very vague sense. The explosion of private security industry as partly been prompted by the illegal entrepreneur's needs for protection.

The existence of cocaine business has clearly worsened the crisis of human rights in Colombia. Many Colombians and their families, mainly from low strata, have suffered the social costs of being double losers to successful drug entrepreneurs and the criminal justice system. Many had to emigrate to the cities to escape rural violence from landowners, paramilitary and guerrilla groups.

Finally, it should be stressed that the most feared and resisted feature of the drug

---

55 The literature on violence in Colombia is vast and impressive. See a.o. Bergquist et al. (eds) (1992); Camacho Guizado and Guzmán (1990); Deas and Gaitán (1995); González et al. (1994); Martin (1996); Palacio (ed.) (1990); Pecaut (1987, 1996); Reyes Posada (1990); Romero (1995); Salazar (1990); Sánchez and Peñaranda (1986) and Uprimny (1994a).

56 For the relationship between cocaine business, violence and human rights, see the excellent research of Uprimny (1994a).

57 See for the development of *sicario* violence in Colombia: Salazar (1990) and Ortiz Sarmiento (1991).

industry by Colombian society has been indeed its resort to violence. This was clear during the 'narco-terrorist' period of Pablo Escobar in the late 1980s and early 1990s. Before and after, people tended to see violence as restricted to the drug business, and cases of external violence such as violence used to buy land, massacres by landowners, or social cleansing in urban slums, were regarded as isolated events. People in Colombia do not primarily link violence with the cocaine business, but with other phenomena such as urban criminality, political war, or personal conflicts.

CHAPTER III

WHITE SHIPMENTS, SOUR TRANSACTIONS

The Dutch Cocaine Market in European Perspective

> "I suppose that its influence is physically a bad one. I find it,
> however, so transcendingly stimulating and clarifying to the
> mind that its second action is a matter of small moment".
>
> Conan Doyle, *The Sign of Four*

3.1 THE EUROPEAN MARKET

3.1.1 Old European cocaine markets

Cocaine in Europe until 1930

Long before Colombia had anything to do with it, Europe already had extensive experience with the pharmacological properties and the economic profitability of cocaine. Although many scientists, explorers and physicians[1] wrote about the coca plant from the sixteenth century onward, it was not until the second half of the nineteenth century that the plant and its properties began to generate a great deal of interest as a 'wonder drug' (Phillips and Wynne 1980: 27).

Cocaine was first isolated and named in 1859 by A. Niemann, a German professor from the University of Göttingen. Both coca and cocaine subsequently acquired sudden fame and popularity in Europe until the late 1920s. These substances were broadly welcomed by physicians in the United States and Europe.[2] The initial enthusiasm about their positive effects and uses as a general stimulant against fatigue or depression, to treat opium, morphine and alcohol addiction, as a local anaesthetic, as an aphrodisiac, to treat asthma, cachexia or stomach disorders, and so on, remained virtually uncontested for 25 years.

---

1   Amongst others Ramon Pave, Tomas Ortiz, Garcilaso de la Vega (Inca), Americo Vespucci, Nicolas Monardes and Humboldt. In 1750, J. de Jussieu was the first botanist to send coca plants to Europe. In 1783, Lamarck classified the plant as the genus *Erythroxylon*. Miller, von Tschudi, Weddell, Pöppig, Prescott, Gibbon and Herndon, Gaedecke, and Markham, from different angles and places, continued experimentation, description and debate in Europe on coca properties during the first half of the nineteenth century.

2   Prestigious scientists such as Mantegazza, De Marles, Fauvel, Aschenbrandt, Palmer, Searle, Christison, Moreno y Maiz, Schraff and von Anrep, Koller, Corning, Bentley, Hammond, Halstead, and, of course, Freud were all strong advocates of the new drug, having high expectations (neglecting thus possible abuse) on its potential positive effects. They should be regarded as the first cocaine 'pushers' and some of them, the first known regular consumers and addicts.

Most of the early experimentation was done with coca infusions, giving rise to all sorts of coca-based drinks and elixirs, presented to the general public as wonder tonics for innumerable disorders. The most successful beverage in Europe came to be *Vin Mariani* (a dark coca-based wine) introduced to the public in 1863 by A. Mariani, a Corsican physician, who quickly gained fame and fortune with his product.[3] In America, an even more successful medicinal tonic appeared in 1886. Instead of alcohol, it was a syrup containing cocaine, caffeine and extracts from cola nuts, mixed in soda water: Coca-Cola was on the market, born from the enthusiasm about the beneficial properties of coca and cocaine.

At the turn of the century, cocaine had already spread beyond the strict medical or para-medical realm to be consumed in a recreational fashion by intellectuals, bohemians, writers, and musicians, as well as by prostitutes, pimps and petty criminals of the main European cities. This potential recreational use of cocaine was pushed forward by the discovery, between 1890 and 1900, of the possibility of sniffing cocaine powder. However, at least until 1910, most of the heavy or chronic cocaine use was still concentrated within the world of 'doctors and patients'.

This expanded and diversified demand (doctors that shoot-up, brain tonic drinking people, sniffing night-life habitués) is clearly illustrated by the increase of coca leaf exports from Peru, the main producer even then: 8 tons in 1877, 580 tons in 1894, 2800 tons in 1906 and 543 tons in 1920 (Escohotado, part II 1996: 84). In Germany, *Merck* had a rather monopolistic control over production by 1885, given that Hamburg was the main trading centre for coca leaf. Willing to promote and sell cocaine as a new panacea, and despite the fact that after 1890 some physicians started to be more cautious about cocaine,[4] the pharmaceutical industry was very active in denying or underplaying undesirable effects, while clearly manipulating some positive statements on cocaine use (Escohotado, part II 1996: 78-79).

Java and the Nederlandsche Cocaïnefabriek

The Netherlands played an important role in coca and, to a lesser extent, cocaine production. In 1878 the first coca plants were brought from Peru to the Dutch colony of Java and during the 1980s commercial cultivation and transportation to Europe expanded with the impulse of the *Koloniale Bank* from Amsterdam. Dutch coca did

---

3   Towards the end of the century, its popularity was immense. Not only amongst doctors that would prescribe it, or people that would buy it in public saloons or popular drugstores, but many celebrities – as in modern advertising – endorsed the wine for its beneficial aspects: Zola, Grant, Bartholdi, Verne, Edison, Ibsen, Sara Bernhardt, the Prince of Wales, the Russian Tsar, or the pope Leo XIII, who decorated Mariani and allowed his effigy to be used on the bottle label.

4   After the first signs of abuse or addiction – including lethal cases of cocaine intoxication among practitioners and patients – were acknowledged between 1880 and 1890, debate within the medical world took virulent proportions and even people like Freud became cautious of earlier statements and research results. In his polemic with Erlenmeyer, Freud calls him a 'crusader', in a prophetic critique against the overlap between pharmacology and morality. However, in his last essay on cocaine, he also recognises premature and blind optimism and revises his own positions on cocaine use against morphinism or alcoholism, and the problem of cocaine tolerance and addiction (Freud 1995: 80).

very well, even surpassing Peruvian production after 1910.[5] Until 1900 crops were mainly sold in Germany, *Merck* being the main buyer. However, that year the *Koloniale Bank* established the first Dutch cocaine factory in Amsterdam, the *Nederlandsche Cocaïnefabriek*. Small in the beginnings, the factory expanded to become the world largest cocaine producer after 1910, maintaining a leading position until 1928, and surviving with the same name until as late as 1975 due to the timely diversification to other hard drugs: novocaine, morphine, codeine, heroin and amphetamines. (Korf and de Kort 1989: 5).

From panacea to evil vice

By the early 1900s, cocaine popularity in European cities slowly started to be the subject of debate and pressure. There were worries along the three fronts of cocaine use: as a therapeutic drug, it was being slowly limited or replaced after increasing doubts and failure; as a popular tonic in patent medicines or drinks, it was increasingly under attack from physicians and pharmacists, and finally, as a recreational drug in underworld and bohemian circles, it became a concern for moral panics and social control campaigners. Counter-reactions to the supposed excesses of cocaine use that eventually resulted in stringent regulation of the drug, first in the United States in 1914 and later in Europe at the end of 1920s, included a mix of medical, moral and social arguments which in many cases reflected or coincided with deeper – and hidden – political and economic anxieties and agendas.

The dramatic change in attitude – from the panacea of 1890 to the most dangerous and evil vice only thirty years later – shows that the real issue with cocaine does not lay in the substance in itself – always a remedy and a poison, always a medicine as well as a potential 'toy'– but rather on the power struggle between distinct social groups – with different social and individual interests – to define and categorise it, and to give the drug one or other social meaning.

A combination of factors can be identified to account for that change. Some refer more specifically to the American situation, but despite some initial opposition due to closer links with cocaine production,[6] Europe followed also the same path.

a) Physicians were increasingly worried about cases of fatal cocaine intoxication, cocaine addiction and, more important, on expansion of non-medical use. With the search for antidotes to cocaine, the substitution with other more secure local anaesthetics such as procaine or novocaine, by the end of the 1920s, cocaine had lost most of its potential usefulness to physicians.

b) Increasing professionalisation and institutionalisation of physicians and pharmacists meant stronger negative attitudes to para-medical products, including

---

5 In 1891, almost 20 tons of coca from Java were sold by the *Koloniale Bank*, which handled yearly between 34 tons and 81 tons until 1900. Java coca exports boomed after that: 200 tons in 1907, 1300 tons in 1914 and 1700 tons in 1920 (Korf and de Kort 1989: 5; Escohotado, part II 1996: 84).

6 France and England followed first, Germany and the Netherlands later. In general terms, European countries had strong interests in production or trafficking of opium and cocaine (colonies, strong pharmaceutical industry, and so forth) and were reluctant to immediately enforce regulation or prohibition.

uncontrolled coca or cocaine-based patent medicines, tonics and drinks. Pharmacists in particular did not want to be seen as responsible for producing cocaine abusers.

c) The popular press was beginning to print horror stories about cocaine addiction, which resulted in widespread, especially middle-class fear of drugs as addicting and vicious (Phillips and Wynne 1980: 57).

d) Non-medical cocaine users, especially those from the lower classes, were considered dangerous to both themselves and society. Cocaine was increasingly linked with moral degradation, and grew to be associated with criminal and violent behaviour, and above all, in America, with 'black' crime.

e) Although in Europe cocaine also started to be associated with prostitutes, bohemians, petty criminals and the decadent night life of Berlin, Paris, Vienna or London, there was also concern about cocaine abuse among soldiers, especially during the First World War. The country to blame was, both as the main cocaine producer and war enemy, Germany.

f) Both in America and Europe, two processes were already under way by the end of the nineteenth century: on the one hand, a revival of traditional theological and anti-liberal discourses, which depicted 'artificial paradises' created by drugs (and drunkenness) as evil and immoral social threats. On the other, the expansion of State interventionism and welfare, that gave room for 'muckraking' social reformers of all sorts, willing both to legislate people's morals and to protect them through the 'therapeutic' State.

Cocaine in Europe 1930-1970

Between 1915 and the late 1920s, Europe went through the process of regulation and finally prohibition. Cocaine still enjoyed some years of underground popularity. The first illegal users were gamblers, prostitutes, pimps, petty criminals, musicians and artists (Korf and Verbraeck 1993: 104). In Germany, illicit cocaine use became a notorious feature of Weimar nightlife. Cocaine was easy available in Berlin, and as the main producing country a source for cocaine used in neighbouring capital cities. The First World War seems to have been both a time for extended illegal use – by soldiers – as well as an opportunity for moving and smuggling cocaine (Phillips and Wynne 1980: 83).

Cocaine was used – sniffed – by some jazz musicians, some of the popular movie actors and by avant-garde and popular writers and artists. This use is reflected in the lyrics of some songs of the era, as well as in the central theme of several novels, plays and movies.[7]

A consequence of anti-drug laws was a temporary enlargement of the underground market for cocaine and a sharp increase in its price. However, that market was based on diversion from legitimate medical sources, and there was a dramatic drop-off in production after 1928. The Council of the League of Nations reported in 1931 that

---

7   Although more notorious in New Orleans Jazz or Hollywood rings, European arts and letters from 1910 to 1930 also reflect cocaine use in many ways: from support and satiric or comic treatment, to moralistic 'anti-dope' melodramas.

compared with 1929, cocaine production declined 58%, while cocaine stocks in manufacturing countries dropped by 85% (Phillips and Wynne 1980: 86-87). Many casual users responded to the price increases by cutting back or stopping consumption, and heavy users moved to alternatives such as heroin or new synthetic stimulants.

Indeed, the major factor accounting for the demise in cocaine's popularity in United States and Europe, and for the fact that for the next four decades, from 1930 to 1970, cocaine remained marginal or very limited for potential illegal drug users, was the result of pharmacological research. After 1932, a new group of synthetic drugs, the amphetamines, were widely and legally available far more cheaply than cocaine. If substantial illegal cocaine production was ever going to re-emerge somewhere again to supply the European market, it was not going to be in Germany or the Netherlands, but certainly much closer to coca leaf cultivation regions.

Cocaine renaissance
The American cocaine revival in the late 1960s and early 1970s, as explained in chapter II, is the result of many factors: growing methadone programmes for heroin addicts that started mixing with cocaine, tighter restrictions on amphetamines making cocaine an attractive alternative, demographic changes and political turmoil increasing the likelihood of young people experimenting with new drugs, open promotion by showbiz celebrities (as it was the case a century before with the *Vin Mariani* endorsed by eminencies), media coverage and legitimising illicit cocaine use as a symbol of sexual prowess, conspicuous consumption and 'white' success. (Courtwright 1995: 215-217).

Supply followed these developments with some delay. A clear bottle-neck occurred during the 1970s between an expanding demand in the United States and a still-to-come massive supply from South America: for a few years cocaine remained scarce, expensive and those who succeeded in the business were people who managed to get the proper contacts at source. In this way, the role played by anti-Castro Cuban exiles first and Colombians later, with their trafficking expertise and their South American connections, was pivotal. Next to them, many individual traffickers could make, during the early 1970s, a couple of smuggling operations a year without fearing police intervention.[8]

However, only some of these factors account for the re-emergence of an illicit cocaine market in Europe. In general terms, two main differences should be indicated between both markets. Firstly, although following the same curve trends, cocaine use did not manage to reach the same epidemic levels in Europe that it did in the States. Both volumes of cocaine seizures and rates of year prevalence consumption in times of market expansion reveal that the European cocaine market never came, during the 1990s, close to American levels.

---

8   See for these early cocaine entrepreneurs the novel of Sabbag (1978) and the ethnography of Adler (1985).

Secondly, the European cocaine market dynamics followed developments in America with a gap of some years. In United States, on the one hand, cocaine dynamics can be broken down into three stages: a) a slow but sustained increase in cocaine use, mostly sniffing, from 1969 through the early 1980s;[9] b) an explosive growth of cocaine sniffing from the early 1980s and crack smoking from mid-1980s; and c) a decline after 1988 among younger, casual and affluent users, though not among low classes and poly-drug addicts (Courtwright 1995: 215). In Europe, on the other hand, market developments can be summarised as follows: a) a limited but slow growing use from 1975 until the late 1980s; b) a fast increase from 1989 onwards; and c) an stabilisation or decline of cocaine use since the mid-1990s among younger and affluent, though a – limited – increase in crack smoking and among poly-drug users, besides market expansion to new regions in Europe (for example, Eastern Europe).

This gap in time – of 6 or 7 years – between American and European developments, is crucial since it partially explains the different magnitude reached by both markets: cocaine arrived in Europe once it had already lost its early uncontested positive and harmless image. Moreover, Europe lacked – only to some extent – both the cultural values associated with cocaine and the deep social conflicts that could make a crack-cocaine culture fully develop.[10]

The reasons for this gap should be sought at the supply side. Massive cocaine import into Europe was only possible once South American cocaine exporters were able to expand to Europe. Maybe also attracted by potential better prices (Van Doorn 1993: 100) and by cocaine availability at source, they required some years to develop new and more entrepreneurial marketing resources (bulk transportation, and so on) and strong business contacts in a more remote and unfamiliar region.

Following the fact that stagnation in United States coincides with expansion in Europe, many authors have indicated saturation of the American market as the main explanation for cocaine expansion in Europe (Lewis 1989: 36; Roth and Frey 1994: 255; Van Duyne 1995: 78). However, this argument seems rather simplistic and difficult to test. First of all, this view ignores the power of demand in drug economies. There is evidence of increased cocaine demand and acceptability from the 1970s among recreational users or heroin addicts in London, Paris or elsewhere in Europe (Lewis 1989: 35 and 41). Secondly, cocaine was indeed supplied through the 1970s and 1980s by individual entrepreneurs, native amateur and part-time dealers, as well as by many groups and individuals belonging to former (or current) European colonies. Besides, the early presence in Europe of leading Colombian entrepreneurs is

---

9   See, for example, the pioneering book on 'drugtakers' (Young 1971) in which the word 'cocaine' is only mentioned three times through the 240 pages.

10   In both 'affluent cocaine sniffing' and 'ghettoised crack smoking' versions, cocaine embodies, as no other illegal drug, key markers of savage capitalism: conspicuous and mass consumption, sexual virility, the search for individual success, power and recognition, high productivity, conformism to dominant values and fast experiences. Cocaine left its footprints in its paradigmatic extreme expressions: Wall Street and the Ghetto.

well documented.[11] They were interested in both doing business and using European financial resources, but they showed slowness or problems in establishing reliable partnerships and opening lines.

3.1.2 Cocaine demand

Trends

Data on cocaine use in Europe is fragmentary; most of the in-depth studies are local and often target a very specific kind of user. Non problematic consumption, users belonging to non-deviant groups, without any contact with police, street corner work or health-care institutions remain a rather unknown quantity. Sometimes the studies follow different methods. Numbers given by European or international institutions, as well as those exposed by media, are at least highly speculative. They tend to overplay the problem or assume that national or local surveys are an underestimation of the real trends (EMCDDA 1995: 6).

Local or regional studies on consumption trends and levels make clear that they can differ from place to place, some witnessing an increase in problematic consumption – crack, poly-drug use, and so on – with new groups of consumers, other showing stabilisation or even decrease, and still others – as for example some East European countries – showing patterns that parallel those found in Western regions ten or fifteen years ago.

As it was suggested before, the European cocaine scene is not a mere retarded emulation of the experience in the United States. Different values and social structure, more popularity of amphetamines as an illicit stimulant, and the new synthetic drugs for younger users, put limits to cocaine-crack demand in Europe.

During the 1980s, cocaine was regarded in Europe as the caviar or champagne among drugs, expensive, and with a generally positive status. On the one hand, cocaine was appreciated and consumed by regular opiate users. *"If God invented anything better, He must have kept it for Himself"* declared a heroin addict from Amsterdam interviewed by Grapendaal et al. (1995: 147-148) referring to the effect of the 'speedball'. The popularity of this combination of – injected – heroin and cocaine, a constant from the 1970s through the 1990s among heroin users, lays in the fact that cocaine allows the addict to continue his hyperactive life, introduces an element of enjoyment, adventure and speed, while controlled by heroin, and is easy to give up, if needed, from time to time.

Cocaine inhalation ('sniffing' or 'snorting') has been a fairly controlled, invisible and sporadic fashion among actors, writers, lawyers, financiers, businessmen, and the traditional professionals, and within the world of advertising, consulting and media

---

11 Rodríguez Orejuela and Jorge Ochoa were detained in Spain in the mid-1980s. Despite the fact that the story of a supposed meeting between Pablo Escobar and Carlos Ledher with a couple of Surinamese dealers in Schiphol, the Netherlands, as early as 1981 is very hard to believe (being the typical fable of those informants or 'repentants' trying to score high with the police and to impress the general public), there are many cases of Colombian and South American entrepreneurs active or imprisoned before 1988 (Bovenkerk 1995b; Haenen and Buddingh' 1994).

(Bieleman et al. 1993: 24). Within this recreational cocaine use among the wealthy and the middle classes, a sharp difference with the United States can be observed: cocaine did not spread so pervasively among European teenagers and youngsters. In 1982 as many as 19% of the age group between 18 and 25 years were estimated to have used cocaine at least once in the preceding year in the United States (Bieleman et al. 1993: 25). For the same age and prevalence group, around a 3% is indicated by the various studies conducted in some European cities for the early and mid-1990s (Sandwijk et al. 1995; Bieleman et al. 1993; OGD 1997a). Lifetime prevalence amongst students 15-16 years old is even smaller, European school surveys indicating a modest 1% to 2% for the mid-1990s (EMCDDA 1998: 19). 'Socially integrated' cocaine users tend to be young male adults aged 25-40 years with above average educational and/or occupational status. They use low doses intermittently rather than frequently, and only a small minority develop a more intensive and problematic pattern of use (EMCDDA 1995: 7). In his study on 'non-deviant' cocaine users in Amsterdam (Cohen 1989) and a later follow-up research (Cohen and Sas 1993), Cohen concludes that the main tendency of experienced cocaine users over time is towards decreasing or ending use. Most display a capacity to control and modify their drug use.

Despite many predictions and panic promoted after the crack epidemic in America, an overwhelming 'crack attack' on the European streets did not occur (Ruggiero and South 1995: 24; Boekhout van Solinge 1996; OGD 1996b). However, modest to sizeable local markets in crack did develop through the early 1990s first in Britain and later in France,[12] especially in cities like London, Paris and Amsterdam (Power et al. 1995: 378). Crack smoking or 'free-basing' in deprived inner-cities or suburban areas has often been linked to economic, social and health problems suffered by both native and ethnic minority groups, mostly young, problems that are again amplified by crack use (unemployment, family break-down, poly-drug use, more contact with health services or police, violence,[13] emergency room episodes, diagnosed 'crack babies', and so on) (OGD 1996a: 79-80; Power et al. 1995: 378). Again, available data make clear that crack use has remained limited, that in fact some users have been smoking a self-made, better quality crack even from the 1980s, and that stories about crack have been over-dramatised (Boekhout van Solinge 1996; OGD 1997a; Kools 1997). Recent Dutch studies have shown a general increase in cocaine sniffing for 1997 (Abraham et al 1999), a 'come back' of coke sniffing amongst 'clubbers and ravers', and a spread of crack smoking amongst deprived

---

12 In both cases, there were Caribbean networks (Jamaicans in London and French Antilleans in Paris) who introduced and controlled retail in these crack markets. (Boekhout van Solinge 1996). Crack use has also been reported in the Netherlands, Germany and Spain.

13 Cocaine – and crack – use has been readily blamed for criminal behaviour. However, most of the studies show that a very small proportion of cocaine users are involved in criminal acts other than drug dealing, basically property offences and *macho* and dare-devil behaviour (Bieleman et al. 1993: 73; Cohen 1989); that its effects are always mediated by the norms, practices and circumstances of their users (Waldorf et al. 1991: 10), and that drug use and crime do not have a straightforward causal relationship (Grapendaal et al. 1995: 197).

neighbourhood youth and homeless drug addicts (Nabben and Korf 1999: 633-641; Boekhout van Solinge 2001).

In quantitative terms, European demand is above world average. Table III shows some estimations on prevalence use rates, number of users and cocaine quantity yearly consumed in the late 1990s. On average, between 1% and 2% of the total European population (370 millions) tried cocaine at least once, between 0,6% and 0,9% used it at least once in the last year, and a core of 0,2% to 0,4% (around 1 million) consumed cocaine during the last month.[14] In Amsterdam, where as in any other large city consumption is high above the European average, the year prevalence of cocaine use shows a relative stability through the years, with some recent increase: 1,5% in 1987, 1,2% in 1990, 1,6% in 1994 and 2,6% in 1997 (Sandwijk et al. 1995; Abraham et al. 1999). The former *Observatoire Géopolitique des Drogues* estimated that, from the five larger countries of the EU, Spain and Britain have the higher consumption rates, followed by Italy, and after that by France and Germany with slightly less consumption.

The OGD suggested that between 120 and 130 tons of cocaine are consumed every year in the EU (OGD 1997a: 77-78). Although this estimation seems a maximum by the year 2001,[15] even 100 tons a year shows the importance of the European market.

The tendencies of European cocaine demand for the second half of the 1990s are somewhat puzzling and suggest many directions:

Table III Cocaine Demand in the European Union,
end of the 1990s (Average Estimations)

	Average Rate	*Number of Users*
Life Prevalence	1,0% - 2,0%	3.700.000 - 7.400.000
Year Prevalence	0,6% - 0,9%	2.220.000 - 3.330.000
Month Prevalence	0,2% - 0,4%	740.000 - 1.480.000
Cocaine Consumed per year in the EU		100-130 tons

Source: Own estimations based on OGD (1997a: 77-78), Sandwijk et al (1995), Bieleman et al. (1993) and EMCDDA (1998: 15-19).

14 Although the main source is OGD (1997a) – a unique study on cocaine consumption in Europe combining interesting qualitative dimensions, own fieldwork and sampling, and quantitative calculations – data presented in Table III are my own estimations based also in other studies and calculations (EMCDDA 1998).

15 Their calculation, based on their own sampling, is unclear and implying very high levels of average consumption per person, since the rates and number of users they handle are not exaggerated. The 100-130 tons of cocaine consumed every year in the EU would represent around the 25%-30% of the world market, estimated in 400 tons per year (Steiner 1997, Rocha 2000). By the year 2000, United States seems to hold 60%-50% of the total consumption (decreasing), leaving the other 15%-20% to the growing Latin American, Asian and Eastern European markets.

a) A general tendency towards stabilisation of cocaine demand in Western Europe from 1995 onwards. Annual international official reports seem to be erratic and inconsistent: meanwhile *"cocaine abuse in most Western European countries is declining"* (INCB 1996), *"increasing cocaine abuse was reported in Denmark, France and Germany in 1996"* (INCB 1997). However, studies all over suggest ageing, fashion changes, awareness about negative cocaine effects and successful replacement by amphetamines or other synthetic drugs as the central factors for a stagnation or decline in recreational cocaine use.

b) Cocaine consumption in the 1990s reaches a more heterogeneous population (Power et al. 1995: 377; Nabben and Korf 1999). Cocaine is no longer the preserve of the elite and the 'yuppies', or of heroin addicts who use it as a 'speedball', but also used by middle-class populations as well as increasingly smoked as crack by younger and more vulnerable individuals in big cities (problematic drug addicts, margined and deprived groups, and so on).[16]

c) Linked with this process of diffusion, cocaine use has become more 'visible' by spreading amongst more problematic (and public) users like homeless addicts and poor youth.

d) Cocaine use has modestly increased in East European countries, following social and economic changes.[17] Although cocaine is increasingly available in domestic Eastern European markets, consumption seems to remain low and limited to specific groups (EMCDDA 1998: 69; INCB 1998a).

Prices
Cocaine prices are very sensitive to various factors, and demonstrate remarkable variations regarding time, space and setting. However, average European wholesale and retail prices follow rather clear patterns through the last two decades. In both cases, prices from the mid-1990s onwards are only half of those in the early 1980s.

Average wholesale European cocaine prices were US$ 52,000 per kg in 1983. They dropped but made a quick recovery by 1987. After that year, prices experimented a sustained decline to average US$ 25,000 in 1993 (Farrell et al. 1996: 267). Since then, a remarkable stability can be found toward the late 1990s. The Netherlands is no exception. In Amsterdam, wholesale prices of US$ 45,000 / US$ 60,000 per kg in the 1980s, dropped to US$ 20,000 / US$ 25,000 in the 1990s (Korf and Verbraeck 1993: 125-126), to remain at that price level after 1993.

Regarding average retail prices, the same pattern should be indicated. They are US$ 105 per gram in 1983 and 1987, with a drop in between. Again, a sustained decrease to reach the average of US$ 65 in 1993 (Farrell et al. 1996: 266). However, retail prices have a wider range of variety, even regarding neighbourhood.[18] In

---

16 For a good overview on the different types of cocaine and crack users in Europe in the late 1990s, especially on the referred heterogeneity, see OGD 1997a: 40-79.
17 The INCB reported increased consumption in Belarus, Latvia and the Russian Federation (INCB 1997).
18 Occasionally making, for example in London, a 30% profit by only crossing the River Thames (Lewis 1989: 47).

Amsterdam, a gram of pure cocaine for specialised customers can cost between US$ 50 and US$ 85,[19] while the same gram sold in the streets in smaller units and with more cuts, can be worth between US$ 100 and US$ 175 (Korf and Verbraeck 1993: 125). In France, retail prices are clearly higher (around US$ 130) and in line with Switzerland and Britain, two other expensive countries (Farrell et al. 1996: 263; Boekhout van Solinge 1996).

Despite the fact that it is quite difficult to determine the main reason for a particular variation in price, it is possible to identify those factors responsible for cocaine price fluctuations:

a) Over-supply due to over-production or to a bottleneck in demand can drive prices down. This seems to have been the main factor for both the fall of cocaine prices after 1987 and the stabilisation after 1993, with supply and demand coming to a balance. In the same way, the price recovery between 1985 and 1987 would have been related to a growing demand not yet satisfied by still-to-come massive cocaine import.[20]

b) Changes in trafficking that lower risks: bulk transportation and more professionalised networks have implied, despite repression efforts, lower personal risks. Insurance mechanisms and over-stocking[21] lower, despite seizures, economic risks. These changes had also an impact in the overall decrease of cocaine prices in Europe.

c) In the opposite direction, an increase in repression (longer sentences and improved rates of interception) has had a negligible effect in driving prices up. As convincingly argued by Farrell (1995), only repressive scenarios with physical violence, life sentences and interception rates above 80% could raise prices, but these scenarios are both undesirable and unattainable. Lenient enforcement policies below a minimum can bring prices down, since more suppliers have been trying to enter the market and compete for the same consumers.

d) Increased competition at wholesale or retail level can account for local decrease in price.

e) Proximity to import, stocking and distribution centres. Wholesale prices (and retail as well) are lower in direct entry countries such as Spain and the Netherlands. Major metropolitan centres often enjoy price advantages.

f) The amount of stages between importer and consumer has a local impact in retail prices.[22] The lesser the stages (the Netherlands, Spain) the cheaper the price. In France, with relatively low wholesale prices (transit between Spain and Italy, French Antilles, and so on), the relatively high retail prices may be partly explained by the

---

19 Dutch wholesale prices are kept in US$, which explains the recent increase in kilo prices from € 25,000 to € 37,000. In contrast, Dutch gram prices are local and do not immediately react to currency changes. Therefore, the US$ retail prices indicated in the literature during the 1990s should be reduced in 20% to account for the current prices.

20 See for changes in cocaine prices in Europe: Farrell et al. (1996).

21 Floating and temporary stocks as a growing integral part of distribution networks have a 'pillow' effect against loses, seizures and theft (OGD 1997a: 20).

22 There are fewer intermediate stages between importer and consumer on European cocaine markets compared to North American markets in heroin and cocaine (Lewis 1989: 46).

presence of more intermediaries willing to introduce a mark-up (Farrell et al. 1996: 265).

g) Differences in transparency of local markets (information transmission) also account for price contrasts, since more transparent markets react quicker to changes in the environment.

h) Retail price varies also regarding purity, amount unit and setting. The smaller the unit and the more impure it is, the more expensive becomes per pure cocaine gram. Street and unconnected dealers handle higher prices than house and well connected ones.

i) Cocaine prices across countries have also some correlation with consumer price indices for legal goods. Switzerland, for example, is the most expensive country in Europe for many things, including cocaine (Farrell et al. 1996: 262).

Purity

The fact that cocaine is sold in powdered form makes it relatively easy to dilute with much cheaper psychotropically-active substances such as procaine, lignocaine, aspirin, paracetamol or amphetamine sulphate, with relatively inert substances such as glucose, lactose, sugar, or mannitol, and even with damaging things like washing powder or lime. Cocaine is usually cut to add weight and increase margin profits.

However, next to the gradual price decrease, cocaine has witnessed a sustained improvement in purity over the last ten years. Cocaine at point of import frequently approaches 80% to 98%. While Britain has witnessed a purity improvement in the last years (OGD 1996a: 79), in France cocaine purity has increased from 55% in 1985 to 75% in 1995 (OGD 1997a: 22). In Amsterdam, meanwhile large volumes seized by the police in 1991 showed excellent purity levels, many retailers also reported some reservations for cutting cocaine (Korf and Verbraeck 1993: 127). Especially in times of increased competition and supply, dealers tend to improve purity as a way of staying in business. Many cocaine traffickers, at all levels, even make the question of 'purity' a matter of personal prestige and reputation as also often happens with legal goods.

In theory, a price decrease and the spread of cocaine use among lower strata should have worked in the opposite direction, reducing purity. However, an overall sustained improvement of purity at retail level has been the case, indicating: a) a strong over-supply as the main cause for price decrease; and b) a strong bargaining position of consumers, pushing for quality improvements (Lewis 1989: 39).

At retail level, purity can vary very much between the middle-class recreational (50% up to 80%) and the street-addict circuits (never below 30%). Those willing to pay less or get smaller units are often confronted with more impure cocaine. Dealers selling small pre-wrapped units in the street, often more interested in rapid turnovers, are able to cut more since testing is impossible, the purchase has to be quick, and customers are more distant and willing to accept poorer qualities. However, individuals who persist in ripping people off with purity levels are often ostracised, expelled from the market, or subject to retaliatory action.

3.1.3 Cocaine supply

Supply and demand trends, although tracking each other in the long run, did not follow the same timing in Europe. These gaps are partly responsible for the changes in price. Until 1987, a growing demand was not followed by a proportional increase in supply. Cocaine was expensive, scarce and erratically available. The period between 1987 and 1994[23] shows a still growing demand, but clearly behind the explosive character evidenced by supply. Why did this occur and what happened with the surplus cocaine?

It was already explained how by 1987-1989 a number of factors coincided that led Colombian exporters to multiply and enlarge cocaine shipments to Europe: a growing demand, very good prices, availability of cocaine at source and the establishment of cargo transportation and business partnerships with local organised groups, which lowered risks and encouraged them to send more and more cocaine.

However, not all cocaine reached European consumers. First of all, given the huge profit margins and the lowered risks involved in bulk operations, Colombian exporters could now afford to lose more cocaine than before. While individual or small entrepreneurs could not sacrifice many kilos without being put out from business, larger exporters (or co-operatives) sending big volumes could, on the contrary, increase the proportion of cocaine loses and still make profits. More cocaine, even in relative terms, ended at the bottom of the ocean or in the hands of the police.[24]

Secondly, with an increased supply, wholesale dealers and distributors could ensure a continuous availability by increasing the so-called 'floating stocks'. Substantial cocaine stocks do not exist but as an integral part of distribution mechanisms (OGD 1997a: 20). Low level distributors can, at times, have some grams stashed as reserve, but in higher levels permanent or even temporary stocks are absent in the cocaine trade. Stashing the drug is indeed one of the most risky and difficult operations in the business, and almost every illegal entrepreneur would try to keep only the exact cocaine amount traded for a minimum time (Korf and Verbraeck 1993: 135). Moreover, the active properties of cocaine start to deteriorate after two years, making cocaine something to be consumed relatively 'fresh'. Abundant stocks kept for difficult times, implying also well organised long-term planning and strategies, are a typical construct pushed by police sources and accepted by some researchers (Van Duyne 1995: 79). The police have never seized any real cocaine 'stock' in Europe, with one exception in Italy.

However, it is possible to talk about a 'mobile' or 'floating stock'. This means that a surplus cocaine is always 'on the road', moving in and through Europe, allowing for continuous supply and neutralising the effects of losses and seizures (OGD 1997a:

---

23 In this period, prices dropped to a half, purity improved by 30% and seizures multiplied sevenfold.
24 Seizures increasing from 5% to 30% of the cocaine volumes actually imported. The meaning of these seizures will be later analysed.

20). Some cocaine, especially regarding big operations, is also aimed as try-out samples or advances.

Thirdly, cocaine entering Europe has also been used, in some cases, as exchange for other illegal goods (weapons, heroin, and so on), delaying deliveries or redirecting cocaine to other markets. Finally, as mentioned before, some increase in demand, especially in East Europe, is not well quantified.

All these reasons explain why in the period of 1987 to 1994 the gap widened between cocaine on the market and cocaine actually consumed. From the mid-1990s on this gap seems to stabilise, with stabilised supply, presumably influenced on the one hand by a saturation point regarding demand and, on the other, by a strong restructuring of cocaine production and export.

Who controls supply in Europe?
If the idea of a few and closed 'cartels' controlling exports was criticised for production countries, that holds even more strongly for supply and distribution levels in Europe.[25] All along the line, cocaine is supplied by different sorts of networks, all very flexible, organised and unorganised, both competing and co-operating, and including a variety of ethnic or national groups.

Some small cocaine laboratories have been found in Europe, especially in Southern countries (Santino and La Fiura 1993: 155). However, they seem to be rare, more the initiative of individual or small organisations than by well-established and diversified groups. Seizures of cocaine base in Britain, Germany and the Netherlands have been indications of such attempts. Small cocaine laboratories controlled by local groups have also been identified in Croatia, Georgia and Lebanon (OGD 1996a: 90; 1997a: 23 and 27). Even with increased control over chemical precursors, the risks involved in establishing illegal laboratories in European territory are still very high.

Cocaine import to European countries is basically organised and conducted by independent groups who manage to establish links with South American exporters (Ruggiero and South 1995: 74). Some of these groups are not local but operate in many countries, and some belong in one way or another to larger and long established illegal organisations active in contraband or other illegal businesses. In some places, as it will be described in chapter V, Colombian or other South American groups and individuals are involved in cocaine import into Europe in many different ways. Spain and the Netherlands are the two countries where Colombians have been more active in import activities.

In contrast with the United States, where Colombian networks controlled wholesale distribution, this market level has been fairly shared in Europe: an international spectrum of local groups, partnerships or individuals selling to lower distributors across the countries.

---

25 After almost twenty years, media and law enforcers still insist in discovering and pointing out the activities and 'representatives' of this or that Colombian 'cartel' (typically, they prefer to refer to the *Cali* Cartel). Many groups – some with no connection between themselves – from the Cauca Valley region have indeed been very active in export to Europe, but also groups based in other cities (Bogotá, Medellín, Pereira, and so on) or countries (Venezuela, Suriname, Brazil).

Both import and wholesale distribution experienced, along the 1990s, a process of professionalisation. As Ruggiero observed:

"Wholesale operations are increasingly conducted by well organised groups who have access to large quantities of drugs and are in a position to invest large quantities of money. In order to minimise risks, but also thanks to the increasing finance at their disposal, these groups undertake a reduced number of operations involving larger amounts of drugs. Wholesalers, in other words, experienced a selective process whereby only those endowed with effectiveness, professionalism and larger funds were left in operation." (Ruggiero 1995: 144)

The idea of an increasing control of import and wholesale distribution by more professional and international organisations has been consistently highlighted by every researcher and source in the field. Some authors, however, have extrapolated and forced this tendency to account for highly structured hierarchical systems (Bieleman et al. 1993: 22), for large and closed groups conspiring and making all sort of secret agreements (Clawson and Lee III 1996: 67-86), or for the existence of 'foreign' criminal groups (Van Duyne 1993a: 14-15). With little more evidence than some – often misinterpreted – 'big cases', these approaches usually ignore that notions of professionalisation and internationalisation can also mean high competition, loose organisations and agreements, less well known criminals and criminal groups, or even small enterprises. In fact, it can be argued that large, hierarchical multinational enterprises are extremely rare (Ruggiero and South 1995; Savona et al. 1993; Dorn et al. 1992), and that their regular detection by law enforcers can also be interpreted as a sign of their weakness.

The general picture differs from country to country regarding each particular involvement. In Spain, the most important bridgehead for cocaine entering Europe, import activities are mainly shared by Colombian and local networks. Despite the presence of small independent entrepreneurs and some Colombian groups[26] operating in Madrid or Andalucia (Savona et al. 1993), most import and wholesale is arranged by Spanish networks, especially from the Galician region. The area, geographically suited to sea smuggling, is the base of groups traditionally dedicated to contraband (mainly cigarettes) and fishing. They have linked – and not replaced – to these activities hashish and cocaine traffic (OGD 1997b). Quite a number of cases involving Colombian and Galician participation are also facilitated by police and customs corruption (OGD 2000: 97). Southern Spain has also been the scenario for business contacts between Colombian and Italian groups (OGD 1996a: 97) and a popular place for money laundering and conspicuous consumption. Again, too often, these international business operations have been wrongly described in terms of 'master mind' agreements between certain cartels, clans, and so on (Van Duyne 1995: 78; Ruth et al. 1996: 265-266).

---

26 The particular role of Colombians and their relation with local groups will be treated in chapters V and VI.

Italy also plays an important role with regard to the organisation of cocaine import into Europe. Import activities are shared by South Americans and groups or individuals linked to *mafia*-type organisations, especially the Neapolitan *Camorra*, which although not making drugs their main source of income, have successfully diversified from heroin to cocaine and been able to construct strong business partnerships with Colombian exporters, not only in Italy (OGD 1996a: 99-100; Clawson and Lee III 1996: 62-66). However, even more emphatically than in the Spanish case, a number of journalists and law enforcement officers have tended to see 'alliances', conspiracies and long-term arrangements between two cities (Palermo and Medellín, for example), or two groups ('the' *Camorra* and 'the' *X Cartel*), things that, of course, do not exist. Colombian-Italian deals can better be seen as single or multiple buyer-seller transactions, some including shipping arrangements, distribution to other parts of Europe, money laundering facilities and even co-operation on intelligence issues. Firstly, evidence shows that money invested into drugs by *mafiosi* has usually been a rather personal initiative and a private affair, which in fact gave some families or groups the opportunity to claim independence from more central bodies and build partnerships with external investors or people. Drug traffic made 'men of honour' mix and go into business with 'ordinary men' (Gambetta 1996: 238-239; Ruggiero 1995: 136). Secondly, many of these Italian illegal entrepreneurs and networks doing business with South American exporters are not even linked with *mafia*-type organisations, but belong to the so-called local 'underworld' (Santino 1993: 111; Bovenkerk 1995b: 210-211; Ruggiero 1995: 135). At the level of wholesale distribution, especially in Rome and several Northern cities, this presence – next to some limited Colombian involvement – is even stronger (Lewis 1989: 40; Clawson and Lee III 1996: 65).

In Britain,

> "free-lance suppliers, South American importers and British professional crime groups
> have all been involved in importation and wholesale supply." (Lewis 1989: 43)

However, the upper level market has been dominated by Britons, with South Americans having difficulty in establishing themselves in the business and forging links with British groups.[27] (Lewis 1989: 43). Next to the professional white illegal entrepreneurs, most with a previous involvement in serious predatory crime and some also active in continental Europe, networks of Caribbean and African (Nigerian) origin are active in cocaine import and smuggling, though moving smaller amounts and usually by plane (Savona et al. 1993). Nigerian networks, organised along ethnic lines and traditionally active in trading and contraband, have increasingly expanded their involvement both in source countries such as Brazil, as well as in other regions of Europe (Germany, Central and Easter Europe), especially as middlemen between larger importers and distributors (OGD 1997a: 15; OGD 1997b).

---

27 Given that the Colombian community in Britain is the second largest in Europe (around 80,000 people) this statement deserves further analysis, also to be discussed in later chapters.

Due to its central position between important cocaine import centres, Germany seems very international regarding involvement in upper levels. Germans, Italians, Dutch, Colombians or East Europeans are among those arrested for wholesale operations, which seem to be shared and splinter by many different groups (OGD 1997b). In cases of Colombian-German co-operation, other groups and individuals are also usually involved (Roth et al. 1994: 278-282). The same international picture can also be drawn for France, combining mixed Colombian-French networks (OGD 1996a: 76), Italian and Spanish wholesalers, and smaller independent smugglers.

Since the early 1990s, South American exporters have also established ties with trafficking groups in Eastern Europe and Russia. Colombians have tried to sell cocaine to local groups in Poland, the Czech Republic, Hungary and Russia, who would buy important quantities both for their expanding markets and for distribution to Western Europe through their own networks there (for example, Clawson and Lee III 1996: 87; Van Duyne 1995: 79). In many cases, Colombians themselves established their own import-export bridgeheads. Members and ex-members of security forces of those countries (secret and national police, customs, and so on) have been involved in these networks in a very active way.

Cocaine import and wholesale distribution in Europe has also made room for Lebanese, Israelis, Portuguese, Croats, Serbs, Kosovars, Argentineans, Peruvians, and many other groups, both working as ethnic or national networks or as individuals belonging to internationally integrated local groups.

With regard to middle-level distribution and retail selling, suppliers are even more heterogeneous and fragmented, their background differing very much as far as place and milieu are concerned. Next to the whole range of consumers that have been drawn into selling, from 'yuppies' to crack smokers, it is possible to find also some people with privileged access to wholesale networks or local groups and individuals involved in trafficking with other illegal drugs. Crack retail distribution has been mainly in hands of distinctive ethnic groups, particularly Afro-Caribbeans. Sometimes as users themselves, crack smoking has been pushed by Jamaicans in London and by Antilleans and later Africans in Paris (Boekhout van Solinge 1996).

Cocaine and colonialism
Cocaine comes from areas linked to the European colonial past. Although tied in different ways, some cultural, economic, political and demographic relations exist between Spain and Colombia, Peru or Bolivia; Portugal and Brazil; the Netherlands and Suriname or the Netherlands Antilles; United Kingdom and Jamaica, Trinidad or Nigeria, and so forth. These ties have obviously played a role in the development of cocaine routes, especially in the early days. Commercial links, frequent flights, constant exchange of people and ethnic communities from ex-colonies living in Europe, combined with their access to supply source, were all factors that allowed these groups to gain a place in the illegal business. Yet not at all of its levels. During the 1980s, when small quantities were smuggled by plane, markets were geographically more fragmented and intermediaries between import and consumption were fewer than today, ethnic groups belonging to former colonies were very active as air couriers. Although some studies on foreign drug couriers (Green et al. 1994;

Green 1996) show the selective practices of customs, it is undeniable that many Nigerians have been found with cocaine in Heathrow or Gatwick, many Surinamese caught in Schiphol, many Francophone Caribbeans in France, and far too many South Americans in Spain and the rest of Europe. However, instead of thinking in terms of some immanent colonial past, the involvement and success of these ethnic groups in the cocaine business seems clearly related to other issues: links and access to exporters and to local distribution networks, willingness and skills to enter, and so on. As I will later show in relation to the Dutch case, Colombians and Dutch can grasp, for many reasons, a position within the market that is sometimes closed to ethnic minorities from the former colonies.

Furthermore, three interrelated developments during the 1990s have made the ethnic or national element within the European cocaine market even more problematic.

Firstly, the explosion of volumes smuggled, from a few kilos by plane to many hundreds by cargo ships. Import, transport and distribution of large shipments required new and more sophisticated tasks, arrangements and infrastructure. Rather than in a primitive flow or presence of 'own' people – ethnic or co-national group – successful organisation of these high levels had to rely on more entrepreneurial considerations and conditions, hardly provided by established groups from cocaine production and transhipment countries. While for the smuggling of few kilos or for retail distribution ethnic ties were and still are important for minimising risks, they turned out to be insufficient and even dysfunctional for providing what is required to organise large-scale cocaine transport and distribution in Europe. Good legal commercial and financial opportunities, strong legal and illegal local networks able to organise import-export operations, and the possibilities of neutralising police enforcement are at the base of the main decisions made by large cocaine entrepreneurs when deciding where and with whom to do business.

Secondly, increased police repression on cocaine trafficking has also weakened those supposed traditional routes and ties. The answer to increasing stigmatisation on particular groups or individuals (Colombians, Nigerians, and so on) was in many cases the search for 'clean' partners or employees, both native or from less known backgrounds. It also gave traditional and new local organisations a stronger position in the business.

Thirdly, the full internationalisation of cocaine market dynamics has also weakened the opportunities for single ethnic groups within it. Ethnic ties may guarantee business at a very local level or in a hardly-to-find point to point line operation, but the fact is that when a kilo is delivered somewhere in Europe, it has already crossed maybe five different countries, often more. Next to that, new European countries gaining a role as transhipment or consumption centres have opened the game for new actors. The fact that cocaine production has also expanded to countries other than Colombia (Brazil, Peru, Bolivia) and export or transhipment to even further latitudes (Argentina, Caribbean, South Africa, Cape Verde, and so on) helped to diversify routes, which in no way follow the historic footsteps of colonialism. Finally, internationalisation of cocaine business has also meant increased integration with other legal (bulk transportation, financial) and illegal (weapons, other illicit drugs) markets, narrowing further the role of ethnicity in the cocaine business. Ethnic minorities linked to the European colonial past (Latin Americans, Surinamese, Nigerians, and so forth) could only survive in strong positions where they were able both to enclose their illegal activities within large migrant enclaves and to establish good links with European and international organisations.

3.1.4 Reading European seizures

Cocaine seizure data, not only that collected by the UNCDP from the Member States or through individual seizure reports – containing additional information on drug origin, smuggling methods and people arrested – but also that reported by newspapers, is a valuable and interesting source of information and analysis when studying the European cocaine market. It allows some questions and hypotheses to be formulated far beyond the problem of law enforcement performance: seizures can also be regarded as clues to uncover smuggling trends and routes, technological and organisational developments within the business, and in a broader sense the interaction between cocaine trade and law enforcement.

Seizures by national law enforcement agencies are very variable and susceptible of being influenced by changes in four different factors. The number of seizures, the average cocaine quantity seized each time, and the total volumes confiscated are always a reflection of:

a Changes in reporting and/or recording (new systems of records, new countries reporting, and so on).

b Changes in law enforcement activities (changes and allocation of material resources, routine checks vs. long-run investigations, priorities on different market levels – transport, import or distribution – or specific products, and so on).

c Quantitative changes in supply-demand dynamic (more or less supply and/or demand, new by-products, new local markets, changes in consumption habits, and so on).

d Qualitative changes in trafficking strategies (changing and diversification of smuggling methods and amount smuggled, changing routes, changing in the nature of trafficking networks – ethnic, international, related to other illegal markets, and so on).

Table IV Cocaine Seizures in Europe 1987-1998 (in kg)

Country	1987	1988	1989	1990	1991	1992	1993	1994	1995	1996	1997	1998
Spain	1134	3461	1852	5382	7574	4454	5350	4016	6897	13743	18419	11688
Netherlands	406	517	1425	4288	2492	3433	3720	8200	4851	9222	11489	11452
France	754	593	939	1845	831	1625	1715	4743	865	1742	844	1051
Germany[a]	296	496	1406	2474	964	1332	1051	767	1846	1373	1721	1133
Italy	321	616	668	805	1300	1345	1101	6636	2603	2379	1650	2144
Belgium	270	404	89	537	756	1222	2892	479	576	838	3329	2088
UK	407	323	499	611	1078	2248	717	2261	672	1219	2074	2808
Portugal	222	302	793	360	1094	1860	216	1719	2116	812	3162	621
Other EU[b]	96	37	118	136	415	171	130	304	200	934	216	786
Non EU[c]	65	245	324	471	761	458	1749	n.d.	n.d.	n.d.	n.d.	n.d.
Total Europe	4163	6994	8113	16909	17265	18148	18641	29125	20626	32262	42904	33771

Source: EMCDDA (1998, 1999). For 1997 and 1998, figures from Europol (Prisma Team 2000). In italics, figures for the EU only.
a Figures for Germany combine East and West Germany for 1987 and 1988.
b EU Member States in 1998 (15).
c Farrell et al. (1996), from UNDCP data.

The most challenging exercise when reading seizures is to identify the extent to which each variable plays a role in local and general terms. Table IV shows cocaine seizures in different European countries from 1987 to 1998. These figures, combined with available data on number of seizures, average seizure weights, price variations, consumption levels, and factual circumstances involved in trafficking operations and police detection, allow for several interpretative remarks.

Naturally, they are not exempt from a certain degree of uncertainty and some are just hypothetical statements that deserve further testing, but many are shared by other's findings and by cocaine traffickers and enforcers themselves as related to me:

a) Sustained growth in seizures from 4 tons in 1987 to 34 tons in 1998 has mainly to do with increased cocaine supply into the continent. However, following from what has been explained in sections 3.1.2. and 3.1.3. on demand and supply trends, some of the increase can indeed be attributed to improved rates of interception. They would have been 10% in the mid-1980s, before the first big shipments started to arrive. Prices were high, supply was still in fact in line or even behind demand growth, cocaine was more carefully taken care of, and police or customs had little experience with large-scale cocaine smuggling, which was not even at the top of enforcement agendas. The average interception rate in the EU since the mid-1990s seems to have improved and stabilised at 25%.[28] Despite more trafficking professionalisation, a clear over-supply of cocaine while a drop-off in prices increased both the amount of cocaine ready to be sacrificed and the competition levels between export-import groups, who increased collaboration with law enforcers against rival shipments and competitors.[29] It can be argued, as a hypothesis, that interception rates tend to improve when the gap between supply and demand expands.

b) Growing international trade and the liberalisation of both trade and money flows are factors that facilitate cocaine smuggling, imposing structural limits to any

---

28 This 25% results from an average of 30 tons seized annually since 1994 upon some 100-130 tons cocaine actually consumed within the EU (OGD 1997a: 79). This estimation is above Farrell (1995: 142), who manages a 30% as the global rate by overstating cocaine production volumes, but in line with all studies indicating global rates of 45% (see chapter II, Figure I).

29 This improvement of 15% should not be regarded, as many law enforcers do, as a 'victory' over cocaine trafficking. It seems to be a logical consequence of drug trafficking rather than a police development, and, to the contrary, shows how illegal entrepreneurs can keep making profits sacrificing more cocaine. The replacement costs (export price plus transportation) of intercepted drugs are so low in relation to the profits made upon sale, that it makes little difference for large exporters and importers to loose 10% or 50% of the shipments. Besides, a price decrease while rates improved evidences how marginal is the impact of interception. Farrell estimates that only interception rates above 75%-92% could drive prices up and illegal entrepreneurs out (Farrell 1995: 145). Furthermore, with demand stabilised or slightly expanding, more seizure rates can only stimulate cocaine production and hit the weaker or the more amateurish illegal entrepreneurs, contributing to the described process of professionalisation. Finally, it is unclear the effect of all the late-1990s police developments – European police co-operation, pro-active intelligence, new control laws, new institutional special bodies, higher performance of customs, and so forth. They are, on the one hand, not primarily aimed to seize more kg – law enforcers usually prefer to get 100 kg with 5 suspects than 500 kg with no detentions. On the other hand, the closer law enforcers get to cocaine entrepreneurs, the more police and custom corruption it is likely to appear – by the way, also a sign of professionalisation – which have a neutralising effect upon possible police improvements.

effort on interdiction or enforcement. The answer from law enforcers has been a constant plea for growing powers and resources. "*Detecting illicit cargo is almost impossible without prior intelligence*", claims the World Drug Report (UNDCP 1997: 231). This false assumption, typical from the 'war on drugs' discourse, is based in the fact that, indeed, more seizures than before are the product of pro-active investigation. However, and especially when analysing cases of sea transportation, tipping from anonymous sources, selective – by some criteria – or routine controls, and chance, are by far the most used methods of detection.

c) Larger shipments by sea during the 1990s, while these have resulted in a sustained increase of the average seizure weight, are responsible for important skews and alterations regarding countries and years, firstly due to periodic spectacular seizures of one or more tons (see Table V), and, to a lesser extent, to changes in sea routes. These large seizures pictured in Table V do not go unnoticed within the national figures of Table IV. In general terms, eight countries concentrate most of the seizures, those countries that are the main import (Spain, The Netherlands) and wholesale distribution (France, Germany, Italy) regions. The still limited amounts seized in Eastern Europe could be partially to do with smaller interception rates than in Western Europe, and with the fact that most cocaine seized transits by land (TIR trucks) and by air, and barely by sea.[30]

d) While European seizures represent the 10% of global seizures, consumption in Europe accounts for around 25% of the total. Large amounts of cocaine earmarked for the European market are then intercepted in production or transit countries outside Europe, especially in South America.[31] This makes Europe the region with less cocaine interception compared with its own consumption. While seizures represent 45% of worldwide consumed cocaine, the European rate floats around the 25%-30%.

e) Cocaine seized in each country often has, more and more, another country as its final destination. Cocaine moving across Europe remains within the European space. This is confirmed by the growing volume of land seizures and their average volume (TIR trucks), and by the multiplication of small vessels and boats involved, both used for transhipping from large cargo ships and as a mean of internal distribution.

f) Air volumes seized kept growing, not in relative but in absolute terms. A stabilisation or even a decrease in the average weight of those seizures implies a multiplication in the number of 'mules', even considering improved interception rates. Far from disappearing, air smuggling is still the only option for thousands of small exporters and importers, who have even professionalised this method of transportation – by transferring new risks to the smugglers, by replacing and using plenty of them, by sacrificing them, by diversifying routes, and so on.

---

30 Even the record seizure of February 1993 of 1,1 tons of Colombian cocaine in Vyborg, near St. Petersburg, was made in a Russian TIR truck container.
31 In March 1995, for example, a Dutch citizen was detained in Brazil with 660 kg ready to be shipped to the Netherlands (*NRC Handelsblad*, 11-3-95).

Table V Multi-ton Seizures in Europe 1988-1999 (relevant cases)

Year	Description
1988	1,0 ton in Irún (Spain). Colombian involvement.
1990	2,7 tons in Ijmuiden (the Netherlands). Harbour warehouse. Colombian involvement. Operation *Holle Vaten*.
	1,2 tons in Madrid (Spain). Loaded van. Operation *Job*.
1991	2,0 tons in the Canary Islands (Spain). Ship *El Bongo*.
	1,3 tons in Ferrol (Spain). Floating in the ocean.
	1,0 ton near Lisbon (Portugal). Ship *Rand*. Spanish operation.
1992	1,1 tons in Amsterdam (the Netherlands). Loaded van. Colombian involvement.
1993	1,1 tons in Vyborg (Russia). TIR truck. Colombian-Russian-Israeli involvement.
	2,0 tons near Cadiz (Spain). Ship *Mar Tere*.
	2,0 tons in Antwerp (Belgium). Harbour storehouse. Dutch involvement.
1994	1,2 tons in Toulouse (France). TIR truck. Italian-Spanish involvement.
	5,5 tons in Turin (Italy). TIR truck. Involvement of former police officers and current customs agents.
	1,1 tons next to Galicia (Spain). Ship *Zwanet*. Colombian-Dutch-Spanish involvement.
	1,4 tons next to the coast (Portugal). Honduran ship. Spanish involvement.
	1,3 tons in Saint-Barthelemy (French Antilles). Abandoned on the beach.
	3,0 tons in Zeewolde (the Netherlands).
	1,1 tons in Amsterdam (the Netherlands). Colombian-Dutch-Surinamese involvement.
1995	2,5 tons in the Atlantic Ocean (Spain). Oil tanker *Archangelos*. Colombian-Galician involvement. Operation *Matorral*.
	1,0 ton in Rotterdam (the Netherlands). Storehouse. Antillean involvement.
1996	2,6 tons in Corme (Spain). Fishing ship *Mae Yemanjá*.
	1,9 tons near Canary Islands (Spain). Swedish ship *Siva*. Operation *Brasil*.
	1,2 tons in Muriedas (Spain). Harbour warehouse.
	1,1 tons near Vigo (Spain). Ship *San José II*.
	1,0 ton in IJmuiden (the Netherlands). Brazilian ship *Odimirense*.
1997	1,5 tons near Canary Islands (Spain). Fishing ship *Martínez Alvarez*. Operation *Manzanal*.
	2,8 tons in Cambados (Spain). Ship *Segundo Arrogante*. Operation *Cabezón*.
	1,2 tons in Zeeland (the Netherlands). Antillean ship *Fogo Isle*. Routine control.
	1,0 ton in Hoorn (the Netherlands). Container and tip from Belgium.
	4,7 tons in Tapia de Casariego (Spain). Hidden in cliffs once unloaded. Tip from neighbours.
1998	1,3 tons in Vigo (Spain), hidden in aluminium cables. Destination Rotterdam.
	1,0 ton in the Canary Islands (Spain) on a sailing boat to the Netherlands.
1999	1,2 tons in France, loaded in a caravan, going to Rotterdam and England.

Year	Description
	4,0 tons in Rotterdam (the Netherlands), in a ship amongst jeans textile in transit to Spain or Portugal.
	1.4 tons in Gioia Tauro (Italy) in frozen fruit juice going to the Netherlands.
	10,0 tons (record) near the Canary Islands (Spain). Operation *Temple*. Ship *De Tammsaare*, with Russian crewmen. Colombian-Galician operation.
	5,0 tons in La Coruña (Spain). Connected with the former case.
	2,0 tons in Amsterdam (the Netherlands), hidden in the structure of the ship *Pearl II*.

Source: Various newspapers (*El País, De Volkskrant* and *NRC Handelsblad* 1988-1998); OGD (1996a, 1997a and 1997b) and Prisma Team (2000).

3.1.5 Lines across Europe: the cartography of cocaine trafficking

Geographically speaking, cocaine forms a cross throughout Europe. Though smuggling and distribution lines can follow almost any available route by air, sea or land, there are four main import centres, not surprisingly located at the four extremes of the continent. They can be considered centres not only for the amount of cocaine entering through them, but for their importance in terms of organisation, operational matters and integration with broader economic or political arrangements. They are, in order of importance, Spain – particularly Galicia; the Netherlands – in fact the centre of a broader set of North Sea harbours including Antwerp and Hamburg; Italy – significant in organisational terms; and East Europe – an emerging diffused centre including the CIS from the Baltic to the Balkan route and other countries such as Poland, Czech Republic and Hungary. These four centres are not isolated from each other. On the contrary, they have become increasingly interdependent in business terms, especially due to all sorts of co-operation, partnerships and deals between groups active in those four regions. These developments have been at least stimulated by several major political changes taking place during the 1990s within Europe. Firstly, the fall of the iron curtain in the former Eastern bloc opened a new market and a centre for organising smuggling into Europe. Secondly, the war in the former Yugoslavia, by intensifying internal diasporas, temporary migration enclaves and the need for essential resources including weapons, affected heroin trafficking along the Balkan Route, pushing Italy and Central Europe to become more active in cocaine traffic. Finally, the opening of internal borders within the EU also encouraged, at least symbolically, the internal movement of people and drugs. However, this may be more true for the movement of small quantities for sale or personal consumption. Large quantities transported by land are rarely detected at border controls. Moreover, these cocaine flows move beyond the Schengen area or even the EU. In fact, although drug entrepreneurs fear borders to a certain extent, they also have more means to control them – by corruption, by studying their routines, by covering the loads, and so on – than to cope with urban or unexpected police surveillance.

Since the Netherlands will be separately treated in section 3.2, I will now give some brief remarks on the other European regions.

Spain and the Atlantic Coast

Spain's role as the major entry point for cocaine reaching Europe has not been contested over the years.[32] By sea, large cargos transporting legal goods – from oil to flowers to jeans – load the cocaine before weighing anchor, while especially rented ships receive the illegal merchandise at open sea. Although variations, these ships often depart from the Caribbean, Chile or Brazil carrying between tens of kilos and 5 tons of cocaine, pass through one or many transhipment or stop points (Atlantic Ocean, West Africa, Canary Islands, Cape Verde, and so on) and approach Spain both delivering the merchandise to smaller – fishing – vessels and speed boats, which reach the coast unnoticed, or by stopping at a port where the cocaine containers can be unloaded. From these two modalities, the first one seems more common in Spain, especially regarding those operations arranged by Galician networks. Cocaine arrives to Galicia through the same fishing and tobacco contraband networks, which at the same time traffic marihuana from South America and hashish from North Africa. Next to the hidden Galician *Rias* around Vigo, Pontevedra and La Coruña, large cocaine shipments also arrive to the Cantabrian coast – from Asturias to the Basque Country –, to the Portuguese ports of Lisbon, Figueira da Foz, Leixoes and Viana do Castelo, and to the Mediterranean harbours of Gibraltar, Málaga and Valencia (OGD 1996a and 1997b). From these areas, the cocaine is transported to Madrid for further distribution or sent directly, by land or by sea, to other European regions. For many years, the Barajas airport in Madrid, although smaller than Frankfurt or Schiphol, has been the main target for cocaine couriers arriving by plane from Latin America.

Spain has also become the largest Colombian drug money-laundering centre in Europe (OGD 2000).

Italy

Although many Italian groups are rather active in organising cocaine import and wholesale distribution, most of the cocaine enters by land from the North (France, Switzerland) than directly by sea. However, some large shipments have arrived to Sicily and to the main ports of Livorno and Genoa. It was here that in 1994 a shipment of 5,5 tons arrived from Cartagena (Colombia). The load was seized in Turin, a European record only broken in 1999 with the discovery of 10 tons near the Canary Islands. In some cases, cocaine lines are channelled by the same networks moving heroin and weapons, especially from and to the Balkan region. In fact, traditional heroin traffic in Italy seems to become more restricted since the mid-1990s, while the cocaine trade has tended to expand (Savona et al. 1993).

Eastern Europe and the Baltic

In 1991, seizures between 30 kg and 150 kg were made in places such as Gothenburg, Helsinki, Gdansk and Prague, most of them in containers, drawing the attention of

---

32 Considering the difficulties in controlling longer coasts with scarce resources and the higher corruption levels, interception rates in Spain can be slightly below European average. The fact that Spain sizes between one third and one half of all cocaine seized in the EU (see Table IV) is a serious indication of such a major import role.

media and law enforcers about the increasing role of Eastern Europe as transit areas for cocaine into Europe, as well as new consumption markets (Van Duyne 1995: 79; OGD 1997a: 29; OGD 1997b; Clawson and Lee III 1996). Since then, continuous seizures have been taken place especially along the many ports of the Baltic Sea, or in their way to further destinations.[33]

Smaller quantities by aeroplane, both for the domestic markets and as first transshipment for Western airports, have been increasingly arriving to the international airports of Warsaw, Prague, Budapest and Moscow. Couriers from several nationalities have frequently been arrested at these airports, while many others in Havana, Buenos Aires, Brazil or Venezuela as they were about to travel to Eastern Europe. It should be noticed that a remarkable number of these shipments, both by air and sea, are destined to the Netherlands and Belgium, where further distribution is arranged.

The Balkan route
Although this traditional smuggling route should still be primarily regarded as the main entrance for heroin coming from Afghanistan and Turkey (Bovenkerk and Yeşilgöz 1998: 77), the growing presence of other drugs, especially cocaine, has been noticed in the region in recent years. In 1995, some 500 kg of cocaine bound for Albania were seized in the Greek harbour of Patras (OGD 1997b). Several reasons can be identified for such a development. Firstly, increasing drug trade internationalisation and integration has 'mixed' more and more different illegal networks, both operating there (Serbia, Croatia, Albania, Bulgarian Black Sea, and so forth) and in other countries such as Italy or Germany (Colombians, Turks, Russians, and so on). Cases involving the exchange of cocaine for heroin or weapons have been occasionally indicated by many sources all over Europe (OGD 1997a and 1997b; Fijnaut et al. 1996). Secondly, radical political changes including market liberalisation, wars, weapon embargoes, etc. have deeply affected countries such as the former Yugoslavia, Albania, Bulgaria or Rumania, encouraging growing local cocaine markets as well as international cocaine lines in all directions.[34] Thirdly, the region is a natural transit area between other old and new cocaine import points: Italy, Lebanon, Syria, Georgia and other Caucasian regions, Russia, and so on. Finally, the growing presence of Greek vessels and harbours can also be indicating a reaction of illegal entrepreneurs against tougher selective controls on cargoes. Due to the huge number of Greek ships in dry dock, and many freight or merchant companies owned

---

33 Many ports are active along the Baltic Route: Rostock, Gdansk, Helsinki, Kotka, Vyborg, St. Petersburg, etc., all of them downloading containers and transporting them by truck to the West Although the 375 kg of cocaine seized in the whole Russia in 1995 seem to indicate low interception rates, many cocaine shipments with such a far destination have been intercepted both at source or during stopovers. Many cocaine loaded trucks have also been seized in Poland and the Czech Republic. Even remote ports such as Archangelsk have been used for large shipments targeting St. Petersburg or Moscow (OGD 1997a and 1997b).

34 Cocaine activity around the region includes: cocaine laboratories in Croatia and Georgia, lines between Venezuela-Romania, Brazil-Beirut-West Europe and Greece-Albania-West Europe, shipments by sea reaching Turkey or moving north to Russia, and so on (OGD 1997a: 27-28).

by Greek and Cypriots having experienced financial hardship, many vessels have been implicated in drug trafficking cases in Poland, Russia, Benelux, Egypt, and on the high seas (OGD 1997a).[35]

Other lines

In between the main sea import routes, countries such as Germany and France have played a role as central wholesale transit areas. In France, more than the 80% of the cocaine seized in 1994 was already in transit through French territory. Beside direct shipments reaching the Atlantic port of Le Havre and the Mediterranean harbour of Marseille, most of the bulk activity seems to be concentrated in the Southern strip between Spain and Italy.[36] This importance of France as a transit country is also revealed by periodic large seizures in the French Antilles and Guyana, a transhipment area for both the American and the European markets.[37] Smaller quantities also enter France from the Netherlands – per land, for limited distribution or personal consumption, including 'drug tourism'– and from North and West Africa – mainly per couriers by plane or by sea through the Mediterranean.

Germany is also an obligatory crossroad between the Netherlands, Italy, Eastern Europe and the Balkan Route. Cocaine arriving by sea is delivered to the harbours of Bremenhaven, Hamburg and Rostock, and then loaded on TIR trucks bound for the Czech Republic, Poland and the Netherlands. Frankfurt Airport, both as a final destination and as a stopover, receives couriers from all over the world. However, most cocaine passes through by land in smaller batches, already belonging to first or second range wholesalers. This is confirmed by the fact that, despite the efforts of the BKA (*Bundeskriminalamt*) and the Federal Customs Service, no spectacular cocaine seizures have been made, with amounts clearly under the European average seizure weight. Especially from the Netherlands, cocaine travels south along *Nordrhein-Westfalen* and up the river Rhein. Next to wholesale, a large number of small distributors and consumers move modest quantities through the Dutch-German border, by car or train.

Separated from the continent, and despite some cases of flight stopovers or involving the *Eurostar* train from London, most of the cocaine entering UK is

---

35 The Panama-registered tanker *Archangelos*, transporting 2,5 tons of cocaine, was boarded by Spanish customs in the Atlantic Ocean in 1995. Although a Colombian-Galician operation, the ship departed from the Greek port of Piraeus, where business contacts were made and illegal companies created (*El País*, 29-1-95).

36 In 1992, 613 kg were intercepted in the Eastern Pyrenees. A year later, 406 kg of pure cocaine were seized in a motorway toll in *Perpignan*. A seizure of 1 ton took place in January 1994, between *Toulouse* and *Narbonne* (Dubois 1997: 33). Finally, a record seizure of 1,2 tons in February 1999 has been made in a TIR truck near Paris.

37 In July 1987, 445 kg of cocaine coming from Colombia were seized in the Marie-Galante Island, in Guadeloupe. In 1990, 551 kg were found in the French part of the Saint-Martin Island and 438 kg in Cayenne. Later almost a ton was seized again in Saint-Martin. The 'good' year of 1994 for French cocaine seizures (see Table IV) has also an spectacular double-seizure in Saint-Barthelemy amounting in total some 1,3 tons.

intended for domestic consumption. Cocaine enters by the several international airports but mainly by sea, both in unnoticed small vessels after transhipment – the Galician method –, and on ferry 'day-trips' by smaller and individual couriers crossing from the continent.

Bi-directional lines and transshipment areas

Cocaine lines are often bi-directional, mainly due to the diversification and democratisation of cocaine traffic. Risk minimising strategies include the mobility of some floating stock through common borders: for example, in 1995 an identical amount of 60 kg of ongoing cocaine was seized in each side of the French-German border (OGD 1997b: 22). It is also very common to find shipments entering one continental extreme that passes through undivided to a very far point, from were distribution starts. Evidence of far-away bi-directional lines includes the Netherlands-Italy, Spain-Italy, East Europe-West Europe, Balkans-Germany or even Denmark-Middle East. France is also a good example of the bi-directional nature of cocaine lines: Spain, the Netherlands and Italy are both sources and main destinations of cocaine passing through France (O.C.R.T.I.S. 1995: 92).

Bi-directionality is also the product of increasingly mixed networks trading different drugs or goods. What was explained before about some mix with heroin routes is even more applicable to cannabis. Large quantities of cannabis coming by sea from South America or North Africa often follow the same cocaine routes, and very often the same importers (especially Dutch, Galician and Colombians) tend to move cocaine and cannabis at the same time.[38]

Diversity in cocaine routes is finally stimulated by the increasing number of transhipment areas of inter-oceanic transportation to Europe. Cocaine transhipment practices are the logical result of the widening of trade lines and flows connected to Europe on the one hand, and the strategies of illegal entrepreneurs to disguise the shipment's point of origin on the other. Since transportation is a minor cost in relation to final profits, location of these areas is important but tied to other factors: economic linkages with source and with target countries, trade restrictions and controls, and so on (Friman 1995: 68). Mexico, the main transshipment area for cocaine to the American market, does not play a role regarding Europe. For this market, the most usual stopovers before crossing the ocean are Venezuela and Brazil (both also real export countries), the entire Caribbean region and Argentina.

Since the mid-1990s, Africa also became a very important transshipment centre for cocaine bound for the European market (INCB 1996). In particular, South Africa, West Africa (Nigeria) and Cape Verde have been involved in large smuggling operations.[39]

---

38 In 1996, 35 tons of cannabis were seized in Colombia on a ship destined for Poland (INBC 1997). Many large combined seizures have taken place throughout the last decade, especially in Spain, the Netherlands and Germany.

39 African couriers, especially Nigerians, have not only been detained in many European airports but also in South America – over 200 were reported locked up in Brazilian jails in 1997 (OGD 1997b). Nigerian networks also organise sea shipments from Brazil to many African harbours – Durban,

3.2 Why through the Netherlands? Some views from traquetos

Why do Colombian *traquetos* move large cocaine shipments through a small location such as the Netherlands? Geography, economy and drug policies are quickly called upon when pointing out the reasons for such decisions:

"The Netherlands has been a site of major illicit trafficking in cocaine (...) The geographical position of the Netherlands, its economic structure, the opening of borders in Europe and some elements of its policy have contributed to that situation". (INCB 1996).

Though the answer remains multi-factorial and in some cases very obvious, general statements particularly from international drug enforcement bodies deserve a closer look. I will try to do this by exploring some thoughts and impressions from the cocaine entrepreneurs themselves.

As with many other entrepreneurs, cocaine traffickers measure risks and local conditions and resources when they have to define the target of any smuggling operation. As explained in chapter II, when the competitive advantage of Colombia was assessed, risks minimising strategies are the main concern of drug entrepreneurs, and local conditions and resources can reduce or increase risks. They generally regard the Netherlands as an overall low risk base, both for import and wholesale distribution operations. Let us see how the different variables are positively or negatively judged and how these judgements fit with reality.

3.2.1 Economic activity and communication infrastructure

A first set of explanations refers to the enormous – concentrated – economic activity of the Netherlands, especially as a major import-export centre of Europe. Since cocaine, as described before, follows routes and uses the same infrastructural resources as legal goods, it is clear that these resources and conditions present in the Netherlands have an effect in lowering illegal entrepreneur's risks. When commenting on this economic environment, they usually refer to four different aspects: a) the huge volumes of airports and seaports such as Schiphol and Rotterdam; b) the good communication infrastructure (trains and roads) and the central place of the Netherlands in between other countries of West Europe; c) the good 'entrepreneurial' atmosphere both regarding the existence of big and small legal import-export firms as well as a more general international 'trading' mentality that speeds both legal and illegal transactions; and d) the existence of enough financial and banking resources.

Miguel is a professional courier who was detained in Schiphol only after an earlier successful 'cross':

Maputo, Cape Verde, and so on – from where the cocaine is sent to Europe by air or sea. A seizure of 350 kg in Hamburg in 1992 turned to be a Nigerian-Polish operation (OGD 1997a: 15). Also countries such as Hungary and Czech Republic have been the targets of Nigerian smuggling operations. Finally, a growing number of shipments passing through Cape Verde Islands are destined to Europe, especially Portugal and the Netherlands.

"You never know what is going to happen. If you are lucky there are many planes coming at the same time, you know Schiphol, people from all over the world. I don't think it is a particularly safe airport, but it's big, many can walk through."

Indeed, movement through the international airport of Schiphol has doubled between 1986 and 1996, from 190 to 335 thousand flights per year, and from 12 to 27 million people passing through its gates (CBS 1997). The fact that it does not have direct flights from and to Colombia does not seem to be a problem for cocaine exporters and couriers, who know the higher risks involved in direct connections from 'hot' places. Miguel:

"It is more dangerous for us [Colombians] but they also know that anyone can be smuggling drugs, from wherever... Of course you change airports, can you imagine a direct flight from Cali? Who would want to take that flight? (laughs)."

Schiphol has very good links with other Latin American and European airports, and of course privileged connections with Suriname and the Netherlands Antilles, both permanently sending and receiving visitors and overseas migrants. Caribbean destinations score high amongst Dutch holidaymakers, and business ties with countries such as Venezuela account for some frequent flyers. However, the name 'Schiphol' is not so familiar in Colombia amongst cocaine entrepreneurs: many considered it just another European airport. In fact, it could be argued that Schiphol Airport has been mainly targeted by non-Colombian individuals or organisations sending small cocaine amounts to Europe: people operating in Venezuela, Suriname, the Netherlands Antilles, Brazil, Chile or Peru.

A much more infamous reputation amongst Colombian cocaine entrepreneurs, when recalled, were the names of Rotterdam and Antwerp. Both places were considered to be rather safe by all people I had contact with. Joel, a Colombian wholesale distributor active in Amsterdam, explains:

"Yes, you can say that a small place is better, but they just keep sending to Rotterdam. Sometimes you lose something, as a month ago when the divers did not find it and I had to pay. I also take risks. Nobody knows what happened, but the thing disappeared. See, what is good in Rotterdam is that it goes fast, you take the thing and you sleep elsewhere [the cocaine container or bulk can be quickly moved to stash]. The mess is often made before, but if you follow the rules, the papers are in order and nobody 'sold' you, man, you 'crown'."

Even those with no personal experience of the harbour, in the Netherlands and in Colombia, always referred to it as being thoroughly praiseworthy.[40] Their impression is well validated by official statistics: a full free transit harbour equipped with modern

---

40 For example amongst peripheral connoisseurs of the illegal business circuit in Colombia, or amongst drug couriers imprisoned in the Netherlands. See also the testimony of the drug entrepreneur B. Gordon (Bovenkerk 1995b: 166).

automated and specialised terminals that in 1997 off-loaded 1.9 million containers and flats transporting 21 million tons of goods. (Hofland et al. 1994; CBS 1998). Although most of them come from other European countries, Asia and North America, some 250,000 containers still arrive in Rotterdam every year from Africa, Central and South America, thus from potential cocaine export and transshipment countries.[41]

However, Rotterdam is only a symbol for a broader positive view about smaller Dutch ports such as Amsterdam, Vlissingen or Ijmuiden. The same goes for Antwerp, widely used and considered by local cocaine importers as a 'local' port. Amsterdam harbour, for example, looks very small with its modest 66,000 downloaded containers in 1996 – in fact an abnormal record year – if compared with the volumes moved through Rotterdam. However, for cocaine entrepreneurs it still generates a great deal of interest: 90% of the containers came from 'sensitive' origins in Africa, Central and South America, and it received four times more containers from Colombia (5,300) than its competitor (CBS 1997). Even small ports such as Delfzijl, Zeewolde or the Texel Island are interesting and have been targeted by smaller boats in operations including containers and cocaine hidden in and under the ship structure.

In the ten years from 1986 to 1996, goods downloaded in containers at Dutch sea harbours increased from 14 to 24 million tons[42] (CBS 1997). The role of the Netherlands as a main 'door' for all sort of goods entering Europe is also revealed by import-export destinations: 415 million tons of goods imported in 1996, from which half from Europe and half from the rest of the world, and 366 million tons exported, from which 90% to other European countries (CBS 1997). The Netherlands is, after Germany, the most important destination for Colombian exports to Europe. In 1998, Colombian legal exports to the Netherlands amounted to € 275 million (EVD 2000).

The variety of goods traded, the number of leading companies involved and the diversity of routes followed by cocaine shipments, suggest that the election of a specific harbour relates to the legal arrangement established for the smuggling: cocaine follows the lines of legal trade, so it is the legitimate business world that in fact decides, even unwillingly, the faith of cocaine shipments.

Tano explains about further communication facilities:

"Joel goes to Antwerp very easily, he goes and comes back the same day. Public transportation here, no, you can't complain, the train and the tram are secure. One is accustomed to larger distances, and the routes there [in Colombia] are like hell. Here you know what you can expect, for example, yesterday they announced the train delay."

---

41 This means almost 700 containers per day entering the port from cocaine export and transshipment regions. In 1998, from the 120,482 containers arrived from South and Central America, only 7,300 came from Colombia. Suriname and Venezuela sent even fewer. More than 50% came from Brazil and Argentina (CBS, Container Statistics 1999).

42 Goods in containers are only a part of the total goods unloaded, which increased from 79 to 85 million tons in the same period.

Good communication infrastructure (train connections, good highways, public and mobile telephone facilities, and so on) are all important for business performance, especially since the cocaine trade consists of connecting people who are distant and do not know each other, and moving merchandise and people through space. Finally, a well developed system of TIR truck transportation ranges the whole continent from Dutch download points, offering cocaine entrepreneurs excellent opportunities to move large drug amounts to further destinations unnoticed.

When asked about the geographical position of the Netherlands for establishing the cocaine lines, none of my informants seemed to take this factor into serious account. The Netherlands are objectively well placed for receiving cocaine – on a sea coast, close to other centres and markets, halfway between West and East extremes – although other neighbouring places share the same features, and countries such as Spain or Russia have even longer and wilder coasts, with larger non populated and inaccessible areas better suited for smuggling and concealing cocaine bulks. However, these considerations were absent in illegal entrepreneur's accounts. It has already been explained that distance does not play an important role for cocaine exporters, for whom transportation costs are very small in comparison to the benefits. All efforts are devoted to reducing risks, and if that implies a particular shipment should enter through the remote port of Archangelsk, Russia, before being returned to Germany, so be it.

Many people suggested that, in the cocaine business, the 'with whom' and the 'how' very often precede and determine further decisions about the 'when' and the 'where'. Ernesto claims to have worked in the heydays of Cali for Santacruz Londoño 'The Student'. He explains about particular choices of location:

> "See, the thing goes in many ways and to many places. Some are better than others, but it all depends on the sort of *flecha* ['arrow', business partner] and the *cruce* ['cross'] you make. First the line, you open the line with some group there or some *paisano* that organises it from there. Then you arrange the *cruce*, and you see the quantity, your financial situation, your contacts and your *tapadera* [front-store]. You know all the possible methods, you can go everywhere. I would say, every operation is unique, especially big operations. The cocaine gets sick before getting there, it travels all over."

Another positive factor indicated by cocaine entrepreneurs in the Netherlands was its 'entrepreneurial' atmosphere and mentality. During the 1990s, the Netherlands opened the door for many foreign companies to establish themselves there by granting business and tax facilities. This meant that not only many leading companies established their headquarters, but also many small import-export firms opened or fixed a branch here, sometimes a single office with one or two employees. An ideal situation for cocaine entrepreneurs. Pollo, a Colombian economist and drug entrepreneur active in Amsterdam, explains:

> "It's not just cocaine. Look what happens here with under and over-invoicing, or with ghost subsidised products. They can do what they want with import-export infrastructure. They talk about us, but they have a longer experience in doing business, all sort of business."

Remarks about Dutch entrepreneurship by Colombian dealers were not only limited to pointing out the actual infrastructure and the long merchant tradition, but also referred to more general cultural features such as the existence of a business 'mentality'. Even when they were negative or derogatory, stressing for example notions of distance, indifference, meanness or materialist interest, they were usually linked to other more positive characteristics around professionalism, efficiency and pragmatism. They were not confined to describing only entrepreneurs, but seemed to be broader and generalising statements about ordinary native Dutch people in their daily environment and social interaction. Pragmatism, for example, is a useful attribute for an illegal business based on flexible arrangements, changing people and strong uncertainties.

Finally, others referred to enough good banking and financial facilities in the Netherlands, which without being exceptional or extraordinary, largely fulfil their needs for moving or sending money away.

The single market

As is the case for legal goods, cocaine import and wholesale distribution dynamics at national level can only be understood within the broader picture of a single European cocaine market. Most of the cocaine entering the Netherlands is intended for neighbouring or far away European countries, the Netherlands being assessed by cocaine entrepreneurs for its role in such a larger context.

In fact, all European entry points are regarded beyond their local dimension. The single European cocaine market is non-transparent, in the sense that gaps in information, law enforcement and opportunities can create over- or under-supply at specific points. Cocaine entrepreneurs react to price changes or local saturation by re-localising trade activities. All interviewed people agreed that although compared with other countries local kilo prices are moderate, the Netherlands shows a remarkable price stability – i.e. mild bottle-necks, no 'over-stocking'– with a fast circulation of the incoming cocaine.

Although somewhat vaguely, people often referred to short distances and to the international environment found in the Netherlands as a positive input for doing business. Tano, for example, liked the fact that English and Spanish were widespread business languages. Joel seemed to be at ease with the fact that business trips, even to Belgium and Germany, were short and rather safe.

3.2.2 The international meeting point

Next to the economic infrastructure, proper human resources are essential for business performance. I already explained that in the European cocaine trade, even at national level, individuals and groups from many countries are involved. Countries or regions either with strong local groups able to articulate upper and lower business levels – for example Galician organisations as middlemen between Colombian exporters and European distributors – or with a local palette of multinational groups and individuals able to operate and get in contact with each other – for example the Amsterdam international legal and illegal business scene – have better chances of hosting a significant share of cocaine transactions.

As I argued earlier, during the 1990s the cocaine business has experienced further processes of internationalisation (geographical dispersion, new routes, and so on), integration with other legal and illegal activities (with other illicit drugs, the weapons industry and the legal economy), professionalisation (more expertise, strategic management, re- and de-qualification in a dual tendency) and flexibilisation (multiple tasks, entrepreneurs without enterprises, increased sub-contracting, temporary and unskilled workers). Local scenarios with various groups or individuals – from legal and illegal entrepreneurs to petty criminals – strongly linked with external resources, networks or markets – such as migrant business, labour enclaves or local middlemen –, certainly offer fertile ground for those tendencies to be pushed forward.

The Netherlands offers an international meeting point for potential partners, operations and intermediations to arise: native Dutch, British, Colombians, Surinamese, Antilleans, Turks, Yugoslavs, Russians, Chileans, Italians, all nationalities likely to be found and linked in the Netherlands. They manage in various forms privileged access to source, transit or destination areas, to heroin or weapons trade and routes, or to international financial resources.

The international nature of the Dutch cocaine business becomes evident not only by analysing detentions in relevant cocaine cases, but also by listening and observing the very actors involved. Former local studies based on in-depth interviewing with cocaine entrepreneurs (Korf and Verbraeck 1993; Bovenkerk 1995a, 1995b) have indicated the international nature of the Dutch cocaine scene. More general surveys on the nature of organised crime, mainly based on judicial dossiers, also highlight the international nature of local 'criminal networks' (Fijnaut et al. 1996; Kleemans et al. 1998). Colombian importers, for example, are often explicitly enthusiastic about the Netherlands as a market place for meeting people from all over. Miguel explains from prison:

"It's nice to do business with Italians. Here in prison we get along very well, we eat together."

And Tano claims that:

"I meet people from places I never imagined before. The owners of the coffee-shop are Dutch, they did time in Spain. Montes is from Venezuela. Then you find Surinamese, Antilleans and Moroccans, all trying to get something when you enter and tell you are a Colombian. Joel sells to Germans, and so on. It is fantastic, so many different people, I learnt a lot in Amsterdam, I don't want to leave."

Opportunities to meet and establish business relations, for example between Colombians and Dutchmen, can also develop far from the *polders*. The Netherlands Antilles, for example, has been repeatedly indicated as a major meeting point for drug entrepreneurs. Many informants stressed the fact that the place is strategically located as transshipment area, that a large Colombian community lives in Aruba, and that mostly Aruba and Curaçao are frequented by Colombian drug entrepreneurs, either for holidays, for family visits or for business. Many deals are closed there, mostly all Colombian cocaine targeting the United States and the Netherlands.[43]

3.2.3 The repression factor

A final issue addressed by cocaine entrepreneurs is the problem of police control and the penal reaction. They do take in account penal answers and strategies, incorporating them into their own practices aimed to minimise risks. As illegal entrepreneurs, they are obsessed with illegality, and spend much time talking about Custom controls, about police moves and corruption, about judicial details concerning themselves or their criminal lawyers, and about prison conditions if they happen to have been caught. Daily life is also shaped by their efforts to avoid detection. Regarding the intensity of law enforcement – one can logically suppose – a drug entrepreneur would rather choose to operate in a tolerant, less punitive country.

The Netherlands is supposed to have a rather mild criminal justice system, being especially lenient with regard to drug offences. Prison conditions are amongst the least bad in the world, while sentences for cocaine smuggling, import and distribution are very flexible depending on quantities and groups involved. For international cocaine traffic, prison sentences can go up to a maximum of 12 years. Still adding fines and economic forfeitures, or additional punishments for 'belonging to a criminal organisation', for money laundering, or for violent offences, the sentence can vary very much according to the amount involved, the personal background, the organisational aspects and other circumstances. It can range from the 1 year given to the vulnerable, first-time foreign courier, to the 16 years imposed upon a leading, well-known – and badly defended – violent cocaine entrepreneur. Medium and large Colombian importers would normally receive between 4 and 6 years. Regarding effective drug enforcement, there is no reason to believe that Dutch cocaine interception rates are lower than elsewhere in Europe. On the contrary, it can be speculated that land smuggling (cars and TIR trucks at cross-borders and inner roads) are even more difficult to control than air and sea shipments; that local pressure for the police to 'score' is high; and that Dutch police and Custom officers are difficult to corrupt.

Although it can be claimed that the mild environment has changed over the last decade, with present Dutch law enforcement at a European average, it is also true that compared with the rest of Europe prison conditions are better, sentences for small quantities or smugglers are still shorter, police violence is lower, and a tolerant social climate is still a diffuse cultural mark.[44] In any case, these 'relaxed' images prevail amongst Colombian cocaine entrepreneurs regardless whether these are real or not.

This has led to the acceptance of a couple of simple assumptions. A first general idea alleges that a more repressive drug law enforcement – by longer sentences, worse

---

43 In 1997, 4,300 kg were sized in the Netherlands Antilles and Aruba.
44 Both as a form of social control and as a mere indifferent attitude about other's choices and businesses.

prison conditions, more effective preventive and repressive police investigation and co-operation measures, and so on – increases drug entrepreneur's risks and shapes his elections about smuggling routes. A second more specific related hypothesis claims that the Dutch mild penal climate has indeed attracted them to deal through the *polders*.

The observations of several drug experts (Bovenkerk 1995b; Caulkins and Reuter 1997; Farrell et al. 1996; Dorn et al. 1992; Friman 1995) suggest that the first claims have weak empirical grounds. Firstly, it is agreed that law enforcement has a disproportional effect: prohibition and a minimum enforcement radically affect risks – so entrepreneur's decisions and drug prices – while enforcement graduations until certain unachievable level has only a marginal effect regarding risks and prices, can be easily manipulated and neutralised by drug entrepreneurs, and in fact only shape more conjunctural aspects concerning smuggling methods or surplus smuggled cocaine. For example, longer sentences or improved interception rates hardly affect drug entrepreneur's decisions, but no control – by impunity or paying-off corrupted authorities – or total control – by physical annihilation or complete interception – may on the contrary play a central role in shaping their choices about where and how to trade.

However, in more concrete terms, a particular multi-ton seizure can affect exporter decisions: he will not send cocaine to the same place in the same way again.[45] He might move to another harbour, or look for new smuggling facilities. The same could happen if particular pieces of the puzzle are suddenly changed – i.e. the importer is caught, a corrupted official turns his back, and so forth. However, this readiness to change arrangements, to keep things moving, is rarely the result of a particular event but a more general and constant attitude of cocaine entrepreneurs who have to remain alert in a highly changing environment.

Secondly, drug entrepreneurs are capable of avoiding controls – by transferring personal risks to other people or keeping innovative and ahead of police developments – or even profiting from a supposedly more effective reaction – by feeding the police with cocaine and small couriers, taking advantage of formal procedural delays, mistakes and abuses, or becoming closer to the criminal justice system and to other illegal markets.

The second claim concerning the specific Dutch case is more paradoxical. The Netherlands is far from being tolerant at the level of cocaine import and wholesale distribution. However, interventions have different intensity regarding diverse law enforcement domains, agencies and market levels. As mentioned earlier, actual prison sentences are on European average for drug offences involving many kilos and organised criminal networks, but remain low, if compared with other European countries, regarding for example the smuggling of a couple of kilos by vulnerable and inexperienced couriers, or for retail selling. Prison conditions are generally better. Miguel:

---

45 Surprisingly, there have been cases of 'serial' seizures, obviously from the same exporter. Depending on his size, he is either wiped out from business or not even bothered about some losses.

"I was 3 years in Portugal and it was the law of the jungle. Esserheem looks like a luxury hotel, even compared with De Koepel."

Yet better prison conditions in the Netherlands do not seem to be taken into account by those people organising cocaine export in Colombia. Marisol, a criminal lawyer from Cali, claims that:

"Many of the big guys are already imprisoned here [in Colombia]. They send people with balls in their stomachs, they tip European airports about their own couriers, and they hardly help them with a lawyer or with money. These people are disposable to them. It doesn't matter what happens after arrest. They only care about the merchandise, and if somebody is caught, about people's silence."

In fact, most of the people making the key decisions about cocaine transports and overseas transactions (i.e. Colombian cocaine exporters) do not have any reason to fear European criminal laws and enforcement as far as they enjoy impunity in their own place of origin or they will not be extradited if caught. This is particularly clear for 'cut out' capitalized exporters well able to neutralise strategic (arrest, charge and conviction) risks (Dorn et al. 1998).

During the 1990s, the Dutch Customs, the Tax Office and the police have developed many specialised bodies (CoPa Team, Prisma Team, FIOD, DIC, Europol Drugs Unit, and so on) and they have joined in many co-ordinated efforts (Schiphol Team, IRT Teams, Hit and Run Container Teams and so on) for fighting cocaine trade. This has meant large budgetary expenses, international co-operation, technological investments and human resources development to a high degree. Colombian drug entrepreneurs do not seem very impressed with computers and complex police investigation. Tano argues that:

"The guys are more worried with random controls. In fact, they feel safe if police is observing them: it means that they are going to stay cool for a while. Yes, everybody imagine DEA officers everywhere, but the people I know do not fear the police here."

Indeed, a rather ambiguous and paradoxical attitude seems to prevail amongst many medium cocaine entrepreneurs (importers and distributors) towards local penal policies and police controls. On the one hand, they either claim to feel unthreatened by criminal laws and police investigation or they accept them or ignore them as given, natural risks inherent to the illegal business. Some make it clear that they more greatly feared the possibility of being killed or ripped-off by people in the circuit than having to go or being already in prison. On the other hand, they do take measures to avoid detection, like phoning from secure phones, avoiding 'hot' places or behaving with low-key profiles. These measures are often aimed to avoid accidental, unnecessary police control rather than to neutralise long-term, complex, strategic police investigation. Explanations for this go in two different directions.

Firstly, they are in many cases unable to undertake complicated intelligence counter-measures: they lack contacts with law enforcers, they simply ignore the details of police surveillance or they lack the infrastructure to neutralise police efforts.

When the Dutch police react astonished about 'amateurish' mistakes made by 'professional' drug dealers – passing sensible information through the phone or working with the 'wrong' people – the truth is that, in many cases, cocaine entrepreneurs cannot do otherwise.[46]

Secondly, they seem to underplay the existence of pro-active police activities, and behave as if the only thing to fear was unexpected detection. They try to avoid trouble, restrict public appearances, or even limit the chances of getting caught on public transport or motorways, acting as if the police did not yet know about them. In other cases, they would acknowledge that they are being 'followed', but would surprisingly underplay the fact all together. Tico explains:

> "Yea, I laugh about the *tombos* [police]. I never saw something more cowardly, compare it with Colombia! They can't cross the line so easily. They take their time to build their case, to observe, to follow people for months before doing anything. It is just gambling to know the space you have to move, but they just let you work. I don't give a shit about the cops."

Many remarks on "poor control" referred in fact about the limited resources to handle illegal activities that are concealed within legal economic ones. In 1996, 157 million tons of goods – dry goods and parcel bulks – were unloaded in Dutch seaports (CBS 1997), more than 430,000 tons a day. The physical control of these goods is technically impossible and would imply the total collapse of Dutch economic activity. Cocaine entrepreneurs reckon on this fact. Other voices stressing the lack of control pointed to the police.

Some referred to the general tolerant climate as a proper environment for doing business. Others claimed, in contrast, that although the police were invisible on the streets and *razzias* on illegal foreigners were rare, control through technological means – video-cameras, high-speed radars, scanners, and so on – was ever present and should be avoided.

In short, Colombian drug entrepreneurs tended to have, despite police and prison developments towards European average, a mild and tolerant image about the Netherlands. There is a number of reasons for this: a) in specific interventions the Dutch system is indeed milder; b) they reproduce known stereotypes often held abroad about tolerance in the Netherlands; c) despite police developments they do not feel threatened by computers or long-term investigations; d) they often refer to broader collective and individual feelings of freedom and social tolerance where they frame the dimension of penal control; and e) there is a lack or deficit of control that is often attributed to the large amount of social and material legal arrangements to be controlled. A couple of informants did however consider social control in the Netherlands to be highly formalised and visible.

---

46   Van de Bunt et al. (1999) argue that the 'arms race' view on the interaction between drug dealers and law enforcement often departs from misleading assumptions: both parties often under- or overestimate each other (Van de Bunt et al. 1999: 400-401).

In general terms, Colombian drug entrepreneurs perceive and comment on the Dutch criminal justice system as being lenient, mild and invisible, often referring in fact to the local social and cultural climate or to the intrinsic limits that a small, democratic country like the Netherlands faces in handling disproportional volumes of legal transactions, businesses and trade routes. These considerations are all important for the identity construction and self-legitimation of drug entrepreneurs, and become in some cases a social censure or a general critical discourse about the Netherlands. However, they are marginal or absent when assessing and explaining the Dutch role in cocaine import, where more positive economic, geo-strategic and logistic factors are by far the most influential.

3.2.4 The obstacles

The Dutch competitive advantage to import cocaine for the European market is nevertheless limited by two negative factors, all referred by Colombian cocaine entrepreneurs. The first one is the difficulty in finding strong and reliable local Dutch partners. Colombians often regard the native drug milieu as polarised between a truly 'Dutch mafia', as they call it, experienced in illegal business, locally and internationally well connected, but more interested in less risky soft and synthetic drugs than in cocaine, and those individuals ready to become business partners, often belonging to the criminal underworld with no connections, no experience and no infrastructure and capability to handle multi-kilo import transactions by themselves. Even when a family tie exists between a Colombian and one of these entrepreneurs, they are portrayed as unreliable, cowardly and ready to talk with the police if necessary. In other words, it is difficult for Colombians to identify native Dutch individuals or groups willing to engage in large import operations who are neither vulnerable members of the so called penose,[47] or drug enforcers trying to get a grip on them. The contrast is always made with regions such as Galicia or South Italy, where native illegal entrepreneurs do count on the protection of local power brokers. However, as explained earlier, this gap is solved by the existence of a very dynamic local market place for multi-ethnic and multi-national groups in which Colombian entrepreneurs can compete and operate by keeping a low profile.

The second obstacle, closely linked with the absence of local mafia-like groups, is the lack of structural corruption within Dutch Custom and police authorities. As a key resource for risk minimising, corruption neutralises criminal justice system intervention, allowing a shipment to pass through, a suspect to remain uncaught, or a penal process to fail. In other countries such as Russia, Spain or Italy better conditions exist for the development of collusion between the State and the illegal business: a) clientelism, b) deficit in accountability, legitimation or democratic control of institutions, and c) existence of strong inter- and para-state power brokers. Colombians often refer to cases of passive and active corruption, but those cases seem

---

47 The Dutch word penose comes from the Yiddish (occupation, livelihood) and refers to the criminal, not powerful underworld.

to be far from their domain: they either make up stories about supposed local protection they enjoy, or they refer to the cases as if they would have only heard about them. In fact, some explain these limitations not so much in absolute terms referring to the context, but in more relative terms regarding their position. Joel:

> "They wouldn't accept my money. The Dutch *mafia*, because there is a Dutch *mafia*, they can bribe whomever they want. For Surinamese people it was also easier, but nobody wants to get involved directly with Colombians, it's too hot. When somebody tells me that he has a cop in his pocket I really doubt, I tell him to watch out."

Colombian drug entrepreneurs feel far removed from local drug enforcers, their strategies being primarily oriented to evading them.

In summary, from the Colombian trafficker's point of view, the Netherlands offers a competitive advantage heavily based on its economic infrastructure and international business environment.[48] It is doubtful that its tolerant penal climate, at least in what still remains milder than the European average, has a real impact on its competitive advantage: even those cocaine exporters and importers who experience a lenient climate do not seem to base their business decisions on those sorts of considerations. This competitive advantage is limited by the lack of *mafia*-type native groups engaged in cocaine import and the absence of structural corruption amongst drug enforcers. The first obstacle is partially overcome by the presence of other multi-national groups in cocaine import, groups in which Colombian nationals play an important role.

---

48 The same point has been suggested or argued by Fijnaut et al. (1996), Farrell (1998: 30) and Van de Bunt et al. (1999: 403). However, the argument has remained hypothetical since empirical evidence is scarce and difficult to operationalise. While my material is also fragmented and only reflects subjective perceptions from Colombian *traquetos*, it clearly provides some evidence that supports the hypothesis. A more refined and localised study – for example regarding different places, transport methods, cocaine entrepreneurs or initiatives – may reveal interesting variations in terms of the primary and secondary factors that shape cocaine routes into Europe.

CHAPTER IV

WITH A CROSS ON THE FOREHEAD

Colombian Migrants in the Netherlands

"¡San Antonio, *dame novio* (give me a boyfriend)!"

Hispano-American invocation, very popular in Colombia

The preceding chapters have outlined the position and relative importance of Colombia and the Netherlands in the global cocaine business. The huge benefits to be made around the export, import and distribution of cocaine in destination countries has clearly intensified a migration of Colombians who struggle to get a share of them. Whether they are proper *traquetos*, adventurers, unskilled smugglers or temporary residents who support themselves by dealing cocaine, these 'migrant-traffickers' (Hernandez 1997: 541) are stimulated by a manifold demand – of illicit drugs, of labour force, of repression – in an industry that heavily relies on human resources. Moreover, this migration has not only been a result but also, like in the US, an important condition for the Colombian advantage.

Before exploring the particular involvement of Colombian nationals in the cocaine business once the merchandise has entered the Netherlands (chapters V to IX), I consider it important to discuss some general features of Colombian migrants in the Netherlands. In order to be able to assess opportunities and limitations for involvement, one should understand who these people are and the nature of their lives. In contrast with other well-researched ethnic minorities in the Netherlands, Latin Americans and particularly Colombians have never been the objects of systematic socio-anthropological research. They remain as an invisible, non-quantified community, which makes their problems more difficult to understand and tackle. This chapter will be devoted to providing some essential data on their migration patterns, their demographic and social profiles, and in particular the several economic activities they perform. I will try to extract conclusions about the nature of this community, testing the applicability of some notions developed by social scientists on migration and ethnic entrepreneurship. Chapter VI will further provide some bases for comparison through revealing the reality of Colombians in the US.

4.1 COLOMBIANS IN THE *POLDERS*

4.1.1 Migration patterns and demographic profile
In contrast to other migrant groups that arrived in one primary wave, Colombians have poured continuously into the Netherlands for the last two decades. However, it

was not until the 1980s that a noticeable group of young Colombian women started to arrive to the Netherlands.[1]

Colombians had already been leaving their country in large numbers, first from the 1930s to Venezuela, and later in the 1950s to the US. These processes only intensified during the 1960s and late 1970s to countries such as Ecuador and Panama. During the 1980s, emigration to other Latin American countries stagnated as they were hit by severe economic recession. Despite the fact that some migrants from the US started to return to Colombia with some accumulated capital made in legal and illegal activities, the outflows did not stop and now were targeted at smaller cities in the US, and other regions such as Europe and Japan.

While cultural links made Spain (Madrid, Barcelona, Valencia) their primary target, previous experience in – and the model of – the US, pushed many to look to the United Kingdom (London). Spain and the UK are followed by France and Germany, which has a large community based in Frankfurt. In smaller numbers, Colombians settled in the Netherlands (The Hague, Amsterdam, Rotterdam), Belgium (Brussels) and Switzerland (Zurich).

In the Dutch case, the large proportion of young women from the very start of the immigration wave (a constant of 2/3) is explained by the main activities that attract them to or keep them in the Netherlands: marriage with a local male partner, and other 'gendered' occupations in house cleaning and prostitution. Some of these migrants had been already abroad – especially in the US, the Netherlands Antilles or Japan – or had some relative in London, Spain or Frankfurt. Many came with small children, others just got them in the Netherlands giving birth to a second generation Colombians.

Once this first group was established – in financial and juridical terms, especially through obtaining the Dutch nationality – it triggered a chain migration that would intensify during the 1990s. More restricting migration legislation, especially measures creating greater obstacles for mixed marriages in 1994, decreased and later maintained the number of legal Colombians residents below the 2,000 mark (see Table VI). The inflow, however, has regained dynamism since 1997, only increasing the number of illegal immigrants, the Dutch born second generation and those ethnic Colombians with Dutch nationality.

Most migrants come from either the main urban areas or have lived there prior to emigration. *Vallunos* from the area around the city of Cali and *paisas* from the Antioquia region (Medellín) constitute by far the two largest groups. There are nevertheless many Colombians from Bogotá, from the 'coffee area' around Armenia, Pereira and Ibague, some *costeños* from Barranquilla and Santa Marta, and some immigrants from smaller regional capitals. In this sense, even with more *vallunos*, Colombian immigrants in the Netherlands come from the traditional emigration areas, which are the most populated and industrialised strips of the country.

---

1   For example as Mediterranean 'guest' workers in the 1960s, Surinamese migrants in the late 1970s, Latin American refugees between 1973 and 1978, or the more recent case of refugees from the Balkans during the 1990s.

Table VI Colombians in the Netherlands (1991-1999)

Year	The Hague Nat	The Hague Ethnic^a	Amsterdam Nat	Amsterdam Ethnic^b	Rotterdam Nat	Rotterdam Ethnic^c	Total The Netherlands M	F	Nat	Ethnic^d
1990	17	n.d.	131	267	64	n.d.	422	716	1138	4943
1991	284	n.d.	180	316	108	n.d.	568	1042	1610	5605
1992	34	n.d.	207	359	139	290	631	1135	1766	6077
1993	362	n.d.	244	403	163	345	706	1285	1991	6552
1994	351	n.d.	276	459	159	355	723	1326	2049	6864
1995	260	835	249	474	140	369	527	1142	1669	6874
1996	23	858	226	477	140	376	488	1081	1569	7078
1997	230	907	232	533	140	401	475	1109	1584	7561
1998	285	1031	215	577	155	n.d.	512	1206	1718	4783
1999	300	n.d.	230	609	170	n.d.	549	1299	1848	6590

Source: CBS Statistics. *Niet-Nederlanders in Nederland (1990-1999)* and *Maandstatistiek van de Bevolking (1990-1999)*. CBS: Voorburg/ Heerlen. Nat: Total of Colombian residents inscribed in the Register Office of City Councils.

^a Dienst Burgerzaken Den Haag. *Bevolking Statistiek 1995-1998*. Residents either born in Colombia or with father and/or mother born in Colombia (includes first and second generation).

^b O+S, Het Amsterdamse Bureau Voor Onderzoek en Statistiek. *Amsterdam in Cijfers 1990-1999*. Residents with either Colombian or Colombian and Dutch (double) nationality (excludes second generation with single Dutch nationality).

^c COS Centrum Voor Onderzoek en Statistiek, Rotterdam. Residents born in Colombia (excludes second generation born in the Netherlands).

^d Until 1997, 'broad' definition of non-native (*allochtoon*) that included persons with Colombian citizenship, born in Colombia, or those with at least one parent born in Colombia. For 1998, the CBS uses a 'narrow' definition, which only includes those persons born in Colombia with at least one parent born abroad, and those born in the Netherlands with both parents born in Colombia. This excludes two large groups formerly taken into account: around 1,300 second generation Colombians born in the Netherlands with one parent born abroad, and between 1,500 to 2,000 adopted children from Colombia (born in Colombia, Dutch nationality and Dutch parents). For 1999, a 'new' definition is adopted recognising all second generation: Colombians are those persons with at least one parent born in Colombia. This still excludes the group of adopted children.

In contrast to the decreasing or rather stagnated population of older Latin American refugees from Argentina, Chile and Uruguay,[2] women and children form the growing Colombian group. Two thirds are women and the average age is very young with 30% below 15 years.

Table VII estimates the total number of Colombians living in the Netherlands by the year 2000. This number is small compared with many other immigrant communities, but it is the largest Latin American group, closely followed by Brazilians and Dominicans. It is of course a matter of dispute whether Colombian adopted children should be counted as Colombians. Many of these children do not speak Spanish and have no cultural or social relation with Colombia or Colombians. However, a growing number of them, some teenagers at the edge of self-sufficiency, seem to be active in reaffirming or rediscovering their 'Colombianess'.[3] Just when the CBS ceased to consider them *allochtonen* (non-native) in 1998 in their statistics, some of these Dutch adolescents started to feel and act 'differently'. While they differ in socio-cultural background to other second generation Colombians (half of which nevertheless have a Dutch father), their increasing 'Colombian awareness' can attract them to other Colombian immigrants.

Table VII Estimation Total Ethnic Colombians (2000)

Group	Number
Colombian Nationals	1,900
First Generation with Dutch nationality	2,700
Second Generation with Colombian parents	500
Second Generation with one Colombian parent	1,400
Colombian adopted children	2,000
Illegal Immigrants	3,000-4,000
Total	*11,500-12,500*

Source: CBS and Colombian Migrant Organisations.

Colombians in the Netherlands do not live together. Despite the fact that half of them live in the province of *Zuid Holland*, they are truly dispersed all over the whole *Randstad* area and its peripheries. In no single street or neighbourhood, do they constitute a visible group in the way they are in Jackson Heights (Queens, New York) or the Elephant & Castle (London). Due to the high number of mixed couples, many of them live in suburban areas or small municipalities: Almere, Alkmaar, Amstelveen,

---

2   The political refugees who arrived in the 1970s were predominantly male and remained more concentrated and closed. The group started to decrease with the return of many during democratisation in the 1980s and 1990s. Some still remained, especially the second generation born in the Netherlands.

3   Maybe the most active and dynamic Colombian organisation during my fieldwork was *Chicolad – Chicos Colombianos Adoptados* (Colombian adopted children) – a teenage group based in Amsterdam that in 1997 grew from two or three enthusiastic youngsters to a countrywide network of more than 100 participants. They organised Colombian *tertulias* (social gatherings), Spanish and salsa courses, cultural activities, 'roots' trips or inquires in Colombia, as well as football or theatre events. Some of them were always visible in broader *Latino* events and settings.

Nieuw Vennep, Haarlem, Zaandam, Purmerend, Rijswijk, Zoetermeer, Noordwijk, Spijkenisse, Capelle aan de IJssel, Hoogvliet, Woerden or Nieuwegein, to give a few common destinations of the Colombian diaspora in the Netherlands.

However, a large group of around 40%, especially Colombian nationals and illegal immigrants, prefers to endure higher living costs in the three larger cities, and stay closer to formal and informal job opportunities, education facilities, or cultural and leisure events. The Hague is by far the city with the most Colombians, followed by Amsterdam and Rotterdam. Again, they do not concentrate in particular areas but rather merge into many immigrant or mixed neighbourhoods: for example in the Laakkwartier, Transvaalkwartier or Den Haag Centrum; in Amsterdam West, Oud Zuid or De Pijp; or in Rotterdam Zuid.

4.1.2 Class background and social capital

The socio-economic and cultural background of Colombian immigrants is heterogeneous, which reflect the different reasons why they come to the Netherlands. They belong to various ethnic groups and different social strata, from low to upper middle classes. While ethnic and regional differences are mitigated during the immigrant experience, class and educational disparities are a permanent source of social fragmentation inside the Colombian group. With very few exceptions,[4] there are no common 'ethnic' activities or businesses that interconnect Colombians from different social classes.

A first group of young women come or stay in the Netherlands primarily because they have met a local partner, most often a Dutchman but also Spanish or Antillean men. I found several cases in which the encounter did not take place in the Netherlands: Dutch entrepreneurs, students, tourists, merchants or sailors who travelled abroad and met a Colombian woman in one way or the other. Others met in the Dutch Caribbean enclaves, places visited and populated by both Dutch and Colombian nationals. Others still met their local partners in the course of a visit to a relative already living in the Netherlands. These 'love' immigrants tend to come from middle classes with at least secondary education completed and some labour experience. Within this group, I met women with degrees in law, psychology, accountancy, journalism, or who were employed in Colombia as secretaries, salespersons, tourist operators or factory workers. As I will later explain, they usually do not keep their occupations or careers once in the Netherlands. Only some, after they learn the language and complete a new study or training, will eventually find jobs appropriate to their educational background. Until then, they either work in unskilled jobs or are financially dependent on their partners or social benefits.

A second group, also mainly formed by women, come to the Netherlands in search of better job opportunities. This labour migration is heavily dependent on personal networks of relatives and friends already established (chain migration) and initially

---

4   The most notorious are the cocaine enterprises that often connect, for example, unskilled workers with
      university degree holders.

targets activities in the informal economy, the two paradigmatic examples being prostitution and housecleaning. These women tend to come from a lower class, but still have basic levels of formal education. Some were unemployed; others had experience in low-wage jobs in the formal or informal economy. In some cases, they have already had a family in Colombia, which either stays behind or is brought over later once settlement has taken place. They often do not plan to stay for long when they realise that formal job opportunities are blocked, but they will stay as long as they are able to support family livelihoods and meet long-desired material aspirations. Many of these women eventually improve their relative situation in the Netherlands by becoming legal residents, again by meeting a local man willing to support them or to provide them with a residence permit. Others return to Colombia after some years, still being followed by other relatives who just walk in their shoes.

There are also some men amongst this second group. They are usually relatives or friends of a 'pioneer' woman of the first or second group who is already established and can assist newcomers with basic needs such as accommodation and employment tips.

The absence of more skilled workers or professional migrants amongst newcomers who can rapidly enter the formal economy is a result of several circumstances. Firstly, restrictive migration laws put a barrier that, in the case of Colombians, is particularly directed at men. Secondly, cultural and language obstacles make these migrants to select other destinations such as the US, the UK or Spain. Finally, those chain migrants described above can neither assist high skilled migrants. Only those who are able to overcome these obstacles (by marrying a local, by retraining in the Netherlands and by actually relying on the Dutch business market) have the opportunity to occupy higher layers in the formal labour market. Exceptions to this are of course the few diplomatic personnel, some temporary managers and employees of the few Colombian enterprises, and some exchange students and internship trainees. However, only a tiny fraction of them actually remain in the Netherlands.

From the small number of Colombian artists (musicians, dancers, painters and writers), only some were already active in Colombia but almost none actually migrated due to their artistic careers or activities. The very small group of officially recognised political refugees tends to come from middle classes and usually have educational levels above average.

Although this heterogeneity is also reflected in the second generation Colombians,[5] this group of children and teenagers displays more common characteristics in terms of formal education, bilingualism, and future perspectives in the Dutch environment. Many of them follow higher education and are starting to get better jobs than their Colombian parents.

However, whilst the Netherlands is not an interesting destination for Colombian professionals, it also does not attract entrepreneurial immigrants. Many Colombians

---

5   During the 1980s, many women came to the Netherlands with their babies or small children. Although statistically considered as first generation immigrants, they show all the traits of their second generation fellows (bilingualism, no intention to return, social mobility, and so on). Thus, I do not make any distinction amongst both groups of teenagers.

have long established trade skills and business expertise, but, as I will soon explain, some of the conditions for the emergence of a local entrepreneurial class are absent. The few entrepreneurs found do not bring capital from abroad but tend to rely on local sources, whether they are savings accumulated from labour or external sources from local (Dutch) partners.

4.1.3 Welcomed?

As Portes (1995) explains, the way in which immigrant groups are incorporated into social and economic local structures is not only determined by their individual human capital and skills. As members of broader structures and networks, the process of assimilation is also affected by their interaction with the social context. Contextual effects are reflected in three different levels of reception: by the government's immigrant policies, by the acceptance from civil society and public opinion, and finally by the nature of the co-ethnic community already present. Let now see how these three levels affect the specific assimilation of Colombians in the Netherlands.

The Netherlands has no prior history of colonial, geopolitical or significant economic domination over Colombia, facts that often influence some destinations of immigrant outflows. The Netherlands is indeed considered as part of the 'advanced West', but it is culturally and geographically far, a truly strange and remote land for those who do not have direct references from friends or relatives. Moreover, the Netherlands has never engaged in systematic labour recruitment from Colombia. However, if – until the beginning of the 1990s – Colombians arrived with no official invitation, from then on their entrance to the Netherlands has been actively combated with increasingly restrictive laws. Newcomers are not assisted and are denied basic rights. Claims for asylum are routinely refused to Colombians, and migration laws even try to discourage locals from bringing a Colombian partner to the Netherlands. Genuine students and tourists are often denied visas even when legal requirements are fulfilled. At this official level, reception for Colombians can be defined as hostile.

A second level of reception involves the social acceptance or rejection from Dutch society, not only in terms of instrumental demand but also in terms of public opinion and images. This level of reaction is more contradictory since different groups or even individuals are accepted/rejected in many ways by various social groups. Colombian architects, for example, have good chances of being discriminated or ignored by their Dutch colleagues, while Colombian prostitutes are not only accepted but also encouraged to come by their many local clients. Colombian women are positively regarded by local men as being exotic, sexually appealing, hot, spontaneous, straightforward, loyal, home loving and hard working. '*What more can you expect from a woman?*' I once heard a Dutchman saying. These images seem to play a positive role in their relative success as prostitutes and potential partners/wives of local men. Further elements contribute to guarantee, at least, further public indifference: they are tolerated as 'Western' and Catholic; they are few and dispersed; most of them are women; their music and dance is very popular in the Netherlands; and so forth.

However, many feel discriminated against and stigmatised by the bad reputation of

Colombia as a source of drugs, poverty and endemic violence. This feeling is particularly noticeable amongst men, illegal immigrants, and those highly skilled or educated. In general terms, however, the social reception of Colombians can be characterised as being neutral or positive.

Finally, a third level of reception is formed by the nature of the Colombian community already established. The assistance of relatives and close friends is essential for almost all Colombian newcomers. These small, personal networks are necessary for securing initial credit, accommodation, employment tips, basic social and psychological support, and cash flows to Colombia. However, these 'ethnic' networks rarely go beyond kinship. In fact, as I will explain, there is *no* Colombian community to welcome or assist newcomers. They are forced to dissolve and be dispersed within other groups of foreigners or native-born, so they are less protected from outside prejudice and culture shock. The lack of substantial entrepreneurial and professional presence reduces the economic opportunities of new arrived Colombians. There is a rather weak reception from co-nationals.

Colombian reception in the Netherlands can thus be conceptualised as officially hostile, socially neutral or positive, and ethnically weak. What sort of immigrant community is shaped under such conditions? Before addressing this question, it is still necessary to show what they actually do in the Netherlands and the obstacles they face.

4.2 SURVIVAL STRATEGIES: *'A COLOMBIAN DOESN'T GET STUCK'*

4.2.1 Colombian jobs and incomes

Informal labour
Maybe one half of Colombian immigrants work in informal activities. The group includes not only the vast majority of illegal immigrants (men and women), but also some legal residents who either get better incomes in the informal economy (prostitution) or just work there part-time to get extra-incomes. It can be argued that many Colombians concentrate in two informal occupational *niches*: prostitution and private housecleaning. Of course, their importance in both activities is not absolute but relative regarding the group's size. Cabeza:

"Most women here [in The Hague] are cleaning. A huge number are just working behind the window. Some retire and new ones keep coming. Some disappear for a while but you see them again after some time."

Prostitution is indeed a major income resource for many legal and illegal Colombian immigrant women.[6] Despite potential higher profits, many women do not want to

---

6   Most Colombian prostitutes work either for legal *sex entrepreneurs* (club owners) or are truly independent (window-rentals). Their activities are informal since they are neither criminally prosecuted nor fully integrated in the legal economy. Only illegal prostitutes complain about being

work in prostitution, do not have the necessary contacts in the circuit or prefer the security of wage labour, so they exploit the local demand for housecleaners and baby-sitters. Both services are more expensive if contracted in the formal economy, so many Dutch households rely on illegal immigrants to get these services more cheaply. These labourers usually work long hours combining many employers, do not have any formal labour protection, and they are paid in cash per hour worked. Some women also clean in bars, offices and studios.

For Colombian men, the Dutch informal economy offers a more limited set of activities. Many are also engaged in both housecleaning and cleaning of (non-Colombian) bars and restaurants, earning the same wages as women. Other people work in seasonal activities linked to gardening and 'green house' agriculture. I also found men working as newspaper or leaflet distributors, illegally employed in dry cleaners, or sporadically contracted to perform small rebuilding or renovation works. Some illegal immigrant men complained about increasing difficulties to find informal jobs, while others suggested that legal workers do not fulfil the increasing demand for unskilled labourers.

Further, some men and women also engage in part-time jobs connected to several circuits. Some people cook and sell Colombian food (*empanadas, tamales, rellena, patacón, arroz con pollo* and so on) for informal restaurants, special events or the street prostitution circuit. Some men also provide informal services for *traquetos* as chauffeurs and telephone operators.[7] Other Colombians give individual Spanish lessons to a varied clientele. Finally, some also perform as translators and interpreters on informal bases.

It should be stressed again that almost all these informal activities are not framed inside any own 'ethnic economy' (Light and Karageorgis 1995). These services and jobs target local clients and employers: prostitutes work for local men, cleaners and baby-sitters work in Dutch households, language teachers for Dutch natives, and so forth. Only a small number of Colombians informally work for other Colombians, essentially cleaning and baby-sitting. In many cases, it is a relative who either works unpaid in exchange for food and accommodation, or, extremely rare, belongs to some family business in which he or she has to help.

Though most of these informal transactions are not inter-ethnic, these job opportunities – especially in prostitution and domestic service – are strongly dependent on tips, contacts and recommendations provided by co-nationals, whether relatives or friends. In this way, a very dynamic demand for these services stimulates a chain (illegal) migration of relatives and friends willing to take these jobs.

For example, Amanda's pioneer arrival in the mid-1980s prompted a chain migration of almost 15 direct relatives and in laws over the past 15 years. All of them work in informal activities, mainly housecleaning, baby-sitting and construction work. Only one woman managed to regularise her situation by re-marrying a local man. The

---

criminalised and persecuted, but in their condition of being illegal foreigners. Even in cases of criminal involvement (traffic in women, pimping, and so forth), the women are considered victims rather than offenders. See chapter VII for a full account on Colombian prostitutes in the Netherlands.

7   See chapters V and VI on informal jobs (*rebusques*) around the cocaine business.

others stay as illegal immigrants either for a couple of years or even longer. Some still have commitments in Colombia – children – and want to go back after accumulating some money, but others prefer and have the opportunity to stay and rebuild their lives in the Netherlands. They all dream with the eventual possibility of finding local partners or being made legal by employers or the state. Only under these conditions, can they seriously think about basic rights, study prospects or a formal job.

Formal employment
A large number of Colombians with work permits or double nationality are wage earners in the Dutch legal economy. Occupationally skilled immigrants, some of them with a technical or university degree and work experience, are often underemployed. They usually follow some training, internship or new study in the Netherlands before getting more highly qualified jobs. Amongst these professionals, there are social workers, psychologists, environment specialists and journalists.

Many Colombians, especially women, work in unskilled jobs on a temporary or permanent basis, mostly through local private employment agencies (*uitzendbureaus*). These jobs are usually combined with another income from a partner or relative, and in many cases, they are performed next to household chores. They are mostly employed in cleaning companies, supermarkets, call centres, catering services, conference halls, hotels, or as administrative personnel in all sorts of firms and institutions, including universities, NGO's, computer companies or chemical factories. Others hold more stable and qualified jobs as secretaries, technicians or low managers in engineer and construction firms, airline companies, or expensive hotels. However, I did not find managers or top employees amongst Colombian immigrants.

Further to this, a very small group work legally in the few Colombian businesses or institutions in the Netherlands. They include some local offices of Colombian enterprises (*Uniban, Transportadora Marítima Grancolombiana*, and so on), the Colombian Embassy and Consulates, some small import-export firms or some bars and restaurants.

Many relatively well educated and skilled Colombians are often willing to accept, at least for a while, harsh jobs in which they can easily earn twice as much as what they could get in a white-collar job in Colombia. Despite the fact that a strong demand seems to exist for many of these legal jobs performed by Colombians, it should be borne in mind that very often this labour is not the primary magnet for these people to come or stay in the Netherlands. In this sense, this labour migration is, in many cases, the result of individual decisions concerning not only economic matters: local partners, (illegal) family reunification, search for new life-styles, knowledge advancement, and so on.

Finally, a number of Colombians sell particular skills related to Colombian culture for the Dutch market, for which a local demand exists. With or without formal training, people work as translators, Spanish and salsa teachers either for schools, institutes or organisations as employed personnel or free-lance contractors. A few professional, mainly jazz and salsa musicians, also manage to survive by playing music for a local audience.

Social Security and partner income

I found many immigrants who received social benefits or relied on their partner's income. Different sorts of Colombians receive social benefits: divorced women with children, artists, unemployed, and even some prostitutes and cleaners who work unregistered. In fact, given the middle class background of many migrants and their consumption expectations, none consider these benefits enough and try to combine them with informal work.

Many women, however, stay at home and have full time jobs as housewives and mothers. Some feel frustrated about a broken career. Others only depend on their husbands for some time but eventually find a job. I found, amongst other Dutch partners, police officers, truck drivers, pensioners, merchants, computer analysts, hairdressers, small entrepreneurs, scientific researchers and construction workers.

Students

There are two types of Colombian students in the Netherlands. The temporary exchange students who only come to the Netherlands with a scholarship and return to Colombia after 6 months/2 years form a first group. They target many disciplines, but concentrate on agricultural (Wageningen), technical (Delft), or development and social studies (The Hague). Especially long established Colombians and second generation teenagers form a second larger – and increasing – group of students. They are dispersed through all sorts of colleges, institutes and universities, and do not form any visible or organised group. Some of these students also work part-time to support themselves.

Colombian scholars, with some presence in other European countries such as Britain, Spain, France or Germany, are almost absent in Dutch academic circles.

Ethnic entrepreneurship: the lack of own infrastructure

Most of the ethnic small enterprises are family businesses organised by Dutch-Colombian couples, in almost all the cases with Dutch capital. A Dutch man married to a Colombian woman, for example, buys Colombian products in Germany (food, handicraft and alcohol) that are sold in the large Dutch cities for extremely high prices. His market stall in *Blaak* (Rotterdam) was closed down when the police discovered that he was selling unlicensed Colombian *aguardiente*. In The Hague, his market shop is frequented by Colombian food cooks and sellers.

The few import-export businesses in Colombian hands – some small-scale including retail of their imported products – are essentially limited to food and handicrafts. Larger import-export businesses dealing with products such as coal, coffee, flowers, textiles, chemicals or industrial machinery are not owned by Colombian entrepreneurs.

There are also some salsa discotheques, bars and restaurants run by Colombians. They are dispersed, and only few of them manage to stay in business for a long time. For various reasons, many do not last more than 2 years: financial troubles regarding debts or taxes, quarrels amongst owners, re-migration, or official close-down due to violent acts or cocaine involvement. Some of them are well known in the *Latino* circuit and have a high degree of visibility. They do not only target Colombians, but also try to reach a broader clientele that includes other Latin Americans, Antilleans, Surinamese and Dutch. I also discovered some travel agencies owned by Colombians.

Some people who started as language or salsa teachers manage to organise their own 'cultural' business offering Spanish, salsa or music courses, in some cases combining them with more 'committed' activities around development projects in Latin America. Some criticised these entrepreneurs for engaging in what some people referred as the 'business of solidarity'.

Other typical 'ethnic' businesses such as grocery shops, financial institutions, bakeries or other retail shops are totally absent in the Netherlands.

4.2.2 Facing obstacles

'Colombiano no se vara' (A Colombian doesn't get stuck) is a popular saying repeated again and again by proud Colombian immigrants about their superb skills for survival. No matter how difficult the situation is, they claim to have not only a positive attitude against adversity but also ready-made solutions for their problems.

What are the major problems of Colombian immigrants? Do they actually organise themselves to overcome them together? Both questions are only partially related. Many problems are not shared and are only experienced by particular groups within this heterogeneous population. Moreover, some problems are in fact felt to be created or amplified by 'Colombia' or other Colombians, so a common answer would be unthinkable. However, many problems are perceived as common and externally created or imposed, and still ethnic solidarity (Bonacich and Modell 1980) does not seem to flourish. After reviewing the main social and personal obstacles both suffered and perceived by Colombian migrants, I will try to illustrate the limits of 'Colombian' organisation and solidarity. I will then identify the factors that plausibly explain fragmentation amongst Colombians in the Netherlands.

Colombia as a trauma

Only very few immigrants come to the Netherlands leaving behind acute poverty. As explained, emigration is a closed road for the most deprived and poor in Colombia. Even when they belong to the lower middle class, their situation was already substantially better than that of their parents. In fact, it can be argued that many come to the Netherlands precisely because they had improved their social position to a level from which further mobility is blocked or uncertain. This symbolic or material relative deprivation takes various forms amongst different immigrants.

Some experience unemployment or can just make ends meet with a high degree of job dissatisfaction. Others have a job, but realise they can never save enough to buy a house or support large households. Some working class Colombians dream about becoming self-employed or small entrepreneurs, for which start capital is required. Others feel excluded from surrounding consumption patterns.

Some migrants suffered violence in Colombia. I met women whose husbands or partners were murdered. Others were threatened and did not want to risk more. Still others were victims of abuses and domestic violence. Despite attempts to present a good country's image, all sort of immigrants had direct experience with violent death: a relative or friend killed, dead in an accident, victimised or persecuted. For many immigrants, the Netherlands represent a sanctuary of peace and harmony.

A small number of immigrants were politically involved in Colombia during the 1980s – in trade unions or guerrilla groups – and had to leave the country as political asylum seekers. In contrast with older Latin American refugees, who expected to go back once dictatorships would disappear, these Colombian refugees have little hopes of short or middle-term changes in Colombia. Most immigrants are rather pessimistic about Colombia's deteriorated social and political situation.

These experiences – economic deprivation, physical violence, and persecution – are by no means closed chapters for immigrants. Some of these traumatic experiences have lasting consequences in terms of fears, suspicious attitudes and self-images. Relatives and friends in Colombia still connect them with those realities. In addition, some newcomers miss their families in Colombia: many left children or old relatives behind.

Legal status and material deprivation
Colombian illegal immigrants always complain about the consequences of illegality. They are denied basic social and civil rights (health, education, housing, vote, retirement and so forth), not only in open contrast with local or legal residents, but also with their own past in which some of these rights were acknowledged. Some feel discriminated against by official institutions (employers, government, and so forth) and ignored or patronised by neighbours. They claim to be ignored or at best tolerated by other legal Colombian residents, the only financial help coming from direct relatives also living in the Netherlands. They also help with initial accommodation, but at the cost of overcrowding. They are later forced to pay high rent prices mostly to local proprietors.

Financial assistance from relatives and rather stable informal jobs prevent them from becoming marginalised, but these immigrants are truly forced to remain at the margins of Dutch society. Work conditions are bad, especially in hard physical activities such as prostitution and housecleaning: they suffer long hours and chronic health problems due to deficient safety or sanitary conditions.

They have few possibilities for moving around. They cannot leave the country even when they have the money, either to visit relatives or for holidays. In fact, they become seldom visitors of public domains: they spend most of their free time at home, restricting their outside social life to private parties and home visits. Those with children also complain about the lack of prospects for them in the Netherlands. Although the Dutch aliens police do not actively track or persecute some of these illegal Colombian immigrants,[8] all of them live in fear of possible expulsion. Anxiety

---

8 Dutch official policies invoke 'humanitarian' arguments both to tolerate illegal immigrants (against *razzias* and police state) and to persecute them (against social and economic slavery). These arguments are combined with a 'law and order' rhetoric about expelling the most socially dangerous (against illegal criminals). In reality, not 'humanity' but 'economic utility' defines who stays and who is thrown out. Those filling the most poorly paid jobs (cleaners) are allowed to stay. Self-employed

and stress are endemic amongst most illegal Colombian immigrants I have met.[9]

For better-off immigrants with legal permits or even double nationality, some of these problems are of course absent. However, even those who enjoy basic securities also feel deprived in various and more subtle ways. Some referred to situations of high dependency on the state and local partners. Others, particularly the high skilled and educated, often argued that they worked under their level and that they earned much lower incomes than their Dutch 'equals'. Some people sending regular remittances to Colombia found it very difficult to save money as originally planned.

Othering the Dutch: self-identity and 'cultural' complaints

Nevertheless, Colombia is not merely seen as a source of problems. Nor is the immigrant's precarious situation a daily subject of conversations. To the contrary, most first generation Colombians place the social, cultural and even weather Dutch conditions at the centre of their daily chats. Colombian pride and self-identity are often reinforced by all sorts of negative references about 'the Netherlands' and the 'Dutch', whether they take the form of jokes, irony, critical remarks, open complaints or back-stage commentaries. The extent to which they pejoratively represent the other vary according to people and settings, but seldom crystallise in open confrontation. People focus on several issues when trying to put the Netherlands down. Around these recurring themes, Colombians feel closer to each other.

A first 'problem' is of course the Dutch weather. Despite the fact that there is indeed a big contrast in terms of temperatures and sun hours, constant references to the weather are used to praise their own hometowns.

Secondly, many complaints target the 'cold' social life and the local ways of relating and expressing emotions. In one way or another, they usually refer to the lack of 'street' and 'night' culture; to people with undeveloped body language; to a tendency to avoid conflict often associated with notions of cowardice and weakness; to a dominant pragmatic and business-like mentality; and to a formal and law-abiding behaviour. From these traits, a whole range of cultural 'differences' appears. It is common to hear that "my husband can not dance at all", "my doctor has done nothing about my stomach pain", or that the party "has been as entertaining as a funeral wake".

Family relations are the next matter of conversation, especially in mixed couples. Since families do not play a central role in daily life, Colombian women for example have mixed feelings about their new Dutch families: on the one hand they point out a sort of indifferent stance, regretting the few and weak interaction between family members. Some women even indicate that "they don't know what I do", "they do not help with the child" or "they hold boring family encounters". Yet on the other hand,

---

(prostitutes) have to go. Moreover, not 'crime' but 'visual pollution' and 'annoyance' are the criteria at work. Smart and more skilled outlaws (drug importers, burglars or fraudsters) are difficult to find or to successfully expel. Street dealers, pickpockets, drug tourists and again prostitutes are considered on the contrary the illegal criminals *par excellence*.

9   These traits of illegal Colombian immigrants have also been found in Belgium (Murillo Perdomo 1996) and England (Pearce 1990).

most seem to enjoy a good personal relationship with their in-laws, enjoying the non-intrusive and non-conflictive attitude from them.

The list of 'cultural' complaints I heard from Colombian migrants is endless: dinner is served too early; lunch is too frugal; Dutch people do not practice any religion (often associated to a materialist mentality); parties are boring and finish too early; and so on.

A very important subject is language. The Spanish language is not only central to Colombian migrant identities, but it is also what connects them with people from a whole continent. It is the key element to feel and act at the same time, for example, as a *paisa* or as a *Latino*. Spanish is considered a valuable asset and, on the contrary, the Dutch language is regarded as difficult and useless, English still considered the language of 'success'. Most first generation migrants speak Dutch after some years since they have to interact with Dutch people at home, work or study. Many prostitutes or illegal Colombian couples only manage to learn a few words or sentences out of necessity. Even amongst mixed couples, I found some of them talking in English or even in Spanish with their partners. In fact, many Dutch partners speak basic Spanish and many really enjoy it. However, it can be argued that the frequent complaints about Dutch language precisely reflect the high degree of interaction with the local environment – through marrying out and working in the formal and informal Dutch economy.

Bored women: "the old man is watching TV"
The rate of mixed marriages – marriage to Dutch natives – amongst Colombians is exceptionally high. In 1997, the CBS reported 908 couples amongst the legal Colombian nationals living in the Netherlands (1584, see Table VI). Only 5% had both partners with Colombian nationality, a 13% consisted of couples with a Colombian man and a Dutch woman, and 77% was formed by Colombian woman and Dutch man[10] (CBS Maandstatistiek van de Bevolking 1998). Even if some of these couples break up after naturalisation, mixed couples continue to be the rule rather than the exception. Although no statistics are available, second generation Colombian teenagers show in my opinion an even higher tendency to mix with non-Colombian boy- or girlfriends.

While, as I mentioned before, Dutch men tended to portray Colombian women in positive terms, an overall positive image was reciprocated from the woman's side. Dutch men were considered a 'good catch': they were usually regarded as either financially solvent or skilled for making money, strong and good looking, sweet and naïve, hard-working, reliable, loyal and ready to accept woman's choices and

---

10 This percentage of 77% is only surpassed by Filipinos (86,5%) and Thais (90,9%), while even more 'integrated' groups such as Surinamese or British show much lower rates of outmarriage. First generation Turkish and Moroccan women, on the other hand, rarely marry native Dutchmen. Further high percentages of outmarriage amongst Polish, Russian and Dominican women suggest multiple interconnections between the prostitution and the marriage markets: arranged marriages to work as a prostitute, ex-prostitutes getting married, prostitutes and partners recruited from the same areas, and so on.

freedom. Of course, every woman pondered these variables differently. Couples ranged from young middle class with rather common backgrounds and interests, to extremely asymmetrical (and instrumental) relations between, for example, a young poor prostitute with basic education and an old Dutch with no financial problems.

Marga, a good-looking illegal prostitute working in Rotterdam, had a marriage proposal from one of her Dutch clients who offered her "*buen eten, buen huis*" (good food, good house). She declined the offer arguing that

> "If I marry I have to stay here, with an older man that I don't love. And my children? No, you see, I have seen many girls that have done it and they are not happy at all."

Although often censured and granted with a low 'moral' status, these 'unhappy' women were often tolerated and never cast out by co-nationals. One way of coping with dissatisfaction was to share it with other *Latinos*, openly degrading their husbands and making explicit the delimitation of social spaces. It was not rare to hear these women, for example at salsa parties, saying that they were bored and that the "fat man", the "bold man" or the "old man" just stayed at home watching TV.

Also women engaged in more even relations had routinely complaints about their Dutch partners or ex-partners. Some condemned them for being mean and tight-fisted. Others were criticised for being too quiet, hardly going out and preferring to stay home in front of the TV. Several women regretted that their husbands did not like Colombian music and that they could not dance.

Second generation: salseros or ravers?

Many children have been born from these and other Colombian couples over the past two decades. While 75% of these offspring have mixed parents (see Table VII), 25% have two Colombian parents, suggesting that many children of illegal Colombian couples are indeed recorded in the statistics. The older ones are teenagers who are leaving school to either follow a study or enter the labour market. Their 'assimilation' patterns resemble that of dispersed working class immigrants (Portes and Rumbaut 1990: 218), with the difference that a large percentage also speaks some Dutch at home. Spanish is, of course, the mother tongue for many, so the tendency is to become limited or fluent bilinguals.

While many remain dispersed and have few contacts with other second generation Colombians (neither in the same neighbourhood nor school), some, for example in The Hague, form *combos* (groups of friends) especially to go out or to visit each other. Robert from Cali is 18 years old and lives close to the Amsterdam RAI. His girlfriend is Linda, the teenage daughter of Omaira from The Hague. He explains:

> "Most of my friends live there in The Hague; we have a nice *combo* on weekends. Look, some Saturdays after *El Caleño* closes at 5 o'clock, we use to continue in some *amanecederos* ['sun rise' discotheques]... I know at least three *amanecederos* here in Amsterdam. They are not open for everybody; you have to know the people to enter. They are just houses; you get some food, strong drinks, and of course music until the next Sunday noon."

As many others, he was rather fed up with Colombian salsa music and bars, and was lately more attracted by the Dutch nightlife around the Amsterdam Rembrandtplein. Many of these boys did not even enjoy *Latino* discotheques, and hung out in Dutch *techno* or *hip-hop* places and concerts. The girls kept somewhat closer to salsa discotheques as well, acting out more explicitly a Colombian profile (actually, in many cases, going out together with their Colombian mothers).

Paranoid distrust and stigmas: with a cross on the forehead

A final obstacle that all Colombian migrants have to deal with does not refer directly either to their Colombian past, their residence status, their socio-economic position, the Dutch culture, their local husbands or their newborn.

Colombians have also to cope with very negative images about them. Constant bad press about the country, reflecting endemic problems of poverty, natural disasters, violence and illegal businesses has a persistent effect on public opinion, according to all Colombians interviewed. In the Netherlands, they feel the target of both international wars on drugs and restrictive migration policies. Both policies combined, Colombian immigrants (or travellers) become Nr. 1 suspects not only for law enforcers but also for a whole range of state agencies. Everybody agreed that crossing borders for Colombians is a nightmare. Marisol explained that having a Colombian passport is like having a

"Cross on the forehead, a mark. Don't we have enough punishment to also suffer this?"

In the Netherlands, as I explained before, a more neutral stance from civil society contrasts with the hostile attitude from official bodies. However, they do have to face a prejudiced stand, especially from those who do not have contact with Colombian citizens. For example, immigrants are believed to be poorer and less educated that what they actually are; they have to face jokes about the cocaine business; and some are even approached asking for drugs.

However, this feeling of stigmatisation from outside does not only lead to collective defences and victimisation attitudes. Many Colombians actually believe that it is not only a matter of bad reputation. Many immigrants, especially middle class women with Dutch partners, artists, students, and even illegal workers, point an accusing finger at other Colombians. Some people claim to avoid contact as much as they can. Others feel uneasy with this extreme solution, but still acknowledge the problem. Aurora:

"It is urgent to improve the Colombian image, I don't know how. It is sad to say but in my experience, where there are Colombians there are problems. (...) We keep much separated among Colombians. We have a bad name and many problems, but it's only a small group who gives bad reputation to all of us. Some are told, even before leaving the country, to avoid contact with other Colombians. I am against that."

Many women understand the situation of Colombian prostitutes, but they also see them as a source of disgrace. They avoid being associated with them, and some even underplay their quantitative importance. Legal residents also feel 'threatened' by illegal newcomers. Hard working illegal immigrants feel uncomfortable with those Colombians making rapid earnings in illegal activities such as cocaine dealing or theft. Some Colombian bars and restaurants have to fight not only against bad publicity, but also for actually keeping the place *sano* (healthy). Gossip travels across cities and towns, since Colombians are dispersed throughout the country. Newcomers have to justify their situation before being helped. The more isolated and 'assimilated' they live, the less responsible they feel for other Colombian migrants. Many fear being cheated and used. Paranoid distrust amongst Colombians is a rather extended pattern.

4.2.3 Dispersion and the limits of ethnic solidarity

The social profile of Colombian migrants on the one hand, and all the obstacles mentioned above on the other, guarantee that Colombians remain unorganised. They lack economic associations and barely have migrant or social organisations.

The few political or cultural committees and initiatives around Colombia are totally controlled by Dutch people, whether leftist sympathisers, human rights activists, salsa aficionados, or even Dutch adopting parents interested in Colombia. Sporadically, some Colombian intellectuals and political refugees try to get involved in these initiatives or to create new groups, but they fail due to a lack of support, interest and personal conflicts. These organisations do not play any role in the daily life of Colombian migrants.

Some social organisations, especially linked to the Catholic church and to the Dutch network of social services, work with the most vulnerable groups amongst *Latinos*: prostitutes, illegal residents, prisoners, ex-prisoners, homeless and drug addicts. While these have more credit and recognition by Colombian migrants, again these institutions are 'external' and not in the hands of Colombians themselves (though some of them volunteer, they are not the most active amongst *Latino* groups).

Some local initiatives are indeed organised by *Latinos*, but they do not last for long. These usually involve established Colombian women who come together to talk and eventually organise some activity. One exception is *Chicolad*, the organisation of Colombian adopted children, which has proved to be very dynamic and successful in bringing people together.

The Colombian Consulate also organises, once a year, an event with food and music to 'unite' Colombian immigrants. However, these and other social gatherings are only seen as nice leisure programmes or, by some, as a good opportunity to make some money. Germán:

> "Last year we cooked and we went to Utrecht with plenty of food. The thing didn't sell."

I witnessed personal fights for organising and selling the food in smaller parties. One Colombian man crudely posed the situation:

"Look, it is very difficult to do things with Colombians. They come for the *rumba*, looking for good cheap Colombian food and *trago [aguardiente]*. They want to be 'served', and will do the minimum to help in advance."

Social interaction and economic cooperation is restricted to the level of kinship. Relatives see and visit each other regularly, since they often live together or in the same area. However, the same does not occur at a broader level. Contacts are irregular and scarce, and many friends only meet in special occasions – birthdays, parties, events, and so on. Those with no relatives in the Netherlands and with a Dutch partner have few contacts with other Colombians, sometimes with no more than 5 or 10 of them.

Why are Colombians in the Netherlands so atomised and unable to cooperate in order to, for example, secure better jobs, fight bad reputations or press for entrance legislation changes? The answer to this question can be formulated by summing up all the characteristics of Colombians in the Netherlands described in this chapter.

Colombians arrived to the Netherlands only recently but not in one single wave. As destination country, the Netherlands is secondary and distant. It is a small group, from which 2/3 are women and 1/3 are children. They live dispersed mainly in urban areas, with no visible Colombian neighbourhoods or streets. They come from the richer areas of Colombia (Cauca Valley and Antioquia), but they also belong to different ethnic groups and social strata.

Many women come as 'sentimental' immigrants to marry a local man and eventually find a job. Others come as labour immigrants to work mainly in the Dutch informal economy – especially in house cleaning, baby-sitting and prostitution – and eventually find a local partner. Both groups prompt a stable chain migration and they explain the high number of women and the strong presence of three groups: illegal immigrants, naturalised Dutch and second generation Colombians. Dutch citizenship is massively obtained through marriage and not through legal residence. There are also some men, but usually connected to a woman (Colombian partner or 'pioneer' migrant). They have good levels of education, but most skilled workers are underemployed and there is a lack of professional immigrants. There are very few political refugees and artists. Students usually do not overstay after their studies. Those who work, work dispersed for Dutch clients or employers. Many depend on partner's incomes and social benefits. More importantly, there is a lack of Colombian enterprises, large or small businesses and even (legal) entrepreneurial immigrants.

All these socio-economic characteristics are embedded in particular social reactions and experiences. Firstly, their mode of incorporation in the Netherlands is mediated by a very hostile reception from official agencies and formal employers, a neutral/positive but still prejudiced stand from civil society, and a weak reception from their own co-nationals.

Secondly, these immigrants face a number of problems that are difficult to overcome. They keep a fresh contact with Colombia through relatives, remittances, visits and also longer stays. However, many also try to place a big gap with uncomfortable past experiences: relative poverty, endemic violence, authoritarian mentality, persecution, *machismo*, and so on. Colombian immigrants in the Netherlands also suffer various forms of material deprivation, dependence and psychological problems linked with the exercise of prostitution or with immigrant laws that keep them in illegality. Although they are economically assimilated and subordinated, only their children start to feel truly 'Dutch'. First generation Colombians remain culturally distant and continue to complain about the local environment: the awful weather, the 'business' and mean mentality, the barbaric customs, the incomprehensible language and boring husbands.

Finally, these immigrants have to face negative stigmas, Colombia(ns) being essentially identified with violence, *mafia*, cocaine, poverty, prostitution, and so on. However, many not only recognise that the crude reality can be even worse than the bad press. Some also feel ashamed of 'undesirable' co-nationals: prostitutes, illegal immigrants, drug entrepreneurs, thieves, and so forth. Distrust, paranoid attitudes and fragmentation amongst Colombians are the result.

All these factors considered together explain what so many Colombians keep repeating: that there is no Colombian 'community' in the Netherlands. However, is there a chance that Colombians in the Netherlands can succeed as cocaine entrepreneurs and employees when they do not constitute an ethnic economy?

CHAPTER V

CROSSING AND CROWNING

Colombian cocaine smugglers and importers in the Netherlands

> "...and a slippery and instant notion of happiness has been fomented upon us:
> we always want a bit more of what we already have, more and more than
> what seemed impossible, much more than what the law allows,
> and we take it no matter how: even against the law."
>
> G. García Márquez, *For a Country within Children's Reach.*

INTRODUCTION

The Sunday Mass given in Spanish was about to begin at the Saint Nicholas church in Amsterdam. A multinational congregation mainly Spanish, Colombian and Dominican slowly filled the benches, while latecomers preferred to stand at the back by the entrance. Amidst the shuffling of feet and the crying of children, the service started. At the entrance, a small group kept coming and going while their ringing mobile phones irritated the adjacent worshippers. While I observed the situation Ana Inés complained to me in a low voice:

> "What a shame, they don't show respect. They could at least wait until mass is over. All openly doing their business here... I don't like it."

Being within earshot it was not difficult to figure out that the people in question were Colombians, and the business was the cocaine trade.

This happened in 1996 when I was just starting my fieldwork in the Netherlands. However, who were these Colombian *traquetos* and the people working for them? What were their motivations, their backgrounds and the risks they faced? Finally, what was their relationship with the local Colombian community (if any) and their specific role in the cocaine business? After two years of fieldwork it was absolutely clear to me that involvement of Colombians in the cocaine business did not stop at export level. There was indeed a significant participation of some Colombian individuals in subsequent stages of trade, here in the Netherlands, from transport and import to distribution and retail selling.

The numbers game

By referring to a 'significant participation' of Colombians in the Dutch cocaine market, I am trying to stay away from the quantitative dimension. How many people are involved? What proportion of the Colombian community has anything to do with the cocaine business? These are two questions that go far beyond the limits of my methodological tool-kit, which is heavily qualitative in nature. Producing empirical evidence to answer such questions would have involved a different approach, not always compatible with my primarily ethnographic stance. Dark numbers are by definition difficult to trace, but calculations in this case are even more problematic for several reasons. Firstly, no study of any sort has yet been conducted on this specific involvement. Secondly, the number of illegal Colombian migrants is a matter of rough estimation. Thirdly, secrecy, flexibility and imperfect information exchange lie at the core of any drug transaction. Fourthly, transactions go beyond the local level, so that patterns of residence and drug involvement do not necessarily coincide. Finally, many of the Colombians involved are not even living permanently or temporarily in the Netherlands.

All this acknowledged, the question of numbers is unavoidable. In fact almost every informant, from Colombian migrants and drug dealers to field experts and practitioners, had some remark to make with regard to the extent of the involvement. However the views were rather divergent, if not contradictory. The police liaison-officer at the Dutch Embassy in Bogotá, for example, stated:

"I estimate that between 100 and 200 Colombians living in the Netherlands have a relation with the cocaine business" (Ab van Stormbroek, 27-8-96, Bogotá).

A former Colombian Ambassador to the Netherlands:

"The group is very small, and most of them are *mulas*. The majority have nothing to do with cocaine." (Carlos G. Arrieta, 1996, The Hague).

Solano:

"At least here in The Hague many Colombians are *untados* [lit. 'smeared', implicated in illegal activities]. Look, I saw more than 100 Colombians, illegal, legal and with Dutch nationality, mixed with the business in one way or another. Not now, but let's say in the last three or four years. I mean people really implicated, *traquetos* and also women, not the prostitutes and the small fry."

Jaime:

"In my experience around here the involvement of Colombians in the business is marginal and those involved are not part of the established community. *Traquetos* do not stay long in one place, you know..."

Amanda:

"...it's only a small group that gives us all a bad reputation..."

Tano:

> "All the Colombians I met come for the same thing, all come to 'work' with it. Once you are in, the only Colombians you meet are *traquetos*, thieves and prostitutes."

Perceptions thus clearly diverged within the Colombian community. In general terms, Colombian officials and community leaders tended to minimise the problem in the same way as those Colombians not involved in the business. On the other hand, those directly or indirectly involved claimed that the group was large and all Colombians came to the Netherlands 'for the same thing'. This divergence of opinion occurs for two reasons. Firstly, it is obvious that people make judgements on the basis of their own social world, and secondly, they may trivialise or amplify the problem to serve personal or institutional interests. In contrast, police sources were often cautious and well aware of selectivity problems: they only knew Colombians involved in the cocaine business.

In 1996, the *Van Traa Report* (Fijnaut et al. 1996) produced a more official picture of the involvement of particular ethnic groups in illicit activities. Referring to the extent of Colombian participation in the local cocaine market, it is stated that

> "Based on what we have found in the Amsterdam case, from which a special report appears in this series, it seems possible to assert that a *considerable* part of the small Colombian community indeed plays, in one way or another, a role in the import and distribution of drugs." (Sub-report I, VII.5, p.176, my emphasis).

and

> "Despite the fact that we cannot attribute the relative success of Colombian [drug] organisations to the local Colombian community, it is likely that *a large proportion* of the few Colombians participates somehow in drug trafficking." (Sub-report I, VII.7, p.179, my emphasis).

While it is impossible to contest these claims with hard numbers, there are enough indirect indicators to state that the opposite seems to be the case: only a small number of Colombians are actually involved in particular levels of the cocaine business.[1] These indicators are as follows:

(i) While most of the people involved are men, the Colombian community in the Netherlands is two-thirds women. Second generation Colombians are hardly involved. As explained in chapter IV, the group does not form an ethnic enclave.
(ii) Many Colombian drug dealers interviewed, contacted or heard of, both in the streets and in prison, were not living permanently in the Netherlands. Some were only coming to perform a specific task in the cocaine business.

---

1   See for a critique of the *Van Traa* Report on the specific issue of Colombians: Zaitch (1997) and Zaitch and Janssen (1996).

(iii) Although the police claim to know less about Colombians than about other groups – thus increasing the dark number of undetected participation – the tasks in which they are involved, as I will show, are those primarily targeted by drug law enforcers.

(iv) Although Colombians in the Netherlands suffer imprisonment rates about 20 times higher than the average,[2] prison numbers cannot be used to make further calculations, not only due to selectivity biases (regarding offence, ethnic origin, vulnerability and so forth), but also to the fact that most of detained Colombians are caught at borders or airports, rendering this rate a meaningless abstraction.

(v) At all cocaine business levels, the ethnic composition has increasingly diversified throughout the 1990s. Whatever the figure, the relative number of Colombians involved has certainly declined in recent years. Changes in law enforcement and in the cocaine market in Europe and Latin America have also contributed to this diversification.

(vi) Finally, as will later be explained, the levels at which Colombians are more involved are either of low labour intensity (importation) or international in nature (transport). For more local and labour intensive levels (distribution and retail selling) disadvantaged competition with other individuals and groups is the case.

It seems impossible to dream up figures from these considerations and one can only think in the terms of hundreds at the most rather than thousands of people. However, what is striking about their participation can only be assessed in qualitative terms. Indeed, many Colombians play roles in the local cocaine trade that they do not play in any other local legal or illegal activity. Their business reputation within the illegal cocaine trade remains, for better or worse, unquestioned. They draw disproportionate police and media attention, while their strong cultural and social impact upon the whole Colombian community is acknowledged even by those who consider them 'marginal'.

Four trade levels: heterogeneity and articulation

The cocaine business, as I pointed out in earlier chapters, should be understood as an articulation of legal and illegal arrangements where various tasks are performed in a flexible way by many different people. The tasks, skills and risks differ to a great extent as do the people involved, the opportunities to enter the business and the chances of succeeding in it. From the time that cocaine leaves the export country to when it reaches the hands of the final European consumer, four different trade levels can be distinguished: transport, import, wholesale distribution and retail selling.

The separation between these levels is not only analytical. In practice, every step in a single trade line involves a mark up in the cocaine price and usually implies distinct actors and economic units. In a few cases two levels can be integrated by one

---

2   In 1997, the average imprisonment rate in the Netherlands was around 82 (inmates per 100,000 inhabitants). With 80 Colombians imprisoned (most of them for drug offences) and a population of around 5,000 – in both cases legal and illegal people only with Colombian nationality – their imprisonment rate rises to 1,600.

economic unit, for instance import-transport or import-distribution. In other cases, a single level can imply the involvement of many economic units, as is often the case in distribution and retail selling. Finally, every single level entails a number of interconnected tasks, some of which link together legal and illegal activities and enterprises.[3] Figure III illustrates those four levels.

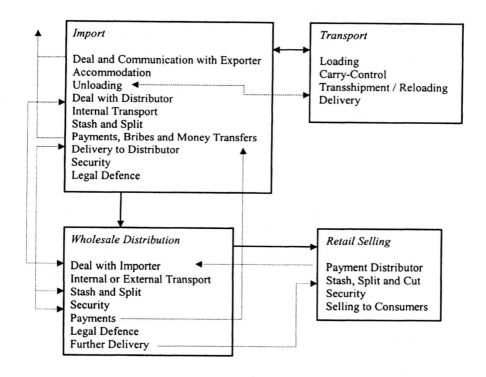

Figure III Four Trade Levels in the Cocaine Business in Europe

Identifying these four levels and the Colombian participation in each of them will allow me to illustrate the complexity and heterogeneity of such an involvement (avoiding simple pictures that hardly distinguish amongst the people engaged) in terms of background, chances, skills, commitments, expectations, social and labour relations, power and gender differences, and so on.[4] This chapter will focus on

3   Chapter VIII will analyse the nature of organisational and labour relations found within and around Colombian cocaine enterprises in the Netherlands.

4   The tendency to stress the ethnic or national dimension can lead, especially in media terms, to present Colombians involved as more or less 'equal', overshadowing internal differences and conflicts. At most, a simplistic dichotomy between 'big shots' and 'small fries' is often presented. A frozen image

Colombians involved in smuggling and import, while the next will depict their roles and activities as wholesalers and retail dealers. I will argue in this chapter and the next that, for Dutch related cases, Colombians have been modestly involved in cocaine smuggling and small import, very active in large import, noticeable but erratic in wholesale distribution and almost non-existent in small distribution and retail selling. This uneven picture, I will also argue, is the result of diverging conditions and variables that restrict and enlarge the opportunities of Colombians at each market level. I will then try to identify those factors and see how they actually shape the involvement of Colombians at each stage. In describing some of their arrangements, risks, opportunities and perceptions, I wish to explore some of the logic behind their successes and failures, their relationship with the local Colombian community and their overall place in the Dutch cocaine market. Finally, a more systematic analysis about the labour and organisational relationships involved will be tackled in chapter VIII.

5.1 SMUGGLING COCAINE

5.1.1 The options

Borrowed from the game of Draughts, in which a single piece is 'crowned' when it reaches the king-row of the board, Colombians commonly use the verb *coronar* (to crown) to refer to any cocaine freight that arrives at the destination without being intercepted. Depending on the amounts involved and the human and material resources available to both the exporter and the importer, there are four different ways to 'crown' cocaine in the Netherlands.

The first method, by means of regular, private or institutional internal post, does not require a smuggler. Despite the increasing variety of techniques to monitor packages – sniffer-dogs, X-ray machines and special scanners – interception rates for such a method of transporting the drug are uncertain. In addition to this, special mail companies have their own internal measures to control freights, tipping the police or Customs in case of suspicion.[5] The Dutch Post Office intercepts around 20 kg of cocaine per month, most of which is discovered in letters or packages sent from Suriname and the Netherlands Antilles (OGD 1997b: 52). However, cocaine by post constitutes less than 5% of total cocaine seizures (Korf and Verbraeck 1993: 107) since the quantities conveyed are rather small. Such dispatches are often performed by small-scale exporters, amateurish adventurers or even by local consumers with friends or contacts in source countries. Risks can be lowered by all sorts of tricks and simple

---

of big and small is also disputable: people present themselves to others as being bigger or smaller than they actually are. I have encountered many small distributors thought to be at the 'top' by law enforcers, while some involved in import were thought to be under 'godfather's' orders, being in fact the heads of their own illegal enterprises.

5   For example, 8 kg were seized in Tilburg in July 1996 after a tip from the courier company. The package came from Curaçao, and the two Dutchmen paid to receive it were arrested.

measures: faking the sender and the origin country, concealing the cocaine within protective materials or disguising it with special products, faking the recipient by writing a false name, simulating ignorance or using safer addresses of employers or friends who are unaware of the illicit content. The use of internal post systems of major, well-established transnational companies or institutions is a safer option when employees are involved as importers or receivers: in January 1997, three Dutch employees of the headquarters of Mercedes Benz in Utrecht were arrested for importing cocaine from Suriname.

A second method of smuggling cocaine is by scheduled flights through international airports. Quantities between half and twenty kilos are regularly smuggled, mainly through the Schiphol airport, by small-time or professional couriers, the cocaine being concealed in all imaginable ways: in hand- or checked baggage, hidden within clothes or objects – for example bike frames, handicraft, baby pampers, CD boxes, tape-recorders, music instruments, food and so forth –, diluted in all sort of liquids, impregnated in textile or swallowed in the form of balls. Large quantities[6] by air arrive as freight or hidden in special cargos.[7] Although the skill of the operation mostly consists of avoiding controls, in some cases the smuggling can be performed or secured by the aid of aircraft crewmen, airport or diplomatic personnel or even military members and resources.[8]

Over the years, the routes for carriers arriving at Schiphol airport have proliferated since transshipments and stopovers are the rule rather than the exception. Although interception data should be cautiously considered due to selectivity biases, smugglers targeting Amsterdam or Brussels have been principally detained in or coming from Paramaribo, the Netherlands Antilles, São Paulo, Bogotá, Caracas, Panamá, Tegucigalpa, Asunción, Quito, Buenos Aires, Lima, Paris, Madrid, Copenhagen, Frankfurt and Moscow. In fact, these are more or less the same places that were repeatedly mentioned during fieldwork. It can be argued that tip-offs from – more familiar – areas such as Suriname and the Netherlands Antilles can lead to more interception and thus over-represent their role as source countries for cocaine arriving by air. However, flights from Colombia, Venezuela or Brazil, also heavily under surveillance, are less frequent and far behind in terms of seizures. Indeed, during the 1990s, at least half of the seized cocaine entering the Netherlands by air came from

---

6   Regarding cocaine smuggling, I consider loads of 100 kg or more to be 'large', between 20 kg and 100 kg to be 'medium-sized' and up to 20 kg 'small'.

7   An unusually large shipment of 142 kg of cocaine dissolved in water inside plastic bags and hidden amongst 5,000 tropical fish from Colombia was seized in Schiphol in February 1996. In May 1999, the Dutch Customs made their record seizure in Schiphol: 700 kg hidden in 144 boxes of fruit and vegetables arriving from Suriname.

8   In September 1995, two KLM employees working in Schiphol (baggage) were involved in several smuggling operations of 14 kg to 21 kg each time. In May 1997, a KLM stewardess coming from Paramaribo was caught with 10 kg. In 1998, some Dutch marines were charged for the smuggling of 125 kg using an *Orion* aircraft from the Dutch Marine, ironically all were posted in the Netherlands Antilles in the fight against drug traffic in the region.

both Suriname[9] and the Netherlands Antilles. African airports as transit points for cocaine aimed at Europe are often used for France, United Kingdom and Spain, but less frequently for the Netherlands.

Small cocaine shipments arriving to the Netherlands by air from Colombia were more common during the 1980s, but sharply decreased in the course of the 1990s. A number of reasons can be given for this development. Firstly, the lack of direct flights from Bogotá to Schiphol makes stopovers necessary. The introduction, in 1990, of a tourist visa requirement for Colombian citizens to enter the Netherlands has, in the second place, partially affected Colombian exporters working with Colombian couriers.[10] A third reason is the increased importance, especially for small quantities, of other transit points in order to obscure 'hot' routes by diverting less obvious couriers through safer airports. This principle applies to all sorts of (cocaine) smuggling, but exporters using air transportation often have more choices available than those who rely on more highly organised – legal and illegal – means. Finally, the decentralisation process of cocaine export during the last decade has reinforced the power of intermediaries and non-Colombian exporters, especially those handling smaller quantities with restricted infrastructure.

Although cocaine smuggled in cargo or scheduled flights seems to be only a fraction of the total, this method accounts for the vast majority of people detained and charged in the Netherlands for international cocaine smuggling. It is difficult to estimate the actual centrality of Schiphol. A total of 2,300 kg were intercepted at this airport during 1996, which represented 25% of all cocaine seized in the Netherlands the same year. Yet this proportion is not stable since sporadic multi-ton seizures, re-allocation of enforcement resources and priorities, and changes in traffic patterns can transform the picture overnight. Neither is it representative of real traffic trends, since it is unclear how interception rates differ for air and sea operations.[11]

A third way to smuggle cocaine into the Netherlands is by land across the Belgian and German open borders, the illegal freight concealed in cars, trucks or small buses. These are (parts of) shipments arriving by sea mainly at the harbours of Antwerp and Hamburg, but actually handled in the Netherlands for further wholesale distribution in

---

9   In 1990, 53 % of the cocaine seized in Schiphol came from Suriname (*Het Parool*, 2-2-91). By 1996, 25% of the couriers detained in that airport came from Paramaribo. There are political, historical and socio-economic reasons that explain the important role of Suriname as a transshipment point for small and medium-seized quantities of cocaine entering the Netherlands. See Fijnaut et al. (1996) and Haenen and Buddingh' (1994).

10 However, in order to overcome this obstacle, it is easier for cocaine exporters to change the nationality of the courier rather than the destination airport, which is often chosen for its accessibility and the nature and resources of the importer involved. Nevertheless, it is a fact that after the introduction of the visa requirement, some Colombian smugglers relocated from Schiphol to Frankfurt.

11 Global interception rates are fairly easy to calculate – see chapters II and III, and Farrell (1995) – but extremely hard to estimate in national, local or sector terms since it is impossible to know how much cocaine passes through specific points. Rough estimations can only rely on subjective risk assessment by cocaine entrepreneurs and smugglers themselves, and on indirect indicators such as the general volume of people and goods moving through a particular spot and the nature and probability of controls.

Europe. In this way, many of these loads ironically come back to those countries untouched. Seizures of these loads are rare and usually involve long-term investigation, tips from or co-operation with the German and Belgian police.[12] In some cases the loads are brought in TIR-trucks of legal transport companies, but in other cases it is the final importer in the Netherlands who organises the smuggling, sending people to collect the shipment.

Finally, the vast majority of cocaine reaches the Netherlands in multi-hundred kilo operations by sea. Quantities from 20 kg to 3 tons are regularly smuggled in various forms by container ships, open cargo or fruit boats, yachts, sailing ships and tankers, all shipped from South American and Caribbean harbours. In the case of Galicia and Cantabria, illegal ships transfer the cocaine load, still out at sea, to smaller vessels or speedboats that reach the coast unnoticed and unload the cocaine in remote uncontrolled spots. In contrast, most cocaine shipments to the Netherlands are smuggled alongside legal merchandise, thus following legitimate commercial routes, transport and unloading procedures. Thus, by far, the most targeted harbours are Rotterdam and Amsterdam, and to a lesser extent Vlissingen, IJmuiden and Zeewolde.[13]

With a varying degree of creativity, the cocaine is often hidden amongst or inside products such as fruits and vegetables from South America, frozen fruit-juice, fish, shrimps, cocoa beans, meat, biscuits, spices, coffee, iron, coal, calcium carbonate, plastic, asphalt, oil, wheelchairs, carpet rolls, furniture, ceramics and sport bags, amongst other things. In most of these cases, the legal cargo is also dispatched by the cocaine exporters, who use either *bona fide* or their own import-export firms. Here, no illegal smuggler is involved: legal shipping, transport and freight companies unwittingly perform the operation, often even unloading and delivering the cocaine to the warehouse.

In some other cases, the cocaine is especially packed and hidden inside the ship or vessel itself: in the engine room, under the keel or within the hull. These operations involve one or more crewmen engaged by either the exporter or the importer to conceal, look after and sometimes supervise other tasks around delivery and unloading. Although many Colombians have been detained performing these smuggling tasks, those involved often belong to transshipment and destination countries (Spain, the Netherlands) or to countries traditionally supplying cheap seamen (Poland, Croatia, the Philippines, Brazil, and so on), even in operations that are completely managed by Colombian exporters and importers. This method obviously involves greater risks than the 'container' method: skilled smugglers and importers, as well as the shipment itself, also risk capture. 'Clean' crew members may

---

12 For example, in 1993, 175 kg were seized in Zaanstad in containers with false coal blocks. In 1997, 1,400 kg were found in Hoorn and Zaandam in containers and a bus with oranges. All shipments came from Antwerp and involved co-operation or tips from the Belgian police.

13 Curiously enough, the 2nd largest Dutch seizure took place in the secondary port of Zeewolde (3 tons in 1994). One cocaine importer interviewed suggested that smaller harbours are attractive since controls are less tight. However, most informants claimed the contrary, implying that multi-ton shipments have better chances of passing unnoticed through large harbours.

inform the authorities about the smuggler[14] and the importer has to undertake the delicate task of cocaine unloading.

Finally, cocaine has also been smuggled by private yachts or smaller sailing ships, either rented or owned by the cocaine entrepreneurs themselves.[15] The main or only aim of the trip is smuggling the cocaine, the smugglers being in these cases either (closely connected with) the importers or subcontracted by them. Whether they are professionally organised or individual adventures, personal risks are again higher: it is cheaper and technically easier to enforce (routine) controls upon suspicious small boats, people or movements than on sealed cargoes of legal merchandise. Indeed, most of the seizures from small private vessels are not prompted by prior intelligence or tips but occur during routine or selective controls.

Cocaine sea routes are more stable and less decentralised than air traffic: they are scarcer, and they involve more complex and risky arrangements that require closer management. Despite the frequent use of transshipment areas – Venezuela, Brazil, Ecuador, Suriname and Trinidad being the most common – or stopovers – Cape Verde, Spain and England – most of large cocaine loads arriving by sea come directly from Colombia. If Suriname and the Netherlands Antilles are the source of at least half of the small and medium-seized shipments by air, with only a very modest Colombian share, this proportion becomes inverted when analysing cocaine seizures of more than 20 kg by sea. Indeed, Colombia is not only the ultimate source[16] but also the main direct cocaine exporter to the Netherlands. Colombians have tried to lower risks by exporting from elsewhere: Colombian ships are suspicious by definition and local harbours have been increasingly controlled. However, there are still many reasons to send cocaine directly from Colombia. First of all, it is difficult and dangerous to move large cocaine volumes within South America: the cocaine can be seized or stolen by hostile authorities and competitors. Besides, many Colombian cocaine exporters are either unable to establish more complex international arrangements – since they rely on local corruption or local resources – or unwilling to sacrifice profit margins in favour of intermediaries, foreign authorities and distant companies.

---

14 In 1996, two Croat crewmen were denounced – and later sentenced – after the captain and other crew members discovered 85 kg of cocaine in their ship sailing to the Netherlands.

15 In 1993, 490 kg were found in a sailing boat in Texel, the cocaine bought and smuggled by two Americans. In 1997, more than 1 ton was seized in Hansweert (Zeeland) in an Antillean ship belonging to the Dutch importer, and other 486 kg were later found in Stellendam in a yacht. The use of these smaller, peripheral harbours is related to the nature, size and ownership of the boats.

16 Although there is growing evidence of cocaine kitchens in surrounding countries, most of the cocaine shipped from Suriname, Venezuela, Brazil and Ecuador is refined in and smuggled from Colombia.

5.1.2 The players

The fall of the independent smuggler

As I explained in chapters II and III, it would not be profitable for Colombian cocaine exporters to sell the merchandise at ports of departure.[17] Their powerful market position has been the result of their ability to 'place' and trade the cocaine overseas, first in the American market and, since the mid- and late 1980s, at European ports. This means that whatever method is used, transporting the cocaine and delivering it to the importer is an important part of their concern, indeed a highly risky and extremely profitable task. Exporters may hire people for transport, may use their own infrastructure or may subcontract the service to others – including legal cargo companies, fishing ships and vessels, or even competing cocaine entrepreneurs from transshipment areas. Cocaine smuggling is indeed in almost all cases both integrated into and subordinated to the exporters' activities, while the people involved in smuggling are employees, subcontracted entrepreneurs, independent organisations or people selling them a service.

There are exceptions. Hypothetically speaking, one could imagine that any person can travel to Colombia, buy cocaine there, smuggle it, and sell it in the Netherlands at import prices, thus becoming an independent smuggling trader. After all, with some infrastructure, contacts and luck, many people would be tempted to take the chance. Even a one-kilo operation could yield many thousand dollars. Yet however easy and logical it may appear, it is hard to find independent smuggling traders in the cocaine business.

During my first stay in Colombia, I was occasionally offered cocaine for personal consumption. I did not ask whether it was possible to buy a kilo on the spot, since a Colombian friend had advised:

> "Do not ask stupid questions that you will regret. It is fine that you write your thesis about us, but don't play the dealer or the policeman. If they offer you a lot, it is to test you; you just stay *sano* [lit. healthy, clean]. They won't sell you anything big, for what? They have people that bring it [the cocaine] for them. No! It's suicidal, for you and for them."

The most I could get, he said, would be an offer to act as a drug courier. Apart from the internal market, nobody would sell cocaine in Colombia that could otherwise be more profitably sold in Miami or Rotterdam. My friend concluded by showing me that even if I could obtain the cocaine, the profit margins were so high that I could easily hire a person to smuggle it for me, and still make money. Cocaine smuggling is almost never an independent activity.

Independent *globetrotters* were in business at a very early stage during the 1960s

---

17   The export price is relatively low, at around US$ 2,000 per kilo. According to time, place and amount, import prices in Europe oscillate around the US$ 24,000 per kilo.

and 1970s, before the consolidation of Colombian exporters.[18] The sporadic occurrence of cases in Europe are usually not linked with Colombia, but primarily with secondary or transshipment countries, and the people involved are often Europeans with their own smuggling infrastructure.

Colombian smugglers in the Netherlands

The opportunities for Colombians to become involved in cocaine smuggling have been favoured by a number of circumstances. Firstly, exporters require close and trustworthy people to perform such a risky task. As personnel remain accountable for possible failure or dirty play and should not talk if caught,[19] the exporter can better control another Colombian by, for example, targeting the courier's relatives for retaliation or compensation claims. A second reason is that drug smuggling is, in some cases, either a career step for 'job promotion' or a task performed by people with a previous or parallel involvement in other activities such as cocaine 'cooking' or security. Many Colombian exporters have indeed started as smugglers, and many couriers are flexible workers for various tasks. Finally, in Colombia there exists a huge 'reserve army' of people willing to take the risk, pushed not only by negative personal circumstances like deprivation, unemployment, debts, social exclusion or specific calamities, but also by a more 'positive' mechanism: the pressure for upward mobility in the context of violent competition and overnight turnovers in which successful role models have made it by illegal means.

However, other circumstances have hindered the participation of Colombian citizens as cocaine smugglers, especially since the mid-1990s. In the first place, Colombians have become increasingly targeted by anti-drug enforcers as potential suspects, so exporters have tried to find less conspicuous couriers such as other Latin American or native European citizens. The result has been a diversification in the social, national and ethnic composition of cocaine couriers, for example old men, entire families with children, young blonde students and European tourists.[20] A second limitation is marked by the developments in large-scale transportation. Professional smugglers with their own legal or illegal infrastructure are often not Colombians, but tend to be linked with transshipment or destination countries. American pilots, Mexican drug organisations, transnational freight or airway companies and the thousands of ships with a non-Colombian flag and multinational crew are the intermediaries that account for the vast bulk of cocaine transported. In

---

18 Before 1980, with a more fragmented supply and with exporters willing to expand sales, the role of free-lance amateur cocaine smugglers buying at source was larger. See Sabbag (1978) and Adler (1985).

19 Although, especially in small scale operations, most of the times the smuggler or drug courier simply ignores the names and whereabouts of both exporters and importers.

20 In October 1991, a Dutch organisation importing cocaine from Suriname and Curaçao was dismantled. Amongst the smugglers, there were 55 young blonde couriers. A 72 years old man smuggling 15 kg was detained in Schiphol in November 1994. A Dutch couple was detained in April 1996 in Copenhagen smuggling 6 kg from Sao Paulo to Amsterdam (Several Dutch newspapers). Cases like these have only increased during the 1990s.

addition, the fact that the role of transshipment countries has grown over the years has increased the diversity of smugglers.

Until the mid-1980s, cocaine smugglers in the Netherlands were predominantly Dutch individuals moving independently. Also during the 1980s, a growing number of Latin Americans from Chile, Argentina, Cuba, Peru and Bolivia were also involved in low and medium-level smuggling positions[21] (Korf and Verbraeck 1993: 104). The period between 1988-1994, a period of consolidation of Colombia as the main exporter to Europe, is marked by a decline of the latter group and the strong leading role of Surinamese air couriers and Colombian smugglers of all sorts. From the mid-1990s, a more diverse picture is the case, with Dutch and non-Latin American couriers increasingly used alongside all the others.

Despite all the changes, a very heterogeneous Colombian participation in cocaine smuggling to the Netherlands has been noticeable during the last ten years. The social composition of this group varies considerably. According to the quantities and the smuggling modalities involved, four different groups can be identified: *mulas* (small air couriers), *boleros* (ball swallowing couriers or 'body packers'), *niñeras* ('baby sitters' and professional couriers) and *tripulantes* (ship crew members).

Mulas

Although this pejorative name[22] primarily evokes exploited, poor, female couriers, all sorts of Colombians have been involved as unskilled air couriers: from desperate young men and women of urban areas to rather well-established migrants in destination countries; from friends and relatives of other drug exporters and couriers to low and middle class adults willing to move upwards; from adventurers to diplomatic personnel and students.

According to those interviewed, the motivations to work as drug couriers are manifold: debts and other money needs, pressures and threats, lack of job or occupation prospects, the ambition to gain more status and material wealth, the desire to travel, to migrate, or to emulate other couriers – whether neighbours, relatives or friends. The broad range of backgrounds and motivations of *mulas* is further evidenced in their payment, which can fluctuate, according also to the amount transported, between US$ 1,500 and US$ 10,000.

The profile of Colombian *mulas* coming to the Netherlands has changed over the years. Despite the fact that some available data either concentrate on specific groups – for example on criminalised female couriers – or refer to a larger population beyond

---

21 This involvement marks the transition from small-scale craft to large-scale organised cocaine smuggling. It was favoured by the growing accessibility of supply sources and the serious economic and political deterioration of the whole region that compelled many Latin Americans to migrate to Europe. Networks of friends and relatives around some of these immigrants became involved in the illegal business.

22 The recurrent use of animal metaphors to describe small drug couriers – referred to as mules, camels or ants – presupposes an emphasis in notions such as physical strength and resistance, docility, exploitation and smart 'instincts' to avoid controls or adversity. Other images regularly presented not only in the media but also by social practitioners and progressive scholars stress their condition of pitiful victims and scapegoats, often invoking drama, sorrow and compassion.

air couriers – such as Colombians imprisoned abroad –, all sources indicate a major shift from 1991 onwards. The period before this time is characterised by the involvement of a relatively larger group with a high number of poorly paid, ill-informed women from large urban centres. These women were, in general terms, from a lower or lower-middle class background, poorly educated, under- or unemployed adults (25/40 years old), alone with many children, and often victims of pressures, threats, violent situations and financial calamities (Del Olmo 1990; Janssen 1994, Cámara de Representantes 1995). However, the situation slowly changed after 1991. Increasing global drug enforcement efforts pushed cocaine exporters to use less vulnerable couriers: more men, younger or older people, better off individuals with steady jobs, frequent flyers, and more Colombians living abroad. In local terms, the introduction of a tourist visa requirement in October 1990 for Colombians to enter the Benelux countries had an impact in this direction. During the 1990s, Colombian air couriers operating in the Netherlands became a more diversified and smaller group. Small in two senses: compared to other nationalities involved in Schiphol and compared to the number of other Colombians arriving at other European airports.[23]

Most Colombians I met or heard of performing as *mulas* were neither established residents in the Netherlands nor complete strangers to the Dutch environment. On the one hand, established Colombian migrants or people with double nationality know the risks the unskilled drug courier usually takes and have better chances of becoming involved in less risky and more profitable activities around import and distribution. Except for some cases involving (ex) prostitutes (usually with residence, debts, good contacts in Colombia and a proclivity for conspicuous consumption) or some VIP frequent flyers (with local support and a strong sense of invulnerability) I could hardly find any Colombian living in the Netherlands as legal or illegal[24] migrant who would work as a *mula*.[25] On the other hand, cases involving unskilled poor couriers from Colombia with no visa permit to enter Schiphol were non-existent. Since it is rather risky and complex to get a visa for a simple courier, cocaine exporters and

---

23 During the first five months of 1997, the Colombian police authorities in El Dorado airport (Bogotá) made 75 cocaine seizures, with a total of 25 people detained and 500 kg seized. In only 4 cases was the Netherlands the final destination (2 cases involving shipments by DHL post), Madrid and Frankfurt far ahead with 21 and 14 cases respectively (Metropolitan Police of Bogotá, Airport Section: 1997). A similar trend is confirmed when analysing couriers detained in European airports coming from Colombia as first place of departure: from July to December 1997, 156 people were detained, among which were a significant number of Colombians. The 5 people detained in the Netherlands contrast with the 67 captured in Germany (Frankfurt) and the 32 in Italy and Spain (Interpol Office, DAS: 1997). Finally, both seizures and detentions in the Schiphol airport show for that period a clear prominence of Suriname, the Netherlands Antilles and Brazil as main source countries, far ahead of Colombian-related cases (Several newspapers).

24 The relationship between drug traffic and illegal immigrants will be dealt with in chapter VII.

25 Couriers visited in prison (Over-Amstel, Haarlem, Esserheem and Breda) as well as cases encountered in the 'milieu' had no fixed address in the Netherlands. Some of them smuggled cocaine before, usually not only to the Netherlands. Others stayed as tourists for a short period. This means a radical contrast with the situation in the US, where at least half of the Colombian couriers detained in the mid-1990s were residents, from which a 30% living in the US for more than 10 years (Ospina and Hofmann 1996).

intermediary organisations only look for Colombians with the access problem already solved: someone with a second nationality or a permit to stay in the EU, the Netherlands Antilles or the US, a relative to visit, a course or study to follow, and so on.

Even when they hold a visa to enter the Netherlands, Colombians are particularly scrutinised upon arrival. The mother of a Colombian woman living in the Netherlands pays a regular visit to her daughter. She explained to me:

> "They see your passport and you notice their faces. You are immediately a suspect. They treat you well, but in the way they treat criminals here. Every time it's a nightmare, first in Bogotá with all the bureaucracy, then at the airport, they ask many questions and often search for drugs. I understand why these people are caught."

Despite her claims, she is the sort of Colombian person targeted by drug exporters to bring a cocaine package to the Netherlands. Most of the cases encountered include entire families travelling as tourists,[26] special travellers with good reasons to visit the Netherlands, and Colombians holding another less conspicuous nationality. Those reasons can be, as the following case illustrates, rather unconventional and seemingly well orchestrated. It was related to me during a service in the Amsterdam Church as a hilarious true story:

> "Two Colombian women, dressed up as Catholic nuns, arrived to Schiphol carrying cocaine in their hand-bags. They were not inspected by Customs, but the police kept an eye on them. They thought they had made it, so already in Arrivals they started to happily kiss many people, laughing loud, and not properly behaving as nuns. They were caught immediately."

Although many couriers claimed to have been fooled about the real content of the transport, a less naïve picture was usually given by lawyers, professional couriers and drug exporters. In most of the cases, the couriers are held fully responsible for the transport. Some argued that the cocaine was carefully weighted and packed in front of them to avoid misunderstandings, others claimed to know just the weight carried and the very basic instructions. Other couriers still allege to have been helped by airport employees in El Dorado airport, handing them the baggage or freight after they have passed migration. A 'clean' employee I interviewed in that airport while he was controlling my luggage for the second time, openly said – I suppose to impress me with a 'before/after' situation – that:

> "In former times, many corrupted employees here would just tell the courier that his package was ready in the roof rack over his seat, but today we control and we get many people. Two hours ago I got a woman, she had too many shoes in her bag, and they were all the same."

---

26 For example, in October 1995, a Colombian couple with three children was caught in Schiphol smuggling 14 kg of cocaine.

However, there are indeed a few cases in which the passenger is completely ignorant of the nature of the freight transported, either given by an acquaintance as a package to hand over to some friend at arrival or, even less common, unwittingly introduced into the baggage by an unknown before or during the journey. Although I could not identify concrete cases like this, many people and signs in Colombia repeatedly reminded travellers, in a rather paranoid fashion, to avoid 'strange' requests and watch out for own bags. This risky method shows the strong asymmetry of the exporter-courier relationship, in which ill- or misinformation is a key element protecting the former and weakening the latter. It demands the extra skill of concealing and recovering the freight from the carrier, with a couple of potential advantages: less vulnerable and conspicuous people who would otherwise not perform as drug couriers can be used; they have less likelihood of behaving tensely even during superficial baggage checks; they are also cost-free in case of success; and law enforcers will not believe them.

The story of Susana, who served time in the women's prison of Breda, shows how some couriers are forced to keep working as a consequence of a previous failure. Susana first smuggled 5 kg of cocaine through the Brussels airport and went to Rotterdam to deliver the merchandise. She almost made it, but two men to whom the importer owed some money followed her and stole the cocaine. She was made fully responsible, and had to keep working in the illegal business to repay the loss. In a second operation involving the land transport of 3 kg, she was finally caught with another Colombian woman.

In another case, the courier was pressured to work for a second time since the previous success was seen by the exporter as a favour. In fact, some couriers claim to have suffered some sort of violent pressure, either in the form of threats, kidnapping or blackmail, especially against relatives. In some occasions these pressures were not explicit. One woman, for example, denied having been pressured but talked and acted as if she felt far from free:

> "Look, they don't tell you the rules but these are the rules and you know what can happen to you if you play smart. I wasn't threatened, they were very gentle, but I knew they would go to them [her family] if things went wrong..."

This is maybe why the claim of pressure, a standard defence strategy in courtrooms, is so difficult to prove.

In any case it should be acknowledged that exporters exercise control over the couriers by a range of measures. They include paying the courier after successful delivery; claiming compensation to relatives in case of failure; and pushing people to work as couriers either as the result of an earlier favour, an unpaid debt, a failure or a previous successful journey.

In sum, Colombian *mulas* found in the Netherlands from the mid-1990s onwards are a very small group of drug couriers. They are first of all people in search of labour opportunities and upward social mobility. In many occasions they have improved their educational levels, but their expectations are truncated either by denied access to the labour market or by unsatisfactory jobs in terms of personal aims and achievements.[27] These aims are strongly influenced by socialisation patterns that regard money, competitiveness and individual success as fundamental values in a cultural context where overnight turnovers is positively valued. They are men and women from lower or middle class, usually adults in charge of a household, some experiencing particular acute economic problems while others just facing few prospects for the future. These couriers do not have a criminal record in Colombia, but many have 'crowned' or have been imprisoned elsewhere before. They normally know the dangerous nature of the job, but their risk perception is often diminished by a number of circumstances. Risk is often underplayed by the suffering of a calamity, by a too fatalistic or too positive attitude towards adversity, by the excitement of potential rewards, by a strong identification with surrounding successful couriers, or by the trust endowed to friends and relatives who often mediate in the recruitment. These mechanisms are further promoted by cocaine exporters with an active policy of misinformation. They do that by denying controls, lying about the freight, trivialising the risks around the delivery, and even hiding the fact that they will be denounced to the police. Finally, most of these couriers live either in Colombia or in places with large Colombian communities such as the US, Spain or Central America. Some have friends or family members in the Netherlands while others are travellers with convincing credentials at Schiphol's migration desks.

Boleros

From the mid-1990s on, a particular way of smuggling cocaine drew special attention amongst European airports, hospitals and media.[28] The so-called *boleros* (body packers) became a particular sub-category of *mulas*. *Boleros* are people who carry between 400 grams and 1 kg of pure cocaine, usually distributed in balls containing 5 grams to 10 grams each.[29] The cocaine – usually packed inside latex fingers made from surgical gloves or condoms – is swallowed or hidden in body cavities, smuggled by many couriers on one or several scheduled flights, and delivered – after being excreted – on arrival.

The method is extremely dangerous for the courier, who risks dying if only one of the balls breaks. Since the mid-1990s, between one and three *boleros* per year are

---

27 See Pulido et al. (1995) for a similar conclusion on Colombian *mulas* detained in the United States. See also Green (1996: 18). Her research on drug couriers in Britain puts all the emphasis on the relative poverty and economic hardship of couriers. Poverty, however, does not explain why they are pushed to 'deviate' from mainstream survival strategies. While I also identified other mechanisms that play a role, I nevertheless share her conclusion that they are double victims of drug entrepreneurs and law enforcers.

28 Far from being new, this method was already in vogue in small scale smuggling to the US during the early 1970s. Unfortunately, detection was normally only prompted by the courier's death. Large scale smuggling to the US and Europe later overshadowed the interest for this smuggling modality. It is nowadays used to transport both cocaine and heroin.

29 Depending on their stomach size, a *bolero* can swallow between 50 and 100 balls.

already dead on arrival at Schiphol Airport, and many others in critical condition.[30] Fatal cases are also regularly reported in Frankfurt and Barajas. Up to seven *boleros* die every year in the route Bogotá-Barajas, either before, during or after the trip, while cases of dead Colombian *boleros* have also been found in Australia, Tokyo, Tel Aviv and New York.[31] They should not be regarded as mere 'labour accidents', as the following case referred to me by an informant illustrates:

> "A Colombian woman arrived to Frankfurt with many balls in her stomach, she was pretty much sick and in pain, but she made it through. When she arrived to the delivery place, she was in very bad shape. Do you think they took her to the hospital? No, they just locked her up and waited until she died, so they opened her belly and removed the balls. The woman was found by the German police chopped in pieces in several garbage bags."

However primitive and small-scale this smuggling method may appear, it has been a cheap, low-risk option for many middle and small cocaine exporters. A number of reasons can be identified for the emergence and vitality of this smuggling method. First of all, it developed out of the fact that until very recently,[32] European airports did not have the proper material and human resources to detect cocaine ball swallowing couriers.

Secondly, despite the dangerous nature of the job, the recruitment of *boleros* does not seem to be a problem for cocaine exporters. On the one hand, these particular couriers are often even more ill-informed than conventional unskilled *mulas:* they are usually made to believe that chances of ball breaking are minimal, rarely fatal, and that it is an easy operation with low chances of detection. In some cases, *boleros* report to have suffered some sort of pressure from the *cargadores* (loaders): psychological blackmail or explicit threats, especially on those who have already crowned before and are seen as owing a favour to the exporter. On the other hand, many people, from South American poor town-dwellers to European citizens, are willing to take the chance for some US$ 1,000 or US$ 2,000.

Thirdly, while this method entails low personal risks for the exporter, who remains out of the picture, it also implies few cocaine losses if one courier is intercepted. By spreading small quantities amongst many people, cocaine entrepreneurs can easily sacrifice couriers – even in a literal sense – losing little cocaine. The police and custom authorities are often more interested in producing detentions than in seizing

---

30 In September 1998, a 21 years old woman from Dordrecht died in Curaçao before catching her plane to Schiphol. The same month another Colombian woman carrying 96 balls died during the flight from Bogotá to Amsterdam (*De Volkskrant*, 15-9-98 and 29-9-98). Many more couriers died coming from Caracas and Paramaribo.

31 Indeed, from the total 32 deceased Colombians reported in 1996 by Consulates in 7 European countries, these were the indicated dead causes: 9 Cocaine and/or heroin ingestion; 6 Homicide; 5 Accident; 5 Natural; 1 Suicide and 6 No Data (Colombian Ministry of Communications 1997).

32 Only as a post-factum reaction, airports such as Barajas, Schiphol or Frankfurt lately introduced special X-ray or 'purge' rooms, first-aid facilities and specialised personnel for controlling and assisting *boleros*.

drugs. On the contrary, cocaine exporters are primarily 'shipment' oriented and very often have no concern at all about the fate of unskilled, replaceable smugglers.

Finally, the increasing number of *boleros* is the result of the further fragmentation of the illegal industry's structure during the 1990s, in which many small exporting groups flourished.

When *boleros* are detained in Schiphol, they are remitted to a penitentiary hospital after an initial check up in the airport. If the balls are not expelled naturally, they are often removed surgically. They subsequently face around one year of prison, depending on their background and their link with the exporter and the importer.[33] The number of arrested *boleros* in Schiphol grew dramatically since the mid-1990s: 17 people arrested in 1994, 87 in 1995, 172 in 1996 and 196 in 1997 (*De Volkskrant*, 27-07-96 and 15-09-98). This improved detection rate of *boleros* is not only the result of more technology and human resources at arrival controls. Airway crew personnel are increasingly trained to recognise *boleros*: they do not eat during the flight and they are often very nervous. However, some help for drug enforcers have also come from the cocaine exporters themselves.

The common practice of sacrificing one or two *boleros* is constantly indicated by couriers and cocaine entrepreneurs. Since many *recuas* (lit. mule train, groups of five to ten *mulas* travelling together) are formed by some *boleros* and some couriers smuggling more quantities, it is wise to entertain the police and the Custom authorities with the smallest and most vulnerable so the largest and less noticeable courier can crown safely. *Boleros* who fall as *ganchos ciegos* (lit. 'blind hooks', decoys) as the result of a tip-off always report the same story: after their passport has been checked, the police either get them on the spot or – more rarely due to the health risks and the small quantities involved – follow them to capture the importer.

Most of the *boleros* arriving to the Netherlands come from Paramaribo and Curaçao and only a small minority are Colombians. A large number are Surinamese women. As explained in 1996 by the head of the *Schipholteam* after a group of 7 Dutch *boleros* were detained:

> "Earlier there came *boleros* from the whole of South America. They were poor devils for whom those earnings of € 1,000 represented more than a year wage. But during the last months we see many Dutch Surinamese that travel again and again. It is unimaginable that they are prepared to take the risk for that money."[34]

His amazement, however, should be cautiously considered. People do not measure risks in the same cold, rational way when they face limit situations or pressure. Moreover, many *boleros* indeed crown successfully, especially those who are better off and less evident. In fact, the less vulnerable the *boleros* are – in terms of gender,

---

33 The fact that sentences for *boleros* in the Netherlands are rather low compared with places like the US, Italy, France or Spain, does not influence cocaine exporter's choices, who could not care less about the fate of a failed *bolero*. However, the couriers themselves often expressed satisfaction in the fact that they had been caught in the Netherlands and not elsewhere.
34 Interview with Mr. De Jong, in *De Volkskrant*, 31-07-96.

age, nationality or legal status, social skills and contacts, and so on – the less they fear detection and the more they are trusted and rewarded. Of course, the additional fear of the balls breaking is also neutralised by misleading information and a strong economic urge, both indicators of some sort of – relative – deprivation. However, not all *boleros* are desperate couriers. Some seem to smuggle in a routine way and achieve the skills necessary to survive many *cruces* (lit. cross, any cocaine export-import operation). As Tico explains:

> "Once I met a *paisano* [Colombian] living in New York, a very normal guy, you could not say that he was in the business. But 4 or 5 times a year he made a cross with some balls, each one with 8 or 9 grams."

Colombian *boleros* – or better still Colombians at risk of becoming *boleros* – always seem to have one or more of the following characteristics: they come from deprived – not the poorest – neighbourhoods with high unemployment rates and large rural-urban migration – for example the San Judas neighbourhood in Pereira or Ciudad Bolivar in Bogotá –, they have friends or relatives either performing as *boleros* or as mediators with the *cargadores*, they have residence abroad – with travelling experience and valid passports to pass migration checks – and/or, they urgently need the money – more often for a relative than for themselves. Adding the fact that drug entrepreneurs always look for new, less conspicuous couriers, the range of men and women at risk is enormous.

Recruitment is usually made by intermediaries, and the courier never gets in touch with the exporter. Two weeks before the trip, the preparation starts. They are trained by swallowing grapes, carrots or banana pieces, and they follow a diet to regularise the digestive cycle. The last two days they eat very light meals: vegetables, fruits and no fat. The painful loading process takes in some cases few hours, walks and massages helping to accommodate the balls, and some yoghurt, olive oil or Vaseline to swallow them. After that, they have at the most 36 hours to expel the balls.

Passing the Schiphol gates does not imply, for some, a guaranteed safe crown. Every year, an increasing number of couriers are treated in Dutch intensive-care units after their cocaine balls break once they have arrived. In order to encourage *boleros* to seek medical help, Dutch hospitals such as the *Kennemer Gasthuis* in Haarlem, the *Academisch Medisch Centrum* in Amsterdam, and the *Dijkzigt* or the *Zuiderziekenhuis* in Rotterdam, have adopted a pragmatic policy based on confidentiality and health priorities: the cocaine balls are handed over to the police as found objects, but the patient is not reported and remains at liberty after recovery.[35] In some cases, the hospital can even turn a blind eye to the whole situation. One informant was rather surprised about a Colombian woman:

---

35   This practice has been a subject of debate since 1998, the medical bodies arguing for 'hospitals as safe havens for everybody' and some politicians for breaking confidentiality and reporting *boleros* to the police. Further, hospitals plead for a more transparent procedure regarding the delivery of the cocaine balls, since the police do not issue any formal receipt (*De Volkskrant*, 15-09-98).

"...she was very critical but we managed to bring her to hospital. She was operated and she had to stay there for three weeks, and everything was for free! I tried to contact the people that would receive her here [in Amsterdam], but of course they were gone. When the woman left the hospital after three weeks, somebody came to her and said: 'you forget something!'. She was given back, in a plastic bag and very discreetly, the remaining removed balls. I don't know, but I think she finally delivered the balls."

Niñeras

Next to the occasional, unskilled couriers, it is also possible to find professional smugglers. While they also transport a few kilograms by air, they usually have a better infrastructure and logistic support. These smugglers are less vulnerable to detection. Some have a better know-how cultivated in earlier operations. Others profit from better operational arrangements by the exporter: contacts or corruption at arrival, better packaging methods, a preferential situation amongst other sacrificed couriers, and so on. In other cases they hold positions that reduce their vulnerability: stewardesses, pilots, military and diplomatic personnel, or merchants. Although there have been particular cases of the latter kind,[36] most of the Colombian professional couriers smuggling cocaine to the Netherlands are just experienced travellers closely linked to the exporters, often already involved in the cocaine business in Colombia.

Professional couriers can also perform as niñeras ('baby sitters'), an ironic name for the people who are sent to covertly escort and control less experienced couriers during their trip. 'Baby sitting' implies a less risky task with a higher status attached, and usually includes keeping an eye on multiple couriers who are unaware of his presence, securing the delivery and handling payments and collections with couriers and importers.

Most of these smugglers, often men with middle or low-middle class backgrounds, are just employees who either combine transportation with other unskilled tasks around production and export, or consider smuggling as a necessary step in their 'career' promotion. Miguel is a Colombian cocaine smuggler in his mid-thirties who embodies this type of professional courier:

"Couriers are selected for their reliability and their chances to crown. You accept the most risky job, but you don't want to stay as a courier, you want more. Patrones are not patrones because they talk nicely, no. They have the 'balls' of being couriers and doing first the dirty and risky work. So you have two sorts of people: the mulas, they are not going to make it. They don't receive much money, but more importantly, they are uneducated, they want to stay where they are. And they don't have the patrón's confidence, they even don't know them. But then you have those who want to climb; you really work for the patrón. It is not only for the money, you see, you want more."

In 1993, Miguel was assigned to travel as 'baby sitter'. He had to look after a Dutch courier smuggling 15 kg to Frankfurt Airport.

---

36 There have been, during the 1980s, isolated cases of Colombian diplomatic personnel and employees of large Colombian companies involved in cocaine smuggling.

"The thing was in a suitcase, put on board by a pilot of Lufthansa. I took the same flight, but he did not know me. European couriers are the best, you see, but when they start you have to watch them. Once in the airport, I contacted the man by a countersign, he crowned easily, and I paid him US$ 10,000."

Miguel delivered the cocaine to some Italian buyers. The instructions were to go with them to Naples, where they would pay him US$ 450,000 for the load. However, the Italians did not want to take him, so after new negotiations with the exporter in Colombia, it was agreed that Miguel would wait in Frankfurt. It was for him a fortuitous change of plans: while returning to Italy by car, the buyers were caught by the *carabinieri*, the illegal freight was seized, and they later received very high sentences. However, Miguel had nothing to fear: he did his job properly and was not responsible for the losses.

"It is very important to perfectly know when your responsibility begins and ends. You have to report everything and always ask for instructions and confirmation."

His problems actually started a couple of months later, when he was caught at Schiphol Airport smuggling a few kilos. Miguel spent almost 3 years in a Dutch prison.

"A courier earns according to who he is and how much he transports. For good couriers getting let's say 5 to 10 kg, you need not less than US$ 20,000 to US$ 30,000, including payment, tickets, accommodation and extras. One rule is that you are not helped if you get caught. Only *traquetos* are helped, but not couriers. They do not kill you, but you are alone. The worst thing that can happen to you is that the police take the thing but let you go. That's very common in Colombia. He [the *patrón*] would think that you are trying to fool him. It is better to go to jail, you see, otherwise the police is possibly sentencing you to death."

Colombian professional couriers do not live in the Netherlands, since they usually travel to many destinations and are close to one or more cocaine exporters in Colombia, for whom they also perform other tasks. As other professional travellers, they can also extend the stop either to arrange money issues or for a short holiday, usually staying in a hotel.

Tripulantes

Far less frequent but more interesting for law enforcement scorers, some Colombians have also been involved as crew members in ships smuggling cocaine into the Netherlands.[37] Large cargo operations often require big financial investments or joint ventures, and require close control by trusted individuals during the whole journey.

Tico, before getting involved in cocaine import and distribution in Amsterdam,

---

37 Since cocaine smuggling through illegal ships, smaller vessels and non-containerised freight require more human resources to load, conceal, control, unload and deal with other procedures, Spain has witnessed a larger involvement of this kind than the Netherlands.

worked for two years as cook on board of a large cruiser for tourists across the Caribbean Sea. He claims knowledge about the wheeling and dealing of Colombian crew members:

> "See, there is a lot of smuggling, but more for yourself, for selling here and there. With *perico* [cocaine] it is different. It depends on the ship and on who is running the operation, it can be one person or the whole crew involved. If the ship is *sano* [clean], you know, a real ship, you have one or two men in charge of the operation, but real sailors, people who know about navigation, about loading and unloading. But let's say the ship is only for the cross. So they want to be sure that everything is OK, somebody has to go to close the deal, to see that the coke is delivered, so they send somebody from the organisation. See, I know cases where the *patrón* in person gets on board."

Unless he means that in some cases the exporter can supervise the freight uploading, his final statement does not seem to have any empirical grounds: exporters never take this sort of risk. The distinction between normal crew members and envoys, however, is a fact with interesting consequences in organisational terms. Whether these crew members are employees of a legal shipping, transport or export company unwittingly involved or recruited for a specific illegal operation, all of them are real contracted carriers with few or no links with cocaine exporters and importers. They truly belong to the maritime environment as corrupted sailors, experienced smugglers or a criminal labour force. In some cases, claims about pressure and involuntary involvement should not be discarded. Tico:

> "You can't run away in a ship. You can shut up and watch the other side, which is the best thing to do. See, it can be like in prison, heavy guys give orders and if you are new and *sano* there is no choice."

The situation of people sent by the exporter is different. Their main task is to protect the freight from dirty play, to transfer information about practical issues, and to negotiate the remaining business deals. In this sense they can be compared with air 'baby sitters'. They are more likely to be found in cases where transport is arranged by importers in ships solely transporting drugs, especially when many parties are involved and when transactions are still open.[38]

All sources indicate that for ships arriving at the Netherlands cases like these are rare. Neither Colombian crew members nor envoys live temporarily or permanently in the Netherlands.

5.1.3 The chances to crown: assessing risks

Cocaine importers and smugglers were rather puzzling when talking about their chances of successfully crowning shipments. Firstly, they always tended to exaggerate

---

38 In August 1994, the ship *Zwanet* owned by the Dutch firm *Mariship* from Delfzijl was discovered near the Spanish coast transporting 1,100 kg of cocaine from Venezuela. Three Dutchmen, three Poles, six Spaniards and one Colombian were detained on board, the Colombian was viewed as the main suspect.

the risks. For people who failed, exaggeration was a way of legitimising their situation. Miguel:

> M: "For every 10 people loaded only one can get away with it."
> DZ: "You mean the other way around..."
> M: "No, no, it is extremely dangerous. I mean... sooner or later you fail."

By overstating risks, those still in business tried to stress, on the other hand, how skilful or lucky they were. For others, it was a good opportunity to gain status or credibility in front of partners and employers, or to present their profits as a deserved price. On a few occasions, the same people seemed to contradict themselves by underplaying law enforcement performance.

Secondly, most of the people contacted could hardly go beyond their personal experience when assessing smuggling risks. People were usually familiar with one method and with people taking the same sorts of risks. The question 'what method is less risky?', I came to realise, made little sense when asked in a broad sense to individuals. A method is primarily determined by the scale of the operation, the capital available to invest and the access to transport and import resources. Less than a choice, for example, air smuggling is the only method available for the vast majority of small exporters since sea lines are scarcer and require contacts and arrangements that are often beyond their reach. For larger exporters handling a shipment of 2 tons, millions to invest and insure losses, and strong contacts with import-export and cargo companies, sea transportation is the natural choice. Risks and chances to succeed are not so much attached to a particular method but to the individual opportunities, constraints, skills and resources deployed in each operation, in which a complex sum of variables play a role.

This explains the contradictory nature of risk perception. Some agreed that smuggling cocaine through small couriers was based upon the principle that there is "less risk involved if large numbers of people carry relatively small amounts of cocaine" (Philips and Wynne 1980: 235). Others claimed, on the contrary, that sea smuggling was safer because it often implies more organisation and local protection at destination points – by powerful illegal entrepreneurs, legal companies or drug enforcement authorities.

5.2 IMPORTING COCAINE

5.2.1 The Colombian share in cocaine import

Colombians have also been actively involved in organising cocaine import into the Netherlands. Far from controlling it, a number of independent Colombian importers both compete and co-operate principally with native Dutch and Surinamese importers, and to a lesser extent with many other nationalities. Colombian participation is modest for small quantities – smuggled by air – but strikingly high for large freights shipped from Colombia by sea. Table VIII roughly illustrates the Colombian share at this business level.

Table VIII Colombian Share in Cocaine Import to the Netherlands (1989-1997)

Up to 20 kg (31 cases)	20 kg to 100 kg (25 cases)	More than 100 kg (48 cases)
Ethnic-national background (main involvement-secondary involvement)		
Surinamese-Dutch 8	Dutch 3	Dutch 4
Dutch 5	Dutch-Colombian 2	Colombian 4
Antillean-Dutch 4	Dutch-Colombian-Italian 3	Dutch-Surinamese 4
Dutch-Antillean 3	Colombian 3	Dutch-Colombian 3
Colombian 3	Surinamese 2	Colombian-Dutch 3
Dutch-Surinamese-	Croat 2	Surinamese-Dutch 2
-Antillean 1	Yugoslav-Antillean 1	Surinamese-Colombian 2
Brazilian-Dutch 1	Surinamese-Dutch-German 1	Antillean 2
Dutch-Brazilian 1	Colombian-Belgian 1	Colombian-Dutch-Irish 1
Dutch-Colombian 1	Chilean-Dutch 1	Colombian-Mex-Dutch 1
Surinamese 1	Dutch-Antillean 1	Colombian-English-
Syrian-South American 1	Dutch-Antillean-Colombian 1	-Surinamese-Greek 1
Spanish-Dutch 1	No Data 4	Colombian-Dutch-Polish-
Dutch-Chilean-Spanish 1		-Spanish 1
		Colombian-Surinamese-
		-Dutch-Bolivian 1
		Dutch-Colombian-French 1
		Dutch-Colomb-Antillean 1
		Dutch-Belgian 1
		Dutch-Antillean-Canadian-
		-Filipino 1
		Surinamese-Togo 1
		Dominican 1
		North-American 1
		No Data 12
Estimated Colombian Market Share[a]		
Dutch M:12 S:14	Dutch M:10 S:2	Dutch M:15 S:9
Surinamese M:9 S:1	Colombian M:4 S:6	Colombian M:12 S:7
Antillean M:4 S:4	Surinamese M:3	Surinamese M:5 S:6
Colombian M:3 S:1		

Source: Own calculations based on the analysis of import cases in Table X (Appendix).
[a] M:x = Cases of main involvement; S:x = Cases of secondary involvement. These rankings are only rough indicators, since the data suffer from biases and limitations. These are: the presence of dark numbers and drug enforcement selectivity (arguably under-representing less vulnerable and less researched importers); media selectivity (more interested in large or 'explosive' cases); incomplete or unclear data on ethnic-national background (absent in some large cases with ongoing long-term investigation, occasionally unclear when ethnicity or nationality is reported, especially problematic for Dutch Surinamese); and, finally, incomplete data on main and secondary involvement. However, these trends have been consistently confirmed by drug experts, enforcers and entrepreneurs interviewed during my fieldwork. See also Van Duyne et al. (1990); Van Duyne (1995); Bovenkerk (1995b) and Fijnaut et al. (1996).

Some reasons are obvious, others deserve a closer look. As I will later explain, there are many import methods implying distinct business arrangements. Normally speaking, cocaine importers have to perform several – sometimes complex – tasks around communication, unloading, internal transport, stashing, selling to distributors and handling payments and money flows. These tasks require a minimum of planning and co-ordination, and often imply the deployment of many human and material resources: skilled and unskilled labour force, communication devices, entrance to restricted areas, cars or other vehicles, houses, hotel rooms, warehouses, import firms, weapons, local contacts with wholesale buyers, and resources to move and deal with large cash amounts.

No wonder that cocaine import into Europe, as indicated in chapter III, is performed by various types of groups. Firstly, by local groups with access and control over those local resources, such as *mafiosi*, legal entrepreneurs or officials. Secondly, by local illegal entrepreneurs protected by them. Thirdly, by ethnic minority groups from source, transit or destination countries with their own local infrastructures, and finally by partnerships between all three mentioned groups. Although these possibilities always coexist, places with strong local groups involved in cocaine import such as Spain, Italy or Russia witness indeed a relatively smaller involvement of Colombians at this stage, especially when these local groups are illegal and effectively exercise social and territorial control.

In the Dutch case, although most of the cocaine imported is indeed controlled by native Dutch illegal entrepreneurs, they are not in a position to effectively deter other groups from entering business. On the one hand, these Dutch entrepreneurs are either too marginal to confront Colombians with resources and know-how (criminal *penose*), too well established and tolerated in other illegal profitable businesses to start a war around cocaine (synthetic drugs, marihuana, prostitution and gambling) or too 'clean' and legitimate to claim control or even involvement in any of these activities (legal importers, policemen, military personnel, and so forth). Colombians, on the other hand, need those people and their resources to import cocaine since they do not hold material infrastructure or social and political local power, the result being a whole range of labour co-operation amongst them and with other individuals (see Table VIII).

Cocaine import is in itself a profitable activity, with mark-ups per kilo of up to US$ 3,000. For Colombian exporters or people close to them it is even more attractive: if they are able to sell directly to wholesale distributors, their mark-ups can rise to US$ 18,000 per kilo. This competitive advantage based on some sort of vertical integration or preferential market situation has been reflected on wholesale prices, which Colombians have managed to lower at times.

Colombian cocaine importers operating in the Netherlands move, on the one hand, in a rather open market place with a clear advantage in terms of supply and prices. They face, on the other hand, a continuous shortage of own material and human resources to safely organise cocaine import. While some have closer links with Colombia, others exploit a particular good local contact. As it was the case with drug couriers, not all importers have the same chances to succeed.

5.2.2 From business envoys to local adventurers: social hierarchies amongst traquetos

Colombian cocaine importers differ very much amongst themselves in terms of social background and skills, place of permanent residence, degree of professionalisation, and indeed material wealth and social prestige. Tano:

> "No, I don't believe there is only one type. Some are educated and others are very simple, speaking as *gamines* [street-children]. You have real professionals, very discrete, others giving *papaya* [showing-off] with gold and looking for problems. Some really believe this is a job, others see it as pure excitement. But all have one thing in common and that's money."

A first clue to understanding these differences lies in the question of initiative. There are two most common scenarios in import operations run by Colombians in the Netherlands. For some the question is: "I have cocaine and I want to deliver it in the Netherlands". In these cases the cocaine exporters take the initiative for setting up operations, either by sending 'own' people to organise the import (envoys) or, less frequently, looking for reliable Colombian groups active in the Netherlands. However, for others the question is the inverse one: "I can sell cocaine in the Netherlands and I am looking for a supplier". In this case Colombian groups or individuals in the Netherlands take the initiative, usually pushed by demand, good marketing or infrastructural conditions or by police infiltration. Of course they exploit a privileged access to source through friends, contacts or even relatives but, as I will explain in chapter VIII, this relationship between local *traquetos* and exporters is problematic, flexible and extremely fragile.

Envoys

A first group of importers is formed by envoys, men working for medium or large export groups. They are sent to the Netherlands especially to receive, stash and sell the shipment to distributors, and eventually arrange financial matters. Far from being, as often depicted, fixed 'ambassadors' of certain 'cartel', these envoys tend to remain in the Netherlands for short periods of time. They usually stay in hotels, have very weak ties with the local Colombian immigrants, and spend a great deal of time travelling and negotiating with business partners and recruited employees. Close to and protected by large exporters, they enjoy the highest prestige amongst *traquetos*. Even when their operations are tracked by the police, they remain as the last and most difficult people to catch: they delegate many of the operational details to others and try to avoid unnecessary exposure. Some grew from low-ranked jobs next to a particular *patrón*, others were successful immigrants in the United States. Others still stayed in the Netherlands longer than expected.

A good example of these envoys is Jairo, a *caleño* detained in September 1992 in Rome during the *Green Ice* operation. He was later convicted to 24 years of imprisonment by an Italian tribunal, and is currently serving time in a Roman prison. During the late 1980s, Jairo worked for some members of the well-known Grajales family from the Cauca Valley.[39] His task was to organise a line in the Netherlands able to receive cocaine freights imported in tropical fruit juice. Although he first lived in Den Bosch for four years, and later in Amsterdam in a rented flat near the *Bijlmerbajes*, Jairo used to travel a lot to Colombia and England to both prepare the operations and arrange money transfers. He had a false Spanish passport to move safely and many nicknames for different people and operations. He spoke good English, but never learned Dutch.

When the police seized 2,658 kg in IJmuiden in February 1990 during the so-called *Holle Vaten* operation, they knew that Jairo was their chief suspect. Eight other people were arrested and convicted, but he remained untraceable in Cali. During 1988 and 1989 he had organised a line and crowned three times before the police finally intervened. Closely following instructions from Colombia, he financed and organised the Dutch import front store, rented the warehouse in IJmuiden, recruited the other Colombians involved, and monitored, especially through the Dutch partners, money transfers and debts from wholesalers.

After this failure, Jairo still tried to organise a new operation for the Grajales, but this time from Colombia. He worked with new people, this time using coal bricks instead of passion fruit juice. In November 1990, and again due to the amateurish mistakes made by those responsible for the import operational details, 600 kg destined for Rotterdam harbour were seized. This was to be his last project for the Grajales family.

In fact, most of these envoys dream of becoming independent exporters like their bosses. They lack capital to invest in a project[40] so they are forced to 'sell' it to large exporters and investors. Only after some successful operations and good skills for replacing or competing with other exporters, they might have a chance of becoming real bosses. However, after failed operations, their usual fate is to end up in prison or, what Jairo did, to look for a new employer.

In 1990 and 1991, Jairo offered two separate projects, both with the Netherlands as final target, to two different exporters. Despite the time and resources invested in travelling and research, none of them were ever realised. His final appearance as an envoy was in 1992, after he and his boss had to appear personally in Rome, trapped by undercover DEA officers in the *Green Ice* Operation.

Line owners

Other Colombian importers are even more independent from the exporters. They stay in the Netherlands in a more permanent basis, but always intend to return to Colombia. Naturally, personal circumstances such as legal status or family bonds also

---

39 Before losing, selling or laundering their companies in the mid-1990s, the Grajales owned the largest winery in Colombia, a leading chain of Department Stores, coal mines and a large agroindustrial business specialised in fruit-juice production and export. They exported large quantities of cocaine to many destinations in the US and Europe, almost always hidden within barrels of deep-frozen tropical fruit-juice. See Castillo (1996: 102-103); Bovenkerk (1995a: 40) and Van Duyne (1995: 81).

40 Since they have the contacts at destination points they could become exporters if they had the money to invest.

influence their decisions, but either failed or successful, they tend to leave the country after some years. These importers usually have been in the Netherlands for some time and are able to mobilise both local and Colombian human and material resources. Some are approached by the exporter and are tested before being accepted as partners. Others work with more than one supplier, who at the same time could be working with two or more independent importers. Others still are poorly connected and have to make a greater effort in building and maintaining supply resources.

I will call this second group of importers the 'line owners',[41] even when the 'line' actually only implies one single operation. Usually male adults, they have a strong bargaining position: much better local contacts, sometimes with legal front-stores or infrastructure, and an even more flexible relation with the exporters who are just business partners. Some often travel to Colombia and most of them have their closest relatives – including a wife and children – over there.

They have plenty of time. Sometimes they stay for months looking for an operation to arise. Before actually becoming concrete, many ideas, attempts or promises lead to dead end. These *traquetos* subsequently take a great deal of time to prepare and monitor the project and then waiting for the shipment to arrive. After a success or a failure, they have to start all over again, sometimes having to find new suppliers and wholesalers. Many of them have enough to do and to earn with two or three operations a year.

'Owning a line' is a rather pretentious notion: it is in fact very easy to lose it. The *flecha* ('arrow'), another name for the line, can be broken at source with suppliers being killed, imprisoned, displaced, retired or moved to other activities; shipment routes can change for safer and more profitable destinations, transport means or partners; importers themselves can face prison or deportation; and finally distributors can also walk away by being imprisoned or by finding better quality or prices. New individuals and groups quickly replace older ones, and they hardly stay untouched for long.

In December 1995, Mocho and other 18 people were detained and 360 kg of cocaine was seized in a German-Dutch police operation involving some unlawful and uncontrolled research and infiltration methods. He was fortunate that these methods were the object of national debate and his case was even discussed by the *Van Traa* Commission: he was first looking at 12 years, sentenced to 8, and later released at appeal along with other 4 Colombians connected to him. Although he and his group were importers supplied by large and well-known cocaine exporters from Cali, the Public Ministry finally lost the case. The intervention of dubious intermediaries working for the police not only explained this failure but also uncovered interesting details about the nature of Mocho's import organisation.

Mocho was not a newcomer. He rented a flat in Amsterdam West, and his nickname was familiar to the local *traqueto* scene. Far from being a 'representative of the Cali Cartel' and although his brother in Colombia was also involved, Mocho

---

41 These Colombian importers usually refer to themselves as *'controlando una línea'* (owning a line, having it under control).

should be regarded as a local independent importer. He was chosen by the exporters after long contretemps. They first wanted to place a shipment in Italy, but a large seizure forced them to re-route the line towards North Europe. After negotiations with two groups – in which police infiltrators helped to find the importers and arrange the transport – Mocho's group got a deal: a large marihuana shipment via Germany, followed by many cocaine freights. As it is the case with many of these Colombian 'line owner' importers, Mocho's group mixes professionalism with improvisation and amateurish mistakes. For example, they failed to recognise many key infiltrators, while they could have realised that they were controlled by just reading the newspapers.[42] They also used to talk openly about business on the phone. In contrast, they managed to get top lawyers, to avoid long sentences and presumably to keep the profits of earlier operations.

Mixed couples
In some cases, the import operation is organised and performed by mixed couples – especially a Colombian with a Dutch, Antillean or Turkish partner. The friends or relatives of the Colombian partner are usually involved as exporters or smugglers, while the local partners often provide infrastructure, financial and marketing resources. Cases can vary from a secondary involvement of a Colombian woman[43] to more leading roles from the Colombian side. Although this 'family business' type of importer also employs all sort of people and in practice does not differ very much from the 'line owners', these couples tend to be more established and integrated – relatives and children around, properties, Dutch language, residence permits or even double nationality. Some have an even lower profile than other *traquetos*, while others are frequent travellers with luxury properties far from the Netherlands.

Alicia comes from Cali and has lived in Rotterdam since 1987. She has three teenage sons with her Colombian ex-husband, and she is now married to a Turkish man. During her trial in 1997 she claimed to have started as a prostitute, but none of the judges seemed to believe her. She was accused of organising the import of 5 kg of cocaine via Antwerp, smuggled in a ship from Peru. While her husband's family indicated that she was the main person responsible, the public prosecutor believed that she only functioned as a mediator. This operation involved Colombian suppliers, Peruvian intermediaries and Turkish buyers – also involved in heroin traffic –, the couple being at the core of the transactions. As it is often the case, evidence against employees or general helpers was stronger than against the importers themselves: she finally got 2 years, only half of the sentence given to the real mediator.

Other couples can move and operate in many countries, being also involved in cocaine export and money laundering. Rosaura and Wilder have Spanish names, but

---

42 In September 1994, 9,200 kg of Colombian marihuana were delivered to Mocho's group under German-Dutch police surveillance. The case was publicly discussed during the *Van Traa* hearings in 1995, and still Mocho was arrested in December during a cocaine related operation.

43 In the fashion of a case described by Korf and Verbraeck: *"... a friend, married with a South-American woman, imported cocaine. Shipments up to some tens of kilos were smuggled to the Netherlands by relatives of the woman..."* (Korf and Verbraeck 1993: 122).

he is Colombian and she is Dutch. They were accused of organising three shipments to the Netherlands in 1991 and 1992, a total of 200 kg having been intercepted before arrival. They were rarely in the Netherlands. After many successful operations, they remained safe by moving between Cali, Bogotá and the Netherlands Antilles, organising more lines from Colombia and Curaçao to the Netherlands and United Kingdom, and of course enjoying high living standards.

The first one to be arrested was Wilder. For many years wanted by the DEA and the Antillean police, he was finally captured on December 1997 in Willemstad (Curaçao) and was immediately extradited to the Netherlands. A short holiday visiting some relatives, even while holding a false identity, ended prematurely. While the Dutch Public Ministry triumphantly presented him as 'head of the Cali Cartel', the Colombian authorities did not consider Wilder to be at the top.

Rosaura was detained only 6 months later when she was about to board a plane in Bogotá. She had been in charge since her husband was captured, mainly operating from Quito, Cali and Bogotá, where they had around US$ 10 million in legal business, properties and other goods.

Adventurers

A final group amongst Colombian cocaine importers is formed by some local adventurers. They are newcomers – usually young men from the middle classes with no criminal record – who after arriving to the Netherlands for adventure, holidays or work become involved in the cocaine circuit. Those with better contacts and skills eventually manage to become independent and to handle their own loads, often small quantities. These *traquetos* who come and go, are locally known within the street Latino circuits, are erratic and vulnerable to repression, and in fact have a close relationship, in social and business terms, to local Colombian wholesale distributors.

Pollo is a young Colombian who used to earn US$ 400 per month in a full-time job in Cali. He has a degree in economics:

"I came to see what happens, I can't do anything with economics in Colombia. I have been in Germany for a while, but here in Amsterdam things are more easy going."

He first worked for other Colombians engaged in import. While waiting for a second operation he became paranoid about DEA officers training Colombians to infiltrate drug organisations, so he decided to go on alone with an associate. He claimed to have risks under control and believed that the only way to survive was working alone or with very few people. Through an old friend he finally found somebody to send him few kilos by plane, which he immediately sold to other Colombians. As a small scale, independent *traqueto* not willing to take many risks, he also acknowledged his limits the last time I saw him:

"I'm empty handed, it's completely *seco* [lit. dry, with no cocaine] at the moment. Either I'm dry or the *manes* [men, buyers] don't buy. And it's not only me, many others complaint as well."

To conclude, the four types of Colombian importers discussed above differ very much regarding specific features. This heterogeneity can be summarised as follows:

	Envoys	Mixed Couples	Line Owners	Adventurers
Social Prestige	++	+	-	--
Infrastructure	++	+	-	--
Residence in the Netherlands	--	+	+	-
Relation with Colombian community	--	-	-	+
Vulnerability	--	-	-	+
Relation with other importers	--	--	+	++

5.2.3 Getting (un)organised

Mobile phones and call centres

Sometimes even outdoing their legal fellows, cocaine importers spend a great deal of time talking on the phone about business matters. Paradoxically, a will to restrict its use for security reasons clashes with more objective needs: personal meetings can be even more dangerous, transactions lack the standardised and bureaucratic procedures and channels available to legal trade, and imperfect or false information force people to stay in touch regularly. Moreover, unexpected changes and improvisation are so common features in the business that traders have to be 'on line' to check, confirm or repeat instructions. After all, deals involving millions of dollars are closed by pure verbal communication.

No wonder therefore that some of the settings in which I met many *traquetos* and made interesting observations about their daily routines are particular budget telephone centres in Amsterdam or The Hague. One of the first things I discovered was that these public telephone centres are not seldom used to make quick, secret phone-calls to Colombia. On the contrary, these places seem to have social life of their own. Some dealers gather there for hours, visit the place one or two times a day, have endless conversations with friends and relatives in Colombia, make also local phone-calls, and use the place and its surrounding bars to meet each other. The phone centres are usually small and very busy, not more than five or six cabins and some mobile phones. Lack of discretion is the rule, but nobody, including the telephone operators, pays any attention to another's business. This double nature of public and mobile conversations effectively restricts the police in any serious attempt to get key information on the operations.

Not only importers, but also wholesale distributors can be found in these call centres. In fact, many of these places function as a real and symbolic bridge between exporters or those responsible in Colombia, and local *traquetos*. In reality, only some of them actually phone Colombia to arrange smuggling details, talk about money issues or discuss problematic delays. For many others, it is just a place to meet the boss to talk about local operational matters. *Traquetos* working for different people occasionally bump into each other to comment on business and social affairs. They stop by to complain about prices and market developments, to warn about other people or the police, or to gossip about common friends in prison. It is the time to specifically show one's own strength and achievements, and to comment about the bad weather, football, a new restaurant, and above all about Colombia. Others still hang around in the hope of getting in touch with the important figures or to find new partners or employees. Indeed, since these centres are also used by Colombian immigrants of all sorts – but especially prostitutes, illegal migrants and newcomers – Colombian importers use the call centres as a suitable recruitment pool. For many Colombians, these budget telephone centres are the very first place in the Netherlands to meet other Colombians.

Ana Inés remembers the circumstances in which she met her first fellow Colombians soon after arrival:

"It was in a call centre in Amsterdam West, a young couple from Cali. We chatted for a while, I told them about Miami, and then we went for a coffee. I realised they were *traquetos* when others arrived and started to talk about enormous amounts of money. He explained me as if I was a friend that 'the market in Amsterdam is in the hands of *Caleños*. We live in Rotterdam because down there it is more quiet, Amsterdam is very hot at the moment.' They did not offer me anything concrete, but they were clearly interested in my past in Miami and the fact that I spoke English. They tried to be friendly but I never phoned back (...) The second time was a man from Cali. He invited me to go out the next night to *El Caleño*, I really wanted to dance and I didn't know the place. We were leaving the phones, another man arrived and they got into a discussion about a debt. Again! I went with him to *El Caleño*; I just wanted to know more Colombians. He was well known there, everybody came to greet him, I suspected already that he was into something, but then he explained me that he was a boss and he worked for people in Cali. I was really scared, he phoned me several times and the last time I told him not to phone again. Luckily he didn't."

Some do not use the call centres, but have their own – bought or stolen – mobile phones, which they use everywhere, even in church. For security reasons, they always take 'pre-pay' mobile phones, which they replace after an operation is closed or after some weeks. Some informants owned various phones that they interchanged all the time.

A safer method to phone abroad was through illegal telephone operators, people with neither a licence nor a public office, offering budget phone calls through a changing network of mobile phones. However, the growth of the pre-paid telephone card system, very popular amongst *traquetos*, has increasingly replaced legal and illegal phone centres by 2001. In this way, they can phone Colombia from wherever they are, avoiding 'hot' own lines or exposure in public telephone centres.

Commercial bridgeheads: front stores vs. bona fide firms
In the case of large quantities arriving by ship alongside legal merchandise, the cocaine has to be imported by legal companies, which knowingly or unwittingly

receive and store the illegal freight. Depending on their resources, experience and contacts, Colombian importers have either created their own 'front stores' or have used non Colombian, well-established import-export firms operating in the Netherlands.

The first method – the creation of own import-export front stores – has been very popular amongst Colombian importers. Firstly, the capital investment is negligible compared to potential profits. Secondly, the timing of the operation can be better controlled through their own front stores. Thirdly, they can easily adapt to the exporter's requirements – in terms of goods traded – and to importer's needs – unloading, storage and so forth. Finally, it is for many the only resource available since the use of existing companies requires the kind of contacts that these importers often lack.

However, the problems and the risks faced by these Colombian front stores in the Netherlands are rather obvious. The first limitation refers to visibility. The volume of Colombian companies – or legal businesses run by Colombians – engaged in import-export in the Netherlands is extremely small, therefore fake companies cannot be so easily concealed behind other legal Colombian affairs. As explained in chapter IV, a very restricted number of formal or informal Colombian business – restaurants, bars, and shops – and in fact the whole Colombian community hardly depend on or consume Colombian imports.[44] Moreover, the main legal imports from Colombia – coal, coffee, food and fruits – are in the hands of non-Colombian enterprises. New, small import-export companies trading goods from South America are indeed priority and easy targets for Dutch Custom or police.

A second problem with these companies refers to performance and management. They hardly really handle the legal goods they are supposed to be importing, so they often attract the attention of trade partners, neighbours or tax authorities for obvious omissions, mistakes or irregularities. The people running these companies are usually either short-term minded – disappearing overnight, letting small problems grow, always improvising – or just not the 'best' candidates for the job – foreigners with no working permits, locals with criminal records, and so on. Illegal entrepreneurs and their employees are dangerously exposed through these *tapaderas* (lit. cover, front store). In fact, front stores are often perceived even by outsiders, and they frequently prompt police intervention. Finally, the vulnerability of these front stores increases when they are also used to launder or transfer money.

In some cases, front stores are more than empty structures. For two years, three Colombians were buying and renting houses in Rotterdam, Amsterdam and mainly in The Hague, and managed to organise a firm with 27 employees – almost all Colombians – including managers and computer personnel, for the import and distribution of cocaine. In April 1993, 120 kg of cocaine were found in Amsterdam's harbour between dry bananas, and the three Colombians were later sentenced to 8, 10 and 12 years (*De Volkskrant*, 20-4-93 and 29-7-93).

---

44 Colombian individuals and business in the Netherlands seem to be well supplied by, for instance, Dutch Department Stores, Surinamese *toko's*, Moroccan butchers or Turkish greengrocers.

In a few cases, they can take the shape of a 'family business'. While playing football in Rotterdam with some Colombians, the following story was told to me by Helmer:

> "There was a *paisa* playing a couple of years ago, he lived in The Hague and every day took the train to Rotterdam. He said he worked in the import-export firm of his father, I think that was true. He said that the business was doing well, that they were very glad, and so on. Well, he was detained between Brussels and Rotterdam with 10 kg and one million *floros* [guilders]."

Helmer continued:

> "Look, when somebody tells me that he has an import-export, I smell dirty business. I also know another *paisa*, and he said he was importing blue-jeans [laughs]...he worked for people in Medellín...he got 8 years and is now in Leeuwarden but he keeps denying, he won't talk to you."

In order to avoid visibility, many Colombian importers would use Dutch or other local groups to set up the import infrastructure. Jairo, for example, paid some Dutch people to organise a tropical fruit import front store. Flor and Nico were once approached by a Colombian couple who proposed that they set up an import firm together for Colombian products. Flor:

> "They had a *tapadera* [front store] in mind. Nico is Dutch and they thought they could easily use him."

Others would carefully choose less conspicuous countries and products, profiting from strong contacts in transshipment areas. Import front stores run by Colombians during the 1990s handled, for example, plastic via Portugal, asphalt barrels from Colombia, coal blocks from Venezuela, iron and aluminium from Venezuela to England and Greece, oil barrels or tropical fruit juice.

Less frequently but far more successfully, Colombians have also used established firms to import cocaine. These *bona fide* companies are real import-export businesses, often active and well-known, and they do not attract the attention of law enforcers. The importers keep out of the picture, while the freights are handled more safely. Non-Colombian enterprises trading with South America are usually targeted, especially those importing food, coffee, fruits, flowers, clothing, minerals or industrial raw materials. In some cases, only special employees or managers are involved, and the operation is performed behind the company's back. Yet in other cases small enterprises in financial need are approached by drug importers, who tempt the owners with overnight profits.

Bona fide enterprises importing cacao, sport bags or carpet rolls have been involved, others dealing with flowers, textile, trees and shoe polish machines are said to have been approached as well (Bovenkerk 1995b: 171).

White, green and brown

Next to legal products, cocaine also gets mixed with other illicit substances imported into the Netherlands. As explained in chapter II, Colombia is also a major producer and exporter of marihuana and heroin, especially for the US market. Although in historical terms each illegal drug has had its own momentum regarding actors involved and market or law enforcement dynamics, the 1990s have witnessed a growing tendency for integration of business networks and marketing procedures. Data available on seizures and detentions for Colombian-US related cases reveal that Colombian cocaine exporters and importers, small or large, have often been involved in marihuana or heroin trade as well.

In Europe, both illegal Colombian products have had a tougher competitive disadvantage. Colombian marihuana is massively imported but it has to compete with North African, Asian or domestic cannabis, while Colombian heroin has – up to now – not been able to gain a share against the long established Asian supply through the Balkan route. The Netherlands being a key entry point for both illegal substances to the European market, the question remains about the involvement of Colombian cocaine importers in marihuana and heroin operations.

Colombian marihuana reaches the Netherlands by ship, usually in 1 to 30 ton loads. It is not rare to find cases in which the same importers are handling, both mixed or alternately, large cocaine and marihuana shipments. During fieldwork in Amsterdam, some *traquetos* eventually referred to these cases. Tano:

> "...20 tons of *bareto* [marihuana] arrived and it is being sold for € 600 per kilo [in February 1997] because there is over-supply. Two months ago they were asking the double."

Cases from the 1990s (see Table X, Appendix) show remarkable regularities for mixed cocaine-marihuana operations. They usually involve large quantities of cocaine – more than 400 kg – and they are handled either by local mixed Colombian-Dutch networks, or by what the Colombians vaguely define as the 'Dutch *mafia*': local marihuana importers, corrupt Custom or police officers, and so forth. In some cases, cocaine is a further step after some less risky marihuana hits. In others, the marihuana only represents the police decoy in 'front store operations' organised by law enforcers themselves.[45] In another case a container holding both cocaine and marihuana was found in Amsterdam. In yet another, still the police found cocaine base while looking for hemp.[46]

The involvement of Colombian importers in heroin shipments is totally different:

---

45 Two large separate cases of December 1994 (1,161 kg in Amsterdam) and December 1995 (360 kg) involved top Colombian importers Lito and Mocho, both later convicted of importing cocaine and marihuana in operations either infiltrated or organised by the police.

46 A container from Colombia with 442 kg of cocaine and 30 tons marihuana remained untouched for 5 months in a shipping company in Rotterdam until the Dutch importer – and CID informant – collected it in Amsterdam in May 1996. In January 1997, 500 kg of cocaine base were found in a farm in Haarzuilens when the police was searching for a 'green house'. Weapons and marihuana were also seized, while two Dutchmen and two South Americans were captured.

they hardly take place, they entail very small quantities, and they are rarely detected. On one single occasion, a Colombian distributor commented:

> "Last week there were two despatches, one 150 grams and the other 200 grams. No, they weren't try-outs, they were for sale."

However, all my informants agreed that in the Netherlands heroin was not a Colombian affair, and that cases connecting heroin and cocaine only occurred at low wholesale and retail levels in the hands of non-Colombian dealers.[47] Smugglers visited in prison often showed a less tolerant attitude towards the heroin trade and consumption, some strongly condemned it.[48]

The 'animals' are coming

Unloading operations are considered extremely dangerous by Colombian importers, especially when local people and arrangements – harbour personnel, police, customs or import-export firms – are not involved. If the operation has been discovered by a tip-off, there is a considerable chance that the police will intervene at that time. If it is screened, those unloading would be identified and followed to capture their bosses. Even when nobody knows about it, the attempt can easily fail by unexpected controls or, as it is often the case, by practical and technical mistakes.

In these cases, one of the major tasks of the importer is to identify the date, time and place of arrival, and to have everything ready to get the *animales* (lit. animals, cocaine load) out. Despite the extensive use of all secret words and codes imagined to pass that information, delays, misunderstandings and last-minute changes often force importers to make real efforts to get in touch with events.

If the freight is concealed in containers or amongst legal merchandise, the actual unloading follows regular procedures and the 'rescue operation' starts once the load has reached certain hangar, warehouse or depot. When the load is hidden inside the ship or under the keel, the unloading becomes in itself a rather complex and risky form of burglary, requiring for example extensive surveillance, co-ordinated moves and even the use of diving equipment.

For the unloading of cocaine freights hidden under the ship's keel, it is rather common that Colombian importers employ one or two divers to recover the cocaine. In January 1997, two divers sent from Colombia went on trial in The Hague after having been captured in a failed operation in Rotterdam. An importer selling to Joel, a wholesale distributor in Amsterdam, has used divers to unload the cocaine from

---

47 However, some Colombian related cocaine-heroin cases have been indicated in other parts of Europe.
48 In this sense Colombian drug entrepreneurs, even when they produce or sell both illegal drugs, usually reproduce the stereotypical dichotomy between 'recreational' and 'functional' cocaine on the one hand, and 'vicious', 'degrading' heroin on the other. Cocaine use, with less stigmas attached, is often seen by them as compatible with ambition and money making, when not a positive sign of wealth. Heroin or 'crack' are framed as negative things for the 'other': American or European junkies, 'losers' and so on.

Rotterdam. Other informants also referred to divers operating in Belgian harbours. A Colombian man I met was asked if he could swim before he was offered the 'easy job' of getting 5 kg cocaine from under the water.

Yet it is far from an easy task, so people interviewed agreed that importers delegate the unloading risks by employing or subcontracting others, from Colombian helpers to harbour personnel. Problems around the unloading are also evidenced by the frequent delays: there are usually days or even months between the ship arrival and the actual unloading. The reasons are manifold, some unbelievable. In some cases it can take a while for the cargo to be finally delivered to the importer's warehouse. For 'burglary' operations I heard stories of unloading personnel not showing up or targeting the wrong ship or container. In other cases, the importers discovered police surveillance and decided to wait until they could move safely. Even fear is a motive for delay. Joel:

> "Can you believe that the thing [cocaine freight] arrived to France but nobody wants to take it out? It is there, and somebody has to go and get it but it looks like a tough one, I think they will abandon it".

Fear and secrecy around an approaching ship contrast with joy and publicity after the load has made it through. When a large shipment crowns successfully, even peripheral people around the local *Latino* street circuit would get the news. Nobody would know dangerous details, but gossip about the quantity and the celebrations would spread very fast. Solano:

> "Two months ago it was a big one. There was lots of money for many people… they are still spending the money. You see it everywhere: with the girls, at the restaurants and at the *rumba*. We sell more food, some people close their debts, see, an endless hangover…"

5.2.4 Further tasks around the importer

After crowning, Colombian importers need people to perform specific business-related tasks. Some of these tasks are part of the core routines and are entrusted to close associates and employees, while others are more peripheral or project-oriented and can be delegated or subcontracted to outsiders, in some cases to people who know very little about what is really going on. The list ranges from internal carriers to security personnel – load-keepers, bodyguards and *sicarios* –, from chauffeurs and hosts to interpreters and phone-operators. Regardless of the status of the importer – temporary envoy or rather established – and maybe with the exception of hired killers, the people involved in these activities are likely to be recruited locally. And in some cases they are indeed Colombians.

Internal transport

Import operations also involve a great deal of internal transportation, since unloading and final stashing points are often far apart – for example from a warehouse in Rotterdam to a flat in The Hague or from Hamburg or Antwerp ports to Amsterdam.

Small importers would take the task in their own hands, but others would just employ or subcontract the services of other people to do this risky job.

After he gained trust with a particular importer as load-keeper, Riverito was asked to unload and transport 50 kg from a ship in Zeebrugge. Although he earned less than the US$ 15,000 originally promised – he was in fact subcontracted together with a Colombian associate – he successfully organised and performed the operation.[49]

When 2,658 kg were seized in IJmuiden in 1990, the police detained five Colombians working for the importer Jairo – who happened to be in Colombia and was only captured two years later in Rome. Two of them were young Colombians who claimed to have been recruited the day before to help with the unloading. They had no criminal record, had been living a very short time in the Netherlands, and had student visas as a cover. The situation of the other three was different. They were older, much better connected in Colombia, and responsible for transporting the cocaine – in three earlier successful operations during 1989 – in a *Traffic* van from the warehouse in IJmuiden to the 'safe house' near the *Stadionplein* in Amsterdam (Bovenkerk 1995a: 36). One of them served 4 years in Spain during the 1980s for cocaine trading.

Security tasks

The *encaletadores* (load-keepers) are people entrusted by the importer to shield and look after the cocaine load from the moment it arrives until it is sold to wholesale distributors. These employees are people close to the *patrón*, and in fact they do little more than what a legal security guard usually does, namely: keep an eye on the freight, listen to music, watch television and the like. However, it is indeed a more dangerous job: they are sometimes involved in unloading and delivery activities, so highly exposed to rip-deals and arrest. In the words of Riverito:

> "It is dangerous, but you don't have to do anything. They carry the stuff in and out; you just stay close to it for one or two days. They didn't give me much, only € 150 or € 200 per day, but they also paid food and drinks."

Many *encaletadores*, like Riverito, consider the job as a temporary step for a future engagement in more profitable deals or tasks as independent *traquetos*.

The presence of professional bodyguards is rare and only limited to cases in which the importer is especially sent from Colombia. Normally speaking, personal security is performed by friends or informal helpers of the *traqueto* and only for situations that involve money or cocaine exchange. The excessive use of bodyguards is considered dangerous and avoided, and many *traquetos* would only bring 'a couple of friends' in extreme cases.

All informants in the Netherlands and Colombia indicated that the use of Colombian *sicarios* in Dutch territory is extremely rare if not completely absent.[50]

---

49 Organisational details and labour relations of this and other Riverito's operations are closely analysed in chapter VIII.

50 Chapter IX on the use of violence will thoroughly handle this issue.

Assassinations in the Netherlands amongst Colombian cocaine entrepreneurs – again hard to find – are either performed by 'helpers', bodyguards and the very drug dealers, or by non-Colombian – usually East European – professional assassins locally contracted. The few cases involving *sicarios* recruited from Colombia to settle scores in Europe usually take place in Spain and often implicate other ethnic groups as targets or contractors.[51] These hired killers are moreover discrete and professional travellers, even able to mislead other people. Cabeza experienced the following:

> "the first time they sent me back I sat in the plane and another Colombian started talking to me. He asked me if I wanted to make *billete* [money]. I said yes, so he told me that the job was to knock off somebody. I was shocked and the man kept asking, but after the third time he desisted and told me to completely forget about it. He then realised, I suppose, that he was talking with the wrong guy."

Logistic tasks

Colombian *traquetos* also request or make use of other Colombians for more peripheral tasks. They are very important in logistic terms, but they imply either a secondary or sometimes unwittingly involvement. This help from local Colombians involves all sorts of people, from long established immigrants moving in the formal or informal legal economy to adventurers surviving through legal or illegal small jobs.

A first matter of involvement refers to accommodation. While established importers would have the problem solved and special envoys from large organisations would stay at hotels or rented flats, many *traquetos* would still need a place to stay and would use the resources provided by Colombian relatives, friends or acquaintances in the Netherlands. In one case, a Colombian woman living in Amsterdam unwittingly arranged the rent of a flat for cocaine entrepreneurs who concealed the real purpose of their visit. However, most of similar cases also involving *bona fide* hosting in own houses, actually regarded Colombian adventurers who would later be involved in wholesale distribution. For accommodation, importers seemed to rely more on other illegal entrepreneurs.

Tico and Tano stayed for a while in a fully furnished small flat in the centre of Amsterdam. Nobody lived there, but the place was kept clean and had a small bar, a microwave oven, a video-recorder and a subscription to a private pornographic TV channel. An annual rent of around € 15,000 was covered by Joel, who used the flat for occasional 'special' guests. Tano:

> "We have to leave tomorrow because a man from Cali arrived, a *duro* with a suitcase to stay for a while. So we come back to Joel's place for 3 or 4 days, and then who knows."

Some of these top-businessmen may need to move around, and instead of renting a car they can arrange things in a more informal way. Manolo is a Spanish immigrant

---

51 For example, according to B. Martens, in 1990 a Dutch importer contracted two *sicarios* to kill a Moroccan man in Marbella (Spain) for an unpaid debt (Bovenkerk 1995b: 117). In 1994, a Galician man was killed in Cambados (Pontevedra, Spain) by two Colombian *sicarios* after he decided to denounce his partners in a large Colombian-Galician import operation (*El Pais*, 29-5-95).

who in the 1970s came to the Netherlands as a 'guest worker' and moved to Rotterdam after an early retirement. He has a teenage daughter with his second and current wife, Colombian Iris from Cali. Once in a while, an acquainted Colombian of Iris' relatives in Cali comes to Rotterdam for a short business trip of two or three days. Manolo is then contracted to be his chauffeur during his stay. The man pays him the petrol, some € 500, and invites the whole family for an excellent dinner in the best restaurant in town. For Manolo the job represents a nice extra income, and he seems to like both the man and the way in which things flow:

> "He is very well dressed and stays in a hotel near Central Station. He never asked me to stay with us. I drive him wherever he tells me, sometimes to Belgium."

Manolo 'knows' about his actual business, but he does not ask questions and sticks to a policy of discretion. Also the man keeps things very formal and distant, and Manolo clearly respects him for being "a man of his word, a generous man". Manolo's help is not only based on economic interest and mutual trust, but on the conviction that the man is to a certain extent clean:

> "I think he doesn't handle the stuff himself, he once suggested that I shouldn't worry because he was *intocable* [untouchable]. He just closes deals or arranges money things, maybe payments and shipments and that sort of things. You know, a business person."

Although in general terms cocaine entrepreneurs operating in the Netherlands show good skills for languages,[52] most Colombian *traquetos* do not speak Dutch and sometimes not even English. Transactions usually take place in Spanish, also as some informants suggested for security reasons. The intervention of interpreters is thus occasionally required. In a rather improvised fashion, trusted – not necessarily involved – people around the *traquetos* are often called to translate to and from Spanish. For example, Solano performed a couple of times as a Spanish-Dutch interpreter in a deal between a Colombian importer and a Turkish wholesaler in The Hague. These Colombians are usually illegal immigrants around the cocaine and prostitution circuits who have already lived in the Netherlands for some time.

Especially around the window prostitution areas of The Hague and Amsterdam, I found Colombians linked to the telephone services often used by cocaine entrepreneurs. Some, as it was the case of an entire *paisa* family in Amsterdam, were running legal businesses targeted at a broader clientele – especially prostitutes and illegal immigrants. Others were just illegally organised, short-lived but very profitable: the so called *teléfonos negros* (illegal call centres). The operators – usually not Colombians and co-organised with other legal or illegal phone operators abroad[53]

---

52 Next to Dutch and English, many Dutch, Surinamese and especially Antillean dealers speak some Spanish.
53 In the three cases I directly contacted, the owners were Dutch, Dominicans and Turkish with the Dutch nationality. However, they all had Colombian young men (often illegal immigrants) employed as telephone-runners.

– would 'hang' to changing lines and offer people, either on the street by mobile phones or from hidden rooms, the possibility of phoning for very cheap rates. Some Colombians or other Latinos were employed to sell the service, which was exclusively targeted for prostitutes and drug dealers. Before he was expelled from the Netherlands, Solano survived for a while in The Hague as a 'telephone-runner':

> "...Two guilders. No matter where you phone it costs two guilders per minute [in 1996]. I go knocking the windows with the mobile phone, and then I get these women for hours on the phone, talking with everybody there [in Colombia]. *Traquetos* also use it a lot but they speak less... I don't get that much, but the boss indeed gets rich because he has the business with a Puertorican operator. They steal the line, they do not pay a cent."

Germán had credit in an illegal budget telephone centre run by a Dominican in the Red Light District of Amsterdam. After ringing the bell three times in one of the prostitution windows, a man who recognised Germán allowed us to enter. The place was a simple room with some chairs and a desk with three or four mobile phones. Two men were making phone-calls in Spanish, and the guy who opened the door was in charge. That first visit did not lead me to believe that this was a 'hot' spot. However, I later discovered that the Dominican owner had already been investigated by the police in a former office he had: they were searching for drugs. In further visits with Germán, I had the opportunity to meet some Colombians there, and it became clear to me that most of them were cocaine entrepreneurs.

CHAPTER VI

SLY *TRAQUETOS*, SAFE HOUSES AND SALSA DEALERS

Colombian cocaine wholesalers and retailers in the Netherlands

"Like an agent, a distributor will usually be a local firm or individual and a specialist
in the requirements of the local market. He or she should be familiar with the
business practices of the area, the structure of the market, local customs,
and the various socio-cultural factors pertaining to the market."

Jobber and Lancaster, *Selling and Sales Management*

6.1 WHOLESALE COCAINE

6.1.1 Locality and the social organisation of cocaine distribution

While people barely linked to the Netherlands can engage in cocaine smuggling and
import, wholesale distribution is an internal market activity reserved for locals.
Whether they are either native, mainstream business groups, come from a middlemen
minority or belong to some ethnic enclave, the opportunities of these local cocaine
wholesalers mirror, with minor distortions, those of legal local traders.

Groups engaged in cocaine import can substantially differ from their legal
counterparts due to the key role played by cocaine exporters or the privileged link
with them. At the one end of chain, the social or ethnic background of cocaine
retailers also tend to vary from surrounding legal (shop) retailers. They are often close
to – or overlap with – the drug consumers they supply, from street crack smokers to
establishment sniffers, and in many cases they alternate with other activities in the
informal economy.

Cocaine wholesale distributors, I will argue here, are local illegal buyers and
sellers not so different from other legitimate distributors, shopkeepers or
businessmen. Although cocaine wholesalers lack legal permits, cannot advertise their
product and have to be ready to use violence, they typically need to combine access to
the required infrastructure, to further distributors or retailers, to cocaine importers,
and enjoy some sort of local protection.

The material and human resources to organise the distribution channels are partly
dependent upon the quantities involved and the local/distant nature of the
transactions, but in general terms are nothing extraordinary. The basic equipment
includes a car or a van for transport, a 'safe house' or store to stash, conceal and
divide the loads, a mobile or public phone, a weapon, and eventually some access to
cash and financial resources through bank accounts, funds transfer companies, cash

carriers, and so on. All kinds of 'front stores' – especially small and with continual movement of people or merchandise to retail such as restaurants, bars, small shops or warehouses – are well-suited and widely used to disguise the illegal transactions. However, a large number of small distributors and intermediates can do and actually operate without them. Finally, tasks to perform or subcontract are less risky and complex than in cocaine import, and even fewer skills are required from those employed by the wholesalers. At this general level, cocaine distribution is a matter for 'local entrepreneurs' – whether local businessmen, shop-keepers, merchants, established migrants, dealers in other illegal goods, and so forth – and in principle restricted for newcomers with no access to these local resources.

The local character of cocaine distribution is further evidenced by another essential asset of wholesalers: their privileged contact with potential buyers – other distributors, smaller dealers, international or foreign wholesalers from destination countries, and so on.

What is easier? To find a supplier when you already have a customer, or to find a customer once you have a supplier? The answers I received from my informants and the observations I made around this question clearly indicate the first option as the more viable one. Even more evident than in legal business, reliable customers are cherished and carefully kept, while suppliers come and go, and are sometimes even switched with respect to the prices and qualities handled. Wholesalers with a solid small clientele are definitely in business, while those who have to 'hunt' for buyers are often expelled early on in the game.[1] In this sense, well-placed wholesalers tend to have strong links with the levels below, exploiting preferential trade lines based in ethnic, cultural and/or purely economic considerations. Again, newcomers or poorly connected migrants lack this sort of advantage to become successful illegal brokers.

Naturally, wholesalers can also derive or strengthen their market position by a privileged link with cocaine importers or exporters. This is particularly the case of some distributors with ethnic or family bonds with those engaged in upper levels. In a few cases, individuals with no capacity to import cocaine can indeed be granted some kilos to distribute from a larger bulk, just because they are trusted blindly by the Colombian exporter. These 'credentials' can also eventually be used by unconnected individuals to move, for example, in middle and low distribution levels, far from the big shots. However, as explained before, people with no infrastructure, no financial capability and no local contacts can hardly become wholesalers, no matter how close they are from suppliers. They have better chances of working for them than working with them.

Finally, the sort of local protection they enjoy further enhances the possibilities of these illegal entrepreneurs to succeed.[2] As priority targets of drug enforcers in a

---

1   They expand the chances of being ripped-off by insolvent dealers or captured by undercover policemen, who more often present themselves from 'below' as potential customers or partners.

2   The proposition advanced by Blok: *"the more successful a man is as a bandit, the more extensive the protection granted him"* (Blok 1974: 100), is also applicable to these illegal traders, whether this protection comes from legal or illegal power brokers. In this sense, success as illegal entrepreneur and protection are inseparably interrelated. See also Gambetta (1996: 226-244).

highly unstable market section, they often rely on measures and social arrangements to ground their position. From 'inside', protection can take the form of physical violence[3] – whether real or symbolic – to neutralise competition and law enforcement. From 'below', it can mean toleration from specific ethnic, business or professional communities that can benefit from their trade – for example, particular ethnic shops, truck chauffeurs, banks and funds transfer companies, and so forth. From 'above', active and passive protection can be delivered by many sort of power brokers: police and military authorities, prison guards, top lawyers, local politicians or *mafia* type organisations controlling illegal markets in specific areas. These forms of social regulation and social control often surround the cocaine wholesaler's activities. Again, individuals or groups able to either get away with violence or to receive the elementary protection tend to be locally established, to already have some knowledge of the cultural environment, and some legitimation as local legal or illegal entrepreneurs.

Cocaine importers sell the freight to what Colombian *traquetos* call the *primera mano* (first hand), top wholesalers who are in a position to buy many kilos, sometimes the whole bulk, and who resell it for a mark up to two or three other smaller distributors (second hand). All the cocaine re-exported to other European countries – as argued in chapter III, most of the cocaine reaching the Netherlands – has already been handled by these first and second hand distributors. Large bulks are further divided amongst smaller distributors who eventually sell per kilo or fractions thereof to local retailers of all sorts.

However, a clean picture of a symmetric pyramidal trade chain is far from reality in the cocaine business. Firstly, the original imported amount can vary from one kilogram to some tons, which of course not only influences the number of possible 'hands' but the actual quantities handled by them. Single wholesalers can handle different quantities in different operations. Secondly, the cocaine loads are sold depending on the financial situation of the buyers and the credit they are granted. Since both things tend to change even per operation, it is not rare to find similar *traquetos* moving different quantities.

Under these circumstances, it is possible to understand the involvement of particular groups in cocaine distribution. Before analysing the performance of Colombian distributors in the Netherlands, it is worthwhile to focus first on the American cocaine market, where they happened to be rather successful. Much can be learned from this comparison.

6.1.2 Back in the States

All sources recognise and stress the key role played by Colombians as major cocaine wholesalers in the US during the expansion and consolidation of the American cocaine market from the early 1980s onwards. Although no study has been conducted about this specific involvement, a broad agreement exists on this point amongst

---

3   However, the use of violence can be an obstacle for business performance (see chapter IX).

Colombian and American researchers.[4] The ethnographic material on street cocaine dealers in New York provided by Williams (1990) and Bourgois (1995) show the absence of Colombians at retail level but their strong position as wholesale suppliers.

Almost all famous cocaine exporters from the first and second generation – thus until the early 1990s – had long experience as successful *traquetos* in Miami and New York either staying there for a while or using local Colombian immigrants as wholesalers. Legends such as Herrera Zuleta and Blanco de Trujillo were present in Miami very early, Escobar went to the US in the 1960s – not yet as a *traqueto* –, Lehder was a truly Colombian immigrant in the US, the Rodriguez brothers and Santacruz Londoño were active in New York, and the Ochoa brothers in Miami. Most of them made their large profits by selling the cocaine to non-Colombian middle distributors. In New York, an early control by Colombians displaced Puertoricans and Americans to lower levels and expelled Dominicans and African-Americans to street retail and crack circuits. In Miami, as I explained in chapter II, Colombian networks managed in the early 1980s to subordinate, after a bloody war, earlier Cuban control on the business. Moreover, in cities like Houston, Detroit, Chicago, Washington DC or Atlanta, Colombians have also been identified as powerful wholesale suppliers. Wilson and Zambrano (1994: 304) rightly question a significant Colombian share in the West Coast, where in fact the Colombian enclave was and remains rather small. An early involvement of US citizens in large distribution (Adler 1985) was followed during the 1990s by an increasing role of Mexico as the main source/transit country and Mexican dealers as growing drug entrepreneurs (Lupsha 1995). However, this Mexican participation seems to be stronger for cross-border cocaine smuggling, Colombians remaining as 'border watchers' and wholesalers (Lupsha 1995: 98).

In general terms, it can be argued with Thoumi that:

> "Independent Colombians control a portion of the wholesale business. Cocaine is sold four or five times before reaching the retail level. Colombians are involved in those stages, but once cocaine is at the retail level, it is in the hands of countless independent sellers who rarely have any connection to Colombian traffickers." (Thoumi 1995: 150).

The many Colombians with whom I spoke confirmed these trends. Joel and his brother, for example, were large distributors in Chicago before they began to operate in the Netherlands. Ana Inés recalls from her times in Miami:

> "In Miami, I had a student visa, but I also worked in a *Latino* bar. The place was really hot, you know, heavy guys and fights all the time. I left the job because I was scared. They offered me many times to do some work, to transport and to distribute the thing...
> I had a boyfriend who happened to be a *traqueto* and went to prison. See, 90% of the Colombians I knew in Miami were involved in drug trafficking. So I later avoided Colombian boyfriends because I had a couple of bad experiences. First you don't know, but later you realise that he is a *traqueto* (...) Once my mother asked me to send her

---

4   See especially Thoumi (1995), Krauthausen and Sarmiento (1991: 150-170), Betancourt and García (1994: 97-100), Urrea Giraldo (1993: 10), MacDonald (1988: 29) and Hernández (1997: 608).

some money. She said to me: 'everybody else there send money home'. So I told her: 'I am sorry mother, but I am not working in that [cocaine dealing] like everybody else you mean' (...) In another occasion, a friend of mine invited me to New York, and he wanted to pay everything. I suspected that in fact he wanted me to transport the thing [cocaine] from Miami to New York so I refused. In Miami they were mainly *paisas*, in New York the *vallunos* controlled the business."

One of Marisol's best friends is still serving a 12-year sentence in an American Federal prison. As she explained to me in Cali:

"She wasn't smuggling, no, she went there as many others around here to organise it. For many years, she enjoyed a high life, or how do you think her family bought all these cars? I visited her last year and it was devastating."

The vast majority of the 6,400 Colombians imprisoned in the United States[5] are, as everywhere else outside Colombia, being punished for some drug offence. Despite the fact that the main fronts of the American war on drugs are either allocated at producing and transit countries (export), at borders (smuggling) and at deprived, ghettoised inner-slums (crack-cocaine retail), there seems to exist a large proportion of local residents and local drug offences (distribution) amongst these Colombians imprisoned. The exploratory research of Ospina and Hofmann (1996) shows indeed for the area of New York, comprising around 40% of the Colombian prison population, that 52% were residing in the US before being detained from which half of them for 7 years or more. Another interesting trend refers to the drug offences: almost 45% are charged with (conspiracy and/or intent to) possession and/or distribution of illegal drugs – typical local activities – while import amounts for 18% of the cases – i.e. smuggling into the country.[6] Even recognising the specificity of the New York case, these numbers are unimaginable in the European context.

While it is difficult to assess the extent of this engagement – presumably very low in quantitative terms regarding the number of migrants and the possible available jobs at wholesale distribution – it is clear that local Colombian networks provided excellent distribution channels to Colombian exporters.[7] Some authors have indicated

---

5 See Ministry of Foreign Affairs of Colombia (1997). The number of Colombians in US Federal Prisons – drug dealing is a Federal Offence – was 4,373 in 1997, representing a 3,3% of the Federal prison population. As explained before, prison statistics primarily reflect criminalisation trends, and only indirectly tell something about the relationship between certain groups and deviant behaviour, due to selectivity biases regarding offence, vulnerability of the offender and enforcement priorities.

6 Other unspecified drug offences with 28%, money laundering with 4%, illegal residence and other crimes with 5% (Ospina and Hofmann 1996: 25).

7 It should be stressed that, whenever possible, this participation has been exaggerated, sensationalised or framed in racial fears and moral panics by American law enforcement viewpoints. During the 1990s, Colombians became suitable enemies of collective anxieties around the crack epidemic, the poor results of drug crusades and the growing urban violence and social unrest in large American cities. This process is superbly exposed by Mike Davis while commenting upon a "Cartel L.A." series published in 1989 by the Herald-Examiner synthesising DEA positions: "...Cocaine...is supposedly warehoused and processed for wholesale distribution by Colombian nationals bound to the cartels by unbreakable *omerta*. Originally estimated to number a few hundred, the Colombians in 1989 suddenly

this fact as a key factor for the success of Colombian drug groups in the American market (Thoumi 1995: 174-175). Once this control was achieved for the mid-1980s, it is also argued that it operated as a symbolic or real pull factor for some Colombians who went and still go to the US to work, many of them as illegal immigrants, in various informal and illegal labour markets (Urrea Giraldo 1993: 10).

In general terms, three reasons stand behind this success of Colombians in the American cocaine market: the nature of the migration enclave, the unbeatable link with supply sources and the business resources deployed for co-operation and confrontation.

A migration flow mainly composed of *paisas* had been pouring to the United States, especially to New York and Miami, since the mid-1960s. During the 1980s, less well-off migrants from all parts of Colombia – including many *vallunos* destined for New York and young black *norteñitos* from the Pacific Coast – kept entering the United States, targeting other regions and cities as well (Urrea Giraldo 1993: 9-10). The result is a very heterogeneous population of more than half a million Colombians rather concentrated in New York and Miami, places in which they are the second largest Latino group after Dominicans and Cubans respectively.[8] In clear contrast with other Colombian communities – for example in Venezuela or Europe[9] – they display patterns of long term settlement with upward mobility, and the development of formal and informal own business and local shops. They also show residential concentration – such as Jackson Heights in Queens, NY, with some estimated 80,000 Colombian immigrants – and, especially before the emergence of an American born Colombian generation, good networks for cash remittances to Colombia and weak loyalties to the United States in terms of political participation, social power or cultural identification.

Next to these well-established Colombians, the number of unskilled illegal immigrants working for low wages either in the informal economy or for co-ethnic employers has also been growing in large cities. Since this group can provide the indispensable unskilled workers who perform flexible tasks for cocaine wholesalers, it has been reasonably argued that some of these undocumented immigrants have also been involved in local cocaine distribution (Krauthausen and Sarmiento 1991: 157-158). Indeed, the presence of illegal co-national immigrants can certainly represent an asset to Colombians organising the cocaine distribution in the US. However, as I will

---

became an 'invading army ... thousands strong' organised into as many as '1,000 cells'. Alarmed by news of the 'invasion', nervous Southern California residents were put on the lookout for 'suspicious' Latin Americans, especially 'polite, well-dressed' families or individuals with penchants for quiet suburban neighborhoods... The Herald-Examiner reassured its readers that 'the 63,000 Colombians living in the Los Angeles area do not all work in cocaine distribution cells' – 'only 6,000'" (Davis 1990: 311-312).

8   They are the largest and oldest South American group in the United States, but smaller than other *Latino* groups such as Mexicans, Cubans, Puertoricans, Dominicans and Salvadorians. However, regarding their socio-economic position – in terms of naturalisation, educational levels, average income, medical care, job and property tenure – they stand above average far better than Mexicans, Dominicans and Salvadorians (US Census Bureau 1997).

9   For the specific characteristics of Colombians in the Netherlands, see chapter IV.

show for the Dutch case, a mechanic relationship between illegal immigrants and cocaine distribution is far from simple or even logical. Krauthausen and Sarmiento, for example, take criminal activity for granted as a direct substitute of labour market success,[10] and wrongly presuppose a natural 'identification' or solidarity between drug dealers and illegal immigrants through mechanisms of trust and loyalty. Their argument forgets that most illegal immigrants work for wages in the general informal labour market; that illegalities are different in nature and not a unified field; that Colombians are doubly suspected and illegal residents more vulnerable; and finally that skills, status, experience or contacts are often more important than mere ethnic or kinship lines to get and keep a job in the cocaine business.

In short, Colombians in the US are in a position somewhere in between Mexican and Cuban immigrants, neither predominantly proletarised in the mainstream economy like the former nor with a fully developed ethnic enclave economy like the latter (Portes and Bach 1985; Portes and Rumbaut 1990). They present some of the characteristics of middlemen minorities described by Bonacich and Modell (1980) such as strong ties with their homeland (mobility, family members, the sending of remittances, and so forth), visible levels of ethnic solidarity (family ties, suprafamiliar institutions, voluntary associations, community leaders and organisations), urban preferences, low political participation, travel experience, hostility from the surrounding society and in some cases the concentration of trade and entrepreneurial activities held in contempt by mainstream economy. However, other key features of middlemen groups are absent. Firstly, they do not perform as real brokers between local elites and subordinate groups. Self-employment in small-businesses and shops exists but is small if compared with Chinese, Indian or Korean diasporas. The image of frugal families dwelling behind their shop, working long hours and ploughing profits back into the businesses, is too narrow and simple. In fact, Colombians are far from the 'trading people with a history of traditional capitalism' (Bonacich 1973: 591-592) often depicted in middlemen theories. They lack the language skills attributed to middlemen, and they push for assimilation through intermarriage or the education system, with relative success. Finally, a heterogeneous class and ethnic composition within the group often limits solidarity to the level of kinship or locality of origin.

It can be argued that some Colombians in the US are linked to the so-called 'ethnic economy' (Light and Karageorgis 1995), a broader and more agnostic notion involving the Colombian self-employed, Colombian entrepreneurs and their Colombian employees. Only some of these immigrant businesses are spatially clustered, have achieved some vertical and horizontal integration, have employed other Colombians and have gone beyond a co-ethnic clientele, which are all further characteristics of full-fledged 'ethnic enclaves' to be found, for example, in the Cuban business concentration in 'Little Havana' in Miami (Wilson and Portes 1980).

---

10 This idea, especially for drug dealing, has been consistently undermined. Recent and weak immigrants have generally fewer opportunities than established ones both as legal AND illegal entrepreneurs and employees (see Reuter et al. 1990; Engbersen et al. 1995; and Butcher and Piehl 1997). For the specific involvement of illegal Colombian immigrants in the cocaine business, see chapter VIII.

Moreover, a visible residential concentration in some neighbourhoods, a large population size providing a core market and a source of labour, good entrepreneurial skills and the availability of capital resources, are additional features that shape the Colombian enclaves of New York and Miami. All these enclave features constitute, as I argued earlier, a fertile soil for both expanding and concealing the networks engaged in cocaine distribution.

Next to the nature of the group, a second reason for their success obviously relates to their privileged position regarding supply sources, an advantage that, for example, Cubans did not have. In a time in which cocaine demand was expanding in explosive proportions (with no moral panics and a few negative stigmas around cocaine), the war on drugs had not even begun and the potential profits were already considerable, why would Colombian immigrants not use their infrastructure to help and profit from the *traquetos* travelling to the States to organise cocaine import? In this way, Colombian *traquetos* and immigrants could profit from each other, the first by concealing transactions and improving business performance, and the second by getting the chance to share the profits as entrepreneurs or employees. Also the way in which cocaine was smuggled in the late 1970s, by plane and in medium or small quantities, allowed for and easier participation of co-nationals even with low levels of organisation.

Finally, Colombian cocaine entrepreneurs in the US showed a remarkable ability to combine mixed business partnerships with extreme violence, or to switch from one to the other whenever required. Changing in time and space, both coexistence with and annihilation of potential competitors are well documented. Thus, on the one hand, Colombians managed in different periods and regions to establish business links – thus up to kilo transactions – with Americans (Lee III 1989), Cubans (Eddy et al. 1992) or Mexicans (Lupsha 1995). On the other, they did not hesitate to use violence to neutralise competitors. I have explained in chapter II that Cubans controlled the marketing channels until Colombians replaced them following the 'Miami Wars' of 1979-1982. New York also evidenced high levels of violence around the control of cocaine wholesale distribution. While some authors have over-dramatised this Colombian related violence (Eddy et al. 1992; Gugliotta and Leen 1990; Mermelstein 1990) others have just recognised it as an important element to explain the Colombian advantage (Thoumi 1995; Bagley 1990). The localised, sporadic violent outbreaks for the control of the illegal business in major American cities – also between Colombian groups themselves – indicate potentially well-placed groups in terms of local networks, business resources and supply access – actually able to perform violence – but temporarily excluded from the market by other dealers and groups better tolerated or protected from 'above'. In a context of market expansion, high competition, enormous profits and police incapability to react, some Colombian groups hostile to local authorities and not protected by other illegal power brokers were able to deploy physical violence to secure their position.

In this way, Colombian *traquetos* managed to become illegal middlemen. With the escalation of the war on drugs and the pumping of their dollars into mainstream US economy, the initial indifference of American traditional mobs – whether Italo-American *mafiosi* or native groups – towards Colombian cocaine wholesalers turned into toleration, shared partnerships or active protection. Cubans were neutralised and only kept some share in Florida, while Puertoricans, Dominicans or Afro-Americans were subordinated and forced to occupy the retail ends in the streets of New York or Los Angeles. More recently, their intensive co-operation and competition with Mexican organisations marks new trends still dominated by Colombian and American wholesalers.

6.1.3 The competitive disadvantage of Colombian distributors in the Netherlands

In contrast to American developments, the involvement of Colombians in cocaine distribution in the Netherlands is highly problematic. Contrary to their rather active role in cocaine import, especially of large quantities by sea, local Colombians suffer a strong competitive disadvantage to engage in further cocaine distribution.

As shown in chapter IV, Colombians in the Netherlands are neither a middleman minority nor an ethnic enclave. It is even difficult to find traces of a mere ethnic economy amongst them. They are few and dispersed, and they lack social or financial capital. Rather than owning businesses, they share with other ethnic minorities the exploitation of particular occupational *niches* in the general economy, usually for local employers or clientele. They also lack the social institutions and the infrastructure required to properly conceal cocaine distribution: retail shops, restaurants, warehouses and other possible front stores. In this sense, other ethnic minorities such as Surinamese or Turks are better positioned to provide a base for the business, leaving aside native Dutch illegal entrepreneurs who in fact dominate at wholesale level.

Moreover, Colombians also lack the main marketing channels towards 'below' – local or European buyers – only developed through active local engagement and some degree of successful economic brokerage. Successful drug entrepreneurs often regard local Colombians as unskilled, socially isolated and too vulnerable. Their marginal position excludes them from the most effective forms of local protection, and they are often forced to truly work 'underground'. In contrast with the US situation, they cannot widely resort to physical violence and get away with it in the Dutch context.

This competitive disadvantage of Colombians at the distribution level can be generalised for the rest of Europe. Even in Spain, with a larger and stronger community,[11] other local or foreign groups seem to enjoy better marketing channels and protection resources.

Finally, the uneven involvement of Colombians in the American and the European wholesale markets has also historical causes. From their perspective, the control on distribution in both places had a truly different meaning. As already explained, the control over the internal market in the United States was simultaneous or even prior (1978-1983) to the consolidation of Colombian groups as main cocaine producers and exporters. Grasping the American market through own distribution channels was

---

11 According to *Latino* migrant organisations in Brussels, there are around 100,000 Colombians living legally and illegally in Spain.

essential for gaining a privileged position over other possible competitors in Latin America. The first Colombians to make cocaine fortunes were those able to import *and* sell kilo quantities in American cities. The high levels of violence around the cocaine wars also reflect such articulation.

Later European developments did not have the same meaning: Colombians were comfortable in control of the export business when they targeted this market. Gaining a position in distribution, though extremely interesting for multiplying profits, was not a condition for their already undisputed leadership as producers and exporters. The lack of strong Colombian networks and the fact that large sea smuggling operations required more entrepreneurial arrangements forced Colombians to deal with other groups or individuals with stronger roots in the local context.

The international palette: dealing in a non-Colombian environment

A salient feature of these cocaine distributors is that they belong to several ethnic and national groups, even more than importers. The international composition is remarkable not only between but also within organisations. It reflects the fact that most cocaine traded is in transit to other European destinations,[12] the market openness beyond any monopolist or regulatory local control by power holders, and to some extent the collusion with other legal and illegal markets and activities at European level.

However, was wholesale distribution, as I argued before, not a truly local activity? It is in fact at this very stage where the local and the global nature of the cocaine business are more obviously related as two faces of the same coin (Hobbs and Dunnighan 1998). An international crowd from source, transit or destination countries can perform as *local* wholesalers, all profiting from different resources and contacts.

Native Dutch cocaine entrepreneurs form a first group of wholesalers. Some researchers have pointed out the ways in which Colombian importers sell to Dutch individuals or groups (Van Duyne et al. 1990: 54-55; Van Duyne 1995: 79; Bovenkerk 1995b: 100-103). Antillean intermediaries facilitate some of these Colombian-Dutch transactions. Others are brought about by mixed couples, the Dutch partner distributing the cocaine after import.

Many of these Dutch cocaine wholesalers, especially those who entered the business during the late 1980s, are 'criminal diversifiers', i.e. existing illegal entrepreneurs that 'diversify' their operations to include cocaine distribution (Dorn et al. 1992: xiii). They have often grown in safer and more tolerated businesses such as hashish/marihuana import and distribution, have good contacts in the local sex industry, and only move to cocaine operations when a good opportunity arises.[13] Some also have experience with heroin and have foreign contacts.

---

12 Since most of the cocaine is bound to other European countries, the Netherlands attracts wholesale buyers from those places, who come to buy cheaper and directly from importers.

13 It is agreed that most of these Dutch illegal entrepreneurs have enough financial incentives sticking to these safer activities, which they know and control, and consider cocaine and heroin two delicate and dangerous businesses. During the 1990s, they had more chances to diversify to the more domestic *ecstasy* than to cocaine traffic.

A good example of these diversifiers was Klaas Bruinsma, a top Dutch drug entrepreneur who became, even before he was killed in 1991, a mythical figure in the Amsterdam drug scene.[14] He bought cocaine from Colombian exporters and importers, engaging for these transactions partners, intermediaries or employees from many places: Surinamese, Chileans, Yugoslavs and Dutch. He cultivated contacts with foreign drug suppliers, with local authorities and did not hesitate to use physical violence (Fijnaut et al. 1996). With a much lower profile, two Dutch brothers I met were also buying cocaine from Colombian importers. They owned a coffee-shop in the centre of Amsterdam, and one of them had spent five years in a Spanish prison for trafficking hashish.

Not all have a criminal background. A number of these Dutch wholesalers belong to the category of 'sideliners', people with legal business enterprises who trade cocaine as a 'sideline' activity on an occasional or regular basis (Dorn et al. 1992: xiii). As was the case with local importers, they enter the business due to financial problems, a strong sense of invulnerability – they are indeed harder to detect – and/or a good contact with some supplier.

However, most of the Colombian importers and distributors interviewed usually preferred to deal with local ethnic minorities (mainly Turks and Antilleans) as well as with all sorts of European groups (Italians, Germans, British, Russians, Yugoslavs and so forth). They often had a negative image about Dutch drug dealers, partly reflecting more general feelings about the local environment. Joel explained:

> "Don't mistake yourself. See, the Dutch *mafia,* yes they run the coffee-shops and all that. They also bring the thing [cocaine] through their corrupt friends. Then you have all over the city [Amsterdam] these small thieves and junks, they want to have something from you, they want to impress you. But you can't trust these people, they come with *cola* [they attract the police], they talk to everybody and they speak if they pull their balls... I sell in Germany and here I deal with Turks and Italians."

Other Colombian dealers made the same sort of remarks, portraying Dutch dealers as too distant, too small or too ready to talk with the police. Additionally, cocaine related cases analysed show some interesting patterns in this direction. In all Colombian-Dutch transactions intended for the European market, Dutch wholesalers seem to be also involved in cocaine import. When Colombians alone control the import operation, they either prefer to sell directly to foreign organisations – avoiding the unnecessary mediation of Dutch wholesalers and a price mark-up – or to some local non-Dutch groups considered safer. Dutch wholesalers are more active in non-Colombian operations, and, of course, when the cocaine is aimed for retail in the Netherlands.

Surinamese and Antilleans are also involved in cocaine distribution. Colombians have more contact with Antillean dealers, who often speak both Spanish and Dutch

---

14 As a product for entertainment, Bruinsma was even portrayed as a *mafia* boss of a criminal 'syndicate' with almost 200 people organised in strict divisions within a hierarchical structure (Middelburg 1992). See for a critique: Bovenkerk (1995b: 108-110).

and who are also trade partners in other business levels like export-import, smuggling or money laundering. Surinamese wholesalers are somewhat further removed from Colombian *traquetos*, either closer to Dutch importers or responsible for channelling small and medium quantities directly imported from Suriname.[15] They profit from their own local infrastructure around their communities in the Netherlands – *tokos*, small import and retail businesses, gold shops, bars and so on – and from local protection in the form of indifference, passive or active corruption (Fijnaut et al. 1996: Sub-reports I and IV on Surinamese and Antillean dealers). They are more oriented to the local cocaine market, supplying the many groups involved in retail and street dealing, which also involve Antilleans and Surinamese especially in the larger cities. In line with drug enforcement priorities, very little is known about these Surinamese wholesalers. Their involvement in export-import or street levels is better documented and ranks higher in media and policy agendas.[16]

Although Turkish and Kurdish drug entrepreneurs have been primarily connected with heroin import and distribution in the Netherlands,[17] they have also diversified to cannabis import and, to a lesser extent, to cocaine wholesale. Many Colombians claimed to have been selling cocaine to the *árabes* (Arabs, a broad label used beyond ethnic or political boundaries), especially in The Hague and Amsterdam. Some of these transactions were facilitated by a sentimental relationship – usually between a Colombian woman and a Turkish man – but in most of the cases referred, they were pure business contacts. Despite the few social and cultural intersections between both groups, Colombians seemed to like Turks as business partners. As Solano recalls from his participation as interpreter in a Colombian-Turkish transaction:

"Here in The Hague you see many Turks buying from Colombians. The Turks are a real *mafia* with their families and so. That is the impression they give compared with the messy Colombians... You can find Colombians saying nasty things about the Arabs, whatever you want. You won't find them together, maybe some Turkish men visit the girls [Colombian prostitutes] but that's all. They go to different churches, bars and discotheques, and if they live in the same flat, they hardly communicate. But I think

---

15 However, in some large 'Surinamese' or 'Antillean' operations, there is a clear link with Colombians at export or import level. In October 1994, 550 kg cocaine were seized in Amsterdam and 17 people detained in connection with a distribution network via Surinamese *tokos* (shops). The cocaine arrived hidden in fruit juice from Colombia.

16 For a complete picture, see Fijnaut et al. (1996). For cocaine export-import from Suriname, see Korf and Verbraeck (1993); Haenen and Buddingh' (1994); Van Duyne (1995: 84-86); Van den Heuvel (1999); Haenen (1999). For money laundering in the Netherlands Antilles, see Nelen et al. (1993); Ilegems and Sauviller (1995); Baars-Schuyt (1996) and Blickman (1997). For retail and street drug dealing amongst Surinamese and Antilleans in the Netherlands, see Gelder and Sijtsma (1988); Sansone (1992: 110-120) and Korf and Verbraeck (1993).

17 Their involvement in the Dutch heroin market can be fairly compared with that of Colombians in the cocaine business in the USA, especially during the 1980s. However, while transit routes in the American case have gained power on their own (Mexico), Turks and Kurds seem to control the whole line through the Balkans and Germany. They also enjoy a less hostile environment in the Netherlands, with degrees of toleration and protection not granted to Colombian *traquetos* in the US. For the involvement of Turks and Kurds in the heroin business in the Netherlands, see: Fijnaut et al. (1996); Yeşilgöz et al. (1996, 1997) and Bovenkerk and Yeşilgöz (1998).

they respect each other. They like dealing with Turks because they are sober and to certain extent trustful. They know the ground and they know how to move the thing [cocaine] all over Europe..."

Indeed, other *traquetos* like Joel also sold cocaine to Turks based in Germany. In order to close the deals, he either went to Germany or they came to the Netherlands. For these and other local Turkish wholesalers it is not only easy but also very profitable to diversify to cocaine. They use the same routes, transport facilities, local infrastructure and international contacts to further sell, next to heroin, cocaine. Colombians systematically played down indications that they also get cocaine from other wholesalers in exchange for heroin (Fijnaut et al. 1996; Yeşilgöz et al. 1997: 61).[18] Moreover, I did not come across any detected or undetected case like this. This cocaine-heroin exchange method, however, might well take place between Turkish and non-Colombian wholesalers.

Some wholesale operations involve British and German citizens. Britain and Germany are closely linked with the Netherlands as direct destination or transit points for the cocaine traded, and Britain plays a central role in terms of financial resources and money laundering. They are very mobile, work close or integrated to other local groups, and often provide professional expertise or material resources in terms of transport, front stores, luxury investments or financial matters. They can more easily afford an – unnoticed – wealthy lifestyle as they belong to the local 'foreign elites'. Some of the cases reported in the media indeed involved exclusive houses and expensive cars. [19]

The presence of Italian wholesalers buying from cocaine importers in major Dutch cities has not only been highlighted by police and judicial sources (Fijnaut et al. 1996), but also consistently confirmed by all Colombian *traquetos* interviewed. Colombians were always positive about Italian partners and acknowledged that Colombian-Italian transactions were cherished, welcome and usually profitable. The role of Amsterdam as a meeting point for these transactions was also emphasised, and so the fact that Italians arrange the transport to Italy (especially Naples) where the cocaine is re-sold. After analysing the material collected by Fijnaut et al. (1996), the available Italian sources on cocaine traffic in Italy and what I gathered from Colombians themselves in the Netherlands, a number of remarks should be made about the nature of this Italian involvement. Firstly, despite a clear tendency during the 1990s towards professionalisation, these Italians belong to many groups and

---

18 Tano, for example, exclaimed: "No, you want to see the money, you have to send it immediately. What do you want Turkish heroin for? Not to bring it back, because we produce and export our own. Neither to sell it here, that's not our business. I told you before, the heroin we get comes from Colombia but is nothing compared with what the Turkish *mafia* handles."

19 In November 1992, the police seized in several places 1100 kg cocaine, more than a ton marihuana, money and nine cars, detaining many Dutch and Colombian importers. The loot included a Porsche containing 126 gold kg bars, both belonging to an Irishman who claimed them back in 1996. In October 1996, 317 kg cocaine were found in the house of a British citizen in Sassenheim, at the time one of the Top-3 most wanted in Britain. The police also found weapons, money and other illegal drugs.

regions in Italy. Next to drug entrepreneurs from Naples – often protected by, more than belonging to some *Camorra Clan*, particularly active in Amsterdam – there have been Italian groups and individuals from Sicily, Calabria, Rome, Milan, Florence, Bari and Genoa. Again, they range from drug entrepreneurs closely protected by local *mafia* groups,[20] to underground organisations such as the Roman *banda della Magliana*, or even to smaller groups from the North. I even found Italian individuals working for other wholesalers, like an Italian chauffeur of Colombian local wholesalers, or living here for many years with no relation with *mafia* groups. Secondly, most of these Italians have been active in all sorts of Dutch cities and towns, from Amsterdam to Zevenhuizen or Barendrecht, dealing independently with different groups. Beyond cliché images of 'pizza' or 'ice-cream connections',[21] the contacts are made in all sorts of settings and the cocaine is transported by car or truck. Thirdly, Italians do not limit their transactions to Colombians but they also buy from Dutch and Antillean suppliers.

Other wholesalers operating in the Netherlands come from Israel, Russia and the former Yugoslavia, all countries directly involved in cocaine import, transit and final retail, and with powerful local groups often dealing directly with Colombians. Jaime's wife Carla:

> "Look, I know cocaine addicts in Russia who bought the drug from Yugoslavs, who bought it here in the Netherlands from Colombians."

Even when they move rather marginally in the Dutch context, they profit from a number of advantages. Firstly, they operate and are dispersed throughout many countries in the chain, like Israelis in Colombia,[22] or Russians and Yugoslavs in Germany. This facilitates international transactions. Secondly, they are also involved in other illegal markets either connected or including the outflow of illegal commodities and assets: weapons, traffic in people, and money laundering. Tano:

---

20 As explained before, *mafia* groups do not engage in cocaine traffic, but individual traffickers protected by or belonging to a specific family do. As political organisations, *mafia* groups simply protect them – granting infrastructure, excluding competitors, and so on – and heavily tax them. In terms of business performance and reputation, it is important for these wholesalers to make appear protection as affiliation to dangerous and powerful organisations, for instance claiming to be part of *the* 'Neapolitan Camorra' in the same fashion than some Colombians claim to belong to *the* 'Cali Cartel'.

21 The role of Italian *pizzerias* in the Netherlands – like in the Campina (Camorra-Pizza-Naples) case of 1992 or more recent cases in Utrecht and Amsterdam – as 'front stores' of these Italian wholesalers, has been overstated (cf. Fijnaut et al 1996). These 'pizza-connections' partly reflect limitations and choices in police research, hunting in rather safe game reserves with a guaranteed score. Two Colombians dealing with Italians had ironic remarks when I asked them about *cocaine pizzerias*: "I won't tell you where we meet, but I prefer Chinese or Argentinean food", said one. "You mean those pizzerias in which suddenly a fat Italian gets a gun from his *pasta* plate? I've seen all that", said the other one.

22 In 1993, the Russian customs seized 1,100 kg of Colombian cocaine in Vyborg, Russia. The operation involved Colombian exporters, Israelis in Bogotá and the Netherlands, and Russians in Belgium and the Netherlands (Clawson and Lee III 1996: 87).

"The buyer was an Israeli guy who also bought a couple of *mazos* (guns)... Yeah, they usually sell them. They know about weapons... but he needed the guns quickly and he got them from Colombians (laughs)."

Finally, especially Russian wholesalers profit from the growing Western (and Dutch) interest to conquer Eastern European markets. Dutch or Colombian importers have used the increasing infrastructure in terms of import firms and transport companies to sell to Russian groups.

Especially during the 1980s, some Latin Americans have also been involved as local distributors. Venezuelans, Dominicans, Argentineans, Peruvians and Chileans have been found, the first three groups mainly performing as partners or employees of other importers and wholesalers and the last two as small independent groups. Chileans were particularly noticeable in the early 1980s, when they were by far the largest *Latino* community in the Netherlands and before the massive arrival of cargo ships from Colombia.

A very interesting peculiarity is the absence of Brazilians at this or other levels of the local cocaine business. Brazil is a major export and transshipment country for cocaine arriving to the Netherlands, and the Brazilian community in the Netherlands is almost as large as the Colombian one.[23] With this in mind, I expected to find Brazilians amongst the many groups dealing cocaine. However, I barely came across them during my research. Wilma, working for the Amsterdam police, was one of the first to point this out to me:

"Some of them are involved in prostitution, and that's it. I never get cases of theft, fraud or drugs amongst Brazilians."

The same trend was noticed when studying the Dutch cocaine related cases for the last 10 years, in which Brazilian citizens only appeared in a couple of small air operations. Colombians and other *Latinos* interviewed explicitly acknowledged the point. Finally, my observations in many Spanish-speaking settings as well as further inquires within Brazilian circuits also confirmed the absence of Brazilian organisations or individuals in cocaine distribution.

The main explanation for this lays, in my opinion, in South America. While Brazil has had a growing role as a transit and export country for cocaine bound to Africa and Europe, those transit operations have fairly remained until now in the hands of Colombian exporters and overseas importers who use Brazilian territory for the transactions. In contrast with Mexico, where powerful local organisations have developed around cocaine transit to the US, Brazilians themselves neither organise export nor large-scale smuggling to Europe. Lacking essential links at export side and the necessary local resources in the Netherlands, Brazilians are also excluded from

---

23 With a fewer number of prostitutes, adopted children, and mixed couples, the Brazilian community is highly concentrated in Amsterdam. Their 'ethnic economy' is not smaller or essentially different than the Colombian one.

import activities.[24] It is this exclusion, which further eliminates them from cocaine distribution.

Many *Latinos* also stressed the fact that Brazilians were a "different group", with their own language, cultural identity or social institutions and networks. Some Colombians felt closer not only to other Spanish-speaking groups, but also to Antilleans or native Dutch with whom they were often married. This distance, at least amongst cocaine entrepreneurs, was less related to cultural differences and more to the Brazilian lack of power, contacts and social prestige in the business. All cocaine wholesale distributors I came across in the Netherlands from export or transit countries – whether entrepreneurs or employees – were either locally strong (Surinamese and Antilleans), closely linked with importers (Colombians) or belonged to countries presently or formerly involved in cocaine export (Venezuelans, Peruvians and Chileans). Their presence and the absence of Brazilians support the idea that some locally weak wholesalers can indeed derive their position primarily from an exclusive access to exporters or importers.

6.1.4 Local Colombian traquetos

There are, in this way, some Colombians involved in wholesale distribution in the Netherlands. After all, some of them have a privileged access to Colombian importers, from which they of course receive or buy the merchandise. Some Colombian distributors are in business only because – and as long as – a Colombian importer would provide them with cocaine to sell. They are easily suspected and they find difficulties in concealing cocaine distribution within larger legal arrangements. Nevertheless, they also profit from some particular circumstances.

If they cannot rely on a strong local Colombian community, at least they can claim indifference, toleration or acceptance from their co-nationals. Some of them are dispersed and often invisible within other social networks. Others stay and deal together, but the police have to invest extra efforts to follow their steps. Police officers interviewed or encountered during my fieldwork acknowledged that they knew much more about other groups easier to police or infiltrate, that informants have to be gathered from other groups (especially native Dutch and Antilleans), that they always need translators and that all these efforts are often focused on import rather than on distribution operations. When Colombian distributors get in touch with the Dutch police, it is usually to be captured. Occasionally they have access to some legal business to conceal their activities. Others profit from their previous experience in distributing cocaine elsewhere. Finally, a number of Colombians can also profit from the reputation they have in the cocaine business. I met many Colombians, especially men, who insisted that they were frequently addressed by people either trying to buy them or sell them cocaine; the only reason being that they were Colombians. Most

---

24 In an exceptional case, 13 kg cocaine were found in Rotterdam in April 1993. The load was smuggled in the fruit ship *Ana Luisa*. A woman from Amsterdam and three Brazilians were detained: one of them came with the ship and the two others had arrived before to organise the import operation.

people rejected the offers, some accepted occasional involvement (especially in peripheral roles and mediation), and others still did not join but kept flirting with the idea of becoming cocaine dealers.

The Colombian distributors I found active in Amsterdam, Rotterdam and The Hague share many common characteristics. They all receive the cocaine from other Colombians, but trade it further to non-Colombian distributors. They form rather small units of two or three people, all independent of each other, and have also a couple of helpers – usually Colombians or other Latin Americans – who either work for them or receive some cocaine to trade it through alternative channels.

However, they also differ from each other. As it was the case with smugglers and importers, I found key differences amongst Colombian *traquetos* in terms of *modus operandi*, the interaction with the local environment, their financial capacity and their lifestyles. Around distinctions in these fields, I identified three types of Colombian distributors: 'conspicuous traders', 'discreet professionals' and 'flexible amateurs'.[25]

Conspicuous traders

A first group of distributors run or use some legal business to cover up cocaine distribution. These businesses, Colombian and non-Colombian related restaurants, bars, salsa discotheques, souvenir shops or telephone centres, are often run by mixed couples or partnerships and in fact do not usually last for very long. As legal businesses they are often poorly managed, surrounded by personal quarrels, unpaid debts and problems with the tax office. In contrast with businesses involved in import – often in industrial or rural areas – these places are central and closer to police detection.

Although some of these Colombians are women, in most of the cases there is a romantic partner – local or Colombian – involved. They tend to be well-established migrants, with children and relatives around. They also have close social contact with other Colombians and are often well known in some institutional or recreational Latino places. These distributors strive to appear as legitimate traders or businessmen, attributing their visible high living standards to some cover-up legal activity. Despite these efforts, most of the people in those circuits are aware of or imagine the illegal nature of their activities. Their reactions, however, ranged from mild condemnation and ironic commentaries to indifference, excluding both total rejection or complete acceptance.

These conspicuous traders are able to handle middle and large quantities of cocaine, but they are often amateurish, only relying on a good contact as supplier and a 'front store', which they quickly burn. While they send some of the illegal profits back to Colombia (usually for buying property there), they also spend money in the

---

25 This typology should be regarded as a mere descriptive device to visualise my own observations and empirical findings. Although clear-cut categories are at this stage less evident than in higher levels – for instance between a '*mula*' and a 'crew member' or between an 'envoy' and an 'adventurer' – these types are rather familiar to the people involved. To some extent, they reflect the conscious and unconscious images that they built from each other. However, they may well overlap with more systematic categorisations; and I doubt if they can be applied to other drug actors and settings.

Netherlands. Most of it, however, goes on conspicuous consumption – leisure, expensive clothing, car, employees, perishable goods, and so on – rather than in local investments or real estate.

A good example of these conspicuous traders are Pacho and Blanca, a Colombian couple who distributed cocaine in Amsterdam between 1990 and 1995.

Blanca and Pacho owned a pizzeria and a restaurant next to the Rembrantplein in Amsterdam. Both places were used as a business meeting point and as a place to stash the cocaine. When the restaurant was closed down in 1995, the police found 10 kg cocaine in the cellar. They did not have the infrastructure to import, so they bought cocaine loads from other Colombians and re-sold them to Italian distributors who came to Amsterdam to close the deals and pick up the merchandise.

Blanca and Pacho had an Italian chauffeur, a strange character who was mysteriously inscribed in a list as tap telephone translator for the Amsterdam police. He was never actually asked to translate anything for them. He was either trying to infiltrate the police or he just had multiple jobs to make ends meet. Two Colombian men were also involved as subordinates. They were in charge of practical matters such as moving the merchandise and arranging the money transfers, for which they used to send Colombian prostitutes to a particular exchange office.

Blanca and Pacho were rather established in Amsterdam, and were well known in many circuits: in church, by their restaurant's legal employees and customers, or by other Colombians around. When their illegal business started to flourish, they decided to bring relatives from Colombia to the Netherlands. First they brought Blanca's mother, later their son, and finally another of Blanca's son from a past relationship. They rented a large house with fashionable decoration in *Amsterdam Oud-Zuid*, they employed a Colombian woman as housecleaner, and bought a new car. Blanca claims that this was nothing particularly luxurious, but it was indeed very exceptional compared to other Colombian *traquetos* who lived more soberly and unnoticed. In contrast to them, Blanca and Pacho had expectations of achieving in the Netherlands not only material wealth but also a noticeable degree of social recognition and prestige. A former employee explained:

> "They are very generous people. I think they did too many favours for people that didn't deserve them. They didn't take care, many people knew about what they were doing."

When Blanca and Pacho moved to their new house in *Amsterdam Oud-Zuid*, they organised a party and called the priest to bless the house. He still remembers the occasion:[26]

---

26 In Colombia, Catholic priests had to compromise with popular beliefs and unwillingly engage in practices of blessing objects or goods in order to drive out bad spirits or influences. A priest told me that "Colombians are so superstitious, that if they don't do it they lose clients to the competition" (sic), especially to commercial magicians, *espiritistas* and *brujos* (witches) of all sorts. However, people seemed to respect the boundaries and complement their services whenever required. For instance, drug

"I entered and saw all those *mafia* type people gathered. The house had expensive furniture, everybody was well dressed and the food looked great. I was a little bit shocked, so I started the ceremony by saying that I wasn't sure if it was the house or the people present that ought to be blessed. There was a silence, but I continued and I blessed the house. But don't get me wrong, I didn't stay for the meal, I left immediately."

Blanca and Pacho were caught after long-term surveillance, which included observation and telephone tapping. He got 4 years and Blanca received 3 years, most of which she served in the women's prison in Breda. The restaurant was closed down, but the pizzeria was under a figurehead name, and remained open.

Discreet professionals
A more successful group of Colombian distributors combine experience with less visibility. They do not rely on legal front stores but on more basic and low profile arrangements such as rented flats in popular neighbourhoods to live and stash the cocaine. Some of them have previous experience in the business, for instance in Colombia, Spain or the US. Although they live in the Netherlands – usually only as long as they are in business – they are less established and return to Colombia after some years. Most of their relatives live there. As Colombian importers, they really feel at home in Colombia. They hardly speak Dutch, move often around the *Latino* prostitution circuit, and even limit themselves to interacting with the few *Latinos* around: helpers, other *traquetos*, incidental travellers or some frequenters of local bars and coffee-shops.

These discreet professionals realise that their access to Colombian suppliers and to potential buyers is not extensive enough to succeed. Lacking infrastructure and protection, their only chance of survival is to behave professionally, or at least to be seen as reliable, concerned, protective and up to the circumstances. Moreover, they have to stay away from the two only things that, in their view, prompt police attention in the Netherlands: money and violence. They send all the money away – to Colombia or elsewhere – and they engage in an active and conscious policy of keeping a low profile.

So low is the profile of Joel, that one can hardly believe he is a wholesaler dealing between tens and hundreds of kilos of cocaine. He lives and works in Amsterdam,

---

entrepreneurs who go to church and respect the Catholic priest's authority for certain occasions (sacraments, blessing of goods, and so on) would also consult a *brujo* before making important decisions, to foresee the future or to bless a cocaine shipment before departure.
Houses can be 'cleaned' *in situ* with the simple blessing of a priest invited to a housewarming party. This practice seems to be restricted to powerful, influential people, who can in fact 'convince' priests to bless their houses. For practical and theological reasons, they have been reluctant to massively engage in this practice. However, for less privileged worshippers, houses can be collectively blessed. During a mass in the famous Cathedral of Buga (*Valle*), I observed how the priest asked the crowd to raise first their small children, later their home's and car's keys, and finally any other object, all to be blessed by him.

buying from importers from Cali, his hometown, and selling especially to Turkish, Italian and German groups.

In contrast with Blanca and Pacho, nobody knows him. He came alone to the Netherlands in 1996, leaving his wife and two teenage sons in Colombia. For some years, he distributed cocaine in Chicago with varying fortunes, until an operation was busted and he had to 'disappear'. His brother, who had worked with him in the US, was already in the Netherlands and convinced him to come. He introduced him to some local as well as foreign buyers. Combined with good contacts at import and export level, he soon managed to be in business.

> "My family lives in Colombia and they tell others that I am in a 'business trip'. I really would like to see my sons. Here, you see, every day is the same. I miss going to play football with them, just a nice picnic. I think I will soon retire, so I go back."

He completed secondary school, and worked as a successful legal entrepreneur until he had to liquidate the business, a company with some small buses for public transport. Both his brother and some in-laws were connected to the cocaine business moving small quantities to the US, so he entered the cocaine business in the hope of making a financial recovery. He would not tell much about his former roles in the business and the way in which he got to the US. He had certainly good and bad times, suggesting a positive balance. However, he also implied that it is hard to make it as wholesale distributor and, before retiring, he wanted to 'crown' a big shipment himself as a nice last job. After retirement, he wants to regain a – larger – bus company, and live quietly in his hometown near his family:

> "My son is already 14 and I would love to be playing basketball with him. You see, with a legal job, you grow slow but you build something. With *traqueteo* [cocaine dealing] you make money fast, but as it comes, it vanishes. (...) I get bored in the Netherlands. Every day the same, and in the weekends to a bar to drink beer."

He does not look like a *traqueto*. He is older than the average – in his fifties – and wears very simple clothes, avoiding all sort of ostentation. He knows when to redraw from *ollas* (drug dealing areas or places) when they become dangerous. He also shrinks from appearing in public places with *Latino* crowds: he does not go to church since

> "...The police has been there before. I don't need to see anybody there and I wasn't going to church in Colombia anyway..."

His brother, on the contrary, is far from discreet. He wears expensive clothes, golden chains and rings, and spent 3 years in a Belgian prison. His infrastructure is very basic. He lives in a normal council flat rented by Simona, a young Colombian woman with a baby and a residence permit. Joel pays her a generous rent, and an additional payment for stashing cocaine there for a couple of days. He also drives a slightly old car, which he tries to use only in Amsterdam. He takes the train to Belgium, and if he has to go to Germany,

"I won't use it [the car] to drive around. I just leave it somewhere, and then I take the tram. A Dutch plate with a Colombian inside is too much for these Germans! (laughs)..."

He also carries a personal buzzer, but no mobile telephone. He goes to bed at 10:00 PM, after which he does not want to be disturbed. When he receives a message from somebody, he phones back from the nearest telephone booth. Curiously, while he takes care about not using hot lines himself, he does not seem to care that much about the numbers he phones. For long-distance arrangements, he goes to budget telephone centres where he often meets his brother, Paisita and some other helpers like Tico (his nephew), Chino and Tano.

He tries to minimise risk by delegating cocaine collection and delivery, and cash transfers or transportation. He only negotiates the terms of the deals, handles the money and stashes the cocaine. He usually buys and sells *escama de pescado* (fish scale) or *concha de nácar* (nacre shell), top quality cocaine known for its pink shining glints.

Joel has an excellent reputation not only around business partners but also amongst close friends and subordinates, especially for being just and jointly liable. Tano:

"He is incapable of killing a fly, and he keeps his word... He lends money, invites dinners, and always asks if everything is OK. Once he helped a friend with US$ 19,000 and he never saw it back. He even helps unknown people. Last week, for example, he gave accommodation to a Bolivian woman, just because she was illegal and had nowhere to go... I don't think these are interested favours, he might have his reasons to help, but he is just like that."

Not all these sort of distributors were men. I found at least two cases of women in charge of distribution networks, though they were also connected with import activities and had always a male relative associated in Colombia.

Flexible amateurs
Finally, a third group of Colombian wholesalers are neither professionals nor full-time distributors. They usually enter the activity through some acquainted importer to whom they remain truly dependent. With no start-up capital, they get some quantity from him, make a mark-up, and pay it back when the deal is closed. They deal smaller quantities, between 1 kg and 5 kg, and often have no previous experience. Since they depend on the importer's – or other distributor's – favour, they tend to see the job as a one-off operation or a sporadic opportunity. They plan very little, and work with very few people. These flexible entrepreneurs mix distribution with other activities, either as employees of other *traqueto*, or as hustlers in the informal economy or other illegal markets. Some of these flexible amateurs speak neither Dutch nor English, and move exclusively in the *Latino* circuit. They are mostly men. Riverito, for example,

can be seen as one of those Colombians who switch many roles in the cocaine business, to eventually engage in cocaine distribution. [27]

Lupo comes from Cali, and he is well established in Amsterdam where he lived for the last 15 years with his Latin American wife. He works in a Latin American restaurant, but he engages in all sorts of informal activities or *cruces* that he either seeks out or happens to come across. In fact, one of his nicknames is *little camera.* Tano:

> "He always has 3 or 4 crazy ideas on how to make money, some are incredible. He talks and talks about his projects, people think that he is in his own film or video..."

However, some of Lupo's businesses are indeed real. Sometimes he works in a restaurant. Sometimes he sells stolen objects like computers, watches or cash registers that he gets from some Colombian *apartamenteros* (burglars) he knows. He first tries to sell them in restaurants or to people he knows, but he often ends up in a pawnshop. He also lends small quantities of money – up to € 2,500 – to friends and acquaintances, charging shark interests for the service. Cocaine distribution is just a side-activity, something to do now and then when he matches a supplier with a potential client. In fact, he does not distinguish very much between cocaine and the other goods he sells, and he does not care much about organisational and security questions. Most distributors contacted in The Hague also belonged to this category of entrepreneur.

To summarise, local *traquetos* engaged in wholesale distribution belong to three groups with distinctive characteristics:

	Conspicuous Tradesmen	Discreet Professionals	Flexible Amateurs
Conspicuous	•		•
Discreet		•	
Underground		•	•
Legal Business	•		
Flexible			•
Full-time	•	•	
Skilled		•	
Unskilled	•		•
Large quantities	•	•	
Small quantities			•

Hanging around distributors: correitos and ASOTRAPO members
As was the case of some Colombians making a living around cocaine importers, wholesale distributors are also surrounded by a number of people who help them in

---

27 See chapter VII for a full description of Riverito's career and involvement.

many ways. These helpers are locally recruited and include illegal newcomers, established migrants or some *traqueto's* relative and friend. They can also be part-time distributors themselves (flexible amateurs) or engage in various legal and illegal activities.

They have to move (collect and deliver) merchandise from one place to the other (*correitos*, local couriers), to collect or transfer cash, to escort *traquetos* and to keep an eye on stashed cocaine. Wholesale distributors do not usually have more than two or three of these flexible labourers.

Paisita works for Joel, but he is his opposite: young, improvised, slightly unstable and rather violent, always threatening debtors. He performs many tasks: usually escorts Joel to close deals, picks up and deliver merchandise, threatens people, and arranges cash transfers to Colombia. He openly wants to become the boss some day, but Joel does not believe in his business skills. Paisita is one of those people who usually end up in prison, but thanks to Joel's professionalism, he has managed to remain at liberty. He shouts about business matters in the telephone centres, and manages to make enemies everywhere he goes.

Tico from Cali has a turbulent past. In Colombia, he used to sniff coke and smoke *basuco*, periodically losing control over his habit. Fortunate enough to avoid the worst prison blocks, he served 2 years in a Colombian prison after killing somebody. There he met major drug exporters from the Cauca Valley region, but did not become involved in their businesses. After living in Miami for 6 months, he was recruited as a cook on a cruiser for tourists where he worked for two years. One of those tourists was a Dutch woman who brought him to the Netherlands. They married and lived for another two years in a small town. He recalls the period as a nightmare:

> "I was going dead there. I did not work, only received social security and completely depended on my wife's family. Sometimes I smoked, but I kept mostly clean. I left her because I needed some action."

His idea was to go back to Miami, but in Amsterdam he found his cousin Chino and his uncle Joel, who was a cocaine wholesale distributor. In fact, there were more *traquetos* in Tico's large family, some of them already dead. They suggested he stay and make some money by helping in the business. He then changed plans and remain in the Netherlands. He rebuilt a violent reputation by talking about his past in Colombia, carrying a knife everywhere, resuming his cocaine/crack habit and showing no sign of fear when working for Joel.

Tano also comes from Cali, but in contrast with Tico and Joel, he belongs to an upper middle class family. He came to the Netherlands following Chino: they were in search of adventure, fun and eventually a qualified job. They could not find the latter, but they found Joel who offered them food, a place to stay and eventually some work. Chino returned to Colombia rather soon after, but Tano stayed and met Tico. Tico and Tano became *parceros* (friends), forming in fact a good business team: Tano had charisma, Tico had the guts. Tano says of Tico:

> "I really feel safe with him. He should get the *flechas* [business lines] if Joel goes back to Colombia. But he should stop smoking that shit [crack]."

Tico about Tano:

> "People like him. He is still green, but people trust him. He gets whatever he wants."

Although Tico and Tano work for Joel, they often owe him money. They are heavy borrowers, they spend more than they earn, and they both sniff some of the cocaine they are occasionally supplied. They hardly survive with the money they make with Joel, which in fact pays very well: € 100 for a cash transfer of € 1,500 or for each kilo moved inside Amsterdam. Tico would have € 500 one day and only debts the day after.

Many of these helpers do not get enough money or excitement as flexible labourers and try to perform as distributors, constituting a sort of underclass amongst *traquetos*. Some of these people were dreamers, others exaggerated their power, and still others systematically complained about the business. However, some jokes reflected their awareness about their lower status. In Amsterdam, some of these people would gather and ask each other if they had already applied for membership to the *ASOTRAPO*, a fictitious *Asociación de Traquetos Pobres* (Association of Poor *Traquetos*) that would protect their interests as a trade union.[28]

Things were not easy for these 'poor' *traquetos*. They were usually promised much more than they actually got. If they got cocaine to sell, they had to be very careful. Tano:

> "In that Brazilian bar a Dutch guy asked me for two kilos. He said that he had cancer and that he badly needed the money. I did not phone him; I believe he was a *tira* (police)."

The irregular nature of distribution forced some of them to combine drug distribution with other illegal activities. Tano again:

> "Sometimes one can wait for months until a *cruce* appears. And what in the meantime? One can't wait and wait. Stealing is more secure, there are less profits but at least they are regular."

Indeed, these poor *traquetos* had many contacts with a number of Colombian thieves active in three modalities of robbery: burglars in large and small cities (*apartamenteros*), armed robbery of specific targets (*quietos*), and various methods of shop-lifting (*escapes, raponeo,* and so forth). Stars amongst these thieves were the *bambero* (jewellery traders) hunters. They worked in groups of three people, renting cars and going after jewellery and diamond dealers who had to move their merchandise by car. Either using tricks or force, they managed to steal a valuable loot that was later sold in major cities.

---

28 *'Trapo'* in Colombian slang means low quality clothing.

Second generation traquetos

Although *traquetos* in the Netherlands are first generation Colombian adults who keep contact with their country, I found, especially in The Hague, a small group of second generation teenagers somewhat close to the cocaine business. They are usually not truly involved, but some of them take the risk of becoming helpers or the victims of physical violence. As I explained before, most Colombian teenagers are rather assimilated, but although they do not hang out at telephone centres or prostitution streets many are indeed regular visitors of the same salsa discotheques and restaurants frequented by *traquetos*. Some follow their example as role models, and just try to imitate them regarding appearance, language and behaviour. However, they seem to restrict these performances to the realm of leisure time. Even when they have nothing to do with cocaine dealing, they enjoy playing the *traqueto* when they go out together.

The boys dress conspicuously, like to show their dance skills, restrict drug consumption to alcohol, and try to be seen as cool, generous and eventually violent. The girls play their part by dressing sexily, receiving lifts, being invited and eventually becoming the objects of dispute amongst the boys. Interestingly, some of the fights or shootings taking place in Colombian salsa bars or restaurants have these youngsters as protagonists.

Relations with *traquetos* are more often mediated through friends and acquaintances than through kinship. Cocaine dealers actually try to protect their own families – and especially children – by excluding them from any business activity. However, this protection does not take place with other's children or teenage sons. Paisita, for example, liked to tell Simona when her little boy started to cry, that she should not comfort him and that he "should learn to become a *traqueto*" (*que aprenda a hacerse traqueto*).

In general, *traquetos* have not tried to target these teenagers as useful recruits: they are considered either troublemakers, too assimilated to accept unskilled risky little jobs or too young to provide contacts, business opportunities and local infrastructure.[29]

Operational problems and daily routines: the 'apartacho'

Colombian distributors use flats or apartments to live, conceal drugs, and socialise with their helpers and friends. These *apartachos* are often provided by another Colombian, and in many cases, they are normal social housing in populated neighbourhoods. The most vulnerable ones are close to the prostitution streets, and are frequented daily by all sorts of people including prostitutes, thieves and drug dealers. Others are much better situated and less noticeable, like Simona's place for example.

They are far from being work offices or permanent warehouses. For most of the time, nothing (illegal) happens in these *apartachos*. People come and go, gather there to listen music, to watch TV or to eat together. At Simona's flat, there was a great

---

29 This situation differs from the one in the US, where some of these second generation Colombians are already adults and Colombian networks are very active in local distribution.

deal of waiting: helpers would stay there waiting instructions from the *traqueto* or for a shipment still to arrive. In these periods, Joel tolerated a degree of relaxation: friends would visit the place and stay overnight and some of his helpers would regularly invite prostitutes. They would also cook Colombian food for many people. Things were quieter if there was some business to do or some cocaine to stash. However, by no means did the place remain closed to trusted outsiders.

Cocaine stash in these *apartachos* is only a matter of few hours or a couple of days, since having the *aparatos* (cocaine kilograms) close is considered by everybody as a very dangerous business.

Favoured by other traquetos

Trusted helpers sometimes had the chance of becoming salesmen on commission. Tano, for example, knew everything about kilo prices since he was occasionally supplied kilo quantities to sell, either getting a fixed € 500 guilders per kilo sold, or everything above a certain price. He always complained about competitors:

> "I just met an Algerian who was offering the kilo at 48 points [€ 24,000] brought from North Africa. We were shocked because it's a good price. At the moment, the competition is very high."

It is thus possible for helpers or even newcomers to become wholesale distributors if they manage to know an importer or another distributor. Several informants report that they have been approached by Colombians in language schools and proposed a deal. Silvio:

> "His offer was: I give you 1 kg or ½ kg and you give me the money as you sell it."

However, the following case illustrates the weak situation of these dealers, who often have to rely on too many favours to survive in business.

Manolo once received a Colombian young man from Cali, an acquaintance of his brother in law, who arrived to the Netherlands to try his luck. Manolo remembers him as an upstanding and extremely polite person. He told Manolo he would try to find something in his former activity: gold export-import. He then stayed in his house in Rotterdam for about two months in perfect and cordial terms. One day he disappeared for a couple of nights. A friend of Manolo saw him hanging out in a night-bar especially frequented by Colombian illegal entrepreneurs. He was handling quite a lot of money, and was clearly involved in cocaine dealing. Manolo heard the story and threw him out of his house. The man did not resent Manolo's decision, and left. In the meantime, the Colombian had already brought his wife and son to the Netherlands. Manolo:

> "I did not want any problem with the police, and he lied to me. (...) He was very stupid. He could have stayed clean because he finally got a job in an oil platform, and he could have obtained a work permit. It was all a big decoy! No gold, but cocaine... He wasn't honest with me; he could have brought me problems. My brother in law is angry with him, see, he feels guilty for having recommended him to me."

Manolo's friend came to the Netherlands to distribute cocaine, everything else was secondary. He worked with somebody connected with Colombian importers. They both received cocaine loads to sell for a mark-up. As partners, they usually shared profits, but in one specific operation, Manolo's friend made the mistake of keeping the assigned load for himself only. When his partner found out, he just denounced him to the police. He was finally detained and imprisoned.

6.2 RETAILING COCAINE

A final market level to be considered is the local retail of cocaine, which of course involves several methods regarding quantities, qualities and social settings involved. Cocaine retail is a truly local business. Wholesale cocaine distribution still involves many foreign buyers since most cocaine marketed in the Netherlands goes through to other European countries. Retail, on the contrary, is a localised operation involving local dealers and consumers, who often belong to the same social or ethnic groups.

The question now is to assess the participation of Colombians in this local trade. To put it in simple terms: if their involvement in wholesale distribution is highly problematic, their engagement in retail selling is almost insignificant within the multi-ethnic range of cocaine retailers active in the Netherlands. Cocaine retail is performed by a countless crowd of individuals or small groups of all nationalities, with a noticeable participation of Dutch, Surinamese and Moroccan dealers, and is spread along various urban settings and consumers.

Away from the streets
Colombians are completely absent from street dealing in major cities. All informants agreed that there is no need for a Colombian who wants to participate in the business of taking the risk of performing as a street *jibaro* (drug pusher). These people are vulnerable and have a fluid contact with the police, often being drug addicts themselves. A Colombian informant explained that

> "If a Moroccan is selling dope, fine. If we would be standing here [Damstraat, Amsterdam], they would start looking for Pablo Escobar."

In fact, nobody wants to see Colombians on the Dutch streets. The police, because they fear an increase of violence and a loss of control. Other retailers, because they fear unfair competition from Colombian dealers who are ready to 'give away' excellent cocaine quality at bargain prices. Finally, Colombian *traquetos*, who do not dare to jeopardise their safer position as importers or wholesale distributors by supplying or having direct contact with these risky types of dealers.

Nor do Colombians retail drugs around the *Latino* prostitution areas or streets.[30] All drug retailers I found close to Colombian prostitutes were Dutch, Dominicans, Moroccans or Antilleans. However, Cabeza claims to have been offered something:

---

30 See chapter VIII for the relation between Colombian prostitutes and drug dealers.

"They know I work here, that I know many women and clients, some young Dutch or Moroccan teenagers. A *paisano* [Colombian] offered me many *cuadritos* [cocaine balls up to 1 gram] to distribute here. I am and want to remain *sano* [clean], I don't want to mess things up, because the *tombos* [police] regularly clean the street, and they go for drug dealers and illegal prostitutes. I tell you, you won't find Colombians selling like these Dominicans."

Bart is a native Dutchman who makes a living as drug retailer in inner Amsterdam. He has been selling, for the last 7 years, cocaine and *trip* (LSD) to consumers both on the street and in coffee-shops or bars, and sells his modest marihuana yield to one specific coffee-shop. Many of his clients are tourists. He insists:

"I have seen all sort of people selling coke [at retail level]: addicts, students, old folks, white Dutchmen, Surinamese, Moroccans, you name it. You hardly see Latin Americans on the streets or in coffee-shops. I only know some Peruvians, pretty known in the city, eh. They are just surviving here; they also live in squats. I think they make it in the old way. They go to Peru and bring back small quantities. They sell them directly with no people in between."

If he knows very little about his own competitors, he hardly knows anything about higher levels of the cocaine business: he does not have a single contact with Colombians, and has no idea about import and wholesale distribution.

There are also no Colombians selling cocaine as house dealers, neither by appointment in well reputed flats for middle and upper class users, nor in the so called *drugpanden* (drug buildings) supplying junkies and drug tourists. I found however a case in which two Colombians sold quantities up to 300 grams to drug tourists for € 20 per gram, who would retail the cocaine at better prices in Paris, the *Ruhr* region and smaller German cities. They did so by smuggling the modest amounts per train, using a method described as 'rail trade' (OGD 1996a: 65-66).

How far from traquetos?
There are other situations as well, in which Colombians sell small amounts of cocaine either to final consumers or retailers.

On the one hand, some Colombian men are often pushed or asked by potential consumers about cocaine. Especially for non-problematic consumers buying quality and larger quantities, to buy directly from a Colombian is seen as an exceptional opportunity. They are seen as closer to the source, so their merchandise is thought to keep original purity levels. Moreover, I noticed that some cocaine consumers in the Netherlands would find it glamorous to have a – rare – Colombian supplier. I found situations in which Colombians not related to the cocaine business liked to 'flirt' with cocaine users, playing a game that enhanced the status of both.

Moreover, street pushers are aware of this situation. During fieldwork in Amsterdam, I was chatting on the street with two Colombian distributors. A Moroccan street dealer approached us and offered cocaine claiming he was Colombian. He had to laugh when the Colombians asked him exactly where in Colombia he came from.

On the other hand, it is also clear that many Colombian importers and wholesalers, especially those handling smaller quantities, always keep some amounts available for either personal consumption or their social circle. In the same fashion as helpers or flexible amateurs who manage to get kilo quantities from *traquetos* to sell on commission, some cocaine trickled to be consumed, given away or traded in gram quantities in bars, coffee-shops or inside some *Latino* circuits.

These people are usually men and tend to be very erratic suppliers rather than professional retailers. They completely depend on a *traqueto* favour and on a particular demand from close people in special settings.

Bars and coffee-shops

In this way, I found few cases of Colombians who sold quantities between 100 grams and 500 grams to (especially foreign) customers of Dutch bars and coffee-shops. In December 1999, for example, the police found 218 ecstasy pills, 300 grams cocaine and a weapon in a bar near the Amsterdam's Rembrantplein. The bar's owner, a DJ, a house dealer and a 25 years old Colombian were detained and later prosecuted.

Tano, Chino and Lupo, sometimes involved in wholesale distribution, were occasionally engaged in retailing cocaine in a couple of bars. However, most of them were once-off transactions and none of them established a clientele or a supply line. They regarded these dealings as mere *rebusques* (hustles, informal activities) in a broader picture. They sold gram quantities while waiting for other jobs in larger operations or while trading other goods.

The paquete: gram distribution inside the Latino salsa circuit

Most cocaine retail in Colombian hands is restricted to circulate within what can be broadly defined as the 'recreational *Latino* market': salsa discotheques, concerts and schools, Brazilian bars, and some other private and public parties and entertainment events. In some of these places, it is not rare to find cocaine consumed by dealers, customers or musicians, discreetly traded in toilets or even openly offered in public. However, not every discotheque or event has the same level of cocaine dealing and use.

For example, in truly Colombian places like *El Caleño* in Amsterdam or *El Llano Bar* in The Hague, with a rather homogeneous ethnic clientele (*Latinos*) and a worse reputation (more presence of *traquetos* and prostitutes), cocaine retail and consumption is less evident and open than in other discotheques and salsa parties. On the contrary, it is easier to find cocaine in more fashionable and established places of the Salsa circuit, with a more mixed clientele of Latin Americans, Dutch and other ethnic minorities. In well known and reputed places in Rotterdam, The Hague and Amsterdam, cocaine finds its way in through security doormen, regular habitués or sporadic retailers.

As a rule, it can be argued that cocaine will be more easily found in places not run or owned by Latin Americans, with a live salsa band playing, and with an ethnically mixed clientele. These – larger – discotheques have better security systems, personnel and controls, which paradoxically allow for more toleration. Silvio, a Latin American salsa musician living and working in Amsterdam for some years, explains:

"...In that place there was a DJ, a policeman himself, married with a Colombian woman, and he seemed to tolerate it if the thing was discreet and did not go out of limits. You should see it by yourself... Of course, people take care. For example, those two brothers going every night to deal cocaine, they only carry small amounts just in case, all night long going out and returning with more. Famous guys, people around here know them very well."

Most of this trade is tolerated but rarely involves the owners or organisers. It is wiser, safer and more profitable for owners, managers and personnel to turn a blind eye or to keep a distance and play a regulatory role. They channel information between clients, dealers and authorities, and they change controls and rules according to several factors. 'Salsa dealers' are left alone unless the police target the place for unwelcome controls, unknown drug dealers appear or drug users cross the line. Further, the danger of violence and personal fights that can damage the place's reputation, the change in clientele profile or the organisation of special nights with unusual profits can also influence the local toleration towards cocaine dealing.

Lupo, for example, used to retail in a Brazilian bar in Amsterdam where cocaine use was a common feature. Another Colombian openly offered cocaine at a big Colombian event organised by a major Amsterdam concert hall:

"I just arrived from the *platanal* [Colombia] with good *perico*. Who wants to try?"

The cocaine offered by these Colombians is usually of excellent quality, commanding gram prices around € 45 in The Hague and € 50 in Amsterdam and Rotterdam.

Even in so called *lugares sanos* ('healthy' places) such as salsa schools that organise parties on weekly or monthly basis with live music, cocaine is also present. In these cases, cocaine retail is not so overt and it is restricted to the people and friends around the musicians, who are often heavy users. Cocaine consumption amongst salsa musicians and their close ring is impressive. Regardless their origin, some salsa musicians are confronted with recreational cocaine use before and during the performance. For some, it can only mean a single *linea* or *pase* (line, fix) during the break. For others, it can rise up to 2 grams for the whole night. Even non-users are often offered the drug several times during the night. However, most seems to be recreational consumption for the occasion rather than the expression of a daily and heavier use.

Amongst *Latino* musicians, cocaine use is fairly open and widely accepted. Everybody knows whom the retailers and pushers are, but many users already bring their own cocaine already purchased elsewhere. Silvio:

"I don't use myself, but when we play I see cocaine all around. We receive a special treatment; you get free drinks but also special prices from people. They won't charge you a gram *f* 100 but *f* 80; they will give you a 'bonus' as courtesy or they will just give you some for free. When somebody gives me a *paquete* (package, ball with 1 gram cocaine) as a present, I give it to somebody else. People criticise me for doing that..."

These gifts are even more common in private Colombian salsa parties, especially when the organisers are cocaine entrepreneurs or people connected to them. Again Silvio:

> "They give everyone in the band a *paquete* and they tell us to ask for more when it's over."

In contrast with public parties, it is hard if not impossible to find there cocaine consumption or retail amongst the assistants. In many cases, the guests are families with children or mixed couples with no connection at all to the cocaine circuit. Meanwhile they eat, drink and dance, most are unaware that salsa musicians receive and sniff coke.

Crack

Finally, only in exceptional cases did the Colombian dealers have any contact with crack-cocaine, which *traquetos* do not regard as a recreational drug and stigmatise as a substance for dropouts.

One of these cases was Tico. He loved crack, and he would go to the streets around the Amsterdam Central Station to buy anything offered to him, sometimes spending up to € 250 in a single day. His friends could never understand this behaviour, since he had easy access to the most pure and white cocaine one can find in Amsterdam. Tico:

> "I don't know. I want to be high and if I have the money, I spend it."

I found also a case in which a Colombian dealer in Amsterdam imported 50 grams of *basuco* for personal consumption and for his closest friends. Colombian *basuco* – cocaine base mixed with tobacco – and European crack are comparable substances in use patterns and effects, and some *traquetos* have smoked it in Colombia. People around were rather surprised about the unusual import. Tano:

> "Who the hell dares to get *basuco* from Colombia to the Netherlands!? He's really out of his mind. It was blown very soon; there are some *sopladores* [*basuco* smokers] around here… [laughs]."

However, the operation was exceptional, a nice surprise for friends that both celebrated their Colombian identity and strengthened his status as drug dealer.

6.3 CLOSING REMARKS

This chapter and the previous one have described the nature and extent of the Colombian participation in cocaine transport, import, distribution and retail selling in the Netherlands. They have made clear that a small but heterogeneous group of Colombians from various geographical, social and ethnic origins is involved in the cocaine business in the Netherlands. Many of them do not even live in the Netherlands, but are only there to perform specific tasks or activities related to the business. Tasks, risks and skills required differ in a great deal, and chances to fail or succeed are very distinct regarding level of involvement, legal status, degree of organisation, and overlap with legal structures and arrangements.

From transport to retail selling, I identified several types of Colombian entrepreneurs and employees who interact in flexible ways. Cocaine transport is performed by Colombian *mulas, boleros, niñeras,* professional smugglers and *tripulantes,* all of them employed by exporters and importers to 'crown' shipments through different modalities and routes. These couriers do not tend to live in the Netherlands and share such a risky job with less conspicuous couriers recruited from many countries.

Cocaine import is organised by four sorts of *traquetos*: envoys, line owners, mixed couples and adventurers. They are again heterogeneous regarding social prestige, vulnerability, infrastructure and connections with exporters, non Colombian importers and other Colombian migrants. Around these entrepreneurs, a number of Colombians are employed or subcontracted to perform important tasks: unloading, internal transport, load-keeping, security and logistic help as hosts, chauffeurs, translators and telephone operators. Although Colombian importers and their helpers have been very active and noticeable in the Netherlands over the past 10 years, they have a subordinate position regarding better positioned Dutch importers.

Colombians have also been involved in wholesale distribution in the Netherlands. However, their position at this level is weak and disadvantaged. I found three types of distributors: conspicuous traders, discreet professionals and flexible amateurs. They also rely on various Colombian helpers even less skilled than those linked to direct import tasks.

Finally, very few Colombians are engaged in retail selling, acting as 'salsa dealers' within the recreational *Latino* circuit.

It is mainly around this circuit where all sorts of *traquetos* also interact with another particular group of Colombians: women working in the prostitution. The next chapter will be devoted to exploring the involvement of Colombian prostitutes and illegal immigrants in the cocaine business.

CHAPTER VII

BAD REPUTATIONS

Cocaine, Prostitution and Illegal Immigrants

"In general, the tendency for a stigma to spread from the stigmatised
individual to his close connections provides a reason why such relations
tend either to be avoided or to be terminated, where existing."

E. Goffman, *Stigma*

"I tell people I'm Spanish."

Germán

During my fieldwork in the Netherlands, I came across many settings in which I could
find both Colombian cocaine dealers and prostitutes. In some cases, they were friends
or acquaintances. In others, they happened to know the same people or use the same
services. They met on the street, at church, budget telephone centres or salsa bars.
They even seemed to help each other. These clues could have led one to consider
these two heavily stigmatised groups of Colombian migrants as a unified ethnic
'underground pool'. Wilma, working for the Amsterdam police, had few doubts:

"It's logical that prostitutes and dealers are connected. It is a simple, evident matter."

The fact that some of these people were illegal immigrants increased the temptation of
blending all 'illegalities' (Foucault 1979: 257) together under the banner of
Colombian vice. However, a closer examination revealed a complex, contradictory
and often limited interconnection between all these Colombians with 'bad reputation'.

This chapter will analyse the relation and possible overlap of Colombian cocaine
dealers with other two groups of Colombian migrants: prostitutes and illegal residents
living and working in the areas of Amsterdam, The Hague and Rotterdam. By
focusing on their interaction and their views about the other groups, I will discuss
their chances of getting involved with, and their reasons for staying away from
cocaine dealers.

7.1 COLOMBIAN PROSTITUTES AND COCAINE

7.1.1 The Colombian prostitution circuit

By the end of the 1990s, between 2,000 and 5,000 Colombian women were working as prostitutes in the Netherlands.[1] They constitute not only a large group within the general Colombian community (I estimate between 15% and 30%),[2] but also, along with Dominican women, the largest group amongst Latin American prostitutes. Smaller numbers from Brazil, Ecuador – especially transsexuals and transvestites – Peru, Argentina and Mexico account for the rest. They concentrate in urban areas of *Zuid Holland* (The Hague, Rotterdam), *Noord Holland* (Amsterdam, Alkmaar, Haarlem) and *Noord Brabant* (Eindhoven), but they are also to be found in Nijmegen, Arnhem, Utrecht and even in smaller towns. Depending on the location, the local policies towards prostitution and their legal status as foreigners, they work in sex-clubs and brothels (Rotterdam and The Hague), windows[3] (red-light districts in Amsterdam and The Hague), private and farm-houses (small municipalities and rural areas) and on the streets (*tippel-* or tolerance-zones in Amsterdam and Rotterdam).

The first wave of women arrived in the Netherlands during the 1970s and early 1980s, following a first influx of women from South-east Asia. Since both groups were recruited by local proprietors keen to enlarge their sex establishments, many of those women arrived through intermediaries who arranged the trip. Other Colombian women, as most of Dominican women at that time, arrived via Panama or the Netherlands Antilles, where they were already working. Many married a Dutch man to make the move, obtaining the Dutch nationality fairly quickly. In general terms, this first generation tended to work in hotels, clubs and brothels under the strict supervision of pimps or sex entrepreneurs, often suffering exploitative conditions. They gradually became more experienced and independent, some eventually moving out from clubs to the windows of, for example, the *Poeldijksestraat* and the *Doubletstraat* in The Hague. In contrast with their Dominican colleagues and the women who later arrived from Africa (Ghana and Nigeria) and East Europe (Poland, Russia, Ukraine and the Czech Republic), this first generation of Colombian prostitutes usually managed to get rid of pimps and build a reputation of independent workers or self-employed.[4] Some came back to Colombia; others married local clients and left 'the life'; others still married their pimps or club managers and started to organise, in the Netherlands or Colombia, the recruitment of new women from Colombia. Finally, some remained active and are still to be seen, already in their forties, working and passing their long experience in the business to a younger

---

1   It is difficult to estimate their actual number since increasing repression against illegal prostitutes have forced them to hide or to move around in the Netherlands and Europe. Most informants in Latino institutions (churches and social services) talked about 2,000 or 3,000, while Polanía and Janssen (1998: 20) put it up to 5,000, overstating also the percentages of women being trafficked.

2   See chapter IV.

3   Window prostitution represents maybe 20% of the total supply in the Netherlands and is particularly popular amongst foreign prostitutes. It consists of a room with a window looking out to the street or corridor, where a woman dressed in lingerie attracts the potential customers. The prostitute pays for the window between US$ 50 and US$ 75 per day for 8 hours.

4   This image (and self-image) of Colombian prostitutes as rather 'entrepreneurial' was confirmed by every informant in the field including Colombian and Dominican prostitutes, social workers, religious leaders and all Colombians involved with the women. They usually contrast them with Dominican women, with a rural and much poorer background.

generation. Most of these women originally came from urban areas of the departments of Cundinamarca, Antioquia, Caldas, Risaralda, Quindío and the Cauca Valley.

Despite the fact that many of these women were followed by a stable chain migration of close friends and relatives, a new influx of Colombian women intensified during the second half of the 1990s. With fewer opportunities to arrange marriages or get legal permits, these very young women, some under-aged, come mainly from the Cauca Valley region – Cali and surroundings – with a striking number from towns like Palmira, El Cerrito, Pereira and Manizales. Most of them are illegal, and are often helped by the older generation.

From this second generation, some have a boyfriend in Colombia. Almost all have families there, and most have young children who they support through regular money remittances. They usually lie to them about their real source of income, and their families will very often pretend they believe them. Some of the jobs mentioned to cover-up their real profession are hairdresser, cleaner, baby-sitter, hotel employee or photo-model. Other women find a local partner in the Netherlands.

Many of these women have not worked in prostitution before and would prefer another job if they could get one in the Netherlands. Aurelia was a young prostitute from Cali working behind a window at the *Doubletstraat* in The Hague. I met her through Cabeza, one of the few men around that she respected as a true friend. She closed the curtain and offered us a cup of coffee:

> "This is temporary, I want something else, even cleaning is fine. The only thing I do not want is baby-sitting, children drive me crazy. I used to work in Cali as a salesgirl, and a good one, eh; maybe I can also sell things here. My sister comes next month and I am looking for a small place for both of us."

She seemed to have strong ethical problems with the job, but other Colombian prostitutes I came across in the same street were not so explicit about this. Some of them were already working as prostitutes in Colombia, and wanted to stay in business as long as they could save money and send it to Colombia.

Although most women come from lower or poor middle classes, most have completed elementary or secondary education. Cabeza explained what he thinks to be the main dividing line between prostitutes:

> "The big difference lays in education. Those who studied and have some idea to progress in life, to go further, in general they suffer a lot and they do it only for a period. Others never studied, and they keep staying until they are too old. See, they like that life, they have no problem in saying that they are prostitutes."

Jessica was a nurse in her country and came to the Netherlands thinking that her diploma would be validated here. She also had intended to go further with her studies and training. However, she desperately needed money for her sister, and ended up working in a window. She pays US$ 40 for the room per (8 hour) day, the owner making some US$ 100 per room every day. Many of these rooms are not well kept.

Illegal prostitutes show a high degree of mobility. Some work during some months, spending the rest in Colombia. Others move through different European countries, especially Germany, Switzerland and Spain. Marga:

"Many women go around Europe. They know when it is better to work in each place. Some regard the Netherlands as a relaxed holiday, you see, less money but much better conditions."

They also move around several cities in the Netherlands, either looking for better profits in certain districts or escaping from police raids or exploitative pimps. I further found Colombian prostitutes who exchanged their posts or replaced each other.

Colombian prostitutes were often seen as market spoilers, working for lower rates or without condoms, working longer hours, and accepting unhealthy working conditions. Many women in The Hague accepted work for US$ 12,50, a rate far below the US$ 20 – US$ 25 asked in Amsterdam. In some cases, they needed the first 4 clients to pay their daily expenses, making profits only with the customers thereafter.

Profits varied a great deal regarding individual cases. They ranged from women that after a couple of years managed to buy one or two houses in their Colombian hometown, to those who hardly accumulated anything. Some even worsened their financial situation after contracting debts that they could not pay off. In general terms, they earned far above their potential average income in Colombia. Many sent regular remittances and gifts and spent Christmas and New Year in Colombia.

Cintia comes from a little village near Manizales, and works as an illegal prostitute in the *Poeldijksestraat* in The Hague. She stays only 8 months in the Netherlands, where she rents a room near the two prostitution streets. The rest of the time she spends in her Colombian hometown with her two small children. As a single mother, the children have to live with their grandmother when she is working in the Netherlands.

"I send money to support my mother and my children, I bought a house for them. You see, it is bad here, but they eat well and wear good clothes."

Cintia is in her late twenties and claims that she knows the 'life'. She seems to enjoy dealing and playing games with her clients. Leticia confirms the claim:

"You should see her talking to those Dutch teenagers, making fun out of them. Cintia likes the job, you see, she got used to it. Only thinking about making more and more money, and the rest is not so important. She is the type of girl that searches for a rich man."

Traffic in women

All Colombian women experienced at least one of three forms of traffic and pimping, which included different degrees of coercion, intimidation and exploitation.

The most common form of trafficking involves intermediaries who recruit women and arrange their ticket and initial accommodation. Despite golden promises, misinformation and lack of certainty about working conditions, the women know that they go to work in prostitution. These recruitment groups are usually small, operate on local basis – explaining the presence of many women from one small place – and heavily rely on family ties for promotion and recruitment. The typical procedure is as follows: a person in Colombia, usually a woman, selects some women willing to go to the Netherlands to work as prostitutes. Most of them receive the offer or the information from friends or relatives, to whom they feel loyal and trustful. The selection is based on anatomic considerations and on their reliability to fulfil future obligations (family background, vulnerability, and so on). The informal contract is closed by taking a shark-debt of around US$ 7,500 to be paid as soon as possible with the initial job's earnings. Although not always explicitly stated, all women know that their relatives stay as a guarantee and can be physically harmed if they do not pay or play dirty. Once they have been selected, the person responsible in the Netherlands, usually a man, flies to Colombia and also gives his approval. He then arranges tickets and car transportation from different European airports. He provides them with a room (which they have to pay extra) and a working setting (a window, a brothel or a club), and ensures that they work. Since they are illegal residents, the man does not insure them if they are expelled in the meantime by the police. Expulsion will only mean a new debt added: he will take them back to the Netherlands for another US$ 7,500, and they will accept it as the only way to repay the accumulated loan. In some cases these mediators do little more than arrange tickets and a contact to phone. Once they have paid off the debt, they are considered independent.

Cintia, for example, paid US$ 7,000 to come to the Netherlands to a Spanish man who runs prostitutes from Colombia. The man was imprisoned there for a while, but was soon released since nobody wanted to press charges against him.

Secondly, though much less frequently than often thought, some women are deceitfully brought to the country. They are offered a job as a dancer or waitress by somebody who pays the ticket and is able to get them through the airport. Once there, they are forced to work in a brothel, club or window by taking their money and passport and threatening them.[5] This is not done overnight, but there are usually one or two weeks of 'adjustment' and slow psychological pressure (even from fellow women already working as prostitutes, often the first 'friends' they can rely on). Under strict supervision, she has to work for months or even a year to 'repay' the accumulated debts (ticket, new 'charges' for the guarantee and mediation, and the daily fee for food and accommodation which is comparable to that of a luxury hotel). She usually accepts this in the hope of better times and because she is not prepared to face a return in failure and shame. These trafficking groups are more distant from the women they recruit, involve closer links with local sex entrepreneurs and often have access to better infrastructure (false passports, corrupted officials, weapons, and so on).

A third form of exploitation refers to more traditional forms of pimping, which can be linked or independent from the former modalities of recruitment. Especially in

---

5   See some Colombian related cases in Stoop (1992); Altink (1993) and Polanía and Janssen (1998).

the beginning, owners or managers of sex clubs and brothels will receive between 20% and 50% of the woman's profits, providing basic protection, working facilities, and clients. Some independent women working in windows often had a 'friend' who helped them to keep an eye on the police, clients and the room owner, and promised them to take them out from the street. Often these men lived from the women's earnings. Finally, very few cases involving mixed couples – Colombian ex-prostitutes and Dutch sex entrepreneurs – integrated recruitment and pimping in a method according to which the woman was practically slaved.

However, in general terms, the trade and exploitation of Colombian prostitutes refers to the initial phase of their work in the Netherlands and it takes the shape of a cut-throat, though rather consensual informal contract. Undoubtedly, the threat of physical retaliation on relatives if contracts are broken is ever present, but in most cases it remains a tacit rule that is only spelled out when problems arise. Factually or symbolically, physical violence remains, as it was the case in cocaine dealing, as a powerful device to regulate and influence behaviour and choices.

Even for those women who feel exploited and victimised by traffickers, there are many good reasons for not pressing charges against them. Firstly, a lack of confidence in the local or Colombian authorities.[6] Secondly, they do not want to be expelled to Colombia. Thirdly, they fear the trafficker's retaliation against their relatives in Colombia. Fourthly, they usually do not want to accuse their friends or relatives who are involved even if they played dirty. Moreover, for other women, a denunciation would mean revealing the real nature of their job to their families. The fact that the women often know or suspect that they go to work in prostitution, make them feel guilty and regard the situation as their own fault.

Vulnerability
Colombian prostitutes complain a lot during their first working year. After that, they either quit in one way or another or they learn the tricks and skills essential to survive the hard reality of prostitution. They get acquainted with fellow women, they learn very essential words to live and work, they get used to the unknown window prostitution system, and they increase their experience in dealing with their clients. These processes are accelerated by three other circumstances: prior experience in prostitution under worse conditions, short-term economic success, and the ability to learn from older prostitutes about how to cope with the job.

In some cases they suffer severe physical problems. They range from physical abuse from clients or boyfriends, sexual diseases, muscular and respiratory disorders, to major complications from ill-treated or ignored existing problems. This later situation has been indeed strengthened by the lack of adequate medical and social services available to them, especially for those with no legal residence permit.

For them, fear for expulsion is always present. Even during periods of relative

---

6   The Dutch police are primarily seen as 'illegal foreign hunters' and never as a possible ally. The judicial system is regarded as unjust, in practice more ready to punish their own work rather than the activities of serious criminals. As illegal residents, they feel they have no rights. Finally, they have even less trust in Colombian authorities who are either corrupt or unable to deliver justice.

calm, women are scared about possible police control and they often react in advance guided by the many rumours that circulate within the circuit. A woman in The Hague:

"The gossip is that on the 31 December there will be a *razzia* in the street, many have already received the letter. For those with no papers things are more and more difficult."

Cabeza has seen many other round-ups before, but regards them as pure 'make-up' operations with little effect in the medium and long run. Cintia also complaints about the regular police raids:

"It is ridiculous. I say, they throw the women out through the door, and they easily enter back through the window. They should give us permits to work and stay, temporary permits, for example for 6 months. They condemn many to live in fear and locked up, for example me, I don't go out very often."

Indeed, by the end of my fieldwork, many Colombian prostitutes had fled the Red Light Districts in Amsterdam or The Hague to work on the street or in private houses and brothels, both regarded less safe than the windows. Finally, some illegal prostitutes would wait 'hidden' in places near the official prostitution zones to be called up by other women or friends who perform as new mediators.

Despite the fact that some of them help each other in terms of accommodation and working facilities, they remain rather isolated and far from institutional frames.[7] Moreover, social exclusion is accompanied by several processes of stigmatisation. Dutch or European women feel contempt for them, claiming that they are unprofessional, dirty and work under the regular tariff. In turn, they accuse them for being selfish and consuming drugs. Colombian prostitutes also look down on Dominican and African prostitutes, feeling less exploited, ethnically distinct, more ambitious and better educated than them. Competition for clients or potential boyfriends can take a virulent form and often constitutes a source of conflict.

These women are further discriminated and discredited by other Colombian migrants. Consular authorities tend to ignore them or express their dissatisfaction. A former consul openly stated that these women were unworthy of being called Colombians. Some ex-prostitutes who stay in the Netherlands rearrange their social identity by changing their name and social environment and breaking with older relations. Other Colombian immigrant women from the same places and social

---

7   However, some women have regular contacts with Latino institutions from the Catholic church, especially *Casa Migrante Amsterdam* and the *Pastoral Latinoamericana Rotterdam*. Other institutions have also tried to help them or recruit them as clients: GG&GD (Health Service), *De Rode Draad* (Dutch union of prostitutes), *Stichting tegen Vrouwenhandel* (Foundation against Trafficking in Women), *Prostitutie Maatschappelijk Werk* (Social Work for Prostitution, Rotterdam), *Prostitution Project* in The Hague, *Foundation A. de Graaf, Funla, Foundation Esperanza, Salvation Army, Humanitas* or the International Organisation for Migration (IOM). Unfortunately, illegal Colombian prostitutes often have more contacts with the *vreemdelingenpolitie* (aliens police) than with any of those institutions.

backgrounds but who work, earning less, for example in cleaning, show more consideration and often have more links with them. However, they accuse them of excessive greed and shameful behaviour. Some complain about sharing some of the discredit faced by the prostitute. Sonia:

> "If I shop in this area [Haarlem], shopkeepers think that I work in the windows over there when I tell them I'm Colombian. One man started to make obscene remarks. I hate the fact that they believe you are a girl [prostitute]."

Better-off women – with legal status, a job and a Dutch partner – alternate between compassion and subtle disapproval, but tend to have little or no contact with the prostitution circuit. Even in church, they do not mix very much. Finally, Colombian men can afford a more comfortable position of 'wise' persons (Goffman 1968: 43), actually engaging in closer interaction with them as friends, partners, protectors, clients or service providers.

7.1.2 Colombians around the women

Colombian prostitutes are vulnerable and remain isolated from mainstream society, but they are not alone. Despite the stigmas attached to their profession and their illegal immigrant status, they are a large group occupying a significant niche and making enough profits to attract other Colombians to their social circle.

Indeed, while they send cash to Colombia, a substantial portion of their income remains in the Netherlands. Next to the money they pay to local operators and entrepreneurs – windows, clubs, and so forth – and the goods they buy locally – supermarkets, transport, accommodation, and so on – some of this income is re-distributed amongst other Colombians. They can either be relatives and friends supported by them, or people from whom they buy services and goods. A short list includes: children and unemployed relatives in the Netherlands, pimps, baby-sitters, window cleaners and administrators, cooks and food sellers, budget telephone operators, chauffeurs, restaurant and salsa disco owners, drug retailers, and even thieves and shoplifters from whom they buy clothes or jewellery.

Some of the women around the prostitutes are relatives or friends who either follow or precede them as immigrants. Some have lost their job or window, while others have just arrived and are looking for a place to start. The financial help ends as soon as a new job appears, and it is often reciprocated if things go the other way around.

If pimps, intermediaries or sex entrepreneurs are involved, they usually are ex-prostitutes and non-Colombian men. In some cases, these men are or were formally linked to them by convenience marriages, for which the women pay around US$ 5,000. In other cases, they just help them with daily things or keep an eye, for what they get financial support. Colombian Amparo from The Hague:

> "Yes, he is a sort of boyfriend. He had a job and keeps promising that he will take me out from here and take care. But he lost his job and now he is helping me here. You see

I have a [false] Spanish passport, but when the people from *extranjería* (aliens police) start controlling the street, he phones me and I hide inside. He also brings me food."

Clients

'Colombiana no chicha calichano' (Colombian women do not fuck Colombian men) is a saying that some of these women repeated to me in Amsterdam and The Hague. Their clients were predominantly Dutch, and especially in cities like The Hague, Turks and Moroccans.[8]

They all explained me that going to bed with Colombian men is an unnecessary source of problems: weak and delicate boundaries between partnership, friendship, kinship and commercial sex are broken, creating problems of rivalry or jealousy amongst the women. One woman explained:

"Many of us have families in Colombia. You don't know if he [the Colombian man] is the boyfriend or husband of a next-door girl, or from somebody you know!"

Moreover, some explicitly want to restrict all possible social embarrassment in their hometowns. One Argentinean prostitute did not want to talk with me because she was afraid that I could disclose her identity in Buenos Aires. In my opinion, many could only cope with prostitution as long as they kept some separation between work – usually referred to in negative terms as the 'other', the 'local', the source of pollution and shame – and social life – reserved for 'their own' as a place for expressing their identities as family members, as women, as *Latinas*, as Colombians, as *paisas*, and so forth. In this sense, the way in which many of these women talked about job details or referred to working conditions and clients did not differ very much from that of some 'straight' women about their local husbands. Many Colombian women preferred thus to deal with local clients, but to go to the restaurant, the salsa bar or the shopping mall with other Colombian women and men.

However, one woman acknowledged receiving Colombian customers, especially *traquetos* willing to pay well not only for sex but also for gifts and *rumba* (dance party):

"See, when he is around he has priority. He pays three times the normal price and he invites me to the restaurant."

Emilio also visited a young Colombian prostitute, but he felt uncomfortable about being 'a friend and a client' at the same time. Explicitly referring to *traquetos*, he further explained that:

---

8   Colombian prostitutes seem to diversify their clientele. Some established prostitutes are able to select, or better refuse, customers. Though difficult to generalise, they often repeat the following scheme: Dutch men are nice but dirty, unskilled for sex – making their work harder – and have a particular taste for 'perverted' practices. Turks and Moroccans, hardly distinguished under the banner of *'árabes'*, are quicker to handle but they are rude, sexist and not gentle. Surinamese and Antilleans are nice but they prefer either black or white women. Finally, *Latino* men ranged from 'totally unreliable', 'dangerous', 'unattractive' to the more positive 'romantic and generous' or 'friendly'.

"The *big guys* do not show up that much with the girls. They go with them, but do not stay in the street. These girls are more used to see Dominicans, Antilleans and Moroccans... and their Dutch managers and their friends."

Even if the men had friendly contacts with Colombian prostitutes, they often desired more 'exotic' local women. Many men vividly referred their experiences with Brazilian, Irish or Dutch prostitutes. Joel had many Colombian prostitutes around, but:

"I like Italian women, I don't know why. I often visit one when I go to the *Albert Cuyp straat*, I don't go to bed with Colombians and I do not go around the Red Light district."

Service and good providers

Colombian prostitutes attract to their environment other Colombians who make a living selling them particular goods and services. Many of them are young men with no residence permits, some with entire families living in the Netherlands. Since most of the goods and services sold are not illicit, their activities are mainly framed in the informal economy (Castells and Portes 1989). Some of these people, as I showed in chapters V and VI, also sell the same services to drug dealers, performing in this way important bridge functions between the drug and the prostitution circuits. They can function as intermediaries for social interaction, facilitating contacts, passing through messages, gossip, news, and so forth. When these services are spatially located, for example in the case of restaurants, discotheques or telephone centres, they bring together prostitutes and dealers around fundamental activities such as eating, calling abroad or having fun.

Many Colombian prostitutes are willing and ready to buy Colombian food on a daily basis. The few formalised Colombian restaurants in cities like Amsterdam and The Hague target a broader clientele,[9] so these women are supplied by a number of informal teams of cooks and food sellers who sell cheaper food, closer to home. While some cook at home and deliver the food to the window or brothel, others improvise temporary informal restaurants in some small flat near the area.

Solano and Jaime sell food in The Hague, making a basic living after long working hours. Jaime lived for a while in Russia, so he also sells *bandejas* (food trays) to Russian, Polish and Ukrainian women. He explains that:

"The competition is high, there are 4 groups selling food at the moment for lunch, each with two or three sellers. And for dinner is even worse, five or six groups. I have 6 established clients and the rest just knock on the windows and offer the food. (...) Sometimes I start at 9:00 and I finish at 23:00."

---

9   These restaurants, some 2 to 5 in each city, are relatively stable if they are not directly involved in drug trafficking. All sorts of Colombian migrants, including prostitutes, go there now and then. Since they are not next to the Latino prostitution streets and do not have delivery services, prostitutes only go there often at night, after or before working.

In Amsterdam, at least two informal restaurants run by Ecuadorian and Colombian women offer basic dishes mainly to prostitutes and *traquetos*. The Solano's brother and his stepson had a little kitchen just a few metres from one of the most crowded streets, and they both delivered and had a couple of tables were the women could eat. Cabeza, for example, learnt to cook in The Hague. He recalls:

> "I had just arrived and a nice woman who was cooking and selling food gave me a place to stay. In return, I worked for her cooking and delivering. In that way, I met the people here [in the prostitution street]."

Jaime has a couple of group pictures taken with prostitutes, but he tries to keep his home separated from 'the street': he is reluctant to talk about the issue at home and he never lets the women collect the food from his own place.

Some Colombian men also offer the women budget international telephone calls, much cheaper than if they would use their own phones. As explained before, they are usually short-lived illegal operators. While some develop closer ties with the women, others treat them as mere clients.

I also found Colombian men managing and cleaning windows for the room owners, and some women cleaning for the prostitutes. For many years, Cabeza was responsible for collecting the daily rent of eight windows in The Hague. He also had to clean the rooms, do the laundry, and solve daily problems related to the women. In return, he received from the Dutch owner a place to live upstairs and some US$ 450 a month. He had a good relationship with the women, but:

> "All are Colombians, Dominicans and Africans. In the beginning, I had more contact with them, but later I decided to restrict it. I don't belong to their world, and in fact I came here to study. I was very naïve to believe that I could just come and study here. Instead of doing a Master on food packaging, I am here cleaning windows amongst pimps. (…) With some *peladas* [girls] we talk about everything, I help them whenever I can. But many stay for a while and suddenly they disappear again."

He still remembered his first impression of the *Poeldijksestraat* in The Hague:

> "From Brussels we took the train to the Netherlands Spoor [The Hague] and we went straight to the street. I was shocked to see all that. Never saw something like that before. I could not even look or talk with the girls, I was really shy, but look at me now!"

Simona used to clean in different houses in Amsterdam. She knew many prostitutes from that period. In The Hague, a Colombian man known as *El Brujo* (The Witch), made a living by cleaning the windows from evil spirits. He claimed to be gifted, but all people around considered him a charlatan. After arrival, he used to frequent prostitution areas offering a wide range of services. He was first addressed by a Venezuelan prostitute with cancer. Later, many women went to see him when they considered that their window was *salada* (cursed):

"They feel that men do not look inside anymore, or they don't know why they have so few clients. They pay US$ 150 for the *arreglo del vidrio* (fixing the window)."

El Brujo cleaned up the windows in a ceremony that included the woman, a bucket with water and some small puppets. He did not perform 'white magic', and claimed that he only cured and never harmed people. When I left the field, he was starting to make lots of money, also travelling to Colombia with special assignments.

Other Colombians around the women offer them expensive transportation. A Dutch-Colombian couple from The Hague used their own car to transport Colombian prostitutes to/from Frankfurt and Brussels airports. They charge between US$ 200 and US$ 1,000 for the ride, and try to keep the number of journeys restricted. Although these Colombian *coyotes* are usually independent and work directly with the women, in some cases professional prostitute recruiters also approach them directly from Colombia. However, some do not see anything wrong in competing with serious train or flight companies.

For a while, Emilio travelled to Germany with a friend in his old small car to pick up Colombian prostitutes coming to the Netherlands:

"We just transported them to the Netherlands for some money, you see, no relation with traffic in women."

Prostitutes with children in the Netherlands also need somebody to look after them. Most of the baby-sitters around the women are Colombian friends or relatives. Emilio transported cash for both prostitutes and *traquetos* whenever he travelled back, also performing bridge functions between both activities.

As these women also spend money in clothes and jewellery for them and their relatives in Colombia, they are also approached by people – including Colombian thieves or shoplifters – who sell their merchandise at bargain prices, basically clothing, cosmetics, jewellery and home-appliances. Tano described how *apartamenteros* (burglars) and *bambero* thieves (people going after jewellery traders) in Amsterdam offer their loot for one third of their market value. Lupo himself use to knock on prostitute's doors with watches to sell. Emilio's ties with many Colombian prostitutes working in The Hague became more solid when he started to work for a Colombian woman who was selling clothing and jewellery to the prostitutes. The merchandise was stolen, but the woman kept on telling Emilio that she had imported it from Germany.

7.1.3 'We are just friends': settings for social interaction

Finally, a number of Colombians involved in drug dealing are to be seen around the women. However, in contrast with the former group, they tend to meet them far away from the brothels, windows or even prostitution streets.

Both prostitutes and *traquetos* frequent some Colombian bars and restaurants in major cities. They gather in separate or mixed groups, and spend above average on food and drinks. Though these places are usually not directly involved in cocaine trafficking, their presence is tolerated and their actual occupations are ignored. In fact, they often keep conversations at social level and do not discuss business matters between each other. Often, gossip about drugs and prostitution are delicately commented on by those not involved in those activities. A Colombian bar keeper in The Hague explained to me:

"I don't want to see this place *dañado* [damaged, spoiled by drugs] as it happened with *El Tamal*. I don't mind what people do for living if they are good people. Here we are just friends…"

This friendship is even more noticeable in *Latino* and Colombian salsa discotheques, around highly valued activities such as drinking, listening to music and dancing. Since many women work on Friday and Saturday nights, Sunday is their favourite day to visit the discotheque. Rotterdam, Amsterdam and The Hague always have one to three places where Colombian *traquetos* and prostitutes are amongst the most visible customers.[10] Neither *traquetos* nor prostitutes work there: they consider the discotheque simply as a place to have fun.

In some cases, their interaction goes beyond a casual encounter. In *Los Compadres*, for example, I met three young good looking Colombian prostitutes who did not dance and looked terribly bored. Every man around was staring at them, but none dared to invite them to the dancing floor. The reason for Cabeza was simple:

"One has a boyfriend in prison for cocaine. The other two entered earlier with some *traquetos*. These are now gone and do not seem to come back, but, you know, it is better to leave the girls alone."

Indeed, these women were treated as the untouchable property of absent people who were to be feared. In some other cases, they just exchanged greetings and went on with different groups. Some prostitutes – the older, more discreet and longer established – suggested that they avoided mixing with *traquetos* altogether. In fact, many of these *traquetos* were to be found accompanied by Dutch white women. On the contrary, few Colombian prostitutes were accompanied by possible Dutch friends or boyfriends.

In the smaller *El Llano Bar*, in the centre of The Hague, I could also find many prostitutes and *traquetos* having fun together. It was a place to go after everything else closed: it really started to get crowded after 4:00 AM. Despite the big sign inside forbidding the use of weapons, *El Llano Bar* was regularly closed down for periodical shootings in- or outside. It was referred by most Colombians as a *hueco* (hole) or *metedero* (a small place to get in), notions reserved for places with extremely bad

---

10 See chapter VI for different types of Colombian salsa discotheques. While *traquetos* and prostitutes visit all of them, they keep a lower profile in Dutch 'salsa-school' dominated environments. In more *Latino* or Colombian establishments such as *Los Compadres*, *El Llano Bar* (The Hague) or *El Caleño* (Amsterdam), they play a leading role by imposing their style, dressing up, spending money more conspicuously and often expressing their conflicts more openly.

reputation. Many young prostitutes, some clearly under-aged, enjoyed dancing together and avoided contact with the men.

In a less playful mood, Colombian prostitutes working in Amsterdam and Rotterdam are amongst the most regular visitors of Sunday's Spanish speaking Catholic masses. Father Wim:

> "They give more money than the others. You can see there has been a *razzia* only by counting the Sunday's donations… (laughs)."

Despite the fact that they usually leave the church rather soon, they still take the opportunity to chat with others, hear the latest news around the *Latino* circuit, find out about possible jobs or accommodation, or look for help regarding health, juridical and financial problems. After the service, some go out for a drink or a lunch with other Colombians, including *traquetos*.

Another meeting place are the many budget telephone centres widely used to call Colombia. In many cases, they function as a first contact point between newcomers, which further develops into a friendship at the discotheque or at home.

Finally, I found many cases in which Colombian prostitutes hung around *traqueto*'s flats. Andrea is a *caleña* from The Hague who has lived there for many years with her Dutch husband and 3 children. Showing me a picture, she told me about her sister:

> "She arrived on Monday, and she was on Wednesday working in an hotel [brothel]. She was doing fine, but soon after she was expelled to Colombia when the police raided a house and found those *pelados* [guys] with coca…she was there with them but she wasn't *untada* ['greased', involved], no, it was just bad luck she was there…or maybe she was lucky because two of them went to jail."

People like Paisita or Tico also knew some prostitutes who would visit them and engage in rather fluid and ambiguous relationships.

Exchange

Despite coming from the same regions, cities or even towns, prostitutes and *traquetos* are usually neither related by kinship nor belonging to the same social groups. Cocaine dealers belong to a much wider social spectrum than Colombian prostitutes, who can, in general, be considered to originate from a lower social stratum.

They consider each other's activities as different in nature. Cocaine dealers tend to grant the women a lower moral and social status, considering them very vulnerable, while prostitutes often have strong reservations against 'real criminals and addicts' and consider drugs to be a risky business. Moreover, they also know that both activities are subjected to a different social reaction. In three opportunities, for example, I met cases of drug dealing women who would pretend to be prostitutes to receive a milder label as exploited victims.

Of course, they have something in common: they are migrants from the same country who either make or try to make profits above the average by engaging in activities legally or morally questioned by others, including other Colombian migrants. However, this fact cannot overshadow the contrasts mentioned above and it is not enough to create a common identity.

In fact, both groups always stressed the fragile nature of their relationship. Prostitutes and drug dealers do not seek each other as members of a common, abstract 'criminal circuit' – spatially, socially or ethnically clustered – but primarily as the result of a material and symbolic exchange.

For the prostitute, a *traqueto* can represent at the same time a privileged source of money and wealth; a potential protection against other non-Colombian men around, including clients, employers and boyfriends; a certain social status in front of other women; and finally, in some cases, even a source of fun and pleasure in a highly hostile environment.

Cocaine in itself is out of the picture. Colombian prostitutes usually do not consume illegal drugs. Some have even strong moral opinions about them. Others, the younger ones, would smoke marihuana or take cocaine and amphetamines now and then. Heroin is of course far from their cultural repertoire. Whenever present, illegal drugs are provided by other women or by the many retailers around, including Dominican, Dutch or Moroccan dealers. Colombian *traquetos* are not sought for their merchandise.

Money, protection, social status and fun: four possible reasons to socialise with *traquetos*. Andrea's sister ended up working in a sex-club in Valencia, Spain. Somebody helped her to get a residence permit, and Andrea seemed positive about her:

"Her Colombian boyfriend was killed long time ago. She has many boyfriends in Spain, but she doesn't want a fixed one. They buy her many things, gifts and so. But not because she hunts for their money, eh, I think she just deserves it."

Cabeza was there and did not agree. He later said:

"No man, many of these women have a *pesos* sign in their eyes."

For the *traqueto*, the prostitute can also mean status and fun. While sex is often absent or a marginal part of the exchange, he can enlarge local social recognition by showing off with her at the restaurant, the shopping centre, and of course at the salsa discotheque. He can first show his financial capacity to her and to other people. Secondly, he can impress others by appearing as a local *mafioso*, seemingly controlling and consuming local resources, including 'his own' women. Further, while being close to prostitutes, some men can reinforce their male identities and behaviours. As objects of sexist jokes, for example, prostitutes are often present in their daily talks. Moreover, they reinforce some of their latent misogynist images about women. Miguel:

"In Cali we used to be around very expensive prostitutes. With all respect for your mother and your wife, women in this society have become an object to buy and sell, like a car."

And Chino:

> "At least these women have the honesty to make it as a profession. Many others pretend they are honest but they are also 'interested' in something material, not in your spiritual qualities."

Some *traquetos* also took pity on these women. Joel thought that these women suffer for being far from their country and their families, and especially in the hands of exploitative sex entrepreneurs, and he tried to help some of them whenever possible. Finally, in some cases, there is also room for sharing deeper emotions, or problematic situations and conflicts. Of course, a common background and a sense of common hardship can facilitate this intimacy. Again, this intimacy is extremely fragile. Whilst he was living in Amsterdam, Riverito had social contact with Colombian prostitutes. Once in prison, he remembered:

> "I knew a woman from Cali, but she never phoned or came to visit me. You know what? It is better in that way. If I phone her, it can mean trouble for her. Besides, I have enough problems myself to receive somebody that comes to tell you this and that. If somebody comes, I don't want to hear more problems."

7.1.4 Prostitutes & cocaine

There are also cases in which prostitutes take an active part in the cocaine business. I could not find prostitutes actively involved in drug smuggling. However, I was told about instances where *mulas* later turned to prostitution. One informant explained that:

> "They only think about money. If drugs are better, drugs. If prostitution is better, prostitution. They know each other, and these women can easily jump. Before, many poor desperate women were working as couriers. That is over now. But some women I knew from those days are now behind the windows."

Rather than showing integration, these cases evidence that prostitution is for some of these Colombian *mulas* an attractive, less risky and profitable alternative.

I also found cases of Colombian prostitutes receiving cocaine in the post. Willem:

> "I used to give language lessons to a Colombian woman, here in this street. I phoned her once and her son told me that she was in prison because she had received from Colombia a mail package with cocaine. Just a small quantity, but it was enough. The police had her telephone tapped, so she may have done it before. But it is the only case I know."

Other informants in The Hague referred similar cases: the prostitutes would use a friend or a boyfriend, usually an old Dutchman, who would unwittingly receive the package at his address. One prostitute told me however that neither the police nor their clients are so stupid to be fooled like that. In the only case she knew, the client was in fact the actual cocaine importer.

A less risky task that prostitutes can perform is carrying important messages between cocaine exporters and importers. They are usually not involved in the operation and limit themselves to handing over the message. A friend or acquaintance in the Netherlands would tell her to phone a person in Colombia who would give her a message for him. In some cases, they are completely unaware of the nature of the message, they are just doing it as an easy favour with no costs or consequences. The following story shows how these messengers can indeed get into trouble.

For two years, a Colombian woman was working as a prostitute in The Hague with varying fortunes. She went back to Colombia and soon after she decided to return to the Netherlands. Before leaving, somebody she did not know asked her to deliver a letter, a small piece of paper, to a friend in Amsterdam. In codified language, the message confirmed the precise arrival time and place of a cocaine shipment. She entered as a tourist through the Frankfurt Airport, where the German police asked her some questions, inspected her belongings, found the message and got suspicious. They eventually let her through, but probably discovered more than she thought and informed the Dutch and Belgium authorities about her and the possible shipment. Once in the Netherlands, she handed over the message with no further problems and stayed for another six months working as prostitute, this time in Amsterdam. In the meantime, the cocaine import operation, planned via Belgium, had to be postponed. The importers realised that the local police had a tip, which in fact matched with the information seen before by the German police. The prostitute, unaware about the situation, became the main – and only – suspect in the case.

The woman had earned enough from her job and decided to return to Colombia. In 1996, she was detained in Barajas while taking a flight. She spent one year in prison in Madrid before being extradited to Belgium for trial. Some people tried to help her from the Netherlands. A Dutch priest visited her in her Spanish prison, but restricted himself to his pastoral mission. The woman was finally extradited to Belgium, where she spent another year in remand. Due to the lack of evidence, she was finally released. Back in Amsterdam, she met a Spanish man with whom she married. The priest describes the wedding party in these terms:

"I was invited. I arrived there and looked around. The place was full of *mafiosi*, in every table there was at least one of these people! I later told her to stay away from them if she did not want to have more problems. She replied, apologising, that they were invited by those who organised the party, not by herself."

As frequent travellers, some prostitutes were also involved in cash transportation. They can do it as a favour or charge up to 5% if the quantity is large. However, smuggling cash is again a risky matter for these women. Germán:

"My wife's cousin has been working for years in The Hague. Two months ago, she went back to Colombia, only for holidays, and the second day she was robbed. They entered her house with guns, tied everybody up, and took the money. She said that there was only US$ 1,000, but I know that she had more than US$ 50,000 from other people."

In fact, Germán himself does not really believe her. She might have been robbed or might have faked everything to keep the money. Whatever the case, she is certainly in trouble with the man who sent the cash.

Cocaine importers and distributors also use prostitutes as flexible unskilled employees, for example to make cash transfer remittances. Both Joel and Blanca involved prostitutes for sending money to Colombia. More than a real engagement in the business, these women are in many cases friends and acquainted who do the job as a – returning – favour, as a once-off activity, or to gain the good will of a generous *traqueto*.

In one case, a woman was involved as wholesale distributor. Jaime:

> "Yes, I know a Colombian prostitute that was involved in distribution, kilo level. She maintained both things separated. I believe that prostitution was secondary for her. A sort of front-store."

Still another case of interwoveness between the prostitutes and *traquetos* can be found at street retail level. At the entrance of the *Doubletstraat* in The Hague, some Dominican dealers were retailing small quantities of cocaine and heroin, either by gram or by 1/5 gr. *balletjes* (small balls or packages). The police regularly raids the street, so some Dominican dealers used to keep small amounts of merchandise hidden by some prostitutes working nearby. In return, dealers would either give them money or gifts, and protect them if necessary. This practice, however, seemed to be restricted to Dominican retailers. Cabeza:

> "There is a huge difference between Colombian *traquetos* and these Dominican dealers around here. Colombians come, talk with the women but they don't stay nor sell drugs here. The Dominicans are a truly street gang, they are very violent, see, believe me, they controlled for a while the street, threatening, stealing and raping newly arrived Dominican women. I am glad the police finally intervened. Some girls convinced a woman to talk. Now the street is quiet, but you never know... Except for these Dominicans, drugs around here are not sold by *Latinos*."

Finally, prostitutes may also be involved in facilitating the arrival of *traquetos*. During a football match in Rotterdam Zuid, I met a *traqueto* who was living in Amsterdam. I was surprised to learn that his wife was a Colombian prostitute. Normally, the man would have suffered a loss of face, while the woman would have afforded to quit prostitution. Further inquiries in Amsterdam clarified the picture: she had the Dutch nationality and it was a marriage of convenience. They led separate lives, and only at a later stage did he actually become involved in drug dealing. In another case, a Colombian prostitute helped people from Mocho's group come to the Netherlands.

Weak business linkages
Almost every informant in the field stressed that these cases of collusion are exceptional: most prostitutes and *traquetos* regard and keep their respective businesses apart. Even when they come from the same places, have close social

contacts, buy goods or services from the same people and are generally stigmatised as part of the Colombian 'underground', their activities remain rather independent of each other. Many reasons explain this fact, some of which have been already suggested.

First of all, both activities imply different skills, risks, moral careers (Goffman 1968: 45) and legal frames. Cocaine import and distribution is illegal and prosecuted, it is very risky especially for roles and positions traditionally occupied by women, and requires differentiated skills such as a violent reputation, discretion and links with the legal economy or with powerful brokers. Prostitution, on the other hand, is tolerated (thus more controlled), it has different risks attached – health related, for example – and requires totally different skills of a physical and psychological nature.

These discrepancies are well acknowledged by both groups. Prostitutes, for example, know the risks of performing as *mulas* and they are not prepared to take them as long as they can work. Nor do they regard drug smuggling as a better alternative to prostitution. Many are truly scared of the drug business and the people involved in it.

Cocaine exporters also consider prostitutes to be extremely vulnerable at airports and borders. They are not only highly visible within their social environment, but also catch the eye of law enforcers and migration officers. Many are refused, detained for interrogation or carefully inspected before being allowed to continue their journeys. In general, *traquetos* treat these women as prostitutes and as such, too close to the police, too unreliable and 'interested', and too loud-mouthed.

Even for tasks as cash transportation they are often vulnerable and easy targets for robbery. Everybody knows and expects that they will return to Colombia with money. In many cases they publicly announce their departure and arrival, and it is commonplace for farewell or welcome parties to be organised. They also want to show off what they have achieved, by letting people know how much they earned, through wearing expensive clothes or giving gifts.

The fact that Colombians are not engaged in street drug retail – spatially and socially connected with prostitution areas, organised in smaller economic units, also tolerated, and so forth – also disables a daily link. On the street, many Colombian women are more exposed to Dominican, Moroccan or Dutch drug dealers. In addition, Colombian women do not tend to consume illegal hard drugs. On the contrary, they generally condemn people who *mete vicio* (take drugs).

One important reason for separation is the relatively independent status of Colombian prostitutes. As explained before, traffic in women exists, but is often limited to forms of intermediation and seldom involves sexual slavery. It can be stated that the less these women are trafficked and the less their activity is regulated by local illegal groups, the fewer the chances are of these women to getting involved in other illegal markets such as drug trafficking.

However, even in Colombian related cases of traffic in women, the overlap with the cocaine business is problematic. All informants tended to minimise the link. In some isolated cases, women traffickers also involved in cocaine trade would not mix the actual items traded (Altink 1993: 54). As a prostitute explained:

"Drug traffic is more risky than traffic in women. The competition is cut-throat and the chances for detection are bigger. For the pimps it is problematic if the police finds drugs by the women." (Altink 1993: 54).

The relative autonomy of both circuits is also enhanced by the lack of local *mafias* having a grasp on many illegal local markets. In this sense, Colombians have to talk with different people if they want to sell drugs or women in the Netherlands. The link from 'below' (through other Colombian immigrants or particular common settings) is not enough to connect the businesses. In this sense, the Dutch case contrasts with contexts such as Japan, also a well-known target for Colombian prostitutes and cocaine. Salazar (1993: 138-148) vividly describes, for the Japanese situation, how Colombians selling drugs or trafficking in women have to deal with local *Yakuza* groups. While these groups directly control prostitution, they also grant cocaine distributors a 'licence' to sell in their areas of influence. The *Yakuza* mediation, however, does not neutralise all the tensions explained for the Dutch case. Furthermore, prostitutes there seem to be scared about drugs and drug traffickers look down on the women, feeling disgust for the Japanese pimps and compassion for the women.

7.2 ILLEGAL IMMIGRANTS AND COCAINE

A second group that has been easily linked with cocaine traffic is that of illegal Colombian immigrants.[11] It is estimated that 3,000 to 4,000 Colombians live in the Netherlands without any residence or work permit.[12] As explained in chapter IV, these immigrants are mostly absorbed in the informal economy by a local demand for services such as prostitution, housecleaning or baby-sitting.

During my fieldwork, I had different levels of contact with more than 30 of these illegal immigrants. In some cases, I visited their relatives in Colombia, in other cases I shared their daily activities or leisure time, and in other cases I met them as 'clients' of one of the three Latino organisations for which I volunteered as a social or cultural worker. Interviews with legal immigrants and social operators who had contact with illegal residents were also an important source of knowledge. While I did not engage in quantitative sampling or analyse police dossiers, I believe this qualitative material can support cautious generalisations. In this sense, they can be coupled or contrasted with the conclusions of earlier research on the relationship between illegality and criminality in the Netherlands (Engbersen et al. 1995; Engbersen et al. 1999).

---

11 'Illegals' reject the use of the word as a noun, widely applied to them as if they *were illegals*. The lack of permits to live and work in the Netherlands is mainly experienced as a restriction – of social and economic rights, of future development, and so forth – and not so much as a state of being.

12 This is an unofficial estimation shared by people interviewed in Colombian related organisations, including *Casa Migrante, Colombia Komitee Nederland* and *Casa de América Latina* (Brussels). The calculation is based on both quantitative demographic developments of the legal Colombian population as well as on qualitative material gathered in their daily contact with illegal immigrants.

In chapters V and VI, I already demonstrated that while many of the Colombians engaged in the cocaine business in the Netherlands are well established migrants, others do not even have a fixed address in the Netherlands since they are only involved in a 'business or work trip'. I explained that certain roles and tasks are more likely to be taken by people with certain skills, gender, social capital and juridical status. Smugglers and 'envoys', for example, are unlikely to live in the Netherlands, while some importers or wholesalers have double nationality and many local contacts.

Still the question remains about the risks and opportunities for those Colombians who, having made it to the Netherlands, do not have a permit to stay and work, but who nevertheless remain as temporary or permanent immigrants. In this sense, I explicitly exclude from this group of illegal residents those persons who enter and leave the country as legal tourists (complying with visa requirements) or with false identities, for performing a specific task or job and with no intention of staying in the Netherlands. *Mulas* who arrive at Schiphol for the first or second time or 'businessmen' who sleep in expensive hotels, but actually live in their *fincas* in Colombia cannot be considered immigrants.

This final part of the chapter will be devoted to analysing why and how some illegal immigrants take part or refrain from participating in drug dealing.

7.2.1 Colombian illegal careers

In their study on illegal immigrants in Rotterdam, Engbersen et al. (1995: 94) identify four types of illegal careers: integrated, stationary, marginal and criminal. The first group, also known in the Netherlands as 'white illegals', are long established migrants, usually belonging to the larger ethnic minority groups, and have access to the formal labour market as well as to public services such as health and education. The second group have a stationary position, arrived after 1992, and do not have access to the formal labour market. They rely on informal jobs and on close social networks of relatives and friends. A third group can neither get formal or informal incomes, nor are they helped by their surrounding social network. They become homeless, keep changing addresses or rely heavily on the support of social, private or migrant organisations. They tend to belong to groups with no migration history in the Netherlands. Finally, a last group is also excluded from the formal labour market and engage, for various reasons, in different criminal activities of a predatory or entrepreneurial nature.

These careers are a result of various circumstances and factors that open and close opportunities to different groups.

A first factor refers to the nature and development of laws and policies regarding foreigners. After regularisation in 1975, restrictions for immigrants have only increased, not only expanding the number, but also deteriorating the situation of illegal immigrants. The access to formal labour markets and to basic social services has been blocked, for example, by the cancelling of tax numbers for illegal immigrants (1991), more punishment for employers (1992) or further exclusion from social services and institutions by the *Koppelingswet* in 1998 (Leun and Botman 1999). In this respect, the sustained group of Colombians arriving during the mid- and late 1990s is, as put by one of them, 'too late for the party'. While many earlier immigrants managed to get the Dutch nationality – especially through mixed marriages – newcomers have been increasingly forced into illegality. Policy changes regarding the restriction of political asylum did not affect the group: the Netherlands has always considered Colombia to be a democracy and neither in the 1970s nor in the 1980s were Colombians granted the status of political refugees. Furthermore, more work controls in formal factories or firms had a marginal effect: Colombians were already absent from formal primary labour markets or from their rather weak ethnic economy – in contrast with 'guest-workers' or 'ex-subjects'. It is uncertain whether the introduction of a tourist visa for Colombians in 1990 had any real effect on the flux of migrants: while it could have discouraged some potential visitors, the core of a chain migration was only about to start due to the establishment of earlier immigrants from the 1980s. Maybe more influential to their situation was the restriction on marriages imposed in 1994. Before then, an illegal immigrant who met a Dutch partner – and this used to be the case for many Colombian women – could immediately get married and obtain social benefits. The situation radically changed ever since, when complex obstacles were put in place to discourage such unions. Also important is the recent active policy against illegal prostitution in major municipalities. While it can have some effect in the long run, in the short term it has only increased the conditions for the exploitation and marginalisation of Colombian prostitutes.

A second factor is the formal and informal labour market open to the illegal immigrants. I have already outlined the various jobs available to Colombians, especially in the informal economy. While most of this labour force, except for prostitution, is tolerated, women still have a wider variety of opportunities than men.[13] Despite all the *razzias*, prostitution is still an important labour market targeted by Colombian women.

Illegal careers are, in the third place, influenced by the group's access to public and institutional services such as education, health, housing and social security. Illegal Colombian immigrants are entitled to none of these rights. They usually pay between 50% and 100% more than legal residents for the rent, and get no social benefits. Many however manage to send their children to primary school (where they are again tolerated) and find a hospital or a kind-hearted doctor ready to treat their most simple complaints.

Another important element to assess the chances of illegal newcomers is their access to social, cultural and financial capital from their own migrant groups. Illegal Colombian immigrants cannot rely on a rather weak ethnic economy to survive. As explained in chapter IV, the Colombian 'community' is dispersed, heterogeneous and unorganised. There are even tensions between different groups, and many legal

---

13 These informal markets are tolerated as long as they remain invisible and have a positive effect on the economy. Illegal immigrants selling T-shirts on the street would be immediately removed and deported, but those cleaning or baby-sitting in private houses can work and not be hassled. The former would be incurring 'unfair competition', the latter would be 'helping to solve a labour force shortage in a context of economic growth' (as posed by economic policy makers).

immigrants (including prostitutes) try to put some distance from the less fortunate. However, most people have some better-off relative or friend from whom they can eventually get financial help, accommodation, tips about jobs or actual contacts to get one. Moreover, most immigrants have completed primary and secondary school, and in many instances some sort of superior education.

Finally, an important factor is the access to specific illegal activities. Colombians, as explained before, have a potential advantage in *some* levels and tasks within the cocaine business.

These elements combined explain why illegal Colombian immigrants present neither 'integrated' not 'marginal' careers. There are no 'white illegals' amongst Colombians, since all of them arrived during the 1990s. Earlier illegal immigrants usually became citizens by marrying a Dutch partner, not by working in Dutch factories or enterprises. Illegal immigrants are excluded from the formal labour market. On the other hand, illegal Colombian immigrants do not tend to 'marginalise'. No matter how difficult the situation would be, they usually show excellent skills for survival. They proudly see themselves as entrepreneurial and creative, with mottos such as '*colombiano no se vara*' (A Colombian does not get stuck) or '*verraco*' (die hard). Some have irregular contacts with private or migrant social institutions (some prostitutes, women with many children, inmates, and so forth), but they only make use of them when needed and do not develop structural dependencies. Most of them have relatives or friends both in the Netherlands and Colombia that prevent them from 'dropping out'. Alcohol consumption (drug dependency is practically non-existent) is also canalised as accepted behaviour and not a source for ostracism. Most people I met preferred to turn back to Colombia than to become a '*desechable*' (in Colombia, a disposable, a throwaway) in the Netherlands. While most of them developed 'stationary' careers (including most of the illegal prostitutes), some had the opportunity to get involved in *some* criminal activities.

7.2.2 Selectivity and specialisation

Illegal Colombian immigrants have very differentiated contacts with the police. Most cases I came across of illegal Colombians detained or deported by the police were prostitutes, people involved in cocaine traffic or people suspected of having links with both circuits. Prostitutes were regularly expelled after *razzias*, simply worsening their debts and pushing them to return. Illegal *traquetos*, when caught, regarded expulsion as a safe way out and not as a punishment. A *traqueto* once told me in a joking mood that if they really wanted to deter people they should forbid them to return to Colombia. Solano was expelled only once in 5 years:

> "The police knew our faces, we hung around the prostitution streets the whole day selling food. They always suspect you are a dealer, of course. They had asked for my passport many times but were not very pushy, so I kept telling them that I forgot it at home and that I would have it ready the day after. I was finally detained, and I remained in Scheveningen for a week before they threw me out. I was back two months later."

In few other cases, they were caught crossing borders, stealing something or travelling in public transport without a valid ticket. Marta and Horacio were both expelled on two different occasions after they jumped a red light with their scooter. Montes was caught in a supermarket stealing food, but could not be deported since they could not find out his real identity. Finally, Solano's wife was caught while returning from Germany by car.

In 1995, some 88 illegal Colombian immigrants were detained in the 4 major cities (Engbersen et al. 1999: 275). Following their estimations, this suggests a group with slightly less contact with the police than average.[14]

Most illegal immigrants I met had no contact with the police. Some were 'left alone' even after two or three encounters with them in the context of accidents, street controls or after being the victim of a criminal offence. People living in smaller municipalities or towns, those cleaning or baby-sitting in private houses, or those dependent on legal relatives or friends also had little or no contact with law enforcers. Furthermore, employees of 'non-ethnic' small businesses were never controlled. The police explicitly told Tano, involved in an incident in which a friend drowned, that it was the dead body and not their illegal status that actually mattered to them. He was even escorted home in a police car. Jaime also recalls one of his encounters with the police:

> "The man who rented us the former apartment happened to be a drug dealer. We didn't know, but one day the police knocked the door looking for him. Thanks God they were not interested in us. I wasn't there and maybe they saw the children, who knows. It can also be that they were only looking for that specific man. But we were scared and we left immediately."

On a second occasion, Jaime was burgled and the police limited their intervention to the routine procedures. I did not meet any case of illegal work controls, I suspect mainly due to the sort of jobs Colombians perform as informal service providers or domestic self-employed. However, these illegal immigrants feared the police and in many cases tried to minimise exposure. Germán, for example, once told me that:

> "I'm not going today [to church] because I heard that the police are controlling in Central Station and I'm not well dressed."

Not all illegal Colombian immigrants had the same chances to be detected or deported. A clear focus on fighting illegal prostitution and drug dealing contrasted with a tolerant attitude towards 'law-abiding' illegal residents. Still, protected prostitutes and discreet professional *traquetos* showed better skills for concealment than visible ones. Some cities tolerated illegal prostitutes, while others engaged in

---

14   They calculate 40,000 illegal immigrants, from which 4,400 were detained by the police (11%). A very conservative estimation of 1,000 illegal Colombian immigrants for the mid-1990s in the 4 major cities (with illegal prostitution still tolerated in The Hague and Amsterdam), and 88 detentions, the percentage is 9%.

razzias. Those who avoided 'hot' places or areas truly believed they had more opportunities to survive. Finally, those involved in profitable activities had more chances of successfully coming back than the rest. All these differences show a process of selective criminalisation, which should not be confused with the notion of discrimination (Bovenkerk et al. 1991: 317).

While this point deserves further investigation – not only through dossier analysis, but through the observation of police practices – it is my impression that the bulk of illegal Colombian immigrants detained for 'illegal residence' are either prostitutes or people suspected of involvement in the drug circuit. From those detained for criminal offences, only some were involved in small predatory crime (especially organised shoplifting, theft and burglary, not 'drug related'), but the majority had committed some offence under the Opium Law. Moreover, I hardly heard of cases of detentions during work controls.[15]

Next to this selective process, and in line with earlier findings for other immigrant groups by Bovenkerk et al. (1991), Bovenkerk (1995c) and Engbersen et al. (1995), illegal Colombian immigrants specialised in certain informal or illegal activities and not in others. Prostitution is, of course, the first and most clear example. The vast majority of illegal prostitutes come or are brought to work as prostitutes. Only very few are illegal immigrants already living in the Netherlands for whom prostitution becomes an alternative option. This reflects a pattern of chain migration, in which connections with intermediaries or women already working is essential to enter.

Most of the thieves I met amongst illegal Colombian immigrants were not pickpockets or drug related thieves, but burglars and organised shoplifters. Although their activities were closer to what De Haan (1993) defines as 'surviving' criminality, some actually seemed to be less marginalised, more profit oriented, switching to drug dealing or other activities if necessary or possible.

The previously explained absence from drug retail selling and problematic consumption is also extensible for illegal immigrants. Colombians are, for example, neither 'drug-tourists' (foreign hard drug addicts) nor do they act as street 'drug runners' or 'drug pushers' as it is the case of some West Europeans, Moroccans and Algerians. Illegal Colombian immigrants tend to perform as a flexible, unskilled, replaceable work force around the import and wholesale distribution of cocaine. In some cases, they can graduate to becoming real *traquetos* and organise themselves the import or distribution operations.

This specialisation is understandable and it fits into the same set of explanations that I developed for the general group of Colombian migrants. However, there seems

---

15 In this sense, the situation amongst Colombians differs a great deal from the general findings of Engbersen et al (1995) on detained illegal immigrants. Their sample, formed basically by Turks, Moroccans, Algerians, Surinamese, Cape Verdians and East Europeans, show a 'young, single man' (90% men and 92% unmarried) detained by the following reasons: 47% for illegal residence; 13% for other minor misdemeanours (illegal work, unpaid travel, disturbance of public order and administrative faults); 26% for minor offences; 5% for major offences and 9% for drug offences. From the 40% detained for criminal offences, 47% for theft (28% for burglary, 17 for theft and 2% for robbery), 22% for drug offences and 14% for false documents (1995: 8 and 92).

to exist specific reasons and chances of illegal immigrants entering the cocaine business or, as they used to say, to remain *sano* (healthy).

7.2.3 Offers that can be refused

There are three types of illegal Colombian immigrants involved in the cocaine business: the *pre-involved*, the *recruited* and the *peripheral*.

The *pre-involved* are people who come to the Netherlands already involved or with the intention to becoming involved in the cocaine business. In other words, their situation as illegal immigrants is a result, and not so much a condition, of their illicit activities. This is the case of some smugglers (*mulas*) who decide to stay after their tourist visa has expired, but especially that of those men and women who stay as *traquetos* involved in import and distribution. In many cases they manage to leave the country for a while and return using safe routes or false identities. Their individual opportunities to enter (and leave) the business have little to do with their juridical status as immigrants. In fact, they regard their 'illegality' as an extra factor to take into account in the management of risk. They fear imprisonment, but not deportation. Nor they are concerned about future perspectives in the Netherlands: the quicker they can make money and eventually return to Colombia, the better. They differ in skills, social backgrounds, professionalism, financial capital, expectations and even lifestyles, but none consider legal work as a serious alternative in the Netherlands. Some develop a cynical or ironic attitude not only about the local context, but also towards those who want to follow the 'long path'. They usually have some close friend or relative in the Netherlands who often brings them over or facilitates their arrival, and are rather quick to develop a social/business network, which includes other legal and illegal immigrants, prostitutes and local entrepreneurs. Joel, Riverito, Pollo and Andrea are good examples of this kind of *pre-involved* illegal immigrant.

A second group is formed by the *recruited*. These people are already in the Netherlands when approached and offered the chance to make some money in the cocaine business. They usually come with the genuine original intention of visiting a relative, to have some adventure, to do some travelling, to follow a course of study or to start a relationship. Others come with the more clear aim of working hard for one or two years, and making enough money to 'start up something' in Colombia. Their plans are eventually truncated and they become frustrated. Some keep searching for a while, but soon realise that few or no alternatives are available. Tano:

> "I first tried as architect, but nothing happened. It was difficult to make the decision, but when I saw it, it looked easy to me and not very dangerous. Brother, you have to eat and nobody helps you when you need it, and they helped me."

Most illegal immigrants interviewed had at least one indirect proposal to get involved in the business. Ana Inés explains that:

"It is very common for *traquetos* to offer you something when you just arrive. You still have nothing, no job and no friends. They do not fear to talk openly; they know you won't denounce them. It is a possibility to do some money very quick."

Indeed, *traquetos* either exploit the weak initial position of newcomers or they approach them after they have suffered their first setbacks. On some occasions, they just help them with small amounts of money. Twice, Chino received US$ 100 as gifts from a *traqueto* with whom he spoke for 5 minutes. In any case, a degree of loyalty is always guaranteed from the illegal immigrant. He or she can, of course, refuse the offer, but would never denounce him nor talk too much about the matter again.

In fact, the chances of receiving or accepting a concrete offer increase if friends or relatives are already involved. People that got involved also tended to underestimate personal risks. However, they usually become 'first liners' as internal couriers, off-loaders, load-keepers, bodyguards or small distributors. They are more vulnerable and exposed than the former group of *pre-involved* illegal immigrants, facing greater risks of prison or death. For instance, one of the two Colombians killed in The Hague in 1996 in a rip-deal had just arrived and had been recruited by a friend who offered him a good deal. Tano felt lucky about his last days in Amsterdam:

"At certain stage everything started to go wrong. I was about to be caught, but I left just on time. The whole thing was getting messy, no, I saved my ass just on time."

For some, the financial aspect is central. They see an excellent opportunity to earn money for whatever purpose they have: to improve their situation or that of their families in Colombia, to pay off debts or get out of difficult situations. Others become involved in the hope of later finding something 'straight'. Most of them are young men: for them there are scarcer informal jobs available, they feel stronger social pressures to succeed economically, and the jobs available in the cocaine business are often male oriented.

Finally, another category of illegal immigrants only becomes *peripherally* involved. They survive in the informal economy, doing or selling things that often put them in contact with the cocaine circuit. They have usually a partner and children in the Netherlands, have some expectation about staying longer, hopefully losing the status of being an 'illegal' alien. Even if they run into financial problems, they carefully measure risks in their decisions. If they do some little job for a *traqueto*, they take care that they keep their regular occupation as cleaners, cooks or telephone operators. They regard their marginal involvement as a safe way of making 'extra' money, but retain their strong ethical reservations about the cocaine business and their participants in it. Solano is a good example of such *peripheral* involvement. He helped and translated for *traquetos* in business deals, and was repeatedly offered to work as a wholesale distributor. He declined:

"I don't want to live like these *duros* (tough guys), it's not just the risks, but I hate their ideology. It's the law of the jungle, and if you survive, you can go to jail."

This resistance was even more evident in many other illegal Colombian immigrants.

7.2.4 Mutual rejection

Illegal immigrants and *traquetos* had also reasons to reject each other. I met many illegal immigrants who did not have any link with criminal activities, condemned drug dealing for various reasons, or explicitly preferred to earn less money in informal activities.

There are structural limits to the potential involvement of illegal immigrants. The first one relates to the number of jobs available. Even being highly competitive and dynamic in terms of circulation of human resources, the Colombian related Dutch cocaine market (import and distribution level) can only absorb a small fraction of the 3,000 or more illegal Colombian immigrants estimated to live in the Netherlands. Leaving aside the *pre-involved*, only some are thus eligible to join as *recruited* or *peripheral*. It is important to bear in mind that, in contrast with predatory crime, cocaine traffic is a limited business not open to everybody.

A second limitation is one of gender. Although I have insisted that many roles are open for men and women (including smuggling, import or distribution), certain roles at lower rank, 'first line' or street level are often fulfilled by men: helpers, bodyguards, off-loaders, and so on. Since more than half of the group is formed by women,[16] already a large percentage has fewer opportunities to get involved.

Many people who rejected involvement did it actively and explicitly. Some did not experienced moral indignation about the cocaine trade, but were against the risks involved and the *traqueto* way of life. Germán was offered work with a woman. He had been in a gang in Colombia, but now had three children waiting for him there. He explains:

> "I know that sort of life. I have enough problems now, can you imagine if I also have to go to jail, with my children in Colombia!"

He considered the price he was paying already high enough. Cabeza was also frequently invited to enter the business. He claims that he was neither pushed nor threatened, and that he even kept contact with the people after a negative answer. When, after much effort, he was granted a student visa, he said:

> "You don't know how long I waited for this. I could have engaged in those things [cocaine trade], you know, but then, I would have never quit that kind of life."

Many illegal immigrants were not only surviving or trying to accumulate some money, but they also wanted to have a *better* quality of life. In Colombia, many faced not only poverty but also personal or political violence, insecurities of all sorts and police brutality. Once in the Netherlands, even if they still did not get any job, they

---

16 This is difficult to estimate. Women constitute 66% of the legal Colombian immigrants. Men have definitively fewer chances of becoming legal residents, but still women have better chances of surviving in the informal economy (including prostitution) increasing the probability for chain illegal migration.

considered their situation as much better than those of the relatives and the pasts they left behind. Jaime, for example, wanted to have a quiet life after having grown up in the Medellín of Pablo Escobar. As long as somebody with this attitude could rely on some financial help from friends and family, they kept an optimistic view about the future. I also met lower middle class immigrants who were fed up of the 'short-term mentality of Colombians' and the materialistic culture around the drug business. Horacio survived for 5 years as illegal immigrant:

> "Many are not like us. Legal or illegal, does not mater, they want to make money very quick no matter how…"

For some of these immigrants, the whole cocaine issue was experienced as a painful stigma, as a heavy obstacle for personal progress in the local environment. Especially illegal Colombian men who did not participate in the business had to learn to develop a cool attitude about the issue. However, many had paranoid attitudes about the police and the cocaine business. The obeyed the most elemental rules (for example, regarding illegal travel on public transport) and avoided 'hot' places like discotheques. In this way, many of them reduced their contacts with other Colombians to small circle of close friends and relatives.

This isolation is an obstacle, not a ground, for further participation in the cocaine business. Indeed, as I suggested before, illegal immigrants have to compete for limited vacancies with better-placed Colombians. Legal residents have a broader social network, more financial and social capital to offer, and, in some cases, know how to get to the 'right' people faster. Further, I found cases of false promises made to illegal immigrants. They seem to occupy a lower position than legal immigrants in both legitimate and illegitimate opportunity structures (Cloward and Ohlin 1960: 150).

Traquetos are often in search for more skilled or connected people. Illegal immigrants are regarded as unfamiliar with the local codes and language, and are less prepared to react in case of problems. Joel, himself a *pre-involved* illegal immigrant, used to help newly arrived Colombians with money, food or small jobs. However, when he had to take an important decision, he stated that:

> "…they [newcomers] are a problem. We had to leave a flat because their *rumba* [party] was loud and neighbours complained… If I leave, the *linea* [cocaine line] remains in the hands of Tico, my nephew, who has 'papers' [residence permit] and speaks Dutch…"

Many drug entrepreneurs needed people who could drive, speak, read signs, negotiate with local or foreign individuals or afford a casual encounter with the police without risking everything. Illegal immigrants cannot offer any legal or illegal infrastructure, often a primary target of Colombian *traquetos*. 'Recruited' illegal immigrants could seldom make a successful career in the drug business, and were continually replaced.

CHAPTER VIII

FLEXIBLE AFFAIRS

Labour and Business Relations amongst Colombian Dealers

"In the life-game of postmodern men and women the rules of the game keep changing in the course of the playing. The sensible strategy is therefore to keep each game short."

Z. Bauman, *Modernity and its Discontents.*

"I came here to *work.*"

Riverito

INTRODUCTION

Chapter II dealt with the social organisation of cocaine entrepreneurs in Colombia, challenging the mythical images of fixed 'cartels', stable enterprises or '*mafia* families' at export level. The preceding chapters V and VI tackled the specific role of Colombians in subsequent business steps in the Netherlands, focusing particularly on individual backgrounds, on social chances and skills, and on operational aspects of their performances. Moreover, a strong emphasis was placed on assessing their share at each level, demonstrating how and why Colombians interact with groups and individuals from transit and destination countries.

While those chapters highlighted the nature of the Colombian involvement in general and of cocaine entrepreneurs and employees in particular, this chapter will be devoted to analysing the most common business and labour relations I encountered during my fieldwork amongst Colombian cocaine dealers in the Netherlands. In so doing, I follow earlier attempts to identify different types of drug enterprises (Dorn et al. 1992; Korf and Verbraeck 1993; Van Duyne et al. 1990) and labour modalities within the drug economy (Ruggiero 1995).[1]

Colombian drug organisations active in Europe have been described either as mere

---

1   See chapter I for a critical assessment of existing approaches on drug organisations. There I reveal the limitations of criminological views revolving around state-sanctioned definitions of *organised crime*, managerial approaches stressing *criminal networks*, and euphemistic macro-economic views, which talk about *transnational corporations* or *cartels*. In contrast, I explain how ethnographic research with a focus on business and labour relations has potential advantages. It can reveal some of the reasons behind internal interaction, changing arrangements, conflicting interests and risk transfer inside the business. It can further contribute to explain the meaning of violence, secrecy and trust for the actors involved. Finally, it can expose both similarities and interconnections with broader social and economic arrangements – with other labour markets, with other legal and illegal businesses or entrepreneurs, and so forth.

representatives or *cells* of all-powerful Colombian enterprises, or as *flexible criminal networks* in which non-criminal roles and relations are, per definition, excluded from the analysis. The first view presents caricatured *branches* and professional business-men. The other offers a chaotic web of underground, international *criminals*. I will first comment very briefly on these two approaches as they empirically refer to the case of Colombian dealers involved in Europe.

A second section will present three cases in which interesting aspects on business and labour relations are revealed. From these and other cases encountered during fieldwork, I will further examine the business and labour modalities involved more systematically.

8.1. BRANCHES, CRIMINAL NETWORKS AND FLEXIBLE ENTREPRENEURS

Most works mentioning Colombian groups or individuals involved in cocaine import and distribution in Europe tend to describe them as *branches*, *cells*, *representatives* or *agents* of the *X* Colombian *cartel(s)*. These descriptions are usually fed by a combination of economic and bureaucratic definitions of organised crime: Colombians are in business and they belong to certain organisations. Whether the emphasis rests in high organised and stable structures (Florez and Boyce 1990), strict labour division, professionalism or vertical integration (Lee III 1989; 1991), the model in mind is that of a transnational corporation. Even when the notion of *cartel* is avoided, Colombian dealers abroad are fixed in large organisational structures. In an interesting attempt to compare the 'narco-business' with any other large company, Zabludoff (1997) argues that

> "...Each cell is organised somewhat along the lines of its headquarters in Colombia. Cells vary in number of personnel according to their responsibilities and the size of the market they serve. Some employ as many as 50 Colombians including a cell leader and several 'vice-presidents' in charge of specific tasks..." (Zabludoff 1997: 35)

Others simply discuss the issue in terms of the activities of 'Colombian cartels' (Savona 1999; OGD 1997a) or 'Colombian families' (OGD 1996a: 67) in the Nether-lands. Some versions of this picture also include an 'alien conspiracy' dimension. For example, Van Doorn (1993) claims that

> "Close family ties at the top and a cell-structure characterize the cartels (...) Arrival and further distribution in Western Europe, is in the hands of high-placed Colombian cartel members who take up residence, either permanently or temporarily... There is a very realistic possibility that the cartels will try to expand their influence in Europe over the next few years by setting up import corporations of their own" (Van Doorn 1993: 101).

Despite the fact that most economic roles and relations amongst Colombian dealers can indeed be compared with those of other legal markets, this perspective tends to institutionalise arrangements and businesses in a holistic way. Moreover, the exclusive stress on professional skilled managers and entrepreneurs simply ignores the reality of the mass of unskilled Colombian employees, often regarded as members and not as victims of the groups they supposedly belong to.

With a stronger accent in economic processes than in bureaucratic structures, Van Duyne (Van Duyne et al. 1990; Van Duyne 1993a; Van Duyne 1995) presents a less static picture of Colombian cocaine entrepreneurs and enterprises. Even though he talks about 'mother organisations' (1990: 55) and mentions *cartels* holding sections of the European market (1995: 80), he pays more attention to business forms as well as to symbiotic relations with the legal economy. He describes 'commercial bridgeheads' and 'pioneer firms' (1993a: 15), which are both flexible and not always a model of professionalism (1995: 82-83). He also identifies enterprises of different size related through intermediaries or brokers. Since only significant detected cases are analysed (through police and judicial dossiers), Van Duyne does not deal with smaller units, more informal coalitions and especially with the labour market of his 'criminal enterprises'.

With a strong entrepreneurial approach, Naylor (1997) criticises the misleading use of economic categories by drug enforcers, pointing out that cocaine trafficking proceeds through a complex of arms-length commercial transactions (Naylor 1997: 20). Other researchers have sustained the same stress on fragmentation as well (Krauthausen and Sarmiento 1991; Thoumi 1995; Kopp 1995). The material presented by Bovenkerk (1995a; 1995b), with a stronger focus on the socio-economic and cultural context of those involved in large cocaine import operations, also reveals more fluid transactions, some levels of autonomy and space for erratic behaviour even amongst top *traquetos*.

From a different perspective, a recent report from the WODC (Research Centre of the Ministry of Justice) (Kleemans et al. 1998) describes Colombian related cases in the Netherlands in terms of 'criminal networks' both facilitated and hindered by the social context. These researchers distance themselves from the economic view as theoretical departure, so they seldom talk about *entrepreneurs* or *cartels*. While they favour notions such as 'criminal networks' or 'co-operation agreements' (*samen-werkingsverbanden*), they still refer to Colombian 'groups' and 'organisations'. Kleemans et al. (1998) also challenge the 'ethnic' tone of the *Van Traa* Report (Fijnaut et al. 1996) arguing that Colombians engage in mixed and international networks since ethnicity is only one aspect of broader social linkages.[2] Their picture, sketched from some dossier-cases involving Colombian cocaine dealers, reveals flexible international co-operation, diversification to other illegal markets at distribution level, and, of course, different operational capabilities regarding contacts in Colombia and the Netherlands. Their view has the merit of recognising flexible relations at the core of any drug transaction.

As earlier explained in this book, the first problem with this approach is the exclusive focus on a-priori isolated 'criminal' relations. 'Non-criminal' relations are considered secondary or analysed as external social context – as 'upper world', as

---

2   See also for the same critique Zaitch and Janssen (1996).

corrupt officials, as spoiled legal businesses, and so on. Secondly, no attention is paid to the meaning that relations have for those involved in the 'network'. During my fieldwork, I met many people who even knowing that they were engaged in illegal activities, did not consider themselves to be criminals: people primarily engaged in legal or informal activities, people who saw themselves as workers, as adventurers or as acting under pressure, and finally those who blamed others for being the 'true criminals'. Illegality is a key factor, but should not be taken for granted when explaining *traqueto*'s social behaviour. People engage in the drug economy attracted by potential large (illegal) profits, but they also do it 'despite' the fact that cocaine is illegal. For example, many informants wanted to step out from illegality as soon as possible, supported drug legalisation, or engaged in legitimate activities that provided greater symbolic rewards.

This approach also tends to portray Colombians as 'co-operative' and 'partners in crime', neglecting internal conflict between different roles and the power relations involved. Finally, this view remains rather a-historic, it does not explain why people behave in certain ways, and it is only secondarily concerned with the economic dimension of the illegal business. Behind flexible networks – whether they are 'criminal' or not – there are flexible entrepreneurs, partners, brokers and employees. Flexibility can be better explained – and compared – when the business and labour relations are the object of analysis.

8.2 SAND THROUGH THE FINGERS

8.2.1 Riverito's four operations

At the time I visited him, Riverito was in his thirties and serving 4 years in *De Weg*, one of the buildings with several Colombian inmates in the Bijlmer prison of Amsterdam. From a middle-class family from Cali, he studied economics at the *Univalle*, where he graduated in 1992. Afterwards he got a reasonably good job with a leading building company in Cali, but he found it routine and boring. During his studies, he worked as a waiter in a famous hotel in the Cali centre, a place where top local cocaine entrepreneurs gathered for business and pleasure. It was in that hotel that Riverito got to know these people and the world of major cocaine producers and exporters. He was at first a simple waiter who knew their tastes and anticipated their wishes. He was later invited to more private events:

> "I was the private waiter of Pacho Herrera [a former major drug entrepreneur from Cali]. Once he gave me a US$ 1,000 tip at the end of a party, I had to share it with some other people."

However, beside this link and the fact that he sometimes easily got hold of some cocaine to retail amongst friends, he did not become involved with those cocaine entrepreneurs. However, his closeness to them had a tremendous impact:

"Brother, you don't imagine how it is until you come close to them. So much money! They impress the people around them, because they are not so different than you or me. They are not old rich bastards, no; they speak the same language as normal people do. Some are gentle and jointly liable. And you wonder: why not me?"

For him, things were not going well in Colombia. He underwent a serious alcohol problem:

"Very rarely a joint or a coke line, no, my true nightmare is the drink: beer, and especially whisky and *aguardientico*. I don't get aggressive, but I lose control. I ruined my marriage in December 1994 due to the drink."

Riverito indeed had an ex-wife, for whom he still felt responsible, and an 8 years old son who lived with her.

In 1995, ten months after they broke up, he decided to go to the Netherlands. He had a sister living there, so he left. Is not clear the main reason behind his decision. He argued during our first meeting that he came to the Netherlands for adventure, that he had nothing else in Colombia and wanted to solve his alcohol abuse by changing environment, but he had not come to deal cocaine. After many encounters, he became more open and forgot his earlier claims:

"I came here to *work* you see, it was the only thing to do. I had no prospects there."

It is reasonable to believe that a number of factors pushed him to decide to move to the Netherlands and participate in the cocaine business: dissatisfaction and frustration with his job, earlier contacts with powerful local cocaine entrepreneurs, a spiralling down that ended in a broken marriage and, finally, the fact that he had a sister in the Netherlands. In the case of Riverito, personal economic problems did not seem to be high on the agenda. Indeed he was interested in making big money quickly, not so much as a path for social improvement, but rather as a disruption, as a possible turning point for a new start. The way in which he became involved in the cocaine business illustrates this. He was not sent by any people nor did he belong to any group or organisation. Riverito went to the Netherlands alone, established contact with local importers and distributors, and eventually used his former contacts within the *Caleño* cocaine circles.

Encaletador

Once in Amsterdam, he shared a room in an attic with other Colombians. Some were already involved in the cocaine business. With these people, he first worked as *encaletador*, the person responsible for keeping and watching over the cocaine loads before they are eventually divided and delivered to wholesalers. He was just an employee, next to other two, of a Colombian cocaine importer. After a couple of operations, in which he demonstrated his competence and gained trust, he was offered a more risky and profitable task: the unloading of several kilograms from a ship in Zeebrugge for which he was offered US$ 30,000, an amount he was meant to share with another Colombian who was supposed to go with him.

Unloading in Zeebrugge

Riverito's operation at Zeebrugge was a successful one, but the US$ 15,000 promised turned out to be just US$ 10,000. Interestingly enough, although he claimed the rest for a while, he just accepted the actual payment that seemed a good deal to him.

> "I wasn't going to create problems, I wasn't in a position to ask for the rest. You see, after all they paid me well. I bought a house in Cali with that money, for my ex-wife and my son."

The unloading operation at Zeebrugge reveals interesting aspects regarding the labour relations involved. Contrary to the idea that a single, well organised group was controlling all the import tasks – for example, with a boss who divided the tasks and paid salaries or percentages to 'his own' people –, the operation involved at least two small independent units.

On the one hand, the Colombian importer and owner of the cocaine load bought to the exporter at US$ 20,000 per kilo – at import port – and sold at a wholesale price of US$ 24,000 per kilo, obtaining gross earnings of US$ 200,000. He worked alone with two informal helpers, both receiving some thousands from him after the operation. While he received information about the *cruce* (sending), he was not responsible for it since he bought from the exporter at the point of arrival. He unloaded the shipment, transported, stashed and divided the merchandise, and delivered it – in this case, three packages – to wholesale distributors. However, he did not do all this by himself. For the most dangerous task, the unloading, he was willing to pay 10% of his profits (US$ 20,000) for to someone else to do it, in the same way, a legal company subcontracts special services for a project. The contractor was in this case Riverito.

Riverito and his companion, on the other hand, were a separate economic unit from the importer. They were not his partners, since they were neither owners nor responsible for the merchandise. They could neither be considered employees like the other helpers, since the contracting relationship ended as soon as the operation had been completed. Riverito and his partner also remained autonomous with regard to the planning and execution of the operation. Naturally, the division was less strict than in legal subcontracting, since Riverito was not in a position to guarantee a refund if the unloading operation failed. In practical terms, the importer worked very close to Riverito, kept an eye on him, provided him with ideas, information and even with a vehicle, though Riverito and his friend had to arrange many technical aspects of the unloading by themselves.

In this way, they were contracted out, as an external labour force, to take over the high risks involved in the unloading. They just offered the importer a highly priced service for this particular operation. In contrast with what happens in legal business, this subcontracting relation had almost no chance of being repeated in future operations: Riverito wanted more, and new personal circumstances allowed him to try on his own.

From unloader to importer to wholesaler

After the Zeebrugge operation, a year after arrival to the Netherlands, his older brother William also came over. Unlike Riverito, he had problems in Colombia with marihuana and cocaine use. They had a good relationship and he wanted to help him, so he convinced him to come to the Netherlands. Together, they started to look for possible opportunities to transporting cocaine from Cali. They had no capital to invest, but they knew many people. Their intention this time was to keep things in their own hands:

> "You see, I work no more with those *paisanos* [Colombians]. Everything fine with them, but I just tried with other people in Colombia. I knew this man from before. He promised to send something, so we waited. We waited, and waited, and nothing happened. He kept giving stupid excuses, I think he liked to talk and tell things he really could not do. Pure bullshit!"

Riverito got what Colombians call a *línea muerta* (dead line), a cocaine line or operation that simply does not exist or is destined to fail. For this operation, Riverito was going to buy in Colombia and sell in the Netherlands, dividing the profits with his brother. They phoned many people in Colombia, but nothing worked out. People who promised things just disappeared. They survived with small jobs as load keepers and internal couriers. In the meantime, their sister had returned to Colombia: she had had absolutely nothing to do with the cocaine circuit.

Finally, in the beginning of 1997, a new operation appeared. It was small, but rather easy and with a good profit margin. They could make a mark up of US$ 4,000 selling a kilo that Riverito had got from another Colombian. Riverito thus suddenly became a wholesale distributor. He bought the cocaine, and his brother William and a *paisa* called Charly entered the deal as his helpers. Charly was a *paisa* that had just arrived and used to repeatedly tell that he had been bodyguard of Pablo Escobar. Charly told Riverito that a friend of him had a buyer for the cocaine kilo. This 'friend', thought to be Colombian by Riverito, turned out to be an Aruban who presumably gave Charly some money to ensure the deal. They followed him to meet the buyers, but things went wrong. Riverito:

> "Man, there was no buyer, there was only a gang of Antilleans who put two guns to our heads and stole the thing. It is a miracle we are alive. I know another *caleño* who was almost killed in the same situation but still walks around with a bullet in his neck."

The man from Aruba did not disappear, but pretended to also have been fooled. As a regular police informant, he could avoid punishment by feeding the police with a 'Colombian criminal organisation' story while he could get away with a loot worth US$ 24,000. After a failed attempt to recover the package from the Aruban – allegedly using violence –, the police raided Riverito's flat in *Amsterdam Zuid*. He and his fellows were subsequently detained. In his last operation, Riverito was the boss.

Riverito's four operations, all taking place with the space of two years, reveal two interesting things. Firstly, that far from a stable and large organisation, a mutating interconnection of small units seems to be the case. Secondly, that this connection changed with respect to people, positions, linkage nature and tasks along the four successful or failed operations in which Riverito was involved. These changing relations and roles are illustrated in Figure IV.

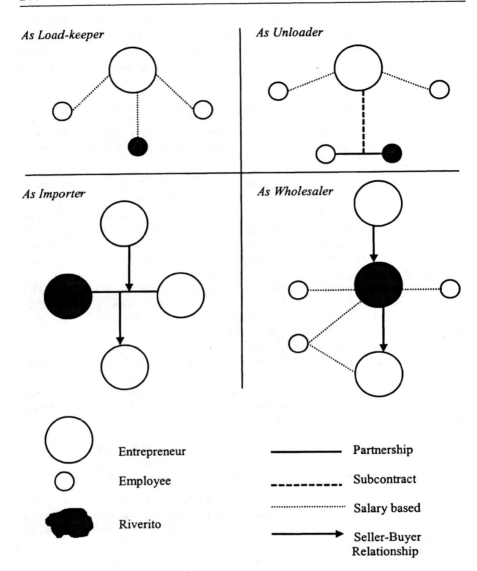

Figure IV Riverito's Business Links in Four Different Operations

8.2.2 *Miguel's many bosses*

Although Miguel primarily addressed himself as an "intellectual mainly interested in philosophy and criminology",[3] he was rather open about his involvement in the business for more than a decade.

He almost made it as a criminal lawyer, but for no clear reason he claimed he was impeded to complete his last year at the University.

> "I felt frustrated and I burned all the books. At that time, I was working in a small secondary school in Cartago as vice-principal and philosophy teacher. I knew some people in Cali, but I did not enter this for the money, I suppose. I think it was out of bitterness."

He was first invited to work as a courier for a small organisation in Bogotá, transporting between 3 kg and 7 kg. He made successful trips to the Netherlands, to Paris, again to the Netherlands, and later to a couple of Central American countries. He was caught in a subsequent trip to Portugal, where he spent 3 years in prison.

> "It was terrible there, the law of the jungle, surrounded by 'garbage' that did not deserve anything. I survived because we have a name, I mean they think it is better not to mess with Colombians".

Back in Colombia, he tried to resume his law studies, but he was again obstructed. Frustration was even more painful since his brother was a criminal judge with many contacts. He started to work in a cocaine kitchen near Cali, a job he regarded as very dangerous:

> "The chemicals are very inflammable, we had to wear rubber shoes cause the slightest spark could provoke an explosion. Everything is very precarious, once a certain amount is cooked the kitchen is dismantled and you are moved to a new one. It is risky, but you get monthly paid."

After that period, and due to the fall of his *patrón* (boss), Miguel returned to Bogotá to resume his job as drug courier, but this time for another organisation. He already had experience, and was no longer regarded as a simple courier. In 1993, he was sent to Frankfurt as a 'baby sitter'. Although he was not caught, the cocaine was seized, some Italian importers were detained and the cocaine remained unpaid for. Shortly after this operation, Miguel attempted to smuggle a few kilos through the Schiphol Airport, where he was caught. My first interpretation was that he had been punished for the failure and 'demoted' from 'baby sitter' to *mula*, but things were more simple

---

3 During our encounters in the prison of Veenhuizen, he commented upon Hegel, Kant, Russell, Bentham and Foucault. He also referred to social utopists such as Owen, Fourier, Saint Simon and Comte, and to authors such as Huxley and Orwell. Quoting Kundera, he finally thanked me for the unique opportunity to share thoughts about these thinkers, implying that he was an exception in that "criminal subculture". Upon this intimacy he also based his willingness to tell me his story.

than that: a new operation for a single courier appeared and he happened to get the job. With a false passport and more than 3 kg cocaine, he was sent via Venezuela and Curaçao to Amsterdam, from where he would have travelled south to deliver the merchandise in Geneva, Switzerland. Miguel explains:

> "You see, I worked for many groups and I never saw anything like a 'cartel'. I don't feel part of a 'cartel'. Every group is more or less independent. Some people know each other, yes, and sometimes a couple of *patrones* could meet and work together. There are also informal rules and codes, but nothing like the *mafia*, people don't really respect them. I believe that the only rule is to survive and get rich."

When asked about his plans after prison, Miguel suggested that he first had to settle things with his most recent boss from Bogotá. After that, he would go back to Cali to "see who is there". He was, however, very sceptical about finding his old employers after so long.

Whatever effort may be made to connect Miguel with a particular group or 'cartel' in Colombia is destined to fail: he moved rather easily from one employer to another, combining or shifting drug smuggling with other roles as 'cook', as bodyguard and as 'baby sitter'.

8.2.3 Joel's loneliness

In chapter VI, I explained why Joel should be considered a 'discreet professional' as a Colombian cocaine wholesaler active in Amsterdam.[4] I then presented relevant information about his career, his daily arrangements, his resources and the ways in which he acts and thinks about the business. What is also interesting about Joel's story is the kind of relations he establishes with business partners and with the people working with and for him.

Joel was usually the boss of his own illegal enterprise. He was clearly what Dorn et al (1998) refer as a *number 1*, 'cut out' from some delicate operational matters such as cocaine transportation and money transfers, but 'hands on' in others such as stashing cocaine. In some cases, he made Paisita his partner – sharing a percentage of the profits –, but only when they sold to a couple of Paisita's clients. Joel was always the investor and he always ran the financial risk of the operations. Interestingly enough, his brother, who invited him to come to the Netherlands and gave him most of the business contacts, worked independently from him, holding a different line. However, they used to work together in Chicago. Tano reveals:

> "Once he went to collect some money, I think a lot of money, and they told him that his brother had already received it. When Joel found him it was already too late, his brother had spent it all in Colombia. I believe they settled the score, but there is always some tension."

---

4   See Chapter VI.

Joel only bought cocaine from other Colombians, but not always in the same way and from the same people. He entered the game per operation. He would receive a message from exporter A from Cali, asking if he wanted to play. Although Joel knew his nickname and a telephone number to contact him, he never met him personally. According to the price and the quantity involved, he would say yes or no. In practice, he always agreed to buy at least part of the cocaine load. Exporter A would arrange the shipment with importer B, mainly through Rotterdam. Joel would also accept sharing the financial risks with importer B, who was also from Cali. In the event that the shipment was lost or seized, he would pay for half of it and he would invite the exporter to verify that no rip-off took place.

The autonomy of the 3 partners in this *linea* (line) or *flecha* (arrow) is obvious not only from the meticulous share of financial risk, but also from the fact that they seldom repeat the same scheme. Importer B and Joel also received cocaine from exporter C, who closed a deal with importer A to use his contacts in the Netherlands. Despite the fact that Joel only bought from importer B – he tried with a second one but he was not satisfied – importer B also sold to other Colombian and non-Colombian distributors.

Joel sold the cocaine to different groups including other local Colombians, some Turks and Italians in Amsterdam, and a couple of groups in Germany and Belgium. However, he never deals with more than two or three clients. On one occasion, Joel was visibly irritated. He explained me that

"Another group of *Caleños*, they sold the thing one point cheaper [a point, referred to the kilo price, is € 500] but we had agreed to sell for 48. Therefore, they sold it and I didn't. I will speak with them..."

While he excluded the use of force, he implied that these informal agreements are common between two or three groups or distributors handling from the same bulk and selling to the same groups. However, even in these circumstances, he admitted the difficulties involved in enforcing these price accords. Other agreements with the importer were often tacit and implied a grey zone of misunderstandings, discussions and conflicts. For example, if the cocaine was not sold immediately, the importer would become rather impatient about the payment.

I met six different Colombians working for or with Joel: Simona, Paisita, his brother, Tico, Chino and Tano. Except for Paisita, who was only on some occasions involved as business partner, none of the others engaged in any stable 'criminal' relation with him. They would not be offered a job either before or after certain operation. Even then, Joel would decide what and when to delegate. I then realised that one of the secrets of Joel's success was that he worked alone. He basically hired people to move the cocaine inside Amsterdam, to receive it and deliver it, and to transfer the money. Some people such as Tano would rotate through all of these tasks. Paisita and Tico could provide the 'violent' image that Joel did not have. Finally, Simona would generally cook and clean for him, and, of course, provide her house to stash the merchandise.

The money transfers to Colombia were arranged in a rather simple way. Sometimes he went to the office by himself, but most of the time, he sent somebody else. He was aware of video cameras and financial legislation, so he used to distribute uneven amounts of about € 2,500 to € 3,500 amongst 6 different people, who would deposit the money in some 4 or 5 well-known funds transfer offices. For this work, Joel also recruited peripheral people – for example, friends of Simona – who would get between € 100 and € 150 for the job. In this way, he managed to send, diverted to different accounts in Colombia, an amount of around US$ 90,000 each time. He avoided sending people to the same office very often, and he occasionally sent cash with trusted travellers. Far from being part of a group – i.e. Joel's organisation – these people were just friends or acquaintances who did not necessarily know each other very well.

Tano described how he delivered the cocaine for Joel:

> "I put the stuff in a big suitcase and I just went alone to meet the buyers. Paisita met me there and we delivered it. Joel paid me € 100 for each kilo transported."

Finally, Joel mentioned some 'projects' – one in Japan and another one in France, both apparently failed – in which neither the people referred above were involve, nor was his precise role in these projects clear to me.

8.3 WORKING WITH/FOR A TRAQUETO

From these three stories and the material presented in chapters V and VI, it is evident that Colombian dealers engage in various sorts of business and labour relations. The following is an attempt to enumerate the most common types of linkages I found during my fieldwork. Since these types are in reality both mixed (for instance partnerships amongst relatives) and mutating (i.e. traffickers change from one method to another), this should serve to grasp the diversity of business forms as well as to identify the most important elements of Colombian cocaine enterprises.

8.3.1 Business types

Individual enterprises
Self-employment, a paramount feature of immigrant economies (Portes 1995), was extremely rare amongst Colombian cocaine dealers. For reasons explained earlier,[5] Colombian smugglers were always employees of somebody else. The few cases were restricted to people mostly involved in wholesale distribution. Joel, for example, acted in most of his operations as an individual entrepreneur helped by ad-hoc recruits. Lupo, in a more erratic fashion, incorporated sporadic cocaine dealing with a larger number of informal or illegal activities in which he engaged alone. Finally, Pollo managed to conduct one single import operation moving on his own.

---

5   See chapter V on independent smugglers.

Partnerships

This was the most common sort of business by far, especially at the level of import and distribution. Most partnerships were between two people. When a third partner was present, it tended to be a non-Colombian associate who provided local resources, infrastructure or further marketing contacts. While some lasted for few operations, most partnerships were temporary coalitions of two persons with a number of helpers, employees and subcontracted personnel. Riverito worked with a partner when he performed as unloader and as an importer (see figure IV). His case, like that of some other adventurers or 'opportunistic irregulars' (Dorn et al. 1992) was to combine or switch from partnerships to wage labour. Some partners were family related, especially brothers and brothers in law.

Thinking in terms of the typology of trafficking 'firms' proposed by Dorn et al. (1992: xiii), it can be argued that none of these Colombian partnerships were 'trading charities' (ideologically committed to drugs) or 'mutual societies' (drug exchange amongst users). Colombian *traquetos* belonged to the other five categories in a very flexible fashion.

Despite the fact that 'sideliners' (legal businesses that trade drugs as a 'sideline') are a common phenomenon in Colombia, no traces of Colombian 'sideliners' in the Netherlands were found. This is due to the lack of legal Colombian entrepreneurship in the Netherlands, which if related to cocaine traffic was already an instrument designed to conceal the illegal business. Naturally, Colombians found partners in local 'sideliners', especially people with import or retail businesses suffering financial problems. If prostitution is considered to be a legal activity, a small number of Colombian prostitutes and ex-prostitutes also 'sidelined' into cocaine by meeting or being related with a drug entrepreneur.

Almost the same can be said about their engagement as 'criminal diversifiers' (existing criminal enterprise that 'diversifies' to include cocaine). Those Colombians who engaged in burglary or shoplifting only entered the cocaine business as temporary unskilled workers, but never as entrepreneurs. In fact, for some Colombians who diversified to other criminal activities and markets in the Netherlands – Mocho, for example, also imported cannabis –, cocaine was the first step and still the most profitable activity. As argued previously, many of these *traquetos* had no criminal record in Colombia. However, many of them engaged in partnerships with local entrepreneurs involved in all sorts of illegal activities.

Though the 'opportunistic irregular' (involved erratically in the irregular economy) and the 'retail specialist' (with a boss employing people to distribute drugs to users) are two categories referring to retail levels in which Colombians were absent, these types were somewhat familiar amongst Colombian entrepreneurs. On the one hand, people like Lupo distributed cocaine along many other small *rebusques* (street informal jobs) he engaged in. Since some *traquetos* only managed 2 or 3 operations per year, their involvement was more 'irregular' than often thought. They reacted to short-term developments, acting as 'jump-up merchants' (Hobbs 1988) when a nice business opportunity suddenly emerged. In this way, they also engaged in temporary partnerships and recruited people for the project. On the other hand, even improvising, the 'groups' assembled had a boss and employees or helpers performing specific tasks.

Finally, Colombian groups or partnerships, especially those involved in cocaine import, were susceptible to dealing with 'state-sponsored traders' (who collaborated with enforcement agencies as informants, infiltrates or undercover policemen). While I could not find one single Colombian willing to become a *sapo* (police informant), many complained of making foolish mistakes by dealing with the 'wrong' people.

Joint ventures

Many partnerships were not only temporary for one or two operations, but involved people already active in other projects with other people. These joint ventures were usually between people holding different sorts of capital resources, all required to put the operation together. One had, for example, the money to invest and a front-store business, while the other provided the supplier in Colombia and the people needed for the operation. Some of these coalitions were 'virtual'. Potential partners spent a great deal of time thinking and talking about projects which never materialised in the end.

Percentage commission

People did not divide profits in an even way. If partners were – or appeared to be – roughly of the same status, negotiations often took place. Even if they knew each other, part of the negotiation was aimed at showing – and often exaggerating – personal credentials: how reliable and profitable each party was. Negotiations also involved discussions about three issues: financial risk, personal risk and material/human resources employed in. The first and third factors were the key ones, while personal risk was difficult to assess, often equally shared or completely passed on to helpers and labourers. When Paisita managed to share profits with Joel, he would only get 30 % for providing the customer, putting some money and arranging the deal. As the main investor, Joel kept the other 70%.

A different picture resulted if partners were very different in size and power: the offer would be accepted with little or no discussion. The smaller party would then receive a percentage commission either in cash from the general profits or in kind from the total amount of cocaine moved. This arrangement was typical in export-import operations involving 'envoys' such as Jairo. Although he organised the import for certain group in Cali – i.e. working *for* them in that particular operation – he became involved as a partner since he provided essential infrastructure, marketing opportunities and assumed high personal risks.

This system should be distinguished from the 'sales on commission' method, widely used amongst small wholesale distributors. As I will explain below, this last contracting arrangement applies less to entrepreneurial partnerships than to flexible labour force.

Family business

None of the cocaine enterprises found were structured along family lines in the style of the 'crime families' described by Ianni (1972) or of 'family businesses' discussed by the vast literature on middleman minorities and ethnic economies. Of course, kinship relations often provided the basis for partnerships, labour recruitment, solidarity and the necessary enforceable trust. Joel or Riverito sometimes worked with their respective brothers, and some couples like Pacho and Blanca or Wilder and Rosaura co-operated in export-import operations. However, most of them had relatives who did not participate in the business, and most commonly dealt with and employed non-relatives.[6] Moreover, the whole idea of 'family labour' was absent. Solano explained:

> "Here in The Hague I met many family members involved: blood brothers and relatives in law. But also close friends, that can be almost the same. (...) I see here many Arabs and they look like a big family, they are closed and they help each other. But Colombians are more individualistic, I don't know why...(...) Yes, family is important, but money makes them blind."

Jairo, who was sent by the Grajales family from Cali, was not related to them. The Grajales 'family business' was in fact a conglomerate of legal and illegal businesses run by different members of a large family, and not a unified structure. Joel and his brother also ran separated businesses. In some cases, the relative primarily provided the know-how, human and financial capital, or infrastructure. This is the case of 'mixed couples' or Colombian couples in which the woman had the Dutch nationality and local contacts. Tano emphatically denied that family ties were important amongst *traquetos* in the Netherlands:

> "Look, you can not do this for many years, so some people try to keep their relatives out of this".

Paisita also insisted on 'Colombian' over family ties:

> "We work with other *calichanos* [Colombianos]. They won't do silly things, you know for sure because everybody has a family in Colombia..."

The centrality of intermediaries and brokers
This system of small, changing and temporary coalitions is certainly invigorated by the essential intervention of a specific type of entrepreneur: the broker. Boissevain (1974: 148) explains that social brokers place people in touch with each other either directly or indirectly for profit.

The usual role of brokers in the cocaine business – also referred as 'go-between', 'intermediaries', 'criminal brokers', and so forth – is to connect potential partners, potential buyers and sellers, and potential employees and employers. In this way, cocaine brokers combine, in a very informal way, some of the tasks usually performed by chambers of commerce, employment agencies, social clubs or financial newspapers in legal business. Nevertheless, they also reproduce other sorts of social

---

6   A more elaborated argument is offered in chapter II on cocaine enterprises in Colombia and chapter IX on the role of trust.

brokerage – amongst friends, relatives, colleagues, co-nationals, and so forth –
present in any other monetary or non-monetary transaction.

Brokers tended to belong to the very social networks being connected. Although
not necessarily cocaine entrepreneurs or employees themselves, they were also not
external 'powerful 'actors such as local politicians, *mafiosi* or migrant community
leaders. During the 1980s, Bettien Martens, for example, managed many contacts
between Colombian exporters and European importers. Although her only capital was
her network, she went beyond brokerage to work for specific groups as an 'envoy', a
money launderer, and so on.

Brokers amongst Colombian *traquetos* included people occupying intersections of
very different networks: illegal immigrants, musicians, frequent travellers, local
dealers, local entrepreneurs, prostitutes, undercover police officers, and so on. Tico,
for example, introduced Tano and Chino to Joel, who later help them in many ways.
Tano acknowledged:

> "Yes, I can work with Tico. He isn't selfish, he didn't know me very well, but he told
> Joel to trust me."

Silvio argued that some salsa musicians in Amsterdam acted as brokers by
exchanging their broad network of potential cocaine users for regular free cocaine
supply for the closest circle. In The Hague, some *Latino* DJ's also knew how to
exploit their contacts with established *traquetos* and 'second generation' Colombians.
I found further cases of brokerage amongst telephone operators, restaurant and bar
tenders, coffee-shop owners, doormen in salsa discotheques and non-Colombian
inmates. They all facilitated new contacts and transactions, and they all did so for
profit.

As explained by Boissevain (1974: 158), the broker's *tariff* (profit) rarely consists
directly of money. Cocaine brokers obtained material and immaterial benefits. The
most common were: credit with *traquetos*; reputation and status; expectation to enter
the business in the future; future possible favours or services; more clients; cocaine
for consumption; moral leadership; and indeed cash. Credit and reputation were very
important since they were key credentials for business success.

Many Colombians refused to perform as brokers when asked by non-Colombian
drug dealers to connect them with the 'big guys'. They did not see any clear benefit in
it. When Cabeza was learning Dutch, two Moroccans approached him at the language
school. They wanted to get in touch with Colombian cocaine suppliers, and wondered
if he could help them. Cabeza:

> "I thought why not, so I found a Colombian and I did the *cruce* [favour]. The
> Moroccans were real *desprolijos* [lit. sloppy, amateurs], and after two failed meetings I
> said: you know what? I cancel the thing and I step out."

However, manipulating *traquetos* with hopes and promises – recommending unreliable people, lying about their skills, making them wait, and so on – was for many
the only way of getting close to a business with such large profits. More than career

makers, cocaine brokers in the Netherlands tended to rely on short-term thinking. The temporary status of cocaine enterprises – in terms of organisation and staff – was then reinforced by a continuous circulation and replacement of brokers as the older ones ran out of credit.

In an attempt to explain diversification of markets and activities amongst Colombian drug entrepreneurs, M. Koutouzis from the OGD in Paris argued that cocaine import was being subsumed into a huge broker operation:

> "It isn't a product (cocaine), but the very network what is really at stake, the real merchandise. The present and future tendency is to buy and sell lines, routes and networks. Internationalised criminal organisations will be able to provide any illegal product." (Koutouzis, April 1997).

Interestingly enough, even considered at local level, this process is reminiscent of homologous trends towards horizontal integration, and flexible accumulation and consumption in late capitalism.

8.3.2 Labour relations

Most of the people contacted during my research were either working or selling a service to some *traqueto*. I have already shown how import and distribution could be both organised as an enterprise or as a job, and that cocaine entrepreneurs had the crucial assistance of all sorts of helpers and employees. I have even described most of their tasks in former chapters. I will now try to characterise this specific labour market, showing the most common contractual arrangements found and the logic behind them. When analysing drug economies, too much emphasis on professionalism has obscured the fact that the 'crime industry also needs a large number of unskilled criminal employees' (Ruggiero 1993: 137) who at the same time pose a major threat to their employers. Reuter (1983) argues that:

> "The entrepreneur aims to structure his relationship with employees so as to reduce the amount of information available to them concerning his own participation and to ensure that they have minimal incentive to inform against him." (Reuter 1983: 115).

Traquetos try to solve this problem by segmenting units, subcontracting, using friends and relatives, avoiding fixed employees, relying on brokers, passing minimal information, providing personal incentives, replacing, intimidating or lowering the number of employees. In sum, becoming flexible and relatively 'unorganised'. After reviewing the specific labour market around Colombian *traquetos*, I will argue that these 'solutions' are part of a wider picture that goes beyond illegal markets. While illegality tends to intensify them, they touch core developments of current capital and labour markets under 'disorganised capitalism' (Lash and Urry 1987), 'flexible specialisation' (Harvey 1989) or 'post-Fordist' economies (Amin 1994).

Skilled subcontractors

Colombian cocaine entrepreneurs relied heavily on subcontracting specific tasks to a variety of individuals and enterprises that provided infrastructure, knowledge or skills for a particular operational aspect. These contractors were usually paid either in cash or kind per individual project. In this way, relatively small economic units were able to operate by integrating flexible layers of contractors and subcontractors.

The subcontract of other illegal enterprises was rare in the Netherlands but very common in Colombia. Cocaine exporters used to contract the services of organisations – some with two or three people – specialised for example in the recruitment and loading of small couriers, in large scale transportation – for example, Mexican groups – or in the exercise of violence – private armies, *sicarios*, and so on.

Other subcontracted businesses had a much better reputation. Whether they were single corrupted employees inside a firm (import-export, freight or transport companies, chauffeurs, bank employees and managers, and so on) or entire small businesses (retail and distribution shops, restaurant owners, and so on), all had in common that they were paid to provide essential infrastructure services, beyond mere know-how or labour force. Almost every single operation that came to my knowledge subcontracted, at certain stage, services from legal companies.

Much subcontracting took place at an individual level, blurring at times the divide between wage labour and entrepreneurship. These people performed more simple tasks, all involving some particular skill and some material resource not provided by the employer. I have explained, for example, how Riverito was contracted to unload cocaine, for which he had to arrange many things for himself. Some infrastructure services were subcontracted in a more continuous fashion: Simona was regularly paid by Joel to stash cocaine in her flat. Some individuals regarded the contract as an extra-income, while mainly keeping more stable sorts of income from jobs or social benefits. Sporadically, Manolo drove an acquainted *traqueto* in his car, but lived from retirement benefits after 30 years of industrial work.

Professionals

Professional skilled workers also tended to be externally hired or recruited. Again, small and temporary enterprises did not allow for stable 'departments' with specialised personnel. Some of these services came from legitimate professionals, who were often paid salaries or fees well above the average. A pool of local or Colombian lawyers specialised in cocaine cases had a remarkable stability in their jobs compared to their clients. Travel and real estate agents were paid excellent prices and commissions. In contrast with Colombia and with local legal and illegal entrepreneurs, I could not find local accountants hired to launder money. This professional service was directly provided by the institutions or the employees involved. In some cases, people with know-how in import-export bureaucracy and in information technologies (IT) were also involved, for example, for organising large import operations. Professional truck drivers were also hired or paid off to transport cocaine in their trucks.

Traquetos also hired a number of people with particular skills acquired by virtue of their full-time involvement in some illegal activity. They included professional smugglers of all sorts, routine burglars (for operations that involved breaking into warehouses, containers or flats) or individual *sicarios* (though rare in the Netherlands). The trend for these 'professional criminals' was to diversify skills and become polyvalent multi-skilled workers. They were good candidates for replacing 'bosses' or becoming their closest employees.

Managerial bodies

The heavy use of subcontractors and 'external' professionals discouraged stable managerial bodies. In many cases, the *patrón* him/herself directly controlled the performance of unskilled workers. When people were sent to the Netherlands to organise the import (envoys), they eclectically mixed functions of managers and entrepreneurs. More specific 'organisers' – sent, for example, to supervise a delivery, assess risk, make a collection or 'fix' a problem – were often focused on one particular operational aspect, closely followed orders from the 'boss', and were more concerned about external relations and arrangements than with internal labour organisation. These people, although highly trusted by the cocaine entrepreneur, did not behave so much as white-collar 'company men' or 'vice-presidents' but often identified with many subordinates in their expectations of 'taking over', 'changing *patrón*' or 'quitting the job' altogether. Hierarchies were understood more in terms of authority and leadership than as compartmentalised, vertical bodies of delegation and control. 'Superiors' and chiefs were often respected for past events or deeds, rather than for present positions and current developments. Moreover, some people suggested the existence of more horizontal relations – in the style of *project crimes* or *crimes in association* (McIntosh 1975) – which involved mutuality beyond the business or labour relation. Miguel:

> "It is not just pure business and cold contracts. Within the group you discuss your personal life, your problems with others or with women, you have fun together."

He even alternated between performing as a supervisor (*baby sitter*) and a worker (*mula*). There were also cases in which 'outsiders' like overseas partners, who for example recruited and dealt with employees, took managerial functions. Sometimes I noticed that tasks and arrangements were simply abandoned to the initiative of those hired to execute them, and that 'bosses' did not have the will or the power to supervise people while the task was being carried out.

Finally, some cocaine entrepreneurs suggested that 'managers' are important but also dangerous, since they know many things that could easily be used against them. Mary McIntosh (1975) made the point in her classic work *The Organization of Crime*:

> "In fact it is not easy to distinguish control over subordinates from control over rivals. A subordinate may at any point cut loose and become a rival; a rival may become a boss, or a subordinate." (McIntosh 1975: 54)

The use of relatives is only a partial solution: pressures to also be 'in charge' are greater amongst close relations, whom incidentally may not always have the organisational skills required to manage people.

Unskilled part-time employees

Unskilled irregulars, people who would perform multiple tasks with different levels of complexity, formed a final and extremely important group of employees. These employees showed high degrees of job dissatisfaction and had no prospect of promotion. For some, the job meant an extra-income next to other legal or illegal occupations. For others, it was a 'last remedy' solution to tackle economic hardship, desperate conjunctures, or no other perspectives. For others still, it was the dream of becoming a *traqueto* some day.

The group included, as described in former chapters, people performing as 'body packers' or small air couriers, local chauffeurs, divers, other unloaders, load keepers, informal bodyguards, internal couriers, cash remitters and smugglers, flat hosts, helpers and peddlers.

They had no job security. As a protection *buffer* to the business, they were placed in the 'front line', and easily replaced when targeted by drug enforcement agencies. Continual replacement not only restricted the flux of sensible information – weakening their bargain position – but also kept labour costs lower than in cases when stronger loyalties were constructed. I found many people 'waiting' to be called by a *traqueto*. Others had done some job for the boss, and were put 'on hold' until the next operation, a process that could take months.

Many of them rotated through different tasks in one or several operations. They had a name for those unskilled helpers doing 'a little bit of everything': *toderos*. They enjoyed the lowest occupational prestige.

These workers were recruited from several networks, but preferably not from established criminal labour markets: relatives of cocaine entrepreneurs, potential, illegal or established migrants, or local drug dealers. In this way, they tended to belong to external labour markets (Tilly and Tilly 1995: 287), evidenced by the lack of career advancement and in many cases criminal records.

While only some of these employees received a salary on a regular or irregular basis, the large majority were given some sort of flexible personal payment for each task performed. Load keepers, for example, were paid by the day. International unskilled couriers were unevenly paid a fixed amount or per kilo transported according to their experience and the financial resources of the exporter. This meant sums of between US$ 1,000 and US$ 10,000 per trip. Internal couriers and cash remitters or smugglers were paid a percentage of the amounts handled. Finally, helpers of wholesale distributors were given a couple of kilos of cocaine and the instruction that they could keep any difference above certain price. Many of these 'salespersons on commission' belonged, in my view, to this type of unskilled, interchangeable labour force.

8.3.3 Post-Fordist arrangements

For the past 20 years, the Fordist organisation[7] of capitalist production experienced a serious crisis that resulted in significant change. While the causes, the extent and the prospects of this transformation remain a matter of debate, little disagreement exists about the main characteristics of so-called 'post-Fordist' conditions of accumulation.[8] Some of the key characteristics of post-Fordism are summarised in Table IX. Hirsch (1993) argues that post-Fordist firms are

> "...increasingly conceived as a "bundle of contracts", none of which requires elaborate headquarters, overhead, staff, hierarchy, slack, or much in the way of organisational memory. These organisational attributes are seen as irrelevant, if not unnecessary and wasteful. Managers are conceived of as interchangeable; specialized skills, if not available in house, can be purchased outside at market prices..." (Hirsch 1993: 148).

The way in which Colombian *traquetos* organise themselves to deal cocaine, from export to wholesale distribution, perhaps represents one of the finest examples of such a firm. In this way, my findings differ from those of Ruggiero (1995), who conducted research on drug economies in Italy and Britain. He found that their labour markets reproduced the Fordist model, in which 'assembly-line delinquents' had clearly divided roles and tasks, within a vertically organised industry. However, he recognises that the overwhelming preponderance of flexible work constitutes an anomaly in his hypothesis, justified by the 'competitive' rather than 'monopolistic' nature of the drug economy. However, he does not explain why such a dynamic business should follow an opposite trend – i.e. Fordist – to other legal markets of the same kind in terms of business organisation and labour relations. In Table IX, I illustrate how most of the characteristics of the cocaine business parallel more general trends of post-Fordist or flexible accumulation.

---

7   The Fordist system basically implied, in the realm of production and labour processes, the following features: mass production and consumption of uniform and standardised goods; vertical integration; displacement of knowledge from labour to managerial bodies; disciplining of labour force; 'Taylorist' segmentation of tasks performed by single workers in a repetitive and alienating way; job specialisation; payment by rate; no or little 'on the job training and learning' and functional as well as spatial division of labour. For an extensive analysis on capital and labour organisation under Fordism, see: Braverman (1974) and Harvey (1989).

8   See Amin (1994); Harvey (1989); Lash and Urry (1987); Jessop et al. (eds) (1991); Wood (ed.) (1989) and Hirsch (1993). It is beyond the scope of this research to thoroughly analyse the nature and implications of post Fordism. In addition, I do not intend to compare businesses at an empirical level. I regard this theoretical exercise, very much inspired by Ruggiero (1995), as a conclusive hypothesis worthwhile exploring in further research.

Table IX Post-Fordism and Cocaine Business Compared

	Post-Fordism	Cocaine Business
Enterprise	Decline of hierarchical management and corporate structure.	No 'branches'. Small firms with arms-length transactions. Flexible 'cocaine' brokers.
	Technological innovation.	New smuggling and packing methods. New communication technology.
	No stocks.	No cocaine stocks.
	Economy of scope in a global market. Flexible and small batch production and distribution.	No 'pipe-lines' but specific operations. European market as an unity.
	Differentiated, non standardised consumption. Demand driven.	New products (crack). Heterogeneous consumers. New markets.
Labour	Dual segmentation towards professionalisation and de-skilling.	Criminal lawyers, legal businessmen, professional smugglers and unloaders VS mulas, boleros, toderos, encaletadores and helpers.
	More horizontal labour organisation.	Despite clear patrones (bosses) and separation of planning and execution: weak managerial structures, many project crimes, little supervision, vertical clashes, workers become bosses.
	Worker's co-responsibility.	Workers take more risks and are expected to solve problems. Little information exchange.
	No job security, poor labour conditions, temporary workers, hire-and-fire.	People hired per operation. Many unfulfilled promises. People 'waiting' for an operation. Many alternating with legal and illegal jobs. Many rebusques. Risk of hopeless imprisonment or death.
	Dispersal, diversification of the spatial-territorial division of labour.	Cocaine consumers in Colombia and Colombian capitalists in the Netherlands. Less regional specialisation.
	(Quasi-) vertical integration through increased sub-contracting and outsourcing.	Many skilled tasks sub-contracted by traquetos: transport, unloading, legal defence and cover, violence, and so on.
	Decline of blue collar working class.	No stable employees, no bureaucracy.
	Elimination of job demarcation. Multiple and rotating tasks.	Toderos. Entrepreneurs also 'hands on'. Polyvalent multi-skilled promoted.
	Revival of domestic and family labour systems.	Kinship and ethnic bonds important, but no 'family business'.
	Personal payment (bonus, flexi-wage, on commission).	Conditional payment if success. Kg sales on commission. Courier's wages very flexible. Gifts when 'crowning'.
	On the job learning and training.	Many people with no 'criminal record'. Improvisation and imitation.

The illegal nature of the cocaine business introduces even more dynamism to all the post-Fordist trends described. No taxes, large profits, no labour regulations and unions, no training costs, not even a company building: the ultimate utopia of those advocators of market flexibility. Undeniably, the lack of stable employees, the massive use of sub-contracting or the reliance on brokers are *also* risk minimising strategies to neutralise repression efforts. Illegality increases the variables that jeopardise the chances of two actors to engaging in the same business or labour relation for a second time. A provisional list of these variables include:

a   Changes in volumes and prices handled; marketing routes; smuggling methods; legal business around the cocaine trade and production or consumption levels.
b   Actor A or B dies; has to 'move'; goes to prison; goes bankrupt; changes expectations, interests, ambitions or reputation.
c   Disagreement; 'dirty play' or dissatisfaction from the first transaction.
d   Police intervention in terms of mutual distrust and paranoia.
e   Police toleration and corruption in terms of new partners; possible alliances and better contacts.

While this 'wild' flexibility may threaten individual entrepreneurs – increasing transaction costs, expelling first-time losers from the game, and so on – it provides to the overall cocaine business with a superb incentive and a competitive advantage.

Although illegality shapes internal business and labour relations, these relations can also de traced in other highly competitive legal markets, which struggle to survive under post- Fordist conditions. These commonalities also make possible the symbiotic overlap between legal and illegal businesses and labour markets.

The impact of illegality upon internal relations can be better observed by focusing on particular resources deployed while doing business. Chapter IX will demonstrate the extent to which violence, secrecy and trust are three important paths for success and failure.

CHAPTER IX

THE AMBIGUITY OF VIOLENCE,
SECRECY AND TRUST

> "The time is past for guns and killings and massacres. We have
> to be cunning like the business people, there's more money
> in it and it's better for our children and grandchildren."
>
> Mario Puzo, *The Godfather*

> "The secret contains a tension that is
> dissolved in the moment of its revelation:"
>
> George Simmel, *The Sociology of George Simmel*

When focusing upon the dynamics of the cocaine business, almost all observers have
highlighted the central role of violence, secrecy and trust in the illegal enterprises or
organisations involved (Arlacchi 1986; Catanzaro 1992; Gambetta 1988, 1996). In
some cases, such as in secret societies or terrorist groups, many authors have stressed
the symbolic nature of these aspects as rituals for internal cohesion, identity construction and social reproduction (Blok 1991a: 142; Blok 2000: 87). However, when
focusing on drug entrepreneurs and organisations, a more instrumental approach has
mainly prevailed in which violence, secrecy and trust are analysed as highly strategic
resources subordinated to economic needs and considerations (Arlacchi 1986;
Krauthausen and Sarmiento 1991; Thoumi 1995; Gambetta 1996). In following this
path, I do not intend to underplay the strong symbolic dimension always attached to
physical violence as a powerful language of honour and respect, reputation and status,
identity and group solidarity, or masculine construction (Blok 1980; Blok 1991b).
Neither do I want to deny the centrality of secrecy in forming the bonds and identities
of secret societies (Simmel 1950).

However, cocaine entrepreneurs, for whatever reason they have to do so, are
mainly interested in making money. Since their business is illegal, risk minimising
strategies are crucial for maximising profits. They resort to violence in the absence of
external regulating devices, they heavily rely on trust in the absence of written
agreements, and they keep their activities secret to avoid detection. This seems
reasonably and widely accepted.

Traquetos, as many other illegal entrepreneurs, are usually portrayed as extremely
violent, highly secretive, and only willing to work with trusted 'equals'. Both in the
existing literature and media accounts, these images are exploited for public
entertainment and commercial success. State agencies and legal entrepreneurs are also
ready to emphasise those elements to highlight a qualitative difference between
gangsters, *mafiosi* or drug dealers on the one hand, and businessmen, bankers or

policemen on the other.[1] Colombian drug entrepreneurs have a particular reputation for being violent and loyal. During my fieldwork, for example, the idea of a dangerous, inaccessible underworld was constantly reflected in the questions I received about my research from the surrounding scientific community. I was told to learn everything about doing 'dangerous fieldwork'. Despite all of the stereotypes and warnings, I soon became amazed about the number of conflicts that did not lead to physical violence and the amount of information that was disclosed to immigrants not involved in the cocaine business. As explained in the introduction, it was a matter of time, common background but especially common sense to become trusted by informants. Dominant perceptions, judgements, images and expectations from outsiders – including those of fellow Colombian immigrants – often clashed with the social reality of drug dealing and dealers, which was more boring, consensual and public than imagined.

However, *traquetos* themselves were often prompted to perform in accordance with the expectations of outsiders and other business insiders. They built violent reputations even against their will, they made promises that were not going to be kept, and they kept secrets that were already known. Next to the real use of violence, secrecy and trust, *traquetos* and their employees often 'acted out' these resources strategically as a form of manipulation and as a way to construct their social and ethnic identities (Siegel and Bovenkerk 2001).

Thus, far from constituting natural, taken for granted features around illegal drug dealing, *traquetos* have tried to carefully administrate these three social resources by using them, avoiding them or acting them out. The result is a complex, almost paradoxical situation in which violence, secrecy and trust are used in ambiguous ways, forming at the same time essential tools and serious obstacles for business success. In the following pages, I will try to illustrate some of this ambiguity.

9.1 VIOLENCE

9.1.1 Paradoxical violence

Illegality turns real or potential violence into a resource with several purposes (Thoumi 1995: 134). Firstly, it is used as a threat to enforce deals or as a conflict resolution system when business deals go wrong. From preventing being cheated to punishing misbehaviour or failure, from 'settling scores' to getting rid of creditors, cocaine entrepreneurs have very often resorted to threats or assassinations, both

---

1   Zygmunt Bauman convincingly argues that 'thanks to the state monopoly, coercion gets split into two sharply distinguished kinds, respectively characterized as legitimate and illegitimate, necessary and gratuitous, desirable and undesirable, useful and harmful. (...) One category of coercion is called 'enforcement of law and order', while the nasty word 'violence' is reserved only for the second. What the verbal distinction hides, though, is that the condemned 'violence' is also about certain ordering, certain laws to be enforced – only those are not the order and the laws which the makers of the distinction had in mind." (Bauman 1995: 141).

toward business partners and their own personnel. Secondly, violence can be used as a threat against competitors to prevent them from intruding in one's market (Arlacchi 1986: 195) or from reporting business activities to the authorities. Good examples of this are the Miami 'cocaine wars' (1979-1982) or the many attacks and assassinations involving Medellín and Cali traffickers. Thirdly, violence protects the illegally obtained property or profits from theft and robbery, both from insiders and outsiders. Finally, it can be used against law enforcers to force policy changes or to avoid capture or seizures. Over the last 20 years, large and small cocaine entrepreneurs have killed politicians, judges and thousands of policemen in Colombia.

Violence has indeed a permanent latent presence in the cocaine business. In contrast with more political organisations – for example, *mafia* groups, guerrilla or paramilitary organisations, and so forth – where it appears as a commodity in itself, for cocaine entrepreneurs violence is one of the resources available.[2]

However, as a 'meaningful' (Blok 1991b) and 'instrumental' means of preventing or solving conflicts, even within the cocaine business, violence seems to be used as a last resort (Krauthausen and Sarmiento 1991: 195).

The nature of the cocaine business places structural limitations to the excessive use of violence. In fact, cocaine transactions are based on agreed exchange rather than on violent extraction, as it is the case in parasitic activities. An ideal deal does not or should not have to include physical violence. Moreover, an overemphasis on market protection and monopolistic tendencies à la Arlacchi ignores that even the people involved recognise the competitive nature of the drug business and act accordingly. I witnessed, for example, how several small Colombian groups peacefully coexisted in the same city – at export level in Cali or at wholesale level in Amsterdam. They often ignored each other or regarded it contra-productive to 'fight' the competition.

More important than the exercise of violence is the 'threat' of violence. A violent reputation – i.e. the conviction that somebody is ready to use violence if necessary – can indeed be enough in many cases to neutralise retaliation or 'dirty play' and push forward a deal. Miguel recalls from a Dutch prison:

"A guy from our group thought that I had something with his girlfriend, which wasn't true. He said he was going to kill me, but the *patrón* told him that he would kill him, his children and the next 5 generations. The day after the guy apologised."

Some Colombian *traquetos* in the Netherlands cultivated a violent reputation by doing nothing more than exploiting a *fama* (fame) or even a surname. One informant was

---

2   Following Blok (1974), Arlacchi (1986) explains that the traditional *mafioso* 'had no hesitation in violating the most deep-rooted cultural and ethical norms' (1986: 14-15). The *mafioso* resorted to physical force in his struggle for supremacy, prestige and honour, and even his legitimate power as protector or mediator was ultimately based on the possibility of successfully administrating, exercising or neutralising violence. The modern *mafioso*-entrepreneur, on the contrary, enjoys a competitive advantage rooted in market forces, and in the ability to combine capital, violence and corruption (1986: 194). A similar dichotomy between power and enterprise syndicates is made by Catanzaro (1994). While the former are specialised in violent social regulation, the latter seek to develop skills and alliances for their illegal activities.

called Escobar, a very common name in Colombia, and he kept telling that he was related to *Don Pablo* when he discovered that the story impressed people. Another man invented the story that he had been a Pablo Escobar's bodyguard.

Too much violence can discourage potential business partners to deal with a reputed violent entrepreneur. The case of Griselda Blanco, 'The Black Widow', is well known. A leading figure in the Miami cocaine wars, her cruelty endowed her with too many enemies. In the same fashion, Tano explains:

> "...Tico was the guy for the job. Not like Paisita who is impulsive and you never know. Tico is perfect; he remains cool no matter what. He looks dangerous and you should have seen these *Suris* looking at him, they were scared. With Tico is much better, Paisita caused lots of problems."

Excessive violence, as I will show later, can also attract the attention of authorities or can provoke an escalation that could damage market performance.

Entrepreneurs themselves use several other mechanisms to prevent or avoid the use of violence. Even when trust has failed there is still a gap before actual violence. For example, in cases of business failure or rip-off, entrepreneurs would first try to get 'civil' compensation: money or a favour in return. In other cases, they would just forget about it or they would be satisfied with an explanation. In fact, the number of conflicts and problems faced by entrepreneurs that are solved in a non-violent way is amazing. Again Miguel, in a joking mood:

> "I had to stop in Venezuela for a couple of days, just two days, but I stayed for a month 'cause I met a beauty. Can you imagine? Yes, you pay with life if you rip-off the *patrón*. He was really worried, so he sent two men after me. They found me, but when I showed them that the merchandise was with me and it was all right, nothing happened. They just told me to move my ass..."

Fear also neutralises violence. So does the threat of being denounced to the police. The frequent use of relatives and old friends also places limitations on the use of violence, turning, for example, a killing into a denunciation. Almost every cocaine entrepreneur in Colombia knows that it is better to bribe a policeman or a politician than to kill him. They have killed a lot, but those using less violence against the state had more chances to survive or even keep in business.

Finally, violence affects their relation with civil society. Again, too much violence would deny them both the acceptance from the traditional elite and the tolerance from civil society that is essential for survival.

The clear success of *valluno* cocaine entrepreneurs after the Medellín group started to collapse in 1991 was less the effect of the so called 'cartel wars' of 1990, than of the fact that they were, at the same time, investing in a legal business empire, cultivating political influence, and, more importantly, adjusting and improving their business methods: reducing risk, achieving economies of scale, just-in-time supply, developing new products – heroin – and markets – Europe and Japan –, and introducing new technologies.[3]

9.1.2 Colombian violence in the Netherlands

The initial quotation from *The Godfather*, to some extent a *cliché* in the mouth of Don Corleone and by no means a general trend in late modernity,[4] expresses, however, the paradox of violence for illegal businessmen. This paradox has been particularly evident in the Netherlands for Colombian *traquetos*: they have had to silence their guns, to restrict settling scores, to rely on reputations, in sum, to behave as civilised people in a pacified country.[5] After briefly presenting some cases of physical violence around the cocaine circuit in the Netherlands, I will argue why they do not happen more frequently.

Dead bodies

The number of cocaine related homicides in the Netherlands involving Colombian victims or offenders is extremely small compared to the situation in Colombia. Many informants had friends or even partners killed there, and some experienced death threats, escaped from desperate situations or were 'sentenced' to death. Miguel told me in prison:

> "The people who sent me will try to kill me. But I'm not going to live in fear. I have two chances: either I go to live in another Latin American country or I face them and tell them 'here I am, let's arrange things right now.' I think I'll do that."

While some people suggested that the situation in the Netherlands had deteriorated over the last 5 years, the number of dead Colombians from liquidations or rip-deals does not surpass one or two per year. Moreover, the cases do not receive much publicity, partly because the police and the Colombian community prefer to keep things quiet, partly because the victims involved are not powerful enough. Father Wim argued that:

> "Colombian violence is entering the Netherlands slightly. This isn't what it used to be. Before they were just settling scores, but today we go from one deadly rip-deal to the next."

---

3   'Colombia's Drug Business. The wages of prohibition', *The Economist*, 24 Dec. 1994 – 6 Jan. 1995.
4   Massacres and guns were still big business in the year 2001, but are now privatised or recollectivised, dispersed, deregulated, neo-tribal, marketed in/by the media, do-it-yourself style, and consumed as shocking stimuli (Bauman 1995).
5   The Netherlands stands as the antithesis of Colombia regarding the state monopoly of physical violence. Following Elias (1982) one could deduce that Colombians tend to be violent in their own country, while they are forced to hand over or repress violence when they operate in more 'civilised', internally peaceful states-societies. However, this idea overlooks the dynamic interweave between state violence and 'drug violence' as well as other factors such as the nature of the Dutch drug market, the drug policy, the Colombian community, the level of corruption, and so forth.

Indeed, 1996 was a particular deadly year. In December, two young Colombians were found shot-dead in a flat in Amsterdam. They were both involved in cocaine import. The case shocked the community since one of them was a woman with children in Colombia. However, nobody wanted to talk. People distrusted the police and feared possible retaliation if they became involved. The Consular authorities wanted to do just the strictly necessary about the case. After some weeks with the unidentified bodies, Father Wim made a dramatic appeal to the community on a Sunday Mass:

> "Let's show to the Dutch police and the Colombian authorities that the people know more than they do! Please, if somebody know their real names and can identify them, I beg you to do it so we can send them to Colombia for burial."

After a month of silence their names were revealed and they could be cremated and sent to Colombia. Riverito knew the couple. He had met them while working in Amsterdam, but he would not say what happened to them. When he was detained, the police found a photograph in which they appeared together. They thought he was connected, but no evidence was found:

> "They tried to incriminate me with those killings because that picture. Ridiculous."

Only one month before, another case had shocked the Colombian cocaine circuit in The Hague. Two Colombian men were found dead by a passer-by, tied inside the trunk of a car in a quiet street in The Hague. The bodies were bound with tape and had more than 30 stab wounds. 'Rambo', one of the victims, was a wholesaler well known in the street prostitution circuit. He was well-established, had double nationality, a car, and a good standard of living. His helper, a 24 years old Colombian, had just arrived two months before. An informant:

> "He hung around the [prostitution] street. He was cooking *arepas* for the girls in a little kitchen. A man lent it to him for a month. When he left the street, nobody saw him again, not alive."

Many stories circulated about the case until suspects could be detained and convicted. The first version, reflected in the first police reports and propagated amongst Colombians, talked about the settlement of a score performed by Colombian *sicarios* sent by a man from Bogotá to whom the victims owed money. The *sicarios* would have entered and left the country unnoticed, so the case was covered by powerful images of professionalism, organised violence and powerlessness. A second more moderated version involved Yugoslav hired killers and 2 kg cocaine. However, things finally changed when the police detained three men accused of the killings. Two Dominicans and one Colombian – respectively 21, 25 and 24 years old – were charged and later convicted with sentences between 15 and 20 years. They killed the Colombians to steal them a little over 1 kg cocaine in a rip-deal.[6] One of the Dominicans was also involved in armed robbery.

---

6   See *De Volkskrant*, 29-03-97 and *Haagsche Courant*, 20-09-97.

A third case was still fresh in the memory of some people. In 1993, two Colombians and one Antillean were selling cocaine to a Turkish wholesaler in The Hague. When the merchandise was being delivered, the Turkish man took a gun and killed the Dominican and one of the Colombians. The other Colombian jumped through a window and eventually told everything to the police. Both Colombians were in fact well known in the local cocaine circuit.

Next to these and other cases, always involving rip-deals, Colombian men are occasionally involved in shootings or fights that bear no direct relation with a drug deal but ensue from personal conflicts, sentimental quarrels or alcohol abuse. They tend to happen at night around the most frequented salsa discotheques in major cities and usually involve non-Colombians as well. In one occasion, Paisita was beaten up by other three Colombians in *El Llano Bar* in The Hague. From the floor, he managed to hear one of them telling to the others '*no vayan a matarlo*' (don't kill him). He left running and never came back to the place.

Sicarios

Some informants in the Netherlands had close experiences with *sicarios* (hired killers). While Miguel was working in a cocaine kitchen near Cali, he shared a house with two *sicarios*, both contracted by his *patrón*. He remembers:

> "It was awful, we were having lunch or dinner and they would go on and on talking about the people they had to *limpiar* [lit. 'to clean', to kill]. They did it in a normal tone, making jokes, being funny, and openly enjoying truculent details while eating. But there was mutual respect. On those days I wore my gun 24 hours a day. I would not kill for money as they did, I would only kill someone who would harm me. For a while I was a personal bodyguard of the *patrón*, but I did not like the job."

A desperate Colombian woman explained that she had a teenage son. She had long been divorced from the father of the child, a Colombia *sicario* who lived in Colombia. However, he kept phoning to his son in the Netherlands to tell him that if he was to become a 'real man', a 'tough guy', he had to be able to kill and he could start by 'cleansing' a *desechable* (disposable), for example, a drunken beggar or a junkie. Even if I find the story hard to believe, the violence of such representation speaks for itself.

In the European context, the recruitment of *sicarios* from Colombia has been restricted to dealing with powerful targets or groups. In September 1994, a Galician from the *clan de los Charlines* was killed by Colombian *sicarios* after having testified against his local associates in a case involving the import of 1 ton of cocaine.[7]

However 'present' the *sicario* is in Colombian experiences and imagination, everybody agreed that it is difficult, expensive and dangerous to import *sicarios* to the Netherlands. Despite a couple of cases during the 1980s in which Colombian *sicarios* were hired by local groups (Bovenkerk 1995b), collected evidence indicates that Colombians use local individuals to settle scores with non Colombians.

---

7   *El País*, 29-05-95.

Many 'violent' people refrained from violence. I found ex-bodyguards dealing drugs, or even score settlers just keeping an eye on their bosses, but as Emilio explained:

> "To kill somebody here, you need protection, you need to be able to *guardarte* [to hide, to conceal yourself]. I am not talking about a rip-deal or a sudden reaction. I mean a planned assassination. No man, it is too risky, too risky... You hear many threats and also some 'pressure', and they are enough. No, everybody has relatives there. They settle their scores in Colombia..."

Drug dealers cannot move with bodyguards unnoticed or tolerated. Even those with clear instructions refused to play the *sicario* for one reason or another. Miguel:

> M: "My instructions were to kill the courier if he stole the merchandise. But everything went fine."
> DZ: "You told me you would not kill for money. Would you have done it?"
> M: "I don't know. I am not a *sicario*. May be not. But then I would have been in trouble myself. I would have followed the guy, get the thing back, and scare him really bad so he learned the lesson."

Others shifted their ethical boundaries. Joel, for example, claimed to be rather peaceful, and many people around confirmed the fact. However, once his nephew in Colombia misbehaved during a particular operation, causing Joel considerable financial damage. He then hired two *sicarios* to punish him. They kidnapped him, and phoned Joel to ask when would they 'break' him. He told them that they had got it wrong, that he did not want a dead body. He just wanted to have him incarcerated for a couple of days. In the Netherlands, Joel did not carry any weapon and only relied on other people for the actual threat of violence. He also denied killing or ever having ordered a killing.

Kidnapping

As a mean to either pressure or punish others, some Colombians resorted to unsophisticated forms of kidnapping. These actions were usually poorly planned and even more badly executed, nothing resembling the accounts of García Marquez (1996) on the kidnapping industry in Colombia.

In 1997, Riverito, William and Charly were detained in an attic in Amsterdam. The police trapped them with no guns (only William carried a knife) and no cocaine. They only had telephone taps and the key declaration of somebody who had been supposedly kidnapped by the Colombians. Riverito:

> "I told you we were robbed. They just took the kilo with pointing guns. We were desperate, we went back home and we took the Aruban guy with us. You see, he knew these people; we just wanted either the thing back or the money. I assure you we only wanted him to help us. But we did not touch him; he was not handcuffed or anything. They were even playing Nintendo with William. He even went out to phone somebody, for sure his uncle, because he is a cop. Since that moment we were tapped and observed and later of course detained."

The victim, however, convincingly told the Court that he had been handcuffed and threatened during those two days. Riverito received 4 years, 2 of which for kidnapping.

> "The police were brutal. They took Charly and they broke his arm, so badly he had to go through rehabilitation therapy. But they scared him and he confessed. I don't blame him. He had too much pressure. But, you see, he was not a bodyguard of Pablo Escobar as he claimed (laughs) (...) it was unfair, that is why we appealed. They gave me two years for the kilo when the rule is only one. Two years more for kidnapping. But first, my lawyer says that the normal would have been 18 months, and, second, it was all a fucking trap. The doctors did not find any sign of violence. It was purely his word. I would have accepted two years, but four is too much."

Indeed, Riverito received a relatively high sentence compared to similar cases. In prison he met another Colombian who received 30 months. He had the same charges, but the victim had cigarette burns on his arms.

In a slightly similar case in 1996, the 15 year old brother of two cocaine dealers was kidnapped from his parent's house in Den Bosch. He was held for some days in order to force his brothers to return 5 kg of cocaine that they had presumably stolen. When it was clear to the perpetrators that the kidnapping was not going to be successful, they decided to release the teenager instead of harming him, despite earlier threats to do so. The police found one kilo and later arrested three people.[8] A Colombian who was not detained had to disappear for a while after telling some people that he had been involved in the case.

In a third case in 1996, Colombian exporters hired a couple of Yugoslavs to kidnap a close associate of a Dutch buyer (main importer). They wanted to force the Dutchman to pay for the 70 kg that he had bought from them and sold on to an Italian group that 'delayed' payment. The kidnapping was 'monitored' by the police and finally forced a new deal. After the event, and despite the fact that no Colombian could be captured, the Dutch police (IRT) decided to intervene in order to preclude further violence.[9]

All cases known involved victims closely related with the business, and were not punitive but were intended to elicit payment.

Going Dutch: low profiles and quiet markets
The actual use of physical violence in the Colombian cocaine circuit was, in the Dutch context, restricted to very specific cases. Dealers tended to keep low profiles, and were rather negative about the use of violence. Most kidnappings and killings were connected with rip-deals and not used as punishments or score settles: violence was regarded as a costly social resource.

Most people did not carry fire-arms. Moreover, they also regarded them as dangerous. Knives were more common, but only to be shown in extreme cases. Some

---

8   *De Volkskrant*, 20-08-96.
9   *De Volkskrant*, 31-01-97.

salsa discotheques tolerated the entrance of weapons, but even in cases of personal fights people tried to calm things down. On two occasions I witnessed how people shouted 'no guns, no guns' when a fight broke out between visitors who were totally drunk.

Again and again, people pointed out that 'threats are enough' and only exploited the Colombian reputation for violence. Powerful *traquetos* seemed to measure more the costs attached to violence, balancing invulnerability, negative costs and symbolic benefits.

Several factors, some not independent from each other, can be identified for the fact that Colombians have tended to keep *cool* while dealing cocaine in the Netherlands.

Firstly, the Colombian community is too small and unorganised to successfully conceal the use of violence. Colombian immigrants are neither intimidated nor protected by drug dealers, so they are also not forced to conceal their actions. In fact, it seems to me that the fragile community 'tolerates' drug dealers as long as they do not engage in internal violence. The high number of women and mixed couples almost certainly has an impact on keeping the resort to violence restricted.

A second factor involves the Dutch social environment. The Netherlands has, certainly in comparison with Colombia, low crime and impunity rates regarding violent crimes. This monopolisation of violence is indeed acknowledged by *traquetos*, who feel more 'exposed' and recognise the risk of 'damaging the market'. Many are aware that stupid fights can invite police attention, so they try to keep out of trouble.

A further element that must be taken into account is the cocaine market dynamic at the level in which Colombians are involved. The market in the Netherlands has remained rather stable, with peaceful competition amongst different groups with no monopolist claims. Furthermore, there has been no interest or power amongst Colombian groups (most of them from the Cauca Valley area) to fight internal wars in the Netherlands. Even those who had clashes in Colombia preferred to ignore each other while operating in the Netherlands. In this sense, the close and constant contact with Colombia constituted an outlet rather a violence source, allowing for many conflicts to be diverted to Colombia.

Finally, low levels of violence are also related, paradoxically, to the lack of an American or Colombian model of internal war on drugs. *Traquetos* in the Netherlands do not have to react against military operations, para-legal violence or summarial executions, actions that would logically expand the number of dead bodies on all fronts. Colombian *traquetos* seem to get the implicit message from Dutch authorities: 'we tolerate you as long as you keep quiet and you don't get rich here'. It can also be argued that state corruption – especially police and customs corruption – and a tied link with local legal arrangements – transport companies, import businesses, banks and so forth – further helps to discourage the use of violence.

9.2 SECRECY

9.2.1 The public nature of traqueto's secrets

It is not difficult to imagine the centrality of secrecy for cocaine entrepreneurs. They have to minimise risks, avoid detection and neutralise competition. Secret measures or practices can be seen at any level: production, smuggling, and so forth. The spread of mobile telephones and even the use of secret words or codes show that secrecy is essential to close deals or pass information. Discretion is highly valued by business partners or employers, and therefore the people who 'keep their mouth shut' also. They cover up their activities, and sometimes they even hide them from family and friends. Arlacchi claims that:

> "A very high degree of secrecy must also be established... Operational secrecy is a crucial element in drug-trafficking." (1986: 196-197)

He also suggests that secrecy is guaranteed by 'common membership to the same culture, the same ethnic and regional community' (1986: 198), in which a 'criminal elite' is formed by members of particular ethnic minorities. This emphasis on secrecy in connection with 'ethnic organised crime' is so popular and accepted that, during my fieldwork, almost every second question I received on my research was how did I manage to get access to my informants.[10]

For cocaine entrepreneurs, secrecy is a social resource, an adaptive device to conceal information, activities and relationships to protect a very profitable business. While even the very existence of the group can be kept secret from some outsiders, cocaine enterprises cannot be considered secret societies[11] but open associations that keep some operational matters secret. As explained in chapter VIII, their flexible arrangements disable any sort of permanent 'secret membership'. They do not move with some secret set of rules, but with very pragmatic and changing measures, which can include secret procedures. Traquetos do not rely on secrecy to maintain an exclusive monopoly on any sort of knowledge, idea, right or leadership.

Naturally, as with any other enterprise that engages in economic competition, a possessed knowledge about contacts, partners, clients, markets and so forth, is carefully protected to gain a power advantage over competitors. This sort of secrecy can be internal and external, and does not differ much from that of craft organisations, guilds or modern corporations. However, cocaine entrepreneurs cannot rely on

---

10 The first question always referred to violence: is it not dangerous?

11 Secret societies are groups whose continued existence relies totally on the continuous concealment of ideas, objects, activities, plans, objectives and membership from outsiders with a high degree of internal secrecy as well (Tefft 1980: 324). Typical examples are religious or political groups such as cults, Mafia-type organisations, revolutionary factions or community groups for ritual socialisation and social mobility (see Simmel 1950; Tefft 1980 and Blok 1991a).

bureaucratised or standardised marketing methods as in legal business.[12] For a single transaction, there are often many contacts made, a good number of meetings, and very long discussions about small operational details (Krauthausen and Sarmiento 1991: 196). This marks a first limit to secrecy: it is not surprising that one of the most successful police methods against cocaine entrepreneurs has been telephone tapping.

On the other hand, secrecy is also directed at concealing the illegal business from social censure and legal punishment. However, more importantly, to conceal information about potential harmful others – thus more powerful – who can take action if that piece of information is disclosed. Chino, for example, occasionally expressed concern about the publication of the material, but not so much for what I could say about him. He was only afraid of one *traqueto* in particular:

> "If he recognises me and discovers that it was me who told you that, I could be in trouble."

Secrecy thus seems to arise more from conflict of interests – between insiders and outsiders, but especially between insiders – than from mutual self-interest. In the drug business, secrets are kept not so much for the sake of loyalty but basically due to fear and self-interest. Here lies a second fragile side of secrecy: since the *traqueto's* loyalty to other groups or individuals (relatives, friends, other immigrants, or, why not, researchers), often supersedes responsibility to their employers and employees, they tend to disclose secrets as soon as they do not feel threatened or they are offered a better deal.

This is why successful operations do not seem to rely that much on keeping shared information secret. To know and exchange the strictly necessary information is often the case along the different levels of a cocaine operation. In this way, secrecy manifests itself as social fragmentation rather than as a bounding or integrative device. Many employees ignore the essential whereabouts of their employers. By keeping employees misinformed – a rule, for example, with drug smugglers – the employer is protected from both capture and betrayal.

In fact, cocaine entrepreneurs seem to dislike secrecy all together. As Ernesto, who was involved in the cocaine business in Cali for a while, explains:

> "...It is a hard life, all the time hiding from police or people who want to kill you. I used to walk all the time looking everywhere. I can range 180 degrees without moving my eyes. I know people like me who left the business because they were just very tired..."

Secrecy also operates as an obstacle in two different ways. In the first place, regarding the business itself. After all, they have a merchandise to sell, and in one

---

12 Allowing for quite impersonal and standardised exchanges, and displacing secrecy to the powerful realm of institutional frames. "A great deal of corporation secrecy is maintained not by conscious design but by the mere fact that the corporation is so complex and has so many diverse operations that even the most persistent outsider finds it hard to learn much about the financial and other economic affairs of the business bureaucracy." (Tefft 1980: 202). These businesses are also better prepared to conceal 'dirty secrets' about illegal activities such as price fixing, tax fraud or money laundering.

way or another they have to advertise it: cocaine entrepreneurs need to let potential partners know that they have a good quality product, that they manage a good price, and that they are able to deliver it. As in any legal business, a good public reputation counts. Naturally, they will try to limit the number of buyers for security reasons,[13] but with too much secrecy they would simply be unable to operate.

Secondly, secrecy creates a clear problem for their social expectations and reconversion strategies. Illegal entrepreneurs want to be recognised as successful entrepreneurs and be accepted as such. They have invested a lot of money and effort to become 'public' figures, in many cases without really hiding their obvious source of income.

The more powerful they are, the more open and public they become. Even Arlacchi acknowledges that:

> "The mafia entrepreneur is a talker, giving regular interviews in which he makes himself out to be a persecuted benefactor. (...) He has got beyond the marked distrust that the old-style *capo* felt towards newsprint, journalists and mass communications media" (1986: 118).

They use – and indeed like – to show up in well-known restaurants, bars or discotheques. It is not rare that they even talk openly about business in these places. For an outsider, it takes only a matter of minutes to recognise them. People will not know about their operations, but will usually be able to point out 'who is who'. In small towns, everybody knows the 'big shots' even by name. In the Netherlands, local dealers working for different *traquetos* immediately knew about busted operations and captured people.

For many business actors, their daily activities are a subject of conversation with friends or close people not involved. Feelings of pride, compassion, regret, hate, fear or misery come up frequently with the job and are often a trigger to talk with outsiders. It is not rare to find people that behind a paranoid discourse on secrecy, in fact talk and share openly their experiences within the cocaine business. Alcohol drinking, and the particular pattern of recreational activities and consumption codes that surround the illegal business, contribute to the disclosure of sensitive information and codes. As explained by Adler and Adler (1980: 459), unless someone shares the knowledge of his activities with others, there is no way he can get the respect and admiration that he has earned and desires so intensely.

As mentioned earlier, I was not only surprised about the amount of information outsiders knew, but also about how much *traquetos* and their employees openly talked and showed me around. Despite some details always remained secret, especially regarding violent acts and specific whereabouts,[14] many things – including incidental

---

13 For exporters and wholesale distributors, the ideal would be to sell large quantities to very few people, maybe two or three. However, this is sometimes difficult for smaller entrepreneurs. For retail dealers, secrecy is even a bigger problem, since they have to compete much more for new and better customers.
14 See section 1.2.4. for fieldwork limitations.

access to a 100 kg cocaine load – were indeed open once acceptable levels of trust were built. Amongst Colombian immigrants, the topic of drugs was present at certain stage of any conversation.

In their pioneering work, Adler and Adler (1980) analysed what they called the 'irony of secrecy' in the drug world. Drug dealers, they found in their research, are torn between conflicting forces that prompt them to both keep and tell their secrets: an erratic movement between purposive and impulsive behaviour, between rational strategies and hedonistic life-styles. However, I am not convinced that this 'irony of secrecy', also visible amongst Colombian *traquetos*, expresses a tension between rationality and irrationality. This juxtaposition seems to be grounded in their romantic believe that drug dealing is above all – which maybe was the case during the 1970s in California – an expressive and hedonistic activity opposed to the logical and mundane routinely world of work and business. For Colombian *traquetos*, I argue here, there are enough rational motives to disclose secrets as there are to keep them.

9.2.2 Public and secret places

A small number of top cocaine entrepreneurs try to avoid public places that they consider to be dangerous.[15] They rarely go to church; they do not hang around prostitutes' windows, and only frequent well-known Salsa discotheques occasionally. They often prefer to go to typical Dutch bars, take-away stores of various kinds, some coffee-shops, or Spanish and Italian restaurants. They avoid large groups and being in public with prostitutes. Some even choose Dutch girlfriends, and try to follow a 'normal' life. Their strategy is to pass unnoticed, not to remain within secret circles. In fact, *traquetos* know that there is nothing secret about *Latino* 'underworld circles'.

Other – usually smaller – drug entrepreneurs and employees behave in a completely different fashion. They could not care less about hanging around in 'hot' scenes. They go to church and the Salsa discotheques in vogue, they walk around the prostitution areas, and they openly advertise their involvement in the illegal business in many ways: they wear expensive clothes, spend lots of money when people are around, talk about the business on ordinary telephones, and even play loud music until late in the places they live, often shared with other Colombians or with passing-by visitors. For them, only operational details are a matter of secrecy.

For both groups, going to the telephone centres to phone abroad means a certain degree of disclosure and publicity. These places are indeed public, anything but discreet, with many people gathering by chance or appointment. Even big *traquetos* have to go there, since talking to Colombia for instructions or information exchange is such a very delicate matter that it is dangerous to delegate. There, secrecy is taken to its ultimate boundaries. Apart from the fact that any person present can hear everything that is being said in the improvised cabins, some people even stay to comment with competitors about prices, the market situation, or to talk about a mutual

---

15 Some of these people are what I refer in chapters V and VI as envoys and discreet professionals.

friend in prison. The telephone centres and the bars around are also used to discuss operational matters or recruit people for particular jobs.

These places are maybe the best example of the structural limits of secrecy for Colombian traffickers.

9.2.3 Nicknames

Joel was rarely addressed by his real name. He was named 'The Uncle', 'uncle J' or 'Charly' by different people around, while in Chicago he used other names still. This was not only the result of a planned strategy on his part to disguise his real identity. Sometimes he liked to use his real name: once he even left it recorded in a message on my answering machine.

Nicknames were ambiguously used and reflected people's intentions to keep distant, feel close or be allusive and parodic (Blok and Buckser 1996). Tico, for example, started to call him 'uncle' being his real nephew. He only became 'The Uncle' when others like Tano or Chino adopted the nickname, showing on the one hand respect but on the other undermining his authority: in hierarchical terms, 'uncles' are not particularly well placed.

The constant flux of names and nicknames amongst *traquetos*, I believe, is only partially related to the secretive character of their activities. It primarily reflects the fluid and ephemeral nature of a business in which very personal relations are paramount, several levels of interaction often mix (for instance including relatives, friends and strangers in a single transaction), and identities and reputations are constantly negotiated and at stake. I seldom found people that could keep a strict separation between names, aliases and nicknames. Some nicknames referred to kinship relations (the nephew, the uncle), while others were simply old nicknames from childhood. Others made reference to a violent reputation (the scorpion, the black widow, the knife), a physical attribute (the fat, the coca queen, the blond), an occupation (the student, the doctor, the engineer), a skill (the rocket, the chess player) or an origin (the *paisa*, the Mexican).

9.2.4 Counterfeit secrecy

On many occasions, people manipulated secrecy for various purposes. A first form of manipulation involved exaggeration or paranoid attitudes. Some people in the business who tended to see 'secret conspiracies' against them – from enemies, competitors, business partners or the police – developed paranoid discourses about secrecy with no real commitment to conceal information. In three different cases, informants would stress in the beginning that 'you do not talk about it' or 'you have to be very careful', but neither they put these ideas in practice nor they could stop talking once they got into the conversation. Others, especially some Colombian immigrants with no relation to the cocaine business, just liked to 'lock' *traquetos* in the realm of underworld secrecy, claiming, for example, that drug organisations were extremely closed. Later in the conversations, however, they would show more knowledge about them than originally indicated. Both forms of self-deception demonstrate how the notion of secrecy can be used to either reinforce a *traqueto* identity as well as to establish social boundaries.

A second and very common form of manipulation involved a game of pretence. Many people around drug dealers were aware of their secrets but pretended they did not know them either to escape stigmatisation, to protect the secret holders, or to preserve the relationship with them. I found cases in which relatives in Colombia were told stories about 'being on a business trip'. Even in cases of imprisonment, I met people who concealed the fact to their families for years. In Colombia, I met a woman who 'thought' her daughter was studying in the States. She was instead facing a 12 year sentence in a Federal prison. Sometimes, friends and acquaintances also faked ignorance or indifference to maintain the amicable relation. A general attitude of distrust amongst Colombians in the Netherlands was accompanied by one of turning a 'blind eye'.

9.3 TRUST

Trust refers to a particular level of the subjective probability with which an agent assesses that another agent or group of agents will perform a particular action, both before he can monitor such action and in a context in which it affects his own action (Gambetta 1990: 217). As a risk minimising strategy, trust is a very important feature for successful business performance. This seems to be true for any sort of transaction involving risks, whether it is legal or illegal. However, the huge profit margins and the absence of a formal juridical apparatus to order and regulate transactions, contribute to an increase in the chances of 'dirty play'. The particular combination of constraint (illegality, few choices), risk (physical danger) and interest (huge profits) seems to call for trust as a social device. Mutual trust, Arlacchi argues, is 'far more necessary among criminals than among businessmen' (Arlacchi 1986: 198). Agreements have a great chance of being transgressed or misinterpreted, and so there are temptations to cheat, steal, denounce or even kill counterparts. For example, expectations for a single successful theft of 100 kg cocaine – worth around US$ 2 million – can prevail over the interest to continue business with an entrepreneur. To avoid rip-off or detection, it is essential to work with trustworthy people, both as employees and as business partners.

During my fieldwork in the Netherlands, trust building was a central part of the research process. Informants only started to be co-operative (and reliable) after a certain confidence was guaranteed. I had to show credentials – by 'receiving' people at my university office – or present my intellectual work and skills – by appearing in public, handing over my publications or engaging in discussions. I also had to gain the good will of influential 'gatekeepers' who gently afforded me access to their social networks. I offered help or friendship to various people who eventually helped me in return. As explained in the introduction, trust was both an essential precondition and a precious result of the interaction with my research population.

9.3.1 Building trust

Cocaine entrepreneurs have many ways of constructing trust. Firstly and foremost, through the use of relatives and close friends. It is extremely common, if not a rule, to find brothers, cousins, nephews, partners and old good friends constituting the core of cocaine enterprises. Bonds created around a common socialisation or kinship are important guaranties for mutual trust. This is the case at all levels, from cocaine production to distribution, and for long distance relationships between different market levels.

Again, the mere instrumental nature that blood or artificial kinship has in the Colombian cocaine business should be emphasised. Organisations do not have any fixed labour, organisational or hierarchical division around kinship. Who owns the business is just a matter of skills, luck or other variables. Two brothers might be partners or one may work for the other. Women might both participate or give orders to their sons or husbands. Many relatives may not be involved at all, and close friends might be, as it is often the case, more important than blood-related people.[16] Colombian cocaine enterprises differ from other illegal organisations where 'clans' or 'families' are basic in their constitution and reproduction. In this sense, the 'collective spirit' that means to trust a relative or a friend has less to do with an abstract identification with 'equals' but more with shared aspirations and aims: to successfully make money and to remain at liberty (Krauthausen and Sarmiento 1991: 43).

A past in common can also facilitate trust, from a shared criminal background to a common past in the police, some guerrilla group or university. However, it is not possible to work only with known people. Another way to build trust is through the intervention of a third common trusted person who can introduce or recommend a newcomer. The closer and more powerful this third party is, the better the chances of gaining trust.

Trust can also be pushed forward by the existence of a power relation. Dependence of any sort can expand unilateral trust, even when it is a pragmatic one. People owing favours, people who have been given a 'second chance', people who can be potentially blackmailed ('he knows my family') or denounced ('he knows many things about me') have some chances to be co-operative. However, as I will further explain, (illegitimate) coercion in fact tends to reduce mutual trust and to provide a weaker alternative means to enforce co-operation.

Further, trust seems also to increase when everybody is happy about profit distribution or remuneration (Krauthausen and Sarmiento 1991: 202). If somebody feels exploited, badly paid or not earning what he or she should be, there are strong possibilities that he would try to look for other partners or employers, including the police.

---

16 It can be argued that some of these social relations constitute a form of artificial kinship (Blok 2000: 87). Friends can become *compadres*, or godfathers and godmothers of other's children. Many *traquetos* treat each other with the word *hermano* (brother). However, the use of this idiom of kinship and blood in social discourses and practices is so common in Colombia that it is questionable if it means anything special for cocaine traffickers.

Above all, as in any legal branch, trust is only gained in doing business: sticking to agreements, achieving maximum labour efficiency, bravely assuming the risks of illegality and protecting personal as well as others integrity. Even between relatives, trust is often afforded to the better qualified. Joel:

> "If I go back to Colombia, Tico [his nephew] will get the *line*. Paisita is too emotional; he can make a mess. Tico has 'papers' and speaks Dutch. He is cool no matter what happens."

Good workers and partners are highly appreciated and carefully kept. On-the-job reliability can only be shown with experience. In some cases, for instance with the contract of hired-killers, after credentials have been accepted, a test or proof can be demanded. Others will have to start from below and go through a trial period to gain know-how and see what the person is up to. There are also 'test-deals' to assess the trustworthiness of certain partner or line.

With this, I suggest that while some degree or provisional mutual trust is a pre-condition for co-operation amongst drug dealers, real trust also seems to appear as a result of co-operation. The cocaine business environment, however, does not stimulate the development and reproduction of 'accumulated trust': flexible relations vanish, many deals result in one-off operations and expectations about future co-operation are rather limited. In fact, *traquetos* provide an excellent case for researching the limits of trust.

9.3.2 Distrust and betrayal

Most informants were obsessed about distrust and betrayal. The scepticism of Tico, for example, was commonly shared:

> "...you can not trust anyone in this business. People will try to steal from you if they can. Police are easier to recognise, but I trust no one..."

An ideal trustworthy person would be a relative who is both responsible and economically satisfied. However, such people rarely exist and only one of the variables mentioned before is too little to gain trust. In fact, in the cases when trust does exist, it seems to be transitory, fragile, always at the edge of collapse.

Betrayal and distrust are also essential resources for survival in the cocaine business. Betrayal between blood relatives is infrequent, though not rare. Joel, for example, worked in Chicago with his brother as a wholesale distributor. Once he had to collect some US$ 150,000 from a client. When he arrived to his debtor's place, he was told that his brother had already collected the money. Joel's brother went back to Colombia and used the cash to pay off personal debts. Joel felt cheated and for a long time did not see his brother again. More mythical cases are often publicised in Colombia: the Ochoa brothers are said to have killed their uncle to get the business in their hands, while a famous operator in Miami known as the 'black widow' had the reputation of having killed a former husband to get control over his assets.

Betrayal between old friends is very common, even between people who have worked together for many years. In fact, familiarity through friendship or kinship tends to expand trust that leads to co-operation only under certain conditions. Firstly, social costs of exit or betrayal have to be high, at least higher than those incurred with strangers. Otherwise, the 'strong tie' only serves to improve, rather than decrease, the chances of betrayal. And even in these cases, difficulties of 'walking away' from friends or relatives can have little to do with trust and much with coercion or fear for punishment or ostracism. Secondly, 'blind' trust (loyalty, global trust beyond local disappointments) often endorsed to friends and relatives cannot only lead to co-operation but to deception as well (Gambetta 1990: 218).

The intervention of a third party or the recommendation by known people is a trust source that cocaine entrepreneurs often regret. As Riverito lamented from prison:

> "These *paisas* are all the same. They are tough and to certain extent trustful but they live from a reputation not always deserved. Look, my friend said that the guy was his friend, but in fact they saw each other only two or three times before! (...) I trusted the guy. He said he had good contacts and spoke with a fluent Colombian accent. I though he was from the [Colombian] coast, but he was from Aruba. He was a thief, and also a *sapo* [police informant]. In fact, I even mistook in trusting my friend Charly."

Trust as a result of 'job satisfaction' or agreed profit distribution is also fragile. If business goes well, usually people would think in terms of more money, better tasks, or in becoming more independent. Even when a cocaine deal is successful for everybody, there is a strong tendency from each party to believe that they are 'smarter' than the other. Even when people want or have many motives to trust, they suspect that the other party wants to play dirty even if it is not so. Finally, trust constructed through work reliability – skills, efficiency, responsibility, and so forth – seems to be stronger, and partly explains the international character of the people involved in the business.

The paradox of trust is that, unlike other devices such as violence, the very same constraints, risks and interests that set the conditions and the need for trust tend to put severe limitations on its development.

Firstly, the need for trust supposes a degree of limited freedom for the two – or more – parties involved. In order to need trust, both persons should be able to freely leave the stage at any time. If only one course of action is possible or even expected from the other (with no alternative for exit, betrayal or defection) trust would not be required. *Traquetos* can only trust each other when they have an alternative (to steal, to deal with other party, to kill, and so forth). However, some informants, especially employees, often claimed to have 'no choice' and participate out of coercion or acute economic hardship. Take the example of the unskilled drug smuggler. He neither has to trust his employer nor does he need to be trusted when the smuggler's relatives can be hurt or his properties seized due to failure or deceit. Illegitimate, coercive constraints based on power differences are common in the business and constitute alternative means for bringing about co-operation. In those cases, distrust is more likely to develop. Coercion and violence, as alternative resources to trust, increase the chances for betrayal and the classic stab in the back.

At the same time, dealers or actors with too many alternatives – for example, the police informant that can receive alternative protection, the dealer that has a large network of business contacts, or even the peripheral adventurer who can easily return to a 'straight' occupation – receive lower levels of trust.

A second condition refers to the nature and perception of risk. I have shown that not only different actors face very uneven degrees of risk, but also that they assess risk in various ways. Again, trust is required but difficult to arise when these differences are so strong. Trust is a highly problematic resource in a business environment so unstable that in any risk calculation – including that of law enforcers – there are always unintended and unforeseen outcomes (Giddens 1991: 112). Many Colombian cocaine entrepreneurs I met were either fatalist or paranoid, and both types had problems with trusting others. People with a fatalistic outlook – often failed dealers but also some who felt immune, powerless or frustrated – showed a resigned acceptance that events should be allowed to take their course. Their appeal to *fortuna* (Giddens 1991: 113) was reflected in many circumstances. Some justified their lot (prison sentence, debts) invoking fate and destiny. Others preferred to give chance almost the same status as risk. For example, for a 'fateful moment' such as the despatch of a large shipment by sea, some exporters would require the advice of experts and outsiders, the counsel of foretellers *and* the help of the Virgin Mary. Finally, some fatalists just 'hoped' that certain persons would help them or leave them alone.

Another attitude was to overstate risks and develop a paranoid distrust about others whether they were individuals or institutions. Paranoid reactions suddenly appeared even inside trusted relationships and challenged the continuity of co-operation.

Economic interest, a major drive behind co-operation in drug enterprises, was also often a weak incentive for trust. Everybody pointed out, especially in Colombia, that short-term 'wolfish hunger' for large profits, and speculative behaviour around an ephemeral economic *boom*, far from propagating trust, increased distrust and the so called 'dishonesty trap' (Thoumi 1995).

Suspicious reputations
That the drug business is at odds with trust is also evidenced by a common attitude found amongst Colombian immigrants in the Netherlands: a basic internal distrust as a weapon to resist stigmatisation, negative images and bad reputations.[17] Even more, as a way of avoiding any sort of problem. Tano explained me that:

> "You don't ask in the beginning 'what do you do for living?'. Nobody asks that question, they will tell you later. A typical answer is: '*y ahi, viendo lo que se hace...*' [well, seeing what's up...]."

---

17 Siegel and Bovenkerk (2001) found the same phenomenon for the Russian community living in the Netherlands. They distrust each other, while they manipulate to their advantage dominant stereotypes about the *Red Mafia*.

In fact, I soon discovered that most immigrants avoided the question when they suspected something. Places with bad reputations were avoided or condemned, and on many occasions people would gossip about 'successful' immigrants. The few legal 'ethnic entrepreneurs' had to battle to demonstrate the transparency of their businesses. Many informants had to 'calm down' worries from home (Colombia) about a possible involvement in drug dealing or prostitution. I found some Colombians who even avoided contact with co-nationals since they regarded them as a source of problems.

9.3.3 Trusting the other: the management of business reputations

Trust attached to particular groups can favour their inclusion or exclusion from the cocaine business. Both *paisas* and *vallunos*, for example, tended to distrust people from the Atlantic Coast, which they felt closer to other Caribbean groups such as Antilleans or West Indians.

I frequently asked Colombian dealers active in the Netherlands about their opinion of the trustfulness, in business terms, of particular ethnic or national groups encountered in Europe. Some had little concrete experience with specific groups but had nevertheless something to say. Interestingly, the reasons given to like or dislike a particular group were remarkably convergent, all revolving around four concrete issues.

A first variable referred to their perceived skills for business performance (professionalism). A second aspect concerned the respect for keeping one's word and sticking to agreements (word). A third issue rested on a vague notion of honour, including readiness to talk to the police, ethical dignity, courage, coolness and 'guts'. Finally, a forth element referred to the degree in which they could access and control the groups (accessibility).

Ethnic groups[18] were indeed perceived as more or less trustful as far as these features were positively or negatively judged. Colombian dealers tended to regard Italians and Spanish as the more reliable, while they were consistently negative about the Surinamese and Antilleans. In general:

	Italians Spanish	Turks	Native Dutch	Russians Yugoslavs	Surinamese Antilleans
Professionalism	+	+	+	+	-
Word	+	+	+	-	-
Honour	+	+	-	+	-
Accessibility	+	-	-	-	+

---

18 Only some came regularly into picture, so I dare to mention them. Some people clearly distinguished between Surinamese and Antilleans, the latter being more positively considered.

The question remains about the extent to which these stereotypes of reliability spelled out by Colombian dealers had a concrete materialisation in terms of co-operation. It is my impression that dealers also tended to reproduce standardised images about the groups, and that trust (or positive image) and actual co-operation did not always coincide. For example, while Turks were regarded as having more 'honour' than Dutch dealers, their business interaction with the Dutch was by far more significant. On the other hand, Surinamese and Antillean groups were negatively depicted as less professional and honorific than the Russians, but their smoother and more fluid contacts with the former groups contrasted with their sporadic encounters with East Europeans.

CHAPTER X

CONCLUSIONS

This book has addressed several questions concerning the involvement of Colombians in the international cocaine trade, particularly focusing upon their participation in the Netherlands as cocaine smugglers, importers, distributors and retailers.

A point of departure for this study was not only the existing gap in empirical knowledge, but also the belief that some of the prevalent methodological and theoretical tools used to approach the issue were either insufficient or misleading to understand the complexity of that involvement. Surrounding images of Colombian 'cartels', *mafiosi* and transnational criminal organisations were enough incentive to enter the field with critical questions about the nature of social relations amongst Colombian *traquetos*.

In contrast to economic-bureaucratic models that portray *traquetos* and their employees as 'belonging' to sophisticated transnational cartels, the present study shows that they mainly engage in short-lived business operations that involve legal and illegal arrangements in which actors and transactions are linked in flexible and changing forms. Against criminological approaches that try to delimit Colombian 'criminal' organisations or networks, my material shows that cocaine ventures involve a wide set of enterprises and people, including *bona fide* companies, law-abiding relatives or friends, and an army of helpers and service providers that are as essential to the business as they are 'disconnected' from it. Finally, the idea of a Colombian ethnic *mafia* is also contested throughout this volume: *traquetos* neither perform mainly as power brokers nor are their relations with overseas co-nationals always smooth, favoured or even sought after.

Chapter II analysed the role of Colombia as the main cocaine producer and exporter in the world, while chapter III dealt with the European cocaine market and the position of the Netherlands within it. In both cases, I tried to highlight historical developments, the business social structure and the ways in which this illegal market is embedded in broader social, economic and political conditions. In chapter IV, I presented the main socio-economic characteristics of Colombian immigrants living in the Netherlands, in an attempt to assess their objective conditions for engagement in the cocaine business. Chapters V and VI showed the ways in which different sorts of Colombians are involved in cocaine smuggling, import, distribution and retail selling in the Netherlands. Chapter VII addressed the question of how two specific important groups of Colombians such as prostitutes and illegal immigrants are linked with the cocaine business. Further to this, chapter VIII examined the specific internal relations between Colombian cocaine entrepreneurs and their employees. In chapter IX, I finally analysed the role of violence, secrecy and trust in the cocaine business.

While some findings in this book are somewhat in line with earlier research results in the field of drug economies, others imply a challenge to official studies purely based on data gathered from criminal justice agencies. Social scientists, and certainly criminologists, have often avoided contact with the very population studied. This fact is partially understandable: these very agencies are often the main (financial) motor behind most research on the subject; researchers are compelled by time or professional duties, or they simply declare that it is too dangerous or difficult to get close to drug dealers in their natural settings.

This research, on the contrary, avoided police and judicial sources as much as possible and relied on long-term interaction (from peripheral participation, observation and open interviewing) with Colombians inside and around the cocaine business in the Netherlands and in Colombia. A first important conclusion of this research is that ethnographic research on drug dealers – and on other forms of contemporary organised crime – is both possible and desirable for the advancement of the field.

Firstly, it is possible. If criminal justice agencies are to become involved in financing ethnographic research, they should grant the researcher enough time, intellectual freedom and operational independence. Other basic requirements are an open mind to hear and reflect on distinct and contradictory voices, and a willingness to build personal relations beyond the mere interviewer-interviewed interaction. Furthermore, researchers should protect their informants and themselves, maintain clear ethical boundaries, and follow rigorous methodological decisions based on openness.

Secondly, it is desirable. Ethnographic research on drug dealers can address often neglected issues behind 'criminal organisations or networks'. It can reveal the socio-cultural context and background of the people involved, and their views about their own activities and the surrounding environment, including their opinions on enforcement agencies, other entrepreneurs and the society as a whole. Moreover, this sort of research has the potential of reflecting internal conflicts and differences between those involved in the cocaine business. It can eventually raise new critical questions about their motives, their risk perceptions, and the rationality behind illegal entrepreneurship.

In these concluding pages, I will try to sum up my main empirical findings and their theoretical implications.

COLOMBIA AND THE COCAINE COMPLEX

Cocaine production and export consolidated 20 years ago in Colombia and somehow mirrored other short-cycle export booms around one particular product. Although stimulated in the beginnings by American demand and traffickers, some Colombian groups managed to gain an early control on cocaine production, export and wholesale distribution in the United States, establishing the refineries in Colombia.

A combination of political, geographic and economic conditions and developments favoured and secured its competitive advantage with regard to other countries: weak state presence; strong local powers and relative autonomic regions; political culture based on 'clientelism' and patronage, with corruption as an outcome; state unaccountability and a long-standing violent institutional de-legitimation; suitable internal geographic features (rivers, coasts, jungle, natural isolation, and so on); long tradition in export contraband, with know-how on marketing routes, foreign contacts and smuggling techniques; expectations of high short-term profits promoted by older booms, around which Colombian capitalism developed; active black foreign exchange market; crises in regional economies; large Colombian migration in the United States willing to enter the illegal business at any price and, finally, early control on wholesale distribution by Colombians themselves.

The Colombian cocaine industry has often been depicted as omnipresent for the country's economy. However, from the material presented in chapter II, it should now be concluded that the size of the illegal industry, although large in relative and absolute terms, has been exaggerated with respect to production volumes and Colombian cocaine income.

Concerning the business social structure, cocaine entrepreneurs and enterprises are far from homogeneous. They firstly vary very much regarding social origins – urban and rural, lower and upper class, and multi-ethnic. This heterogeneity can be explained by a number of reasons: the rather 'open' nature of the cocaine business, the fact that it is not restricted to one particular set of political actors or social conflicts between specific groups, the prospects for quick upward mobility for all (both included and excluded from legal activities) and the relative wide range of social acceptance, toleration and legitimacy attached to this activity, at least until the mid-1990s.

They secondly differ regarding regions. The distinct social dynamics, political environments and cultural markers of Colombian regions have shaped six cocaine 'centres' or focuses, each one with its own importance and momentum. The existence of these focuses, however, does not mean that they are the only places where cocaine enterprises are active, or that each focus functions as a unified and homogeneous group.

A third difference is a generational one. After the death, imprisonment or retirement of older and better-known bosses, a younger generation of *traquetos* has taken over. Many of them have no criminal background, and they have invigorated the illegal business by further flexibility, internationalisation, re-localisation, and risk management.

Fourthly, cocaine enterprises in themselves are heterogeneous and the mutating product of fragile agreements between people and flexible articulation between legal and illegal enterprises. Some exporters have achieved a remarkable vertical integration, but normally cocaine production and transportation are separate economic units, subcontracted by exporters. Powerful organisations using many resources and performing many tasks, can in fact be subcontracting most of them – transport, military and security resources, professional expertise, money laundering services, labour force, and so forth – whereas they do not have a strict and rigid labour division. Typically, a division can be made between bosses, assistants, professionals and unskilled, flexible mass labourers. Tasks, methods and enterprises change according to the dynamics imposed by illegality, which allows independent and sporadic entrepreneurs to survive alongside the larger ones.

The concept of 'cartel' is totally inappropriate to refer to cocaine enterprises, even to those moving in a relative oligopolist market sector. They are more often decentralised, amorphous and fragmented networks – basically dyadic ones – articulated by precarious and variable transactions. They move from co-operation, by developing systems to integrate smaller investors to the illegal business and to co-ordinate military actions, to savage competition, by killing, stealing or denouncing competitors or their own people.

The further atomisation of export groups after repression efforts intensified in Colombia during the second half of the 1990s (reintroduction of extradition, forfeiture legislation, capture of large exporters, and so on) provides a clear example of how illegality disables 'large', stable and bureaucratic structures, and actually push enterprises to remain sporadic and mutating.

Far more noticeable than the economic impact, the social and political impact of cocaine entrepreneurs in Colombia has been enormous. They have indeed used social and political resources to protect their activities, and they have tried to gain social recognition by a number of reconversion strategies. Since some have transformed accumulated money into social power – founding politicians or expanding local loyalties and support – many authors have used the notion of *mafia* to portray these drug entrepreneurs. However, if compared, for example, with the Italian case, quick analogies should be avoided. *Traquetos* are not *mafiosi* since they do not perform as power brokers. Italian *mafiosi* and Colombian drug organisations differ very much regarding historical origins, organisational models, and in their relations with the state and the civil society.

The activities of illegal drug entrepreneurs in Colombia have had very negative effects in social and political terms. The existence of the illegal business has definitely contributed to further state de-legitimation by growing corruption, use of violence and in very few cases task competition. It has spread feelings of impunity, while reinforcing models of individual success 'at any cost'. It has turned foreign policies and international relations with Colombia into a matter of 'narco-diplomacy'. Long-suffered internal armed conflicts have been worsened by the cocaine business collusion with guerrilla and paramilitary activity. In particular, the link between traffickers and paramilitary groups has deteriorated the human rights situation in Colombia. Furthermore, although the cocaine business has often been too simply associated with all sorts of violence in Colombia, it has undeniably amplified many violent social conflicts.

THE EUROPEAN AND DUTCH COCAINE MARKET

Further in the marketing chain, cocaine is exported to Europe to be distributed and retailed. What are thus the main characteristics of the European cocaine market and what is the role of the Netherlands in it?

The material presented in chapter III shows that, in contrast with Colombia, cocaine has a long tradition in Europe. Cocaine production and use underwent a four-phase development since it was first isolated in 1859. Until the early 1900s, it was regarded as a 'wonder drug', broadly used by physicians for various purposes. All sorts of coca infusions, syrups and elixirs reached the general public during the 1880s. Germany and the Netherlands were the main cocaine producers, importing coca crops from Peru and Java.

A second phase runs from the turn of the century until 1930, a period in which cocaine lost its positive image and became illegal. Growing scepticism about its medical uses and its expansion as a recreational drug amongst intellectuals, bohemians, artists, jet-setters, soldiers, as well as all sorts of outlaws, pushed a crusade that included a mix of medical, moral and social arguments. The counter-reaction was joined by physicians, stronger medical bodies, more controlled pharmacists and social reformers in the frame of 'moral Welfarism' and post-liberal States. Social fears were reflected in the popular press and in political debates about urban dangerous classes, decadent life-styles and violent crime.

The third phase ranges from 1930 to 1970, in which cocaine literally disappeared from the European scene. The first illegal users rapidly replaced expensive cocaine by legally available and far cheaper amphetamines. A final period since the 1970s is marked by a renaissance of cocaine as an illegal drug. In fact, Europe followed trends in the United States with a gap of some years (only after smuggling by sea became possible). However, the European market never reached the magnitude of the American cocaine epidemic: a different cultural and social environment set a limit, and by the late 1980s cocaine had already been stigmatised. Better prices, an increasing demand and new transport methods, rather than a saturation of the American market, explain expansion to Europe.

Different sorts of users consume cocaine in Europe. Many regular opiate users have been using heroin and cocaine together ('speedball') from the 1970s on. Cocaine powder is sniffed in a rather invisible and recreational way by all sorts of people: professionals, artists, wealthy middle-classes, and so forth. The socially integrated, occasional 'sniffer' is a young male adult aged 25-40 years with above average educational and/or occupational status. Lifetime prevalence amongst underage students is rather low (1%-2%) compared with the United States. Modest to sizeable local markets in crack-cocaine developed since the early 1990s in major European cities. However, crack use has remained very limited.

Cocaine demand in Europe is above world average, with a monthly prevalence of around the 0,2% – 0,4% mark and an average of 90 to 100 tons consumed every year within the EU. There has been a general tendency towards the stabilisation of cocaine demand in Western Europe since 1995, especially due to replacement for other substances. However, next to local recent signs of use increase, the user population has become more heterogeneous than ever before, with more problematic users. Cocaine has also reached new markets in Eastern Europe. Over the past 20 years, wholesale and retail prices have dropped 50% while purity levels have substantially improved.

This demand, and the large illegal profits to be made along the marketing chain, has certainly attracted many people and groups to participate in the cocaine business. Cocaine is supplied in Europe by various flexible groups that compete, co-operate and include several national and ethnic groups. They are mostly independent groups that manage to establish links with South American exporters. Import and wholesale distribution experienced a process of professionalisation during the 1990s. The most successful groups are those able to handle large quantities of cash and cocaine, and to combine local and international resources. This necessarily implies rather small and dynamic groups or partnerships able to quickly react to market changes and neutralise repression efforts.

In Spain, most cocaine is imported by Galician groups traditionally dedicated to contraband and fishing, usually working close to or with Colombians. In Italy, a close Colombian-Italian co-operation has also been the case. Despite cases of local protection by *mafia*-type organisations (for example the Neapolitan *Camorra*), cocaine entrepreneurs either operate under private, personal initiative, or are totally unconnected to those groups. Cocaine import in Britain is mainly organised by Britons and Nigerians, while Germany and France show a more international composition of cocaine entrepreneurs mostly engaged in wholesale operations. Colombian exporters have increasingly targeted Eastern Europe during the 1990s, both selling to local groups as well as trying to import from these areas. The evidence of various Colombian-local mixed groups at import level in several European countries illustrates the strong Colombian bargaining position as main exporters.

Former colonial ties between Europe and places like South America, the Caribbean or Nigeria (in cultural, economic or demographic terms) have played a role, especially during the 1980s, regarding cocaine routing and people's involvement (for example in transport, import or retail selling in metropolitan centres). However, during the 1990s, routes became more diversified and business composition more international with the increase of large-scale operations, the growing repression and stigmatisation of particular groups, and the market integration with other legal and illegal activities.

More cocaine intercepted in Europe for the past decade has mainly been related to the expansion of the cocaine supply into the continent. However, it also reflects improved interception rates (from 5%-10% to 30%), because over-supply and huge profits allow large exporters to easily sacrifice more cocaine. Despite claims that prior intelligence (for example through infiltration) is essential for police performance, most large cocaine seizures are still made in selective or routine controls, following anonymous tips, or by chance. Countries receiving cocaine by sea (mainly Spain and the Netherlands) show the highest seizure levels, with multi-ton operations quite noticeable in the statistics. Europe is by far the region with less cocaine interception (10% of the global) regarding its own consumption (25% of the global). Cocaine smuggled by air has been growing in absolute terms, this method still being the only option for thousands of small exporters and importers.

Cocaine routes into Europe form a cross, with four import centres at the extremes. Spain, the Netherlands, Italy and Eastern Europe (from the Baltic Sea to the Balkan route) are these four centres, increasingly interconnected by political changes, economic integration and migration diasporas. The cocaine loads are often trans-shipped once or twice and are the object of several stopovers. Once in Europe, the cocaine moves rather freely by land in bi-directional lines.

For the last decade the Netherlands has played, after Spain, the main role in the import and wholesale distribution of Colombian cocaine into the Europe. From the point of view of cocaine traffickers, the Netherlands brings together good local conditions and resources for cocaine import and wholesale distribution. Colombian *traquetos* explicitly mentioned three aspects that make the Netherlands attractive: its economic activity, its international human resources and its penal climate.

First and foremost, all considerations about the enormous economic activity in the Netherlands reflect the extent to which the cocaine business is certainly embedded in the legal economy. Colombian cocaine entrepreneurs interviewed referred, tacitly or explicitly, to four specific issues when they talked about the Dutch economy: a) the huge dimensions of Schiphol and Rotterdam; b) the excellent communication infrastructure (trains and roads) and the central position of the Netherlands in Europe; c) the good entrepreneurial environment (both in terms of mentality as well as regarding the large number of import-export firms); and d) the existence of enough banking resources to move cash. Even peripherally involved people in Colombia with a superficial knowledge about the Netherlands shared these ideas and images.

A second – positive – aspect refers to human resources. Colombian *traquetos* regard the Netherlands as an international meeting point with well connected groups and individuals. While the presence of other Colombians (usually relatives) was mentioned in some cases as an advantage, others stressed the quantitative and qualitative limitations of these contacts. Positive remarks about local human resources concerned a broad group of people including Dutch legal and illegal entrepreneurs, petty criminals, some coffee-shop owners, and especially wholesale distributors linked with destination countries (Italy, Germany, Eastern Europe and so on) belonging to various ethnic and immigrant groups.

The absence of local *mafia*-type organisations engaged in cocaine import facilitates the involvement of all sort of illegal entrepreneurs and employees, including Colombians. Many *traquetos* also expressed their inability to buy protection from Dutch Customs and police officers, feeling in this respect truly disadvantaged compared with local groups.

All people interviewed finally had some remark to make about the drug enforcement strategies and controls. Both entrepreneurs and employees tried to avoid detection concealing their actions in various ways. Despite Dutch repression at import level effectively being on the European average – certainly above countries receiving cocaine loads by land – Colombian *traquetos* regarded the Netherlands as a mild, tolerant country with respect to law enforcement. While some people – especially illegal residents – feared routine and unexpected police controls, most informants were not intimidated by drug enforcement strategies. Shorter sentences or better prison conditions are often acknowledged *post factum* by vulnerable inmates. More capitalised and successful *traquetos* – those engaged in decision-making in Colombia or the Netherlands – are able to transfer strategic risks to others. Their concerns are mainly focused on potential interception (only sometimes, since they are also ready to sacrifice cocaine and smugglers to feed the police), on employees (to guarantee their silence) and on competitors or partners (to avoid deceit and physical damage).

In this sense, these three positive conditions for importing cocaine through the Netherlands have nevertheless a different impact on the views and decisions of various Colombian traffickers and their employees. For those at the decision-making level, the interesting position of the Netherlands has little to do with the 'repression factor' and is mainly based on its economic infrastructure and facilitating human resources.

A COLOMBIAN ENCLAVE IN THE NETHERLANDS?

Colombian cocaine exporters could hypothetically find that infrastructure and human resources amongst the Colombian immigrants living in the Netherlands. Overseas ethnic enclaves or middlemen minorities can provide good import and distribution channels for the drugs exported by co-nationals. This has been, for example, the case of Colombian networks in the United States for the last twenty years: they have enjoyed a privileged access to *traquetos* while they have also met some objective conditions for engaging in the illegal business.

However, are these conditions also present amongst Colombian immigrants living in the Netherlands? From what has been exposed in chapter IV, I argue that Colombians in the Netherlands lack essential characteristics to possibly consider them either an ethnic enclave or a middleman minority.

Firstly, there is no Colombian enclave economy. The lack of Colombian capital (in terms of businesses, enterprises, and so on) is very evident, while Colombian labour is mainly oriented to the Dutch market (local enterprises or clients). The few legal or informal businesses, though they can employ other Colombians, are weak, short-lived, dispersed, and not specialised in one branch. Neither are they clustered and interconnected. Most of them are ethnic in the sense that they sell a 'Colombian' product or service, but they are not framed in any ethnic economy that would involve ethnic capital, labour and business expertise. Most Colombian businesses are established with Dutch capital and credits, and very often involve mixed couples with Dutch participation.

Secondly, the group can neither be conceptualised as a middle(wo)man minority. These immigrants lack essential social characteristics typical from these groups. Ethnic solidarity is weak, the tendency for outmarriage is enormous, and their offspring tends to 'assimilate' through mainstream schooling and socialisation. They do not have organisations at suprafamilial level, neither voluntary, charitable or self-help associations that can, for example, exercise internal social control. In economic terms, they are also far from forming any sort of commercial or entrepreneurial brokerage between dominant and subordinated local groups. As I explained, they do not practice any local legal trade activity but rather concentrate in ('gendered') labour specialisation as housewives, house-cleaners and prostitutes. Typical middlemen family owned and operated small enterprises are, again, absent amongst Colombian migrants in the Netherlands.

At the most, it can be argued that Colombian entrepreneurship in the Netherlands manifests itself through the – partial – colonisation of particular occupational *niches*. The clearest examples are prostitution and other informal jobs mainly performed by women, such as housecleaning. Although this labour force does not involve any web of independently owned firms, it neither develops into a classical wage 'ethnic' proletariat. They tend to remain as a flexible, often self-employed, work force ready to exploit various activities. These activities can also be, as I found out during my fieldwork, illegal activities in the cocaine business.

The evidence that Colombians in the Netherlands do not form any ethnic enclave or middleman minority is certainly relevant for this study. Historically speaking, immigrant groups that have succeeded in organising and controlling particular illegal businesses are groups that developed minimum levels of entrepreneurial life, or at least some sort of ethnic economy. For example, in the US, all groups found to be historically involved in 'ethnic organised crime' are in fact the same groups also described as successful trading minorities or ethnic entrepreneurs: Jewish, overseas Chinese, Lebanese, Cubans, and so on. Even large proletarian migrant enclaves like Irish, Italians and more recently Mexicans in the US, or Turkish in Germany, can also turn into 'trade' if a number of conditions are also present, one of them being the development of a web of own ethnic shops. Illegal businesses, and especially international drug trade, do not flourish in a vacuum, but within broader political and mainstream economic structures with which they are fully interdependent.

TRAQUETOS AND OTHER COLOMBIANS INVOLVED IN THE COCAINE BUSINESS

Despite their weakness, I found Colombians engaged in all four levels of the cocaine business in the Netherlands: transport, import, wholesale distribution and retail selling. However, my findings bring bad news for those who frame this participation in the realm of ethnic *mafias* or transnational 'cartels'.

It is a small and changing heterogeneous group, with a variety of geographical, social and ethnic origins, which for the last 15 years has nevertheless drawn disproportionate police and media attention, has kept a name and reputation in the cocaine business, and has deeply affected, at least in symbolic terms, social relations amongst Colombian immigrants.

Many of them do not even live in the Netherlands or only stay temporarily. The tasks, risks and skills required differ a great deal, and chances to fail or succeed are very distinct with regard to the level of involvement, legal status, degree of organisation, and overlap with legal structures and arrangements.

Various Colombians are involved in cocaine transport to the Netherlands. Whatever the method, these couriers are never independent but employed by exporters and importers to 'crown' shipments through different routes. They do not tend to live in the Netherlands and share such a risky job with less conspicuous couriers recruited from many other countries.

Some circumstances favoured, especially until the mid-1990s, the opportunities for Colombians to become involved in cocaine smuggling. Firstly, exporters need close and trustworthy people who can be controlled. Secondly, drug smuggling is, in some cases, either a career step for 'job promotion' or a task performed by people with a previous or parallel involvement in the business. Thirdly, Colombia has a large 'reserve army' of people willing to take the risk, pushed not only by negative personal circumstances (deprivation, calamities, and so forth) but also by more positive expectations of quick social mobility at any cost. However, other circumstances have hindered their participation. Colombians have become increasingly targeted by anti-drug enforcers as potential suspects, this resulting in a social and national diversification of drug couriers. The development of large-scale transportation and the proliferation of routes and transshipment countries have also increased the diversity of smugglers.

According to the quantities and the methods of smuggling involved, I identified four different groups of smugglers: *mulas* (small air couriers), *boleros* (ball swallowing couriers or 'body packers'), *niñeras* ('baby sitters' and professional couriers) and *tripulantes* (ship crew members). This study reveals that cocaine smugglers are the double victims of *traquetos* and law enforcers. The cost for their highly risky service is almost negligible if compared with the potential profits of their employers, turning smugglers into an expendable and replaceable labour force.

Colombian nationals have also been actively involved in organising cocaine import into the Netherlands. Far from controlling this level, a number of independent Colombian importers both compete and co-operate principally with native Dutch and Surinamese importers, and to a lesser extent with many other nationalities. Colombian participation is very modest for small quantities – smuggled by air – but strikingly high for large freights shipped from Colombia by sea.

Colombian importers experience conditions that both promote and limit their opportunities for involvement in import. On the one hand, and regardless their degree of proximity to exporters, they are attracted by two circumstances: a privileged contact with supply in Colombia (financial advantage) and a rather peaceful and open local business environment with no single group able or willing to restrict competition. On the other, their participation is clearly hindered and limited by the lack of own infrastructure and human resources in the Netherlands and the access to legal arrangements (corruption, import and transport firms, and so on).

Cocaine import is organised by four sorts of *traquetos*: 'envoys', 'line owners', 'mixed couples' and 'adventurers'. They are again heterogeneous with respect to social background and prestige, vulnerability, infrastructure and connections with exporters, non-Colombian importers and other Colombian immigrants. Only a small minority are envoys sent from Colombia by export organisations. They only stay temporarily, have weak contacts with local Colombian immigrants, and enjoy the highest social prestige amongst *traquetos*.

'Line owners' are more independent from exporters. They stay in the Netherlands on a more permanent basis, but always intend to go back to Colombia. Even when their suppliers are friends or relatives, they operate independent as entrepreneurs taking financial risks. These *traquetos* have difficulties in mobilising human and material local resources. Some are approached by exporters and are tested before being accepted as partners. Others work with more than one supplier, who at the same time could be working with two or more independent importers. Others still are poorly connected and have to strive to build and maintain supply resources.

Yet a third type of importer is the 'mixed couple', Colombians with a local partner. Friends and relatives of the Colombian are usually involved as exporters or smugglers, while the local partner provides the necessary infrastructure, financial and marketing resources. Some are frequent travellers, but they tend to be more established and integrated in the Netherlands.

Finally, a number of 'adventurers', usually newcoming young men from middle classes and with no criminal record, also engage in the import of smaller quantities of cocaine. These *traquetos* come and go, are locally known within the street *Latino* circuits, are erratic and vulnerable to repression, and in fact have a close relationship, in social and business terms, with local Colombian wholesale distributors.

In general, it can be concluded that Colombian importers are more vulnerable than Dutch ones since they have trouble in either using or constructing import-export firms or arrangements. The unloading of cocaine shipments is considered to be particularly problematic by Colombian importers. Around these illegal entrepreneurs, a number of Colombians are employed or subcontracted to perform important tasks: unloading, internal transport, load keeping, security and logistic help as hosts, chauffeurs, translators and telephone operators.

Colombians have also been involved in wholesale distribution in the Netherlands. However, their position at this level is even weaker and more erratic than in import, showing a clear disadvantage regarding other local operators. In contrast with the American case, local Colombian networks lack the essential characteristics required for a successful engagement in commercial distribution: no infrastructure, no protection, and weak marketing channels. They profit nevertheless from indifference or toleration from co-nationals not involved, from police difficulties in infiltrating or gathering information about this group, and from the reputation they have in the business. In this study, I claim that the few number of Colombians involved in cocaine distribution in the Netherlands exclusively derive their position from a privileged access to other Colombian importers and distributors, from which they are supplied.

They all sell kilo quantities to various groups, either local intermediaries or European wholesalers. They form rather small units of two or three people, all independent from each other, and have also a couple of helpers who either work for them or receive some cocaine to trade it through alternative channels. I found three types of Colombian distributors: 'conspicuous traders', 'discreet professionals' and 'flexible amateurs', all showing different degrees of social visibility, skills, commitment, and links with legal arrangements. Discretion and low profiles were regarded by everybody as the key factor for success. As was the case with Colombian importers, their profits are not invested in the Netherlands but are moved away through 'smurfed' remittances and cash transportation. Some money is spent in conspicuous consumption of services and perishable goods.

They also rely on various Colombian helpers even less skilled than those linked to direct import tasks. Some of these helpers can also be seen as 'poor' *traquetos* who have to struggle to get the cocaine entrepreneur's favour, live in permanent financial problems, and often combine drug dealing with other *rebusques* or illegal activities. Finally, the participation of Colombians in retail selling is almost insignificant within the multi-ethnic range of cocaine retailers active in the Netherlands. Colombians are completely absent from street dealing in major cities. Neither do they retail drugs around the *Latino* prostitution areas or streets. Further, they do not perform as house dealers. The few cases found are restricted to the recreational *Latino* circuit, and to a lesser extent the bars and coffee shops frequented by Colombians. These 'salsa dealers' are usually men and tend to be very erratic suppliers rather than professional retailers. They depend on a *traqueto* favour and on a particular demand from close people in special settings: salsa discotheques, concerts and schools, Brazilian bars, and some other private parties or events.

In some of these places, it is not rare to find cocaine consumed by dealers, customers or musicians, cautiously traded in toilets or even openly offered in public. It can be argued that cocaine is easier to find in places not run or owned by Latin Americans, with a live salsa band playing, and with an ethnically mixed clientele.

COCAINE, PROSTITUTION AND ILLEGAL IMMIGRANTS

Amongst Colombian immigrants, two groups are the usual suspects for maintaining connections with the cocaine circuit: prostitutes and illegal immigrants. The question is thus to what extent this relation is real and what are the reasons behind involvement or social distance.

A significant group of Colombian women work as prostitutes in the Netherlands in different cities and under various conditions. A first wave preceded the influx of cocaine from Colombia by some years; the second one, mainly illegal prostitutes, follows a chain pattern and retains a high degree of mobility. In general terms, they are more independent and entrepreneurial than other foreign prostitutes. Most of their pimps, sex entrepreneurs and clients are not Colombian, but instead Dutch, Turkish and Moroccan.

Traffic in Colombian women is mainly limited to forms of intermediation or to the initial work phase, taking the shape of a cut-throat, rather consensual informal contract that represents a large initial debt for the woman. Many traffickers are mixed couples of a Colombian ex-prostitute and a Dutch sex entrepreneur.

They are extremely vulnerable, suffering chronic physical and financial problems. In particular, illegal prostitutes are very exposed to regular police controls, and they are isolated from institutional and social services. They are further discriminated against by other Colombian migrants, mainly other women who feel unfairly stigmatised.

However, they tend to develop a social network formed amongst others by Colombians. Firstly, the women support relatives and unemployed close friends. Secondly, many Colombians make a living selling them several goods and services: food, telephone calls, cleaning, transportation, baby-sitting, clothes, jewellery, and even witchcraft. Some of them also have contacts with drug dealers, in this way performing important bridge functions between the drug and the prostitution circuits.

Many of them do socialise with *traquetos*. They often come from the same areas in Colombia, but they are not blood related and they tend to belong to a lower social stratum. They meet far from the 'street', especially in bars, restaurants, discotheques, churches, budget telephone centres and common flats. They regard each other's activities as different and separate. Cocaine dealers tend to consider the women as vulnerable, pitiable or unreliable. Prostitutes, on the other hand, have strong reservations against 'criminals' and drug addicts, and consider drugs a risky business. They do not seek each other as members of a common, abstract 'criminal circuit', but mainly as the result of a material and symbolic exchange. While Colombian prostitutes do not usually consume illegal drugs, they seek *traquetos* for money, protection, social status and fun. For drug dealers, prostitutes also represent a source of fun and status, sex often being absent or only marginal part of the exchange. They also reinforce their male identities.

I argue in this book that prostitutes are only marginally involved in the cocaine business. They can eventually act as package receivers, cash transporters and remitters, messengers, retail helpers or migrant facilitators, but they do not engage in central roles of import and wholesale distribution. These weak business linkages can be explained by a number of reasons. Both activities require or imply different skills, risks, moral careers, legal status and criminal policies. These differences are recognised by both groups, which despite the intensive social interaction try to keep their businesses separate. The fact that Colombians do not engage in street drug retail, and that often Colombian prostitutes do not consume cocaine drugs are two further reasons for market delimitation. Most importantly, the rather independent status of Colombian prostitutes also helps to keep a distance from possible illegal traffickers and market operators. While traffic in women and in cocaine is usually run by different people and their relation remains problematic, it is also true that women with lots of debts have more chances of accepting risky jobs in the drug traffic. Finally, the lack of local *mafias* that control and articulate prostitution and drugs also discourages further market integration.

Illegal Colombian immigrants also constitute a relatively important group amongst migrants. Though officially recorded as illegal foreigners, many Colombians involved and caught in drug trafficking, such as *mulas* or 'envoys', neither live in the Netherlands nor can be considered immigrants.

Excluded from the formal labour market as well as from institutional services and – non-existent – migrant organisations, illegal Colombian immigrants nevertheless combine good social capital and skills with some personal social networks of friends and relatives. They are neither 'integrated' nor they tend to 'marginalise'. Instead, they engage in many activities in the informal economy – especially housecleaning, but also prostitution – and develop 'stationary' careers, while some of them manage to get involved in different criminal activities of a predatory or entrepreneurial nature.

They face differential chances of being detained or deported. Most have no contact with the police. The less touched are those living in smaller municipalities or towns, those cleaning or baby-sitting in private houses, those dependent on legal relatives or friends and those employed in 'non-ethnic' small businesses. Protected prostitutes and discreet professional *traquetos* also demonstrate good skills for concealment. A clear focus on fighting 'visible' illegal prostitution and drug dealing increase the chances of deportation for those illegal immigrants hanging around the street prostitution circuit. Finally, those involved in profitable activities tend to successfully return to the country despite deportation.

Alongside this process of selectivity, illegal Colombian immigrants develop opportunities to engage in some informal and illegal activities and not in others. Cleaning, baby-sitting and prostitution are good examples of such specialisation. Regarding illegal activities, most of the thieves are not pickpockets or drug related thieves, but burglars and organised shoplifters. They abstain from drug retail selling – as 'drug runners' or 'drug pushers' – and from problematic consumption as 'drug-tourists'. Illegal Colombian immigrants tend to engage as a flexible and unskilled labour force around the import and wholesale distribution of cocaine. In some cases, they can become real *traquetos*.

I have identified three types of illegal immigrants involved in the cocaine business: the *pre-involved*, the *recruited* and the *peripheral*. 'Illegality' assumes a different meaning for each group, they tend to occupy different positions and they perform distinct tasks. They also face varying degrees of risk of being captured and succeeding as illegal workers and entrepreneurs. Several reasons can be identified for the involvement of *recruited* and *peripheral* illegal immigrants. In line with many other immigrants, from prostitutes to cleaners to merchants, these reasons involve the possibility of procuring money for whatever material or symbolic purpose. However, their chances of entering seem to be both connected with their opportunities in other legal or informal activities, as well as with finding a proper contact with *traquetos* beyond superficial and unreliable offers.

I finally conclude that, compared, for example, with better and longer established immigrants, illegal Colombian newcomers have fewer opportunities in the drug business than in other informal activities and that they have fewer opportunities to establish a solid and reliable link with cocaine dealers when they are not a relative or a close friend.

Indeed, illegal immigrants and *traquetos* have reasons to reject each other. The cocaine business can only offer a very limited amount of jobs to a small fraction of the 3,000 or more illegal Colombian immigrants estimated as living in the Netherlands. Another limitation refers to gender. While many illegal immigrants are women, many roles at lower rank, 'first line' or street level are often fulfilled by men. Many people reject involvement actively and explicitly. While some do not see the cocaine trade as morally wrong, they oppose the personal risks involved and the *traqueto* way of life. Illegality is for many a source of enough problems. Others reject the whole drug business as they connect it with traumatic experiences, violence, and a source of stigmas and shame.

Many illegal immigrants even limit their social contacts with other Colombians. They avoid 'hot' places and develop paranoid attitudes about police controls. This isolation reduces their opportunities while they compete with legal immigrants in terms of information, self-promotion, contacts and job offers. Moreover, from the *traquetos*' point of view, illegal immigrants can only offer some loyalty around their vulnerable situation. However, they are unfamiliar with local codes and language, are less prepared to react in case of problems, and they lack local contacts. They cannot drive and cannot offer legal or illegal infrastructure. Illegal immigrants are regarded, as it is the case with prostitutes, as a vulnerable social group.

FLEXIBLE INTERNAL RELATIONSHIPS: THE POST-FORDIST NATURE
OF COCAINE ENTERPRISES

When focusing upon the internal relations inside Colombian cocaine enterprises operating in the Netherlands, I found enough elements to critically question two dominant frameworks on the issue: the 'economic-bureaucratic' and the 'criminal network' approaches.

The first model, adopting an economic-bureaucratic approach, tends to see fixed 'branches' of cocaine cartels. It allows for comparison and further research on the interwoveness of legal and illegal economies. It fails, however, in not providing evidence for the organisational models and structures assumed: Fordist, monopolist transnational corporations with rigid pyramidal hierarchies and labour division. While it refers to a model that has either been transformed – Fordism – or does not apply to the reality of very competitive markets, it also neglects the impact of illegality upon the cocaine business. Within this bureaucratic model, others prefer to use the more militaristic notion of 'cells'. They also fail by placing the drug economy and their actors in the realm of hyper-organised international conspiracies. They have in mind the model of 'terrorist' threats and enemies, and feed the rhetoric of 'war on drug' crusaders. This notion hinders any attempt to understand drug dealer's practices in relation to broader socio-economic relations and contexts.

The second approach, with the stress on 'criminal networks', has the merit of capturing the flexible and dynamic nature of more micro, interpersonal interaction. However, it only relates flexibility to the illegal dimension of the phenomenon, setting the cocaine business and its actors out of the economic action. In this way, it does not allow cocaine dealing to be understood within the broader picture of profit making, while it neglects the 'non-criminal' aspects of social relations. Internal conflict and collusion with legal structures are also secondary aspects of 'criminal networks'.

By studying internal business and labour relations, I tried to capture both the economic and the dynamic dimensions of cocaine enterprises. I found that Colombian cocaine firms are informal, small, mutating and decentralised. Some are individual enterprises; others adopt the form of temporary partnerships between two or three people. These coalitions are often formed solely for a single project, with some of the people involved also engaging in legal activities or in other coalitions. In many cases, a percentage system is used to divide profits, and payments in kind are not rare. A further conclusion of this study is that despite the importance of kinship ties and the frequent use of relatives, none of these enterprises are 'family businesses'. Brokers (people with contacts) play a central role in bringing about these coalitions and transactions.

Labour relations are also characterised by a high degree of flexibility. Far from restricting their involvement to one role, most people either change or systematically switch tasks and employers. Many tasks are sub-contracted to transfer financial risk and allow for (quasi) vertical integration while keeping the business small. Subcontractors range from skilled professionals or legal enterprises selling their specialised services, to multi-skilled cocaine entrepreneurs who buy off particular risky operational tasks. Nevertheless, the most dangerous ones are performed by an unskilled, replaceable workforce. These people are hired, again, either for specific operations or for doing 'a little bit of everything' (*toderos*), and they are paid with some sort of flexi-wage. They have poor skills, no promotion perspectives, and they face death or imprisonment with no security for them or their families. They are irregulars, some alternating with other legal, informal or illegal activities. Many of them had no criminal record, and learnt the job by doing it.

Against the popular belief, these enterprises do not develop stable managerial bodies. Bosses often work 'hand in hand' with their helpers, some of which also have their 'own' businesses or eventually replace them if they are caught. Despite a clear division between capital and labour, between bosses and subordinates with different power and status, labour division is not rigid and compartmentalised in vertical lines, but shows a more horizontal fragmented structure. Some people erratically switched roles between what Mike Davis has called 'lumpen capitalists' and 'outlaw proletarians' (Davis 1990: 310), especially subordinates, brokers and subcontractors. Finally, flexible payments included 'on commission' and 'bonus' systems, gifts or other incentives if things went as planned. Personal failure and conflicts, or even business delays or seizures, meant usually payment cuts or no payment at all.

As a tentative conclusion, I claim that these characteristics regarding enterprise structure and labour relations resemble Post-Fordist legal businesses. Illegality only accentuates a 'wild' flexibility (regarding production, labour and service contracts, or capital accumulation), which is in fact a normal feature of any other highly competitive market under contemporary forms of capitalism. These commonalities certainly contribute to the symbiotic overlap between legal and illegal businesses and labour markets.

VIOLENCE, SECRECY AND TRUST

Also exploring internal relations, I further discovered that Colombian *traquetos* resort to violence, secrecy and trust in ambiguous ways. These social resources both serve as essential tools for business performance, but they also constitute obstacles for success. *Traquetos* use violence in the absence of external regulation, they heavily rely on trust in the absence of written agreements and due to the good chances of 'dirty play', and they keep their activities secret to avoid detection. They are successfully portrayed as being very violent, highly secretive, and only working with trusted 'equals'.

However, these images from outsiders often contrasted with the social reality of drug dealing and dealers, which was more mundane, consensual and public than imagined. Moreover, *traquetos* themselves were either pushed to perform in accordance to those perceptions or simply exploited violent or secretive reputations. Next to the real use of violence, secrecy and trust, *traquetos* and their employees often 'acted out' these resources strategically as a form of manipulation, to either defend themselves, to gain power or to construct their social or ethnic identities.

Violence has a permanent presence in the cocaine business. In contrast with political organisations like *mafia* groups or paramilitary organisations, violence does not appear as a commodity in itself, but as an instrumental resource that is carefully measured. The cocaine business imposes structural limitations to the excessive use of violence. Transactions are consensual and not based on violent extraction. The actors involved usually recognise the competitive nature of the drug business and act accordingly.

More important than the exercise of violence is the 'threat' of violence. A violent reputation can indeed be enough in many cases to neutralise retaliation or 'dirty play' and push forward a deal. Excessive violence can discourage potential partners to deal with a reputedly violent person, can attract the attention of authorities or can damage market performance. *Traquetos* will first try to get 'civil' compensation: money or a favour in return. Other conflicts are just 'forgotten' for various reasons: fear, threats or the use of a relative. Violence also damages their expectations of being legitimated by broader social groups.

In the Netherlands, Colombian *traquetos* tend to restrict the use of physical violence and keep a low profile. Cases of kidnappings and killings occur but are rare, usually connected with rip-deals and not used for punishment or to settle scores. Fire-arms are carefully avoided. Most people use threats and a mere reputation as effective measures.

Several factors can be pointed out for the fact that Colombians have restricted the use of violence in the Netherlands. Firstly, the Colombian community is too small and unorganised to successfully conceal, accept or tolerate the use of violence. A second factor refers to the Dutch social environment: low crime and impunity rates regarding violent crimes (state monopoly of violence) increase the visibility and vulnerability of violent *traquetos*. A further element to take into account is the cocaine market dynamic at the level in which Colombians are involved: no local or Colombian group 'fights' for monopolist control, all respecting a stable and peaceful competition. Finally, low levels of violence are also related to the lack of any internal war on drugs. Drug dealing is relatively tolerated as long as no violence or conspicuous money making are involved. *Traquetos* seem to respect this unofficial policy. Corruption and collusion with the local legal economy also discourages violence.

Operational secrecy is also important for cocaine entrepreneurs to minimise risks, avoid detection and neutralise competition. Secret measures and practices are common at any level: mobile telephones, passwords or codes, cover-ups, and especially discretion. Secrecy functions as a social resource, an adaptive device to conceal information, activities and relationships and protect a profitable business. However, cocaine enterprises cannot be considered secret societies, but instead open associations that keep some operational matters secret. Trade secrets are more difficult to keep than in legal business, which rely on bureaucratised and standardised marketing methods. For a single transaction, there are often many contacts made, meetings, and long discussions about small operational details. This marks a first limit to secrecy for *traquetos*. Further, secrecy is also directed to concealing the illegal business from social censure, legal punishment and conflictive interests. In the drug business, secrets are kept not so much for loyalty but basically out of fear and self-interest. A second fragile side of secrecy is marked by the fact that *traqueto's* loyalty to other groups or individuals often supersedes responsibility to their employers and employees. They tend to disclose secrets as soon as they do not feel threaten or they are offered a better deal.

Successful operations seem to rely on ignorance rather than on secret shared information. Secrecy appears as social fragmentation rather than as an integrative device. *Traquetos* dislike secrecy. Excessive secrecy can exclude them both from business and from the possibility of public recognition and respect. They enjoy 'public' life, especially when they are successful. They like to talk about the business, even with outsiders.

Places like the telephone centres reflect the boundaries of secrecy for all *traquetos*, whether they keep low profiles or they show-off their involvement. Their nicknames also reveal the tension between secrecy and open identities. Finally, secrecy is a device for manipulation. People construct their social identity and establish social distances or links through exaggerating or pretending secrecy.

Trust, as a risk minimising strategy, is finally another resource for successful business performance. The particular combination of constraint (illegality, few choices), risk (physical danger) and interest (huge profits) makes trust a necessary tool. Agreements have a great chance of being transgressed or misinterpreted, and so the temptations to cheat, steal or kill counterparts. To avoid being ripped-off or detected, it is essential to work with trustworthy people, both as employees and as business partners. *Traquetos* have many ways of constructing trust. Firstly, using relatives and close friends. Bonds created around a common socialisation or kinship are important guarantees for mutual trust. A past in common can also facilitate trust: a shared criminal background, a common past in the police, some guerrilla group, and so forth. Another way to build trust is through the intervention of a third common trusted person who recommends a newcomer. Trust can also be pushed forward by the existence of a power relation. However, illegitimate coercion tends in fact to reduce mutual trust. Further, trust increases when everybody is satisfied about profit distribution or remuneration.

Finally, as in any other business, trust is also a result and not a pre-condition of successful co-operation. Good workers and partners are highly appreciated and carefully kept.

The cocaine business environment, however, does not stimulate the development and reproduction of 'accumulated trust': flexible relations vanish, many deals result in one-off operations and expectations about future co-operation are limited.

Most informants were obsessed about distrust and betrayal. They seem to be also essential resources for survival in the cocaine business. Betrayal between relatives is infrequent, though not rare. Betrayal between old friends is very common, even between people working together for many years. Familiarity through friendship or kinship only expands trust under certain conditions. Firstly, social costs of exit or betrayal have to be high. Otherwise, the 'strong tie' only serves to improve, rather than decrease, the chances of betrayal. Secondly, 'blind' trust (loyalty) often endorsed to friends and relatives cannot only lead to co-operation, but to deception as well.

The intervention of a third person or the recommendation by known people is a trust source that cocaine entrepreneurs often regret. Trust as a result of job satisfaction or agreed profit distribution is also fragile. For people with 'no choice' (through coercion, economic hardship, and so on) trust is not even a problematic issue. Trust is also difficult to build amongst people who assess risk in different ways.

Many Colombian *traquetos* develop either fatalist or paranoid attitudes about trusting others. Economic interest, a major drive behind co-operation in drug enterprises, is also a weak incentive for trust in a business based in short-term high profits.

The cocaine business spreads distrust to the whole Colombian community. Most Colombian immigrants in the Netherlands distrust each other as a weapon to resist negative images, bad reputations and possible problems.

Trust over particular groups can favour their inclusion or exclusion from the cocaine business. Colombian dealers trust other groups following some vague notions of professionalism, given word, honour and accessibility. From more to less reliable, they mention Italians and Spanish, Turks, native Dutch, Eastern Europeans, and finally Antilleans and Surinamese. Dealers tend to reproduce stereotypes and standardised images about these groups. Trust over them and actual co-operation does not always coincide.

APPENDIX I

MAP OF COLOMBIA

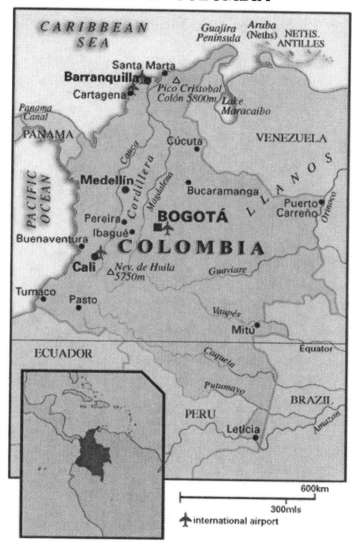

APPENDIX II

COCAINE RELEVANT CASES IN THE NETHERLANDS

Table X Cocaine Seized in the Netherlands 1987-1998 and Relevant Cases 1989-1997

1987	1988	1989	1990	1991	1992
406	517	1425	4288	2492	3433

1993	1994	1995	1996	1997	1998
3720	8200	4851	9222	11489	11452

Year	Description
1989	April, 100 kg in Rotterdam, tanker ship *El Pionero* from Colombia, no arrests.
	December, 330 kg in Rotterdam, tanker ship *EWL Paramaribo*. Three men and one woman arrested (all Dutch). Later a Surinamese military official involved.
	December, 244 kg in Rotterdam. W.S. sentenced in April 1991 to 12 years.
1990	February, 2,658 kg in IJmuiden in a fruit ship. Operation *Holle Vaten*. Line Colombia-Amsterdam since 1988 (4 or 5 successful operations). Passion fruit exported by Grajales and received by Dutch people in Haarlem (Lida and former kick-boxing trainer). Colombian Pepe at the top but escaped. Money was sent by cheques from *Thomas Cook*. Three Dutchmen and five Colombians arrested, including R.G. Londoño (engineer), O.F. Rivera and H.A. Ospina. Londoño was sentenced to 16 years in 1991 and in January 1992 escaped from Sittard. His brother in law (Rivera) escaped in 1991 from Arnhem-Zuid.
	April, 140 kg in a warehouse in Amsterdam Westhaven. The load was hidden in 30 tons of cacao beans, moved first from Colombia to Suriname, and from Paramaribo shipped in the *Kingston* of Nedlloyd. The police was tipped and waited until unload. Six people were arrested: The 33 years old Dutch owner of the transport firma, his girlfriend, two other men from Amsterdam and two Colombians. They were 27 and 41 years old and stayed since one week in a hotel in Amsterdam. The older Colombian was a lawyer, carried € 75,000, and was the main suspect.
	June, 87 kg in Schiphol. Connected with the case of 244 kg in Rotterdam. Five arrests (one customs officer) plus a military official from Suriname, and a German later extradited to the Netherlands.
	October, 41.5 kg in Rotterdam from Curaçao. Two people arrested, later released.
	21 kg in Vlissingen in the Colombian banana ship *Swan River*, several times involved in cocaine transportation via Belgium.

Year	Description
1991	January, 105 kg in a container in The Hague (December) and 60 kg in Rotterdam in containers with plastic from a ship from Colombia to Rotterdam via Portugal. Two people arrested: a 49 years old Dutch engineer from Delft who ran *La Malinche Import-Export Bv* and used its bank account to launder money, and a 44 years old former chauffeur from the Mexican Embassy in The Hague. They received 9 and 5 years. Police could not investigate the role of the Embassy, but it is clear that at least two top officials were involved (first secretary later transferred). Two Colombians also involved as organisers, but could not be detained.
	February, 650 kg in Oudenhoorn, smuggled from Trinidad to Rotterdam in asphalt barrels. Public prosecutor asked between 4 and 10 years for five suspects, and in February 1994 a court from The Hague sentenced Jesse J. to 10 years. Bettien M. also involved.
	May, 357 kg in Rotterdam on Danish ship *Elisabeth Boye*, coming from Suriname. Five persons detained after delivering in Breda. Four (three brothers) sentenced to 18 months for cocaine unloading. Later in 1995, main suspect with excellent contacts with Surinamese military asked 16 years. No direct Colombian involvement.
	May, 120 kg on the ship *EWL Paramaribo*. 100 kg more in a taxi, by two men coming from the ship. Other 150 kg found in two houses. Dutch court sentenced a man from Togo to 10 years and one from Suriname to 8 years, for the smuggling of 286 kg.
	July, 92 kg under the keel of a Colombian ship, and 2 kg more by people on board. One Colombian arrested.
	October, 46 kg in Paris by six Dutch people, four young couriers and two receivers. Later 70 people detained in 5 places (French Guyana, Curaçao, Paris, Brussels and the Netherlands), from which 55 young, native blond couriers. Two lines: Antilles-Brussels-Amsterdam and Suriname-French Guyana-Paris-Amsterdam. 40 years old M.A. organisator sentenced to 9 years in the Netherlands, his daughter to 3 years. Still two suspects free in Suriname.
1992	January, 845 kg in a warehouse in the Harlemmermeer.
	November, 1,100 kg hidden in a vehicle and in oil barrels in a warehouse at Amsterdam Westhaven. Five Colombians and four Dutchmen detained in Amsterdam, Aalsmeer, Abcoude, The Hague, Hoofddorp and Dordrecht. Big operation including other seizures: 1,100 kg marihuana in a warehouse of Hardinxveld-Giessendam, money and nine cars. Report *Lucrativo* from the CRI: Money laundering via the own *Dutch Change Office Enigma BV*, which changed € 14 million. Two Dutch brothers organised the money laundering and were involved, next to an old Irish criminal and a Dutch, in an import operation in 1991 of 1,500 kg from the Antilles to Europe. Also, *Thomas Cook* and *Holland Casino* were used. Money transferred to England and then to other places. In April 1993, the public prosecutor asks 15, 8 and 5 years for 4 Colombians. One of them already had escaped in the beginning of 1993 from Sittard. 36 years old Francisco G. is the main suspect, and 45 years old Horacio N. is an economist, director of a radio and sub-director of a hospital in Colombia, also founder of a psychiatric institution for drug addicts. In June 1996, Irishman M.G. asks Dutch Justice to have back 126.7 kg gold seized in a Porsche in 1992.
1993	April, 350 kg in Colombian ship in Rotterdam. No detentions.

Year	Description
	April, 200 kg in Amsterdam.
	April, 13 kg in Rotterdam. One Dutch woman from Amsterdam and three Brazilians detained. Smuggled in the fruit ship *Ana Luisa*. One of the suspects came with the ship. The other two came earlier to organise the import and stash.
	April, 120 kg in Amsterdam harbour between dry bananas. Nineteen men and eleven women detained (27 Colombians and 3 Dutch) mainly in The Hague, connected with a large coca front store. Operation in 15 places: one in Rotterdam, seven in The Hague and seven in Amsterdam. Seizure of cars, a complete administration with computers and € 80,000 in an investigation that started in September 1992. Three Colombian, well-off entrepreneurs (28 years old F.R.M., his brother C.R.M. and 29 years old L.S.Z.) were organising the illegal business for two years, renting and buying properties. In July 1993, a court from The Hague sentenced them to 12, 10 and 8 years. The Colombian exporter was known but could not be detained.
	May, few kilos in Amsterdam's bar and three Colombians detained.
	June, 175 kg in a warehouse in Zaanstad. Five containers with false coal blocks from a group of 100 containers from Antwerp shipped from Venezuela in June. Operation with the Belgium police, with two Dutchmen detained and a total amount of 2,200 kg, mainly in Belgium. Two Dutchmen detained in Zandaam and Harlemmermeer.
	July, 490 kg in a little boat in Texel. Two Americans detained, later convicted to 8 and 6 years. The coke was bought in Venezuela and smuggled to Texel in a sailboat.
	September, 18 coke-dealers detained, almost all Antilleans, in connection with a coca-line from Curaçao.
	September, Operation *Golfslag*, Nine men and two women detained in Amsterdam.
	800 kg in a warehouse north of Rotterdam, hidden in iron blocks. International group moving large quantities from Venezuela to England, the Netherlands and Greece. Seven people detained: Three Colombians, two Surinamese and two Greeks. In Blackpool (England) 900 kg more and four Englishmen and one Colombian detained. Own import-export front store in England and Greece: *Coldo Inc.*, exporting iron and aluminium from Colombia to Europe and the US.
	120 kg in a container in Rotterdam. Customs officials noted overweight, but as it was handled by a *bona fide* firm. They let it through to capture the importers. Two Colombians living in the Netherlands, both with two helpers, were finally detained next to the load in Betuwe and Brabant.
1994	January, 15 kg on a Colombian fruit ship in Amsterdam Westhaven. Customs officer killed by Dutch J.B. who was involved in the earlier kidnapping of Heineken. Typical case of Dutch *penose* moving into cocaine import. Dutch customs had a tip from the DEA. J.B. was asked life sentence in December 1994.
	Early in the year, 70 kg with seven detentions.
	March, 15 kg in a fish ship from Suriname in Vlissingen. Two Rotterdamers detained.
	March, 3000 kg in Zeewolde (record) on a ship from Venezuela. Fourteen Dutchmen detained, all released two days later. Probably from Suriname.

Year	Description
	March, the Colombian police seized 1753 tons of chemicals, mostly MEK, from the firm *Holanda Colombia* (Operation *Volatile*). It was an affiliated company of Holland Chemical International.
	April, 9 kg in fish containers in a warehouse in Vlissingen. Two women detained.
	June, 862 kg in Amsterdam Westhaven. One person detained and two others escaped.
	June, three people detained in relation with a coke-line between Groningen and Brazil. A bar was closed down.
	July, 150 kg in Vlissingen from Suriname. Eight people detained.
	August, Dutch firm *Mariship* from Delfzijl is the owner of the *Zwanet*, a ship discovered in the Spanish coast with 1,100 kg from Venezuela. Next to three Dutchmen, there were one Colombian (main suspect), three Polish and six Spanish detained.
	September, 10 kg and four people captured. In December 1995, a 22 years old customs officer was sentenced to 4 years and 6 months for allowing the shipment to pass through.
	October, 550 kg in Amsterdam, hidden in fruit juice from Colombia. The new IRT Team detained seventeen people, mainly linked with a distribution network via Surinamese *Toko's* (shops). The Surinamese-Dutch importer had an import-export firma in Amsterdam.
	October, 250 kg in Amsterdam.
	November, 15 kg in Schiphol in the baggage of a 72 years old man from Curaçao. Another person detained.
	November, 519 kg in Breda. The coke arrived to Hoek van Holland from Curaçao via England, hidden in lamb meat. Infiltration by the setting up of coca-firm in co-operation with British police. Amongst three Surinamese detained: 43 years old I.S. who worked between 1974 and 1981 for Narcotics Police in Suriname, later sentenced to 14 years. In May 1996, sentence reduced to 9 years because the import of 250 kg by the CoPa Team in 1993 was covered during the trial. The case was discussed during the *Van Traa* hearings. I.S. received the coke from Colombians.
	December, 1,161 kg in Amsterdam, hidden in fruit barrels in a ship from Colombia via Spain. Twenty-four detentions by police from The Hague (Colombians, Bolivians, Surinamese and Dutchmen between 18 and 46 years old). Main suspect is A.C., 26 years old Colombian, considered "the leader of the Dutch section of the Cali Cartel", later sentenced to 14 years. He was in the Netherlands since 1992 and was accused for the import of 12 tons of marihuana and smaller cocaine quantities. Amongst those captured there were also the daughter and the son in law of the Minister of Social Affairs of Suriname. Defence based on illegal methods used by the police (Langendoen and Van Putten) was finally successful: in January 1997 Colombian G.B. and Dutch J.H. were released due to police illegal methods after staying in prison for three years. They also got financial compensation.
1995	January, 435 kg in Rotterdam Haven hidden in a calcium carbonate load in a ship from Colombia. Customs and the FIOD detained three people during the unload and seized two weapons in a searching.

Year	Description
	February, 35 kg of cocaine base in a container in Apeldoorn, from a ship via Antwerp coming from Colombia and hidden in ceramic and rolling-chairs. Discovered by customs, FIOD and the Amsterdam Police using tips and infiltrators. Thirteen detentions from which nine Dutchmen, one Colombian and one Venezuelan. Police methods were later under discussion during trial. Connected with the *Octopus* organisation (Johan V.), linked with the killing of Bruinsma in 1991.
	February, 60 kg in Rotterdam port within sport bags. Five people detained: four Chileans and one Dutchman.
	February, 26 kg in Bratislava Airport smuggled by a 32 years old Dutch from Venezuela hidden in porcelains. Sentenced to 8 years and 6 months in 1996.
	March, 660 kg in the port of Capuaba (Brazil). The load was hidden amongst spices and was to be shipped to the Netherlands. A Dutchman living in Brazil, with contacts with Colombian exporters, was arrested.
	March, a cocaine laboratory (kitchen) discovered in the Schilderwijk (The Hague). Three people between 32 and 34 years old arrested.
	May, 18 kg in Schiphol. Smuggled in fresh vegetables from Suriname.
	May, 95 kg in a house in Amsterdam, where police found a large arsenal of weapons and ammunition. Two Dutchmen detained, one owning a coffee-shop.
	May, 3,5 kg in Schiphol. Line Aruba-Curaçao-the Netherlands run by a 33-years-old man from Kerkrade, using more than eight small couriers. No relation with Colombia.
	June, 156 kg in a container in Rotterdam coming from Colombia, hidden in sport bags. Possible involvement of a well-known harbour's firm.
	July, 100 kg in Amsterdam harbour found by the FIOD in a container of a fruit ship from Colombia with Poland as final destination.
	July, 180 kg in Rotterdam in sport bags, similar and connected with the case of 156 kg in June.
	July, 45 kg in Schiphol hidden between 1,200 trekking shoes from Ecuador. Discovered in a routine control. A 35 years old Amsterdamer detained when collecting the shoes.
	August, 32 years old Colombian woman died in a flight between Caracas and Amsterdam, carrying 110 grams in a plastic ball in her vagina. Police claims that this case is the first one in its sort.
	August, 134 kg in Amsterdam port, in a container with cookies from Colombia. Discovered by customs officials in a routine control, with no people detained.
	August, 86 post packages containing between 100 grams and 5 kg, mostly by plane, were intercepted with X-rays and sniffing-dogs, and destroyed.
	August, 188 kg in a Dutch boat in the Azores Islands. Three men and one woman arrested, from which two Dutchmen.
	August, 24 Colombians arrested at *El Dorado* Airport (Bogotá) when trying to smuggle cocaine in 30 suitcases to Sint Maarten (the Netherlands Antilles).
	August, Dutchman from Oss linked with a large network of amphetamine producers is arrested, also involved in cocaine import from South America.

Year	Description
	September, two Dutchmen working for KLM in Schiphol (baggage) are charged for cocaine transport. *Marechaussee* controlled the network since 1994 and seized 700 kg since research began. The group had people at airports in Colombia, Venezuela, Panamá, Aruba and Curaçao. Deliveries made in bags and suitcases, between 14 and 21 kg each time. One man was released soon after and the other one, a 42-years-old Amsterdamer, was sentenced to 8 years in 1996.
	October, 14 kg in Schiphol smuggled by a Colombian family with three children.
	October, 1,000 kg in containers in Schaardijk, Rotterdam East, coming from Ecuador hidden in deep-frozen shrimps (*Iglo* case). Although nine men and one woman were arrested, a couple (main suspects) came back to Curaçao. 'Controlled delivery' used by the police in this and earlier connected cases (cocaine in pepper), provoking a scandal. In 1996, there was a car bomb attack in Krimpel aan de Ijssel on the wife of one of the suspects. In May 1996, a lawyer from Schoonhoven was suspected to have laundered money by buying art works and properties in the Antilles, and set up import front stores.
	November, 27 kg in Amsterdam port in a container ship from Colombia. During a routine control: seven people were arrested. A man from Amsterdam had 16 kg on his clothes, the rest was found on board.
	December, 360 kg in ship from Colombia and 19 people detained. German-Dutch police co-operation from mid 1994, using infiltrators, front-stores and 'controlled deliveries'. 9.2 tons of marihuana were allowed to pass in September 1994, and 21 tons marihuana were later seized in Hamburg. Public prosecutor asked high sentences for six Colombians, but only five (Kike Group) were convicted to shorter sentences: Kike and Angelica to 8 years for organising import and the other three to between 8 months and 4 years. The court found police methods (before and during *Van Traa* hearings) unacceptable and dismissed many evidence. They all went in appeal and were released in October 1997.
	December, seventeen people arrested in Amsterdam Westhaven for the smuggling and stealing of an earlier captured container with 15 ton marihuana from Colombia. Two former workers of the CTA (Combined Terminals Amsterdam) involved, in total having imported 800 kg coke and 70 tons marihuana.
1996	January, 325 kg in St. Maarten seized by Dutch and American Coast Watch. Shipment was directed to the US hidden in plastic and jute bags.
	January, cocaine line Curaçao-Schiphol dismantled. After a shooting, two men from Zaandam and Amsterdam were arrested, both working at the airport. Other five also arrested: a man with US$ 800,000 in a suitcase, going to Curaçao, two in the Netherlands and two in Curaçao.
	January, 26 kg in Amsterdam harbour in a tanker from Colombia, discovered by customs officials and the FIOD.
	February, increasing number of Dutch couriers – especially young native female – are detained in Moscow Airport with quantities around 5 kilos, some flying Panama, Cuba or Colombia-Warsaw-West Europe. High sentences, later drastically reduced in appeal and by presidential decree (in 1997).

Year	Description
	February, 142 kg of cocaine in solution in Schiphol. Discovered by customs officials, hidden in plastic bags between 5,000 tropical fishes coming from Colombia. Two 24 and 25 years old Amsterdamers arrested and later sentenced to 4 and 8 years.
	March, 50 kg in Schiphol. A woman from Suriname was arrested and later sentenced to 6 years. She accused Brunswijk (Surinamese Jungle Commando leader) as the main organiser. He sat next to her during the flight.
	March, 10 kg in Madrid (Barajas) by a Dutchman. It was a stopover from Guatemala to Brussels.
	April, 6 kg in Copenhagen airport smuggled by a Dutch couple from Sao Paulo to Amsterdam. Increased use of Danish airports. Also a Dutch 19 years old woman with 5 kg detained in Zaventem (Brussels) doing Sao Paulo-Amsterdam.
	April, around 12 kg in Zaventem airport (Belgium) smuggled by three Dutchwomen, two young and one 60 years old, from Aruba. The operation was organised by two Dutchmen from Enschede and Rotterdam, and a woman from Groningen who recruited and paid the couriers. The group was active since 1994.
	April, 1,200 kg in Suriname (record) transported in a small plane from Colombia. Twelve Surinamese and four Colombians, including the pilot, arrested. The police was tipped off. Later six more detentions amongst inhabitants of the small indian village Casipora and one million dollar in cash found buried.
	April, 10 kg in Schiphol hidden in whisky bottles and suitcases and smuggled by four South American couriers. Two other couriers with 3 kg in a laptop computer, which resulted in further searching in Zaandam and Amsterdam. A network smuggling cocaine from Colombia was hit with ten arrests in Amsterdam and one in France. Four Syrian brothers, all illegal residents, were the organisers and had properties in the Netherlands and France.
	April, 85 kg on board of a ship in the Bay of Biscay in its way to the Netherlands. Two Croat crewmembers were arrested in IJmuiden and later sentenced to 5 years for drug smuggling. The captain and other crewmembers asked for police intervention when discovered the cocaine load on board.
	May, 52 kg in IJmuiden hidden inside the engine room of a coal ship with Panamanian flag coming from Colombia. Discovered by customs officials and the FIOD.
	May, 442 kg in the Amsterdam port in a container from Colombia with other 30 ton marihuana. The container remained untouched since January in a transport and shipping company in Rotterdam. A 42 years old Dutch, informant of the CID and organiser of the import operation, received 6 years.
	May, alarm for the increase of ball swallowing couriers (body packers). Forty-five arrested in Schiphol during the first five months of 1996, and three dead during the flight. In 1994 there were only 17, and in 1995 some 87 cases. There were many Surinamese women amongst them.
	June, 800 kg in Saint Barthélémy (French Antilles). Three Dominicans arrested, all based in Sint Maarten (the Netherlands Antilles).
	June, a 31 years old man died in the flight between Paramaribo and Amsterdam carrying cocaine balls in his stomach.
	July, 87 kg in a boat in Vlissingen, in a container with frozen cassava coming from Suriname. The owner of the receiver company was arrested.

Year	Description
	July, five ex-military members from Seedorf were sentenced for import and distribution of drugs (also cocaine) in small quantities.
	July, two Surinamese working as civil servants in the Haarlem and Amsterdam courts were arrested, accused of organising cocaine import to the Netherlands.
	July, 1,000 kg in IJmuiden in the sail ship *Odimirense* coming from Brazil. Eighteen people were arrested: Dutchmen, Colombians and Antilleans. By further search by the 'Prisma-team', some weapons, money and 145 kg more were found. The police began investigations a year before. The sailboat stopped in Trinidad.
	July, 4 kg in Schiphol distributed in seven – four men and three women – body packers coming from Paramaribo. All had only the Dutch nationality. The number of *boleros* seems to double in 1996: more than 100 in the first six months.
	July, around 8 kg in Tilburg by post from Curaçao. Customs officials had a tip from the courier company: two Dutchmen from Eindhoven arrested, who were paid to receive the sending.
	September, 6 kg at Barajas airport (Spain) smuggled by a 55 years old Dutchman. The flight was Panamá-Brussels with a stop in Madrid. Six other Spaniards with 5 to 11 kg each were also arrested.
	October, 317 kg in Sassenheim, in the house of a British citizen, one of the Top-3 most wanted in Britain. Also weapons, money and all sorts of illegal drugs. In June 1997 sentenced in The Hague to 12 years.
	November, 108 kg in Amsterdam seized by customs during a control in the harbour, hidden inside furniture. The shipment was coming from Ecuador. Six detentions, money and weapons seized. Later, only one Amsterdamer sentenced to 7 years. The man had worked in Streetcornerwork.
	December, 300 kg in Hazeldonk (A16 border) in a container truck (TIR) hidden within carpet rolls. Truck belonged to a West Brabant transport company. The chauffeur was arrested.
1997	January, 140 kg in Drenthe and Friesland. Dutch distribution network destroyed.
	January, 558 kg in a motor boat north of Aruba and Bonaire. Antillean-Aruban Coast Watch with Dutch infrastructure support. Five people arrested.
	January, three Dutch employees from Mercedes Benz use MB headquarters in Utrecht and internal post to smuggle small quantities (kg) from Suriname to the Netherlands.
	January, 500 kg of cocaine base in a farm in Haarzuilens. Police was looking for hemp. Two Dutchmen and two South Americans arrested, and infrastructure, weapons and marihuana seized.
	January, three Dutchmen and one Venezuelan arrested from a major import group dealing with Colombians and Italians. Extensive IRT research. They were responsible for some operations in 1996: 26 kg in a container in Amsterdam, 38 kg in a boat in Ireland, and 83 kg in Antwerp and Zeebrugge, all discovered. Police intervened before expected to avoid more violence – a kidnapping had already taken place.
	February, 170 *boleros* arrested in Schiphol in 1996.
	February, 2 kg under the clothes of a 51 years old Dutch Catholic priest in the Caracas airport, smuggling the cocaine from Suriname to Schiphol. Rotterdam's church sent € 30,000 to help him. Later released for procedural mistakes.

Year	Description
	February, 200 kg in a container with sport bags and coffee in a ship from Colombia. The police was tipped from Colombia. Seventeen weapons were also found in the container, and three people were arrested.
	February, 3 kg in Amsterdam by post from Curaçao, detected by customs. Later, four people from Zwolle and one 'foreigner' arrested.
	March, 35 kg by post from Venezuela to The Hague. The receiver, a shop owner, did not know anything about the package and delivered it to the police.
	April, 10 kg in the Lima airport by three Chileans and a 72 years old Spaniard in a KLM flight to Amsterdam.
	April, 1,236 kg in Hansweert (Zeeland) in the Antillean ship *Fogo Isle* from Curaçao. Police found it during a routine control. Six people detained: three Filipinos, one Canadian, one Antillean and one very wealthy Dutchman who was living in Zeeland with a couple of boats from the Fogo Isle.
	May, 115 kg and € 400,000 in the Rhein-Main airport by two Dutch persons coming from Ecuador and going to Amsterdam.
	May, 10 kg in Schiphol, during a routine control, in the bag of a 27 years old KLM stewardess from Amsterdam, coming from Paramaribo. Later sentenced to 4 years.
	June, 400 kg in Zaandam, in a small bus hidden in boxes with oranges. Three people arrested.
	June, more than 1,000 kg in Hoorn in a container with oranges coming from Belgium. The police from Zaanstreek-Waterland had a tip from the Belgian police. Case connected with the 400 kg in Zaandam.
	July, 2 kg in an Indonesian airport smuggled by a Dutchwoman. There were 8 Dutch couriers imprisoned in Indonesia.
	August, 68 kg in the Rotterdam port. A Croat sailor was arrested.
	September, 486 kg in Stellendam in a yacht during a routine control. Four people arrested.
	September, 57 years old Colombian Angelo Ospina tried to be rescued from the Geerhorst prison in Sittard. Old Dutch fellow prisoner approached the place by helicopter, but he crashed down. Ospina got 9 years for the IJmuiden case in 1990, with two other Colombians that already escaped in 1991 and 1992. Ospina also escaped in 1993 from the Schie (Rotterdam) but he was recaptured immediately after.
	October, cocaine import organisation dismantled in Arnhem and 10 people arrested. At least 250 kg imported to the Netherlands, the UK and especially Belgium. Many seizures during long investigation.
	November, 130 people arrested by the Amsterdam police in the Operation *Tango*, against 6 'large' cocaine and heroin import-export organisations: Turkish, Dutch, Syrian-Lebanese and Colombian groups.
	November, 50 kg in Bolsward in a *bona fide* firm coming from Colombia hidden within carpet rolls. Frisian police and FIOD from Rotterdam did not make any arrest. Dutch-Antillean *Zwarte Cobra* later detained in Fuengirola (Spain) to be extradited to the Netherlands. A 27 years old Yugoslav sentenced to 9 years in 1998 as main suspect. He was going to kill *Zwarte Cobra* and his son. Also other marihuana shipments from the Netherlands to England.

Year	Description
	November, eight Dutchmen prosecuted for cocaine import. Main suspect was a 45 years old ex-policeman from the Rotterdam drug brigade. Two others were an ex-*Maracheussee* and an ex-prison guard. Cocaine was imported from Colombia in banana shipments and by couriers with cocaine base solved within their clothes.
	December, 45 years old Colombian A. Quiceno Botero (alias Lucho Palmira) was arrested in Curaçao by the Dutch police and sent to the Netherlands. Although denied by Colombian authorities, indicated as a 'top' man from Cali, heavily wanted in the US, with a strong line in Europe. Involved in three sendings to the Netherlands in 1991 and 1992, all seized. Public Prosecutor asked for 8 years in September 1998.

Source: For cocaine seized in the Netherlands: Bijkerk and Grapendaal (1999). For cocaine cases: *De Volkskrant, NRC Handelsblad, Algemeen Dagblad, Het Parool, Rotterdams Dagblad, Haagsche Courant, Trouw, El País*, (many years); Korf and Verbraeck (1993); Van Duyne (1995).

APPENDIX III

OVERVIEW OF INFORMANTS

Table 11 presents an overview of the people formally and informally interviewed for this research. The table includes all people addressed in the Netherlands, Europe and Colombia during the process of participant observation, as well as those especially contacted. While the degree of interaction and the level of information obtained varies per individual, they are all considered important direct informants that consciously told me their stories, helped me to contact other informants, talked about others, or offered me their expertise. While many remain anonymous or are vaguely referred, others are (nick)named along the book. The table excludes people met in innumerable casual encounters, especially in Colombia, whose accumulative, unconscious contribution was nevertheless precious.

Table XI Overview of informants

Category	Number	Named in the book
Latino community leaders (Brussels 1, Rotterdam 2, Amsterdam 6, Colombia 2)	11	Camilo
Religious leaders (Amsterdam 2, Rotterdam 1, Colombia 2)	5	Wim
Import-export entrepreneurs, employees and authorities	5	--
Colombian related Human Rights activists	6	--
Colombian illegal immigrants (not involved)	14	Germán - Sonia - Jaime - Carla - Marta - Horacio
Colombian prostitutes	10	Aurelia - Jessica - Marga - Cintia - Leticia - Amparo
Colombian drug couriers	8	Miguel - Susana
Colombian cocaine importers, distributors and retailers (Importers 10, distributors 13, retailers 3)	25	Bart - Tico - Chino - Tano - Joel - Paisita - Lupo - Pollo - Riverito - William - Charly - Blanca - Pacho - Don Anibal - Alicia
Helpers and employees	10	Solano - Simona - Ernesto - Emilio - Manolo - Montes - Brujo
Mixed couples (not involved)	16	Ana Inés - Estela - Flor and Nico - Amanda
Colombian political refugees	4	Helmer
Musicians and DJs	3	Silvio
Other Colombian immigrants	21	Cabeza - Robert - Linda - Omaira - Iris
Colombian parliamentarians	1	--

Police and custom authorities (Holland 3 - Germany 2 - Spain 2 - Colombia 3)	10	van Stormbroek
Diplomatic authorities	4	Arrieta
Criminal Lawyers	3	Marisol
Interpreters and translators	2	Willem - Wilma
Social Workers	3	Elvira
Drug and Organized Crime researchers and experts (Cocaine market 6, Organized crime 2, Prostitution 1, Colombia 7, Drug trafficking 8)	24	Janssen - Bovenkerk - van Gemert - Korf - Boekhout van Solinge - Jelsma - Romaní - Koutouzis - Kopp - Salazar - Ruggiero
Journalists	6	Haenen - Blickman
TOTAL	*191*	

APPENDIX IV

GLOSSARY

Aguantadero: place to hide somebody hot, illegal drugs or weapons. Also place to close drug deals. Also *caleta.*

Amanecedero: literally, place to stay during sun-rise. Special Colombian places (private parties or public bars) where the *rumba* continues after other salsa places close (around 4:00 am or 5:00 am). Also *hueco* and *roto.*

Ambiente: somebody has *ambiente* when is friendly and enjoys the *rumba* (party) very much.

Animales: literally, animals. Cocaine freight.

Aparato: a kilogram cocaine.

Apartacho: apartment to stay or store drugs.

Apartamentero: burglar.

Apuntada: system through which investors, mainly due to the lowering risk of joint export ventures, put up some capital to buy cocaine in Colombia to send it to the main markets. The system, equivalent to selling shares in several shipments, has been used to engage individuals with a clean record, and to increase the social and political support for the industry.

Aventar: to tip off somebody to the police.

Bajada: cocaine unload.

Balacera: shooting, cross-fire.

Bambas: golden chains, necklaces, rings, earrings and so forth, used by drug entrepreneurs to show off. *Embambado,* wearing *bambas.*

Bambero: person selling or dealing jewellery on mobile basis, often targeted by Colombian thieves.

Bareta/o: most common name for marihuana. Also *maracachafa, María* and *marimba.*

Basuco or bazuco: cocaine base smoked as cigarettes mixed with tobacco. Also *surungo, tierra, susto, soplete, soplagen.*

Billete: literally, banknote. Money. *Hacer billete,* to make quick money. Also *guita.*

Bisnes: cocaine business.

Bolero: body packer, ball swallowing drug courier.

Boleteo: 1) form of extortion. The term derives from the means – the short, anonymous, often hand-written notes, or *boletas* – used to convey threats and terms to victims, usually rural property owners. Widespread during 'The Violence' period, the *boleteo* is once again common in many rural areas. 2) also, somebody is *boleta* when having to be discreet attracts too much attention.

Bolitas: small cocaine balls usually smuggled inside the body (stomach, vagina). *Bolitas* are also the cocaine balls (up to 1/4 or 1/5 gram) sold on the streets.

Bravero: person who refuses to pay or give money back and threatens to settle the problem on the spot, usually with a gun or a knife.

Caballo: somebody who does not use drugs. *Descaballarse,* to try drugs for the first time.

Cachaco/a: person from Bogotá. Also *rolo.*

Caleño/a: person from Cali.

Caleta: small place to hide people, drugs or weapons, usually a false or double wall or floor. Also *aguantadero.*

Calichano: Colombian. Used in Holland by drug entrepreneurs to avoid pronouncing the word *colombiano*.

Caliente: hot place or person.

Calle: street. *Latino* prostitution street scene.

Camello: literally, camel. Work, usually a very hard one, used also by drug entrepreneurs. *Camellar*, to deal drugs.

Caucherazo: from *cauchera*, elemental weapon to throw stones to the birds. In the seventies, operation with American pilots taking cocaine out from Colombia in little planes.

Cocina/Cocinero: kitchen/cook. Laboratory or refinery to produce cocaine, and the skilled people employed there (chemist).

Cola: followed by the police. To come with *cola*, to bring the police.

Combo: teenage gang, peer group of friends.

Coronar: from the game of Draughts, to crown. To make the cocaine shipment arrive to the destination point without problems or delays.

Correo: drug courier. *Correito*, a small transport of cocaine, usually from one stash place to another.

Cortar: to cut cocaine with other substances.

Cosa: literally, thing. Cocaine.

Cristal: crack, rock.

Cruce: drug deal. In broader terms, any informal business agreement. A *cruce* also means the cocaine export-import operation. Also, *hacer un cruce*, to do a favour.

Cuadrito: cocaine ball up to 1 gram. See *bolitas*.

Chicharro: last bit of a marihuana joint.

Choro: thief.

Chuspa: little plastic bag to put up to one gram cocaine.

Chuzar: to stab with a knife.

Dar el paseo: literally, to go for a walk. To kill somebody.

Desechable: literally, disposable. In Colombia, name often given to homeless vagabonds, street children, heavy addicts, beggars, and other marginalised people, all of them victims of the so called *limpieza social* (social cleansing). In Holland, junkies.

Desordenar: to ruin a deal or a business.

Dinero caliente: hot money, money from illegal business.

Duro: tough, heavy person belonging to the drug scene. Also *mafioso*.

Embalado: high on cocaine.

Empacar: to pack the cocaine.

Enrumbado: completely into the party, enjoying music and dancing. It also means using drugs alone, usually in a closed place.

Escape: unarmed robbery. Stealing and running, also a rip-deal.

Facultad: literally, university faculty. Prison. Also *universidad*.

Faltón: unreliable. Person who does not pay debts, arrives late to appointments, cuts cocaine or does not cumply with agreements.

Ferretería: literaly, ironmonger's shop. From *fierros*, weapons. Place to store weapons.

Fierro: gun. Also *mazo*.

Finado: dead person.

Flecha: literally, arrow. Business partner at the other side of the ocean, exporter-importer relationship. Also *línea*.

Floro: from *florín*, guilder.

Fufurufa: in Cali, pejorative name for those women going out with drug entrepreneurs. Often their mistresses, they wear expensive sexy cloths and receive from *traquetos* gifts and invitations, increasing social status and recognition.

Gamba: hundred gilders or hundred kilograms cocaine.

Gancho Ciego: literally, blind hook. Decoy. In the cocaine business, small drug couriers, especially *boleros*, who are sacrificed – unwittingly tipped-off to the police – to allow larger couriers or shipments to arrive safe.

Gil: victim of a robbery or a rip-deal.

Giro: money transfer or remittance to Colombia. Also *girito*.

Guardado: Hidden. Somebody who does not show up in the regular places.

Guardaespaldas: bodyguard.

Guitarra: from *guita*, money. Used by Colombian illegal entrepreneurs in Holland. Also *platica* and *billete*.

Hueco: small salsa place with bad reputation, usually hot and opening until the next morning. Also *amanecedero* and *roto*.

Jíbaro: street drug dealer. *Jibarear*, to sell drugs.

Lavaperro: literally, dog-cleaner. In Cali, pejorative name for those performing the most unskilled jobs for the drug entrepreneurs, including gardening, car cleaning, and so forth. *Lavaperros* gain social recognition and status for working nearby *traquetos*.

Ley (la): the police. Very common among Colombian drug dealers. Also *tombo* and *vigilante*.

Limpiar: literally, to clean. To kill somebody.

Línea: line of cocaine, but also a particular network composed by the exporter, the importer and the wholesale distributor. Also *flecha*.

Llevar: to involve somebody into the cocaine business.

Llevado: person in very bad financial situation or very addicted to hard drugs.

Maduro: literally, a mature plantain. *Basuco* mixed with marihuana.

Mafioso: cocaine entrepreneur. Also *traqueto* and *duro*.

Malandro/malandrín: used by Colombians, anyone belonging to the underground scene, especially pimps, thiefs and small time dealers.

Man: guy, fellow.

Mandadero: person who performs small unskilled tasks for the cocaine entrepreneur. Also *todero*.

Marimba: marihuana.

Mazo: gun. See also *fierro*.

Mercancía: cocaine. Also *merca*.

Metal: knife. Used in Dutch prisons by *Latino* inmates.

Meter: literally, to put. To use drugs. *Metedero* is a place to use drugs, implying a filthy, underground place.

Moño: cannabis bud.

Muestra: cocaine free sample carried by illegal entrepreneurs in small plastic bags to show the quality they are offering.

Mula: literally, mule. Drug courier transporting up to 10 kg hidden in clothes, body or baggage. Usually pejorative for female, poor smugglers.

Muñeco: dead body. *Muñequear*, to kill somebody.

Narcoguerrilla: term coined by the US for the left guerrillas involved in drug production and trafficking to finance their activities.

Narcotraficante: drug dealer.

Negocio: cocaine business, including all stages from production to middle level distribution. Also *bisnes*.

Niñera: literally, baby-sitter. Trusted person who travels with the shipment, controls that the smuggler arrives without delays, sometimes pays him or her, and receives the money in the case the operation was not closed in advance.

Olla: literally, pot. Place or point where drugs are sold, usually in marginal and deprived urban areas or neighbourhoods. Also *sopladero*.

Paisa: person from the Antioquia region.

Paniquear: to panic, to become paranoid.

Pantalla: literally, screen. 1) Person attracting too much attention to the police, with the risk of becoming hot. Also *boleta*. 2) Front store, decoy. Also *tapadera*.

Papaya (dar): to draw excessive attention showing off or by other means, to almost call for being stolen or detained.

Paquete: package of 1 gr. cocaine. Also *bolita* or *cuadrito*.

Parche: peer group or gang. From street-children language, also used by drug dealers. Also *combo. Parcero* is the closest friend inside the group. Also *llave*.

Pasada: in the early days, payment to the smuggler (American pilot) once the cocaine had been entered.

Pase: fix, dose of cocaine.

Papeleta: *basuco* wrapped in a piece of paper.

Paras: paramilitary armies in Colombia.

Patrón: chief. Among Colombian cocaine organisations, disregarding their size, the most common name given to the main boss.

Pelado/a: child or teenager. Also means without any money.

Perico/a: most common name for cocaine.

Pesado: heavy, dangerous man.

Pinta (el): man, person who closes the drug deal.

Pistolo: *basuco* cigarette.

Platanal: Literally, banana plantation. Name for Colombia, used in Holland to avoid pronouncing the very word.

Plon: joint drag.

Poner: literally, to place. As used in legal business, to place somewhere a cocaine bulk.

Propio (el): person who performs as intermediary between different parties from which they remain independent. They transmit messages, arrange appointments or pass information amongst *traquetos*, employees, lawyers, prisoners or policemen.

Pueblo: Colombia. Used abroad to refer to the country.

Quebrar: literally, to break. To kill somebody. Also *quiñar*.

Quedar mal: to break promises or agreements within the business. Also *faltonear*.

Quieto: literally, freeze! Armed robbery.

Raponeo: mugging.

Rebusque: small informal or illegal job, hustle.

Recua: literally, mule train. A group of *mulas* travelling together.

Rumba: salsa and merengue dance party.

Ruta: a secure way for transporting cocaine.

Salado/a: something that has a curse on it.

Sano/a: literally, healthy. Person who do not belong to the drug or prostitution circuit.

Sapo: literally, toad. Police informant. *Sapear*, to tip off.

Seco: literally, dry. Without coke supply, used by big distributors when they run out of stock.

Sicario: hired killer, used to eliminate adversaries. Widely – but not exclusively – used by drug organisations. In Colombia, commonly organised in youth gangs from poor urban areas.

Soborno: bribe.

Sopladero: houses or places where *basuco* is sold and used, usually with very bad reputation. Also *olla*.

Soplador: basuco smoker. Also *basuquero*.

Soplón: police informant.
Subir: literally, to put up. To place the cocaine somewhere.
Tapadera: legal front store business to cover up illegal businesses or activities. Also *pantalla*.
Teléfono negro: illegal telephone line used to call abroad for very cheap rates.
Tieso: dead body.
Tira: police informant.
Todero: from *todo*, all. Person who does everything, especially small unskilled jobs, also in the cocaine business. Also *mandadero*.
Tombo: the most common name for policeman. Also *polocho, chupa, verde, tira* and *vigilante*.
Torcido: rip-deal.
Traba: the state of being stoned. *Trabado*, stoned.
Trabajar: to work in the cocaine business. Also *traquetear* and *camellear*.
Transar: to deal drugs. Also, *transar un tombo*, to bribe a policeman.
Trapicheo: to buy and sell all sorts of illegally owned goods, especially stolen goods, but also small amounts of drugs.
Traqueto or **Traquetero**: in the early days, trusted individuals sent by the cocaine exporters to the US to organise the distribution channels. Nowadays, name given to every Colombian cocaine entrepreneur working abroad or travelling often. It includes importers and distributors. *Traquetear*, to work abroad in the cocaine business.
Tumbar: to rip-off. Also, to kill somebody.
Universidad: prison. *Estudiar en la universidad*: to be in prison.
Untar/untado: literally, to smear. To be directly involved in some illegal business. Also, to bribe, to grease the hand of somebody or to receive dirty money. *Untado* also means hot, too much exposed through direct involvement in the cocaine business.
Valluno: person from the Cauca Valley.
Ventana: Window where the prostitute works. Also *vidrio*.
Vicio: drug addiction. *Vicioso/a* is a drug addict.
Vigilante: policeman. Also watchman, cocaine load keeper.
Visaje: suspicious move that attracts police attention. Also *boleta* and *pantalla*.

BIBLIOGRAPHY

Abadinsky, H. (1990) *Organized Crime*. Chicago: Nelson-Hall.

Abraham, M.D. et al. (1999) *Developments in Drug Use in Amsterdam 1987-1997*. Amsterdam: CEDRO.

Adler, P.A. (1985) *Wheeling and Dealing; An Ethnography of an Upper-Level Drug Dealing and Smuggling Community*. New York: Columbia University Press.

Adler, P.A. and Adler P. (1980) The Irony of Secrecy in the Drug World, in: *Urban Life*, 8, pp. 447-465.

Adler, P.A. and Adler P. (1987) *Membership Roles in Field Research*. London: Sage.

Agar, M. (1973) *Ripping and running: a fomal ethnography of urban heroin addicts*. New York: Academic Press.

Altink, S. (1993) *Dossier Vrouwenhandel NL*. Amsterdam: Sua.

Alvarez, E. (1995) Economic Development, Restructuring and the Illicit Drug Sector in Bolivia and Peru: Current Policies, in: *Journal of Interamerican Studies and World Affairs*, vol. 37, 3, Fall.

Ambos, K. (1997) Attempts at drug control in Colombia, Peru and Bolivia, in: *Crime, Law and Social Change*, 26, pp. 125-160.

Amin, A. (1994) Post-Fordism: Models, Fantasies and Phantoms of Transition, in: A. Amin (ed.) *Post-Fordism. A Reader*. London: Basil Blackwell.

Arango, M. (1988) *Impacto del Narcotráfico en Antioquia*. Medellín: Editorial J.M. Arango.

Arango, M. (1990) *Los Funerales de Antioquia la Grande*. Medellín: Editorial J..M. Arango.

Arango, M. and J. Child Vélez (1984) *Narcotráfico: imperio de la cocaína*. Medellín: Editorial Percepción.

Arlacchi, P. (1986) *Mafia Business*. London: Verso.

Arlacchi, P. (1993) *Leven in de mafia, het verhaal van Antonino Calderone*. Amsterdam: Nijgh & Van Ditmar.

Arlacchi, P. (1994) *Addio Cosa Nostra, la vita di Tommaso Buscetta*. Milano: Rizzoli.

Arrieta, C. et al. (1990) *Narcotráfico en Colombia: dimensiones políticas, económicas, jurídicas e internacionales*. Bogotá: Tercer Mundo Editores.

Baars-Schuyt, A.H. (1996) *De Nederlandse Antillen en Aruba in relatie tot witwassen: een literatuurverkenning*. Den Haag: WODC.

Bagley, B. (1990) Colombia y la Guerra contra las Drogas, in: J. Tokatlian and B. Bagley (eds) *Economía y política del narcotráfico*. Bogotá: CEI Cerec.

Bailey, T. and R. Waldinger (1991) Primary, secundary, and enclave labor markets: a training systems approach, in: *American Sociological Review*, 56, pp. 432-445.

Bauman, Z. (1995) *Life in Fragments*. Oxford: Blackwell.

Bauman, Z. (1997) *Modernity and its Discontents*. Cambridge: Polity Press.

Bayona, J. and G. Vanegas (1995) Redes de poder local y violencia: el caso de la región valle-caucana, in: *Prospectiva*, 2, October, pp. 77-108, Univalle, Cali.

Becker, H. (1963) *Outsiders. Studies in the Sociology of Deviance*. New York: The Free Press.

Bergquist, Ch. et al. (eds) (1992) *Violence in Colombia. The Contemporary Crisis in Historical Perspective*. Wilmington: Scholarly Resources Inc.

Betancourt, D. and M. Luz García (1990) *Matones y Cuadrilleros. Origen y evolución de la violencia en el occidente colombiano*. Bogotá: Tercer Mundo Editores.

Betancourt, D. and M. Luz García (1994) *Contrabandistas, marimberos y mafiosos: historia social de la mafia colombiana*. Bogotá: Tercer Mundo Editores.

Bieleman, B., A. Díaz, G. Merlo and Ch. D. Kaplan (eds) (1993) *Lines across Europe: Nature and extent of cocaine use in Barcelona, Rotterdam and Turin*. Amsterdam: Swets and Zeitlinger.

Bijkerk, R. and M. Grapendaal (1999) *In beslag genomen verdovende middelen 1997 en 1998.* Zoetermeer: CRI Afdeling Onderzoek en Analyse.

BKA (1998) *Lagebild Organisierte Kriminalität. Bundesrepublik Deutschland 1997.* Wiesbaden: BKA

Blickman, T. (1997) The Rothschilds of the Mafia on Aruba, in: *Transnational Organized Crime,* vol.3, 2, Summer, pp. 50-89.

Block, A. (1991) *Perspectives on organized crime. Essays in opposition.* Dordrecht: Kluwer.

Block, A. and W. Chambliss (1981) *Organizing Crime.* New York: Elsevier.

Blok, A (1974) *The Mafia of a Sicilian Village, 1860-1960.* Illinois: Waveland Press, Inc.

Blok, A. (1980) Eer en de fysieke persoon, in: *Tijdschrift voor Sociale Geschiedenis.* June 1980, pp. 211-230.

Blok, A. (1991a) *De Bokkerijders.* Amsterdam: Prometheus.

Blok, A. (1991b) Zinloos en zinvol geweld, in: H. Franke et al. *Alledaags en ongewoon geweld* Groningen: Amsterdam Sociologisch Tijdschrift / Wolters-Noordhoff.

Blok, A. (2000) *Honour and Violence.* Cambridge: Polity Press.

Blok A. and A. Buckser (1996) Nicknames as symbolic inversions, in: *Focaal,* 28, pp. 77-94.

Boekhout van Solinge, T. (1996) *Heroine, cocaïne en crack in Frankrijk. Handel, gebruik en beleid.* Amsterdam: CEDRO - Universiteit van Amsterdam.

Boekhout van Solinge, T. (2001) *Op de pof. Cocaïnegebruik en gezondheid op straat.* Amsterdam: Stichting Mainline.

Boissevain, J. (1974) *Friends of Friends. Networks, manipulators and coalitions.* Oxford: Basil Blackwell.

Bonacich, E. (1973) A theory of middleman minorities, in: *American Sociological Review,* 38, pp. 583-594.

Bonacich, E. and J. Modell (1980) *The economic basis of ethnic solidarity.* Berkeley: University of California Press.

Bourgois, P. (1995) *In search of respect. Selling crack in the Barrio.* Cambridge: Cambridge University Press.

Bovenkerk, F. (1992) *Hedendaags Kwaad. Criminologische opstellen.* Amsterdam: Meulenhoff.

Bovenkerk, F. (1995a) Cocaïnesmokkelaar in Colombiaanse dienst, in: *Vrij Nederland,* 15 April 1995, pp. 36-45.

Bovenkerk, F. (1995b) *La Bella Bettien.* Amsterdam: Meulenhoff.

Bovenkerk, F. (1995c) A Delinquent Second Generation?, in *Research Notes 1995.* Amsterdam: SISWO.

Bovenkerk, F. (ed.) (1996) *De georganiseerde criminaliteit in Nederland.* Deventer: Gouda Quint bv.

Bovenkerk, F. (1998) Fenomeenonderzoek. Of hoe de etnografische criminologie haar onschuld verliest, in: Justitiële Verkenningen, jrg. 24, 8, pp. 27-34.

Bovenkerk, F. (2001) Organized Crime and Ethnic Minorities: Is There a Link?, in: P. Williams and D. Vlassis (eds.) *Combating Transnational Crime. Concepts, Activities and Responses.* ISPAC, Frank Cass Journal.

Bovenkerk, F., W. de Haan and Y. Yeşilgöz (1991) Over selectiviteit gesproken!, in: *Tijdschrift voor Criminologie,* 33, pp. 309-321.

Bovenkerk, F. and Y. Yeşilgöz (1998) *De maffia van Turkije.* Amsterdam: Meulenhoff / Kritak.

Braverman, H. (1974) *Labor and Monopoly Capital. The Degradation of Work in the Twentieth Century.* New York: Monthly Review Press.

Bunt, H. van de et al. (1999) Georganiseerde criminaliteit en het opsporingsapparaat: een wapenwedloop?, in: *Tijdschrift voor Criminologie,* jrg 41, 4, pp. 395-408.

Butcher, K. and A. Morrison Piehl (1997) *Recent immigrants: unexpected implications for crime and incarceration.* Working Paper 6067. Cambridge: National Bureau of Economic Research.

Camacho Guizado, A. (1988) *Droga y sociedad en Colombia: el poder y el estigma.* Cali: CIDSE.

Camacho Guizado, A. (1994) Empresarios Ilegales y Región. La gestación de clases dominantes locales, in: *Delito y Sociedad,* 4/5, pp. 163-182, Buenos Aires.

Camacho Guizado, A. and A. Guzmán (1990) *Colombia, ciudad y violencia.* Bogotá: Ediciones Foro Nacional.

Cámara de Representantes de la República de Colombia (1995) *Informe sobre Presos Colombianos en Europa.* Bogotá: unpublished.

Castells, M. and A. Portes (1989) World Underneath: The Origins, Dynamics, and Effects of the Informal Economy, in: A. Portes et al. (eds) *The Informal Economy. Studies in Advanced and Less Developed Countries.* Baltimore: The John Hopkins University Press.

Castillo, F. (1987) *Los Jinetes de la Cocaína.* Bogotá: Editorial Documentos Periodísticos.

Castillo, F. (1991) *La Coca Nostra.* Bogotá: Editorial Documentos Periodísticos.

Castillo, F. (1996) *Los Nuevos Jinetes de la Cocaína.* Bogotá: Editorial Oveja Negra.

Catanzaro, R. (1992) *Men of Respect. A Social History of the Sicilian Mafia.* New York: The Free Press.

Catanzaro, R. (1994) Violent Social Regulation: Organized Crime in the Italian South, in: *Social & Legal Studies,* vol. 3, pp. 267-279.

Caulkins, J. and P. Reuter (1997) *What Price Data Tell Us About Drug Markets.* Maryland: paper unpublished.

CBS (1997 and 1998) *Dutch Statistics on sea and air navigation, import, export, and transport of goods.* Den Haag: CBS.

Chambliss, W. (1975) On the Paucity of Original Research on Organized Crime: A Footnote to Galliher and Cain, in: *The American Sociologist,* vol. 10 (February), pp. 36-39.

Chambliss, W. (1978) *On the Take: From Petty Crooks to Presidents.* Indiana: Indiana University Press.

Chambliss, W. (1988) State Organized Crime, in: *Criminology,* vol. 27, 2, pp. 183-207.

Clawson, P. and R. Lee III (1996) *The Andean Cocaine Industry.* London: Macmillan Press.

Cloward, R.A. and L.E. Ohlin (1960) *Delinquency and Opportunity. A theory of delinquent gangs.* New York: The Free Press.

Cohen, A. (1955) *Delinquent Boys: The Culture of the Gang.* New York: The Free Press.

Cohen, L. and M. Felson (1979) Social change and crime rate trends: a routine activity approach, in: *American Sociological Review,* 44, pp. 588-608.

Cohen, P. (1989) *Cocaine use in Amsterdam in non deviant subcultures.* Amsterdam: Department of Human Geography, University of Amsterdam.

Cohen, P. and A. Sas (1993) *Ten Years of Cocaine; a follow-up study of 64 cocaine users in Amsterdam.* Amsterdam: Department of Human Geography, University of Amsterdam.

Colombian Ministry of Communications, Enlace Project (1997) *Deseased Colombians in Europe.* Bogotá: unpublished.

Conan Doyle, A. (1992) *Introducing Sherlock Holmes. The Sign of Four.* Hertfordshire: Wordsworth.

Cortés, F. (1993) *Rodríguez Gacha "El Mejicano".* Bogotá: Intermedio Editores.

Courtwright, D. (1995) The Rise and Fall and Rise of Cocaine in the United States, in: J. Goodman et al. (eds) *Consuming Habits.* London: Routledge.

Cressey, D. (1969) *Theft of the Nation: The Structure and Operations of Organized Crime.* New York: Harper & Row.

Davis, M. (1990) *City of Quartz: Excavating the Future in Los Angeles.* London: Vintage.

DEA (1995) *Illegal Drug Price/Purity Report.* Washington: DEA.

Deas, M. and F. Gaitán Daza (1995) *Dos ensayos especulativos sobre la violencia en Colombia*. Bogotá: Tercer Mundo Editores.

del Olmo, R. (1990) The economic crisis and the criminalization of Latin American women, In: *Social Justice*, vol. 17, 2, pp. 40-53.

del Olmo, R. (1992) *¿Prohibir o Domesticar? Políticas de Drogas en América Latina*. Caracas: Editorial Nueva Sociedad.

del Olmo, R. (1996) Drogas: Discursos, Percepciones y Políticas, in: X. Arana and R. del Olmo (eds) *Normas y culturas en la construcción de la "Cuestión Droga"*. Barcelona: Editorial Hacer.

Doelder, H. de and A.B. Hoogenboom (eds) (1997) *Witteboordencriminaliteit in Nederland*. Deventer: Gouda Quint.

Dombois, R. (1990) ¿Por qué Florece la Economía de la Cocaína Justamente en Colombia?, in: J. Tokatlian and B. Bagley (eds) *Economía y política del narcotráfico*. Bogotá: CEI Cerec.

Doorn, J. van (1993) Drug Trafficking Networks in Europe, in: *European Journal on Criminal Policy and Research*, 1, 2, pp. 96-104.

Dorn, N. and N. South (1990) Drug markets and law enforcement, in *The British Journal of Criminology*, 30, 2, pp. 171-178.

Dorn, N., K. Murji and N. South (1992) *Traffickers. Drug markets and law enforcement*. London: Routledge.

Dorn, N. et al. (1998) Drugs importation and the bifurcation of risk, in: *The British Journal of Criminology*, 38, 4, Autumn, pp. 537-560.

Dubois, R. (1997) *Rapport sur les acteurs du Narco-Trafic en France*. Paris: OGD.

Duyne, P. van, R. Kouwenberg and G. Romeijn (1990) *Misdaadondernemingen*. Den Haag: WODC - Gouda Quint bv.

Duyne, P. van (1991) Crime Enterprises and the Legitimate Industry in the Netherlands, in: C. Fijnaut and J. Jacobs (eds) *Organized Crime and its Containment. A Transatlantic Initiative*. Deventer: Kluwer.

Duyne, P. van (1993a) Organized Crime in a turbulent Europe, in: *European Journal on Criminal Policy and Research*, vol. 1, 3, pp. 10-30.

Duyne, P. van (1993b) Organized crime and business crime enterprises in the Netherlands, in: *Crime, Law & Social Change*, 19, pp. 103-142.

Duyne, P. van (1995) *Het Spook en de Dreiging van de Georganiseerde Misdaad*. Den Haag: Sdu.

Eddy, P. et al. (1992) *Las Guerras de la Cocaína*. Bogotá: Círculo de Lectores.

Elias, N. (1982) *The Civilizing Process: State Formation and Civilizations*. Oxford: Blackwell.

E.M.C.D.D.A. (1995) *Annual Report on the State of the Drug Problem in the European Union*. Lisbon: E.M.C.D.D.A.

E.M.C.D.D.A. (1998) *Annual Report on the State of the Drug Problem in the European Union*. Lisbon: E.M.C.D.D.A.

E.M.C.D.D.A. (1999) *Annual Report on the State of the Drug Problem in the European Union*. Lisbon: E.M.C.D.D.A.

Engbersen, G. et al. (1995) *Over de verwevenheid van illegaliteit en criminaliteit*. Utrecht: Rijksuniversiteit Utrecht.

Engbersen, G. et al. (1999) *Inbedding en uitsluiting van illegale vreemdelingen*. Amsterdam: Boom.

Escohotado, A. (1996) *Historia de las Drogas. Vol 1-3*. Madrid: Alianza Editorial.

EVD (2000) *Statistics on Colombian-Dutch Trade, 1998*. On-line publication: www.evd.nl

Farrell, G. (1995) The Global Rate of Interception of Illicit Opiates and Cocaine 1980-94, in: *Transnational Organized Crime*, vol. 1, 4, Winter, pp. 134-149.

Farrell, G. (1998) Routine activities and drug trafficking: the case of the Netherlands, in: *The International Journal of Drug Policy*, 9, pp. 21-32.

Farrell, G., K. Mansur and M. Tullis (1996) Cocaine and Heroin in Europe 1983-93. A Cross-national Comparison of Trafficking and Prices, in: *The British Journal of Criminology*, vol. 36, 2, Spring, pp. 255-281.

Ferrell, J. and M. Hamm (eds) (1998) *Ethnography at the edge: crime, deviance and field research*. Boston: Northeastern University Press.

Fijnaut, C. et al. (1996) *Inzake Opsporing. Eindrapport Georganiseerde Criminaliteit in Nederland*. Den Haag: Sdu.

Florez, C.P. and B. Boyce (1990) Colombian Organized Crime, in: *Police Studies*, vol. 13, 2, Summer.

Foucault, M. (1979) *Discipline and Punish. The Birth of the Prison*. London: Penguin Books Ltd.

Franke, H. et al. (eds) (1996) *De georganiseerde criminaliteit in Nederland. Tijdschift voor Criminologie*, jrg 38, 2.

Freud, S. (1995) *Coca e cocaina*. Roma: Newton Compton editori s.r.l.

Friman, H. (1995) Just Passing Through: Transit States and the Dynamics of Illicit Transshipment, in: *Transnational Organized Crime*, Vol. 1, 1, Spring, pp. 65-83.

Gambetta, D. (1988) Fragments of an Economic Theory of the Mafia, in: *Archives Europeennes de Sociologie*, 29, 1, pp. 127-145.

Gambetta, D. (ed.) (1990) *Trust. Making and breaking cooperative relations*. Cambridge: Basil Blackwell.

Gambetta, D. (1996) *The Sicilian Mafia. The Business of Private Protection*. London: Harvard University Press.

García Marquez, G. (1994) Por un país al alcance de los niños, in: *Política y Gestión Universitaria*, 17, October. Cali: Universidad del Valle.

García Marquez, G. (1996) *Noticia de un Secuestro*. Bogotá: Grupo Editorial Norma SA.

Geertz, C. (1979) Suq: The Bazaar Economy in Sefrou, in: C. Geertz et al. (eds) (1979) *Meaning and Order in Moroccan Society*. New York: Cambridge University Press.

Gelder, P.J. van and J.H. Sijtsma (1988) *Horse, Coke en Kansen; sociale risico's en kansen onder Surinaamse en Marokkaanse harddruggebruikers in Amsterdam, I & II*. Amsterdam: Department of Human Geography, University of Amsterdam.

Gemert, F. van (1988) *Mazen en Netwerken, de invloed van beleid op de drugshandel in twee straten in de Amsterdamse Binnenstad*. Amsterdam: Department of Human Geography, University of Amsterdam.

Giddens, A. (1991) *Modernity and Self-Identity*. Cambridge: Polity Press.

Goffman, E. (1968) *Stigma. Notes on the Management of Spoiled Identity*. Harmondsworth: Pelican Books Ltd

Gómez, H.J. (1988) La economía ilegal en Colombia: tamaño, evolución, características e impacto económico, in: *Coyuntura Económica*,18, 3.

Gómez, H.J. (1990) El tamaño del narcotráfico y su impacto económico, in: *Economía Colombiana*, 226-227, February-March, Bogotá.

Gómez, H.J. and M. Santa María (1994) La economía subterránea en Colombia, in: *Gran Enciclopedia Temática de Colombia*, vol. 8. Bogotá: Círculo de Lectores.

González, F. et al. (1994) *Violencia en la Región Andina. El caso Colombia*. Bogotá: CINEP-APEP.

González-Arias, J. (1998) Cultivos ilícitos, colonización y revuelta de raspachines, in: *Revista Foro*, 35, September 1998.

Granovetter, M. (1995) The Economic Sociology of Firms and Entrepreneurs, in: A. Portes (ed.) *The Economic Sociology of Immigration*. New York: Rusell Sage Foundation.

Grapendaal, M., E. Leuw and H. Nelen (1995) *A World of Opportunities. Life-Style and Economic Behavior of Heroin Addicts in Amsterdam*. Albany: State University of New York Press.

Green, P. (1991) *Drug Couriers*. London: The Howard League for Penal Reform.

Green, P. (1996) Drug Couriers: The Construction of a Public Enemy, in P. Green (ed.) *Drug Couriers. A New Perspective*. Howard League Handbooks II. London: Quartet Books.

Green, P., C. Mills and T. Read (1994) The Characteristics and Sentencing of Illegal Drug Importers, in: *The British Journal of Criminology*, vol. 34, 4, Autumn, pp. 479-486.

Green, T. (1969) *The Smugglers. An Investigation into the World of the contemporary smuggler*. London: Michael Joseph LTD.

Gugliotta, G. and J. Leen (1990) *Kings of Cocaine*. New York: Harper.

Haan, W. de and F. Bovenkerk (1993) Moedwil en misverstand; Overschatting en onderschatting van allochtone criminaliteit in Nederland, in: *Tijdschrift voor Criminologie*, jrg 35, 3, pp. 277-300.

Haan, W. de (1993) *Beroving van voorbijgangers*. Den Haag: Ministerie van Binnenlandse Zaken.

Haenen, M. and H. Buddingh' (1994) *De Danser. Hoe de drugshandel Nederland veroverde*. Amsterdam: Uitgeverij De Arbeiderspers.

Haenen, M. (1999) *Baas Bouterse*. Amsterdam: Uitgeverij Balans.

Haller, M.H. (1990) Illegal enterprise: a theoretical and historical interpretation, in: *Criminology*, 28, 2, pp. 207-235.

Hartlyn, J. (1993) *Drug Trafficking and Democracy in Colombia in the 1980s*. Barcelona: Institut de Ciències Polítiques i Socials.

Harvey, D. (1989) *The Condition of Postmodernity*. Oxford: Basil Blackwell.

Henman, A.R. (1981) *Mama Coca*. Bogotá: El Ancora/La Oveja Negra.

Hernández, M. (1997) Comportamientos y búsquedas alrededor del narcotráfico, in: F. Thoumi et al. *Drogas ilícitas en Colombia. Su impacto económico, político y social*. Bogotá: Ariel - UNDP - DNE.

Hernández, J. and N. Téllez (1990) *Aproximaciones al estudio sobre el impacto del narcotráfico en la región valle-caucana*. Cali: Centro de Investigaciones y Documentación Socioeconómica, Universidad del Valle.

Heuvel, J. van den (1999) *De jacht op Desi Bouterse. Hoe het Suri-kartel de Nederlandse drugsmarkt veroverde*. Den Haag: Bzztoh.

Hirsch, P. (1993) Undoing the managerial revolution? Needed research on the decline of middle management and internal labour markets, in: R. Swedberg (ed.) *Explorations in Economic Sociology*. New York: Russell Sage Foundation.

Hobbs, D (1988) *Doing the Business: Entrepreneurship, the Working Class and Detectives in the East End of London*. Oxford: Clarendon.

Hobbs, D. (1995) *Bad Business*. Oxford: Oxford University Press.

Hobbs, D. and C. Dunnighan (1998) Glocal Organised Crime: Context and Pretext, in: V. Ruggiero et al. *The New European Criminology. Crime and Social Order in Europe*. London: Routledge.

Hobsbawm, E. (1986) Murderous Colombia, in: *New York Review of Books*, 20 November 1986, pp. 27-35.

Hofland, G. and J. Remie (1994) *De haven van Rotterdam: volledig vrije doorgang?* Utrecht: Willem Pompe Instituut.

Hoogenboom, A.B. et al. (1995) *Financieel recherchen*. Den Haag: Vuga.

Huisman, W. and E. Niemeijer (1998) *Zicht op organisatie criminaliteit. Een literatuuronderzoek*. Den Haag: Sdu Uitgevers.

Ianni, F.A. (1972) *A family business: kinship and social control in organized crime*. New York: Russell Sage Basic Books.

Ianni, F.A. (1974) *Black Mafia. Ethnic succession in organized crime*. New York: Simon & Schuster.

Ilegems, D. and R. Sauviller (1995) *Bloedsporen; een reis naar de mafia*. Amsterdam: Atlas.

INCB (1996) *Report of the International Narcotics Control Board for 1996*. Vienna: INCB.

INCB (1997) *Report of the International Narcotics Control Board for 1997*. Vienna: INCB.

INCB (1998a) *Report of the International Narcotics Control Board for 1998*. Vienna: INCB.

INCB (1998b) *Report of the International Narcotics Control Board for 1998 on the Implementation of Article 12 of the United Nations Convention against Illicit Traffic in Narcotic Drugs and Psychotropic Substances of 1988*. Vienna: INCB.

Inciardi, J. et al. (1993) *Women and Crack-Cocaine*. New York: Macmillan.

Interpol Office, DAS (1997) *Colombian courriers detained in Europe*. Bogotá: unpublished.

Jackson, J. et al. (1996) Examining Criminal Organizations: Possible Methodologies, in: *Transnational Organized Crime*, vol.2, 4, Winter, pp. 83-105.

Janssen, J. (1994) *Latijnsamerikaanse drugskoeriersters in detentie: ezels of zondebokken?* Arnhem: Gouda Quint bv/Willem Pompe Instituut.

Jaramillo, J. et al. (1986) *Colonización, Coca y Guerrilla*. Bogotá: Universidad Nacional de Colombia.

Jelsma, M. (2000) *The Vicious Circle. The Chemical Spraying of Drug Crops in Colombia*. Amsterdam: TNI.

Jessop, B. et al. (eds) (1991) *The Politics of Flexibility*. Hants: Edward Elgar.

Jobber, D. and G. Lancaster (2000) *Selling and Sales Managment*. Harlow: Pearson Education Limited.

Johnson, B.D. and T. Williams (1986) *Economics of Dealing in a Nonmonetary Labor Market*. Amsterdam: Mimeo.

Kalmanovitz, S. (1990) La economía del narcotráfico en Colombia, in: *Economía Colombiana*, 226-227, February-March, Bogotá.

Kalmanovitz, S. (1994) Análisis macroeconómico del narcotráfico en la economía colombiana, in: R. Vargas (ed.) *Drogas, Poder y Región en Colombia*, 1. Bogotá: Cinep.

Kennedy, M., P. Reuter and K. Riley (1993) *A Simple Model for Cocaine Production*. Santa Monica: RAND Corporation.

Kleemans, E. et al. (1998) *Georganiseerde criminaliteit in Nederland*. Rapportage op basis van de WODC-monitor. Den Haag: WODC.

Kleemans, E. and Kruissink (1999) Korte klappen of lange halen? Wat werkt bij de aanpak van de georganiseerde criminaliteit?, in: *Justitiële Verkenningen*, jrg. 25, 6, pp. 99-111.

Klerks, P. (1996) *Ondergrondse organisaties in vergelijkend perspectief*. Rotterdam: Erasmus Universiteit Rotterdam.

Kools, J.P. (1997) Gekookte coke is geen crack, in: *Mainline*, 1, pp. 10-11.

Kopp, P. (1995) Colombie: trafic de drogue et organisations criminelles, in: *Problèmes d'Amérique latine*, No.18, juillet-sept 1995, pp.21-39.

Kopp, P. (1997) *L' èconomie de la drogue*. Paris: Éditions La Découverte.

Korf, D. and M. de Kort (1989) N.V. de witte waan, de geschiedenis van de Nederlandsche Cocaïnefabriek, in *NRC Handelsblad, Zaterdags Bijvoegsel*, 13 May, p. 5.

Korf, D. and H. Verbraeck (1993) *Dealers and Dienders*. Amsterdam: Criminologisch Instituut 'Bonger' - Universiteit van Amsterdam.

Krauthausen, C. (1994) Poder y mercado. El narcotráfrico colombiano y la mafia italiana, in: *Revista Nueva Sociedad*, 130, pp. 112-125.

Krauthausen, C. (1998) *Padrinos y mercaderes: crimen organizado en Italia y Colombia*. Bogotá: Planeta Colombiana Editorial.

Krauthausen, C. and L.F. Sarmiento (1991) *Cocaína & Co.* Bogotá: Coediciones Tercer Mundo - Instituto de Estudios Políticos de la Universidad Nacional de Colombia.

Labrousse, A. (1993) *La droga, el dinero y las armas.* México: Siglo Veintiuno Editores.

Labrousse, A. (1996) Les routes de la drogue et l'approvisionnement du marché européen, in: Leclerc, M. (ed.) *La Criminalite Organisée.* Paris: La documentation française.

Labrousse, A. (2000) *Drogues. Un marché de dupes.* Paris: OGD.

Langer, J. (1977) Drug Entrepreneurs and Dealing Culture, in: *Social Problems*, vol. 24, pp. 377-386.

Lash, S. and J. Urry (1987) *The end of organized capitalism.* Cambridge: Polity Press.

Leal, F. and A. Dávila (1991) *Clientelismo: el sistema político y su expresión regional.* Bogotá: Tercer Mundo Editores.

Lee, R.M. (1995) *Dangerous Fieldwork.* London: Sage.

Lee III, R.W. (1989) *The White Labyrinth: Cocaine and Political Power.* New Brunswick: Transaction Publishers.

Lee III, R.W. (1991) Colombia's cocaine syndicates, in: *Crime, Law and Social Change*, 16, 1, pp. 3-39.

Leun, J. van der and S. Botman (1999) Uitsluiting van illegale migranten na de Koppelingswet, in: G. Engbersen et al. (eds) *Arm Nederland. Armoede en verzorgingsstaat.* Amsterdam: Amsterdam University Press.

Lewis, O. (1964) *The Children of Sánchez.* Middlesex: Penguin Books.

Lewis, O. (1968) *La Vida.* London: Panther books.

Lewis, R. (1989) European markets in cocaine, in: *Contemporary Crises*, vol. 13, pp. 35-52.

Light, I. and S. Karageorgis (1995) The Ethnic Economy, in: N.J. Smelser and R. Swedberg (eds) *The Handbook of Economic Sociology.* Princeton: Princeton University Press.

Lupsha, P. (1995) Transnational Narco-Corruption and Narco Investment: A Focus on Mexico, in: *Transnational Organized Crime*, vol. 1, 1, Spring, pp. 84-101.

MacDonald, S.B. (1988) *Dancing on a volcano: the Latin American drug trade.* London: Praeger Publisher.

Martin, G. (1996) Violences stratégiques et violences désorganisées dans la région d'Urabá (Colombie), in: G. Bataillon *Survivre. Reflexions sur l'action en situation de chaos.* Paris: L'Harmattan.

McCoy, A.W. and A. Block (1992) *War on drugs: studies in the failure of U.S. Narcotics Policy.* San Francisco: Westview Press.

McIntosh, M. (1975) *The Organization of Crime.* London: MacMillan.

Medina Gallego, C. (1990) *Autodefensas, Paramilitares y Narcotráfico en Colombia.* Bogotá: Editorial Documentos Periodísticos.

Medina Gallego, C. (1993) La violencia parainstitucional en Colombia, in: A. Guerrero Rincón (1993) *Cultura Política, Movimientos Sociales y Violencia en la Historia de Colombia.* Bucaramanga: Universidad Industrial de Santander.

Mermelstein, M. (1990) *The man who made it snow.* New York: Simon and Schuster.

Metropolitan Police of Bogotá, Airport Section (1997) *Local statistics on cocaine seizures and related cases.* Bogotá: unpublished.

Middelburg, B. (1992) *De Dominee, opkomst en ondergang van mafiabaas Klaas Bruinsma.* Amsterdam: L.J. Veen.

Middelburg, B. (2000) *The Godmother.* Amsterdam: Contact bv.

Middelburg, B. and K. van Es (1994) Operatie Delta: hoe de drugsmafia het IRT opblies. Amsterdam: L.J. Veen.

Ministry of Foreign Affairs of Colombia, Sub-secretary of Colombian Communities Abroad (1997) *Colombian citizen detained abroad.* Bogotá: unpublished.

Molano, A. (1987) *Selva Adentro.* Bogotá: El Áncora Editores.

Molano, A. (1997) *Rebusque Mayor. Relatos de mulas, traquetos y embarques.* Bogotá: El Áncora Editores.

Murillo Perdomo, A. (1996) *Problemática psicosocial de los colombianos indocumentados en Europa.* Brussels: Casa de América Latina.

Nabben, T. and D. Korf (1999) Cocaine and Crack in Amsterdam: Diverging Subcultures, in: *Journal of Drug Issues*, Summer 1999, pp. 627-652.

National Institute on Drug Abuse (NIDA) (1994) *National Household Survey on Drug Abuse (NHSDA) 1994.* Rockville: US Government Printing Office.

Naylor, R.T. (1997) Mafias, Myths and Markets: On the Theory and Practice of Enterprise Crime, in: *Transnational Organized Crime*, vol. 3, 3, Autumn, pp. 1-45

Nelen, H. and J.J.A. Essers (1993) *Veel voorkomende criminaliteit op de Nederlandse Antillen.* Arnhem: WODC/Gouda Quint.

Nelen, H. and V. Sabee (1998) *Het vermogen te ontnemen; evaluatie van de ontnemingswetgeving; eindrapport.* Den Haag: WODC.

O.C.R.T.I.S. (1995) *Usage et Trafic de Stupefiants en France.* Paris: O.C.R.T.I.S.

OGD (1996a) *The Geopolitics of Drugs. 1996 Edition.* Boston: Northeastern University Press.

OGD (1996b) *Atlas Mondial des Drogues.* Paris: Presses Universitaires de France.

OGD (1997a) *Où va la cocaïne en Europe?* Paris: OGD.

OGD (1997b) *The World Geopolitics of Drugs 1995/1996. Annual Report.* Paris: OGD.

OGD (2000)) *The World Geopolitics of Drugs 1998/1999. Annual Report.* Paris: OGD.

Omaña, E. (1995) *Análisis sobre el Uso en Colombia de Sustancias Químicas Precursoras y sus Mecanismos de Control.* Bogotá: Dirección Nacional de Estupefacientes (DNE) and UNDCP.

Ortiz Sarmiento, C.M. (1991) El Sicariato en Medellín: Entre la violencia política y el crimen organizado, in: *Análisis Político*, 14, Sep-Dec.

Ospina, S. and A. Hofmann (1996) *Perfil de la Población Carcelaria Colombiana en Nueva York.* New York: unpublished report from the New York University.

Palacio, G. (ed.) (1990) *La Irrupción del Paraestado. Ensayos sobre la crisis colombiana.* Bogotá: ILSA-CEREC.

Passas, N. and D. Nelken (1993) The thin line between legitimate and criminal enterprises: subsidy frauds in the EC, in: *Crime, Law and Social Change*, 19, pp. 223-243.

Pearce, J. (1990) *Colombia, inside the labyrinth.* London: Latin American Bureau.

Pecaut, D. (1987) *Orden y Violencia. Colombia 1930-1953.* Bogotá: Siglo Veintiuno Editores.

Pecaut, D. (1996) Pasado, Presente y Futuro de la Violencia en Colombia, in: *Desarrollo Económico*, 36, 144.

Phillips, J. and R. Wynne (1980) *Cocaine. The Mystique and the Reality.* New York: Avon Books.

Polanía Molina, F. and M. Janssen (1998) *I never thought this would happen to me. Prostitution and traffic in Latin American women in the Netherlands.* Amsterdam: Fundación Esperanza.

Polsky, N. (1969) *Hustlers, beats, and others.* New York: Anchor Books.

Potter, G.W. (1994) *Criminal Organizations.* Illinois: Waveland Press.

Portes, A. (1995) Economic Sociology and the Sociology of Immigration: A Conceptual Overview, in: A. Portes (ed.) *The Economic Sociology of Immigration.* New York: Russell Sage Foundation.

Portes, A. and R. Rumbaut (1990) *Immigrant America. A Portrait.* Berkeley: University of California Press.

Portes, A. and L. Jensen (1987) What's an ethnic enclave? The case for conceptual clarity, in: *American Sociological Review*, 52, pp. 768-771.

Portes, A. and R. Bach (1985) *Latin Journey: Cuban and Mexican Immigrants in the United States*. Berkeley: University of California Press.

Portes, A. and J. Sensenbrenner (1993) Embeddedness and Immigration: Notes on the Social Determinants of Economic Action, in: *American Journal of Sociology*, vol. 98, 6, May, pp. 1320-1350.

Powell, W. and L. Smith-Doerr (1995) Networks and Economic Life, in: N.J. Smelser and R. Swedberg (eds) *The Handbook of Economic Sociology*. Princeton: Princeton University Press.

Power, R., A. Green, R. Foster and G. Stimson (1995) A Qualitative Study of the Purchasing and Distribution Patterns of Cocaine and Crack Users in England and Wales, in: *Addiction Research*, vol. 2, 4, pp. 363-379.

Prisma Team (2000) *Criminaliteitsbeeld 2000*. Den Haag: Prisma Team.

Pulido, H.C. et al. (1995) *Estudio Descriptivo para Caracterizar los Ciudadanos Colombianos Detenidos en el Exterior por Delitos de Narcotráfico*. Bogotá: Ministry of Justice and Law (unpublished).

Puzo, M. (1970) *The Godfather*. London: Pan Books.

Reuter, P. (1983) *Disorganized Crime. The economics of the visible hand*. Cambridge: The MIT Press.

Reuter, P. (1992) After the Borders are Sealed: Can Domestic Sources Substitute for Imported Drugs? in P. Smith (ed.) *Drug Policy in the Americas*. Boulder: Westview Press.

Reuter, P. and M. Kleiman (1986) Risks and Prices: An Economic Analysis of Drug Enforcement, in: *Crime and Justice*, vol. 7, pp. 289-340.

Reuter, P. et al. (1990) *Money from Crime: A Study of the Economics of Drug Dealing in Washington D.C.* Santa Mónica: RAND Corporation.

Reyes Posada, A. (1990) La Violencia y la Expansión Territorial del Narcotráfico, in: J. Tokatlián and B. Bagley (eds) *Economía y política del narcotráfico*. Bogotá: CEI Cerec.

Reyes Posada, A. (1991) Paramilitares en Colombia: contexto, aliados y consecuencias, in: *Análisis Político*, 12, January-April, pp. 35-41.

Reyes Posada, A. (1997) Compra de tierras por narcotraficantes, in: F. Thoumi et al. *Drogas ilícitas en Colombia. Su impacto económico, político y social*. Bogotá: Ariel - UNDP - DNE

Rhodes, W. et al. (1994) The price of cocaine, heroine and marijuana 1981-1993, in: *Journal of Drug Issues*, 3, pp. 383-402.

Rocha, R. (1997) Aspectos económicos de las drogas ilegales, in: F. Thoumi et al. *Drogas ilícitas en Colombia. Su impacto económico, político y social*. Bogotá: Ariel - UNDP - DNE.

Rocha, R. (2000) *La economía colombiana tras 25 años de narcotráfico*. Bogotá: Siglo del Hombre Editores - UNDCP.

Rodríguez Ospina, E. et al. (1992) *Encuesta nacional sobre consumo de sustancias psicoactivas 1992*. Bogotá: Dirección Nacional de Estupefacientes (DNE).

Romero, M. (1995) Transformación rural, violencia política y narcotráfico en Córdoba 1953-1991, in: *Controversia*, 167, Oct-Nov, pp. 95-121, Cinep, Bogotá.

Roth, J. and M. Frey (1994) *Het verenigd Europa van de Mafia*. Amsterdam: Van Gennep.

Ruggiero, V. (1993) Organized crime in Italy: testing alternative definitions, in: *Social & Legal Studies*, 2, 2, pp. 131-148.

Ruggiero, V. (1995) Drug Economics: A Fordist Model of Criminal Capital? in: *Capital & Class*, 55, pp. 131-150.

Ruggiero, V. (1996) *Organized and Corporate Crime in Europe*. Hampshire: Dartmouth Publishing Company.

Ruggiero, V. and N. South (1995) *Eurodrugs. Drug use, markets and trafficking in Europe.* London: UCL Press.

Sabbag, R. (1978) *Snowblind. A brief carrer in the cocaine trade.* London: Pan Books.

Salazar, A. (1990) *No Nacimos Pa' Semilla.* Bogotá: Cinep.

Salazar, A. (1993) *Mujeres de Fuego.* Medellín: Corporación Region.

Salazar, A. and A.M. Jaramillo (1992) *Medellín. Las subculturas del narcotráfico.* Bogotá: Cinep.

Sánchez, G. and D. Meertens (1983) *Bandoleros, gamonales y campesinos. El caso de la violencia en Colombia.* Bogotá: El Áncora Editores.

Sánchez, G. and R. Peñaranda (eds) (1986) *Pasado y presente de la violencia en Colombia.* Bogotá: CEREC.

Sandwijk, J.P. Cohen, S. Musterd and M. Langemeijer (1995) *Licit and illicit drug use in Amsterdam II. Report of a household survey in 1994 on the prevalence of drug use among the population of 12 years and over.* Amsterdam: Department of Human Geography, University of Amsterdam.

Sansone, L. (1992) *Schitteren in de schaduw.* Amsterdam: Het Spinhuis.

Santino, U. (1993) La mafia siciliana y los nuevos mercados de drogas en Europa, in: A. Labrousse et al. (eds) *El Planeta de las Drogas.* Bilbao: Ediciones Mensajero SA.

Santino, U. (1994) *La Borghesia Mafiosa.* Palermo: Centro Giuseppe Impastato

Santino, U. and G. La Fiura (1993) *Dietro la Droga.* Turin: CISS - Centro Giuseppe Impastato - Edizioni Gruppo Abele.

Sarmiento, E. (1990) Economía del Narcotráfico, in: C. Arrieta et al. *Narcotráfico en Colombia: dimensiones políticas, económicas, jurídicas e internacionales.* Bogotá: Tercer Mundo Editores.

Savona, E. (1999) *European Money Trails.* Singapore: Harwood Academic Publishers.

Savona, E., N. Dorn and T. Ellis (eds) (1993) *Cocaine Markets and Law Enforcement in Europe.* Rome: UNICRI.

Shaw, C. and McKay, H. (1972) *Juvenile Delinquency and Urban Areas.* Chicago: University of Chicago Press.

Siegel, D. (2001) *Russian Biznes in the Netherlands.* The Hague: WODC Rapport (forthcoming).

Siegel, D. and F. Bovenkerk (2001) Crime and manipulation of identity among Russian-speaking immigrants in the Netherlands, in: *Journal of Contemporary Criminal Justice,* vol. 16. (forthcoming).

Silva García, G. (1997) *¿Será Justicia? Criminalidad y justicia penal en Colombia.* Bogotá: Universidad Externado de Colombia.

Simmel, G. (1950) *The sociology of George Simmel* (edited and translated by K.H. Wolff). New York: The Free Press.

Sluka, J. (1990) Participant Observation in Violent Social Contexts, in: *Human Organization,* vol. 49, 2, pp. 114-126.

Smith, D.C. Jr. (1975) *The Mafia Mystique.* New York: Basic Books.

Smith, D.C. Jr. (1982) White-Collar Crime, Organized Crime, and the Business Establishment: Resolving a crisis in Criminological Theory, in: P. Wickman and T. Dailey (eds) *White Collar and Economic Crime.* Toronto: Lexington Books.

Smith, P. (1992) *Drug Policy in the Americas.* Oxford: Westview Press.

Steiner, R. (1997) *Los Dólares del Narcotráfico.* Cuadernos Fedesarrollo 2. Bogotá: Tercer Mundo Editores.

Sterk, C.E. (1999) *Fast lives. Women who use crack cocaine.* Philadelphia: Temple University Press.

Stoop, C. de (1992) *Ze zijn zo lief meneer.* Leuven: Kritak.

Sutherland, E. (1949) White-Collar Criminality, in: *American Sociological Review*, 5, pp. 1-12.

Sykes, G. and Matza, D. (1957) Techniques of Neutralization: a Theory of Delinquency, in: *American Sociological Review*, 22, pp. 664-673.

Taylor, I. (1999) *Crime in Context*. Oxford: Polity.

Taylor, L. (1984) *In the Underworld*. London: Counterpoint.

Tefft, S. (1980) 'Introduction' and 'Secrecy as a Social and Political Process', in: S. Tefft (ed.) *Secrecy. A Cross-cultural Perspective*. New York: Human Sciences Press.

Thoumi, F. (1995) *Political Economy & Illegal Drugs in Colombia*. London: Lynne Rienner Publishers.

Thoumi, F. (1997) Tramas de lo legal y lo legítimo en la industria colombiana de las drogas, in: R. del Olmo (ed.) *Drogas. El conflicto de fin de siglo*. (Cuadernos de Nueva Sociedad N° 1) Caracas: Editorial Nueva Sociedad.

Thoumi, F. (1998) *Why some countries produce illegal drugs and others don't*. ISPAC Paper: unpublished.

Thoumi, F. (2001) Illegal Drugs in Colombia: from illegal economic boom to social crisis, in: *Annals of the Academy of Political and Social Sciences* (forthcoming).

Tilly, C. (1985) War Making and State Making as Organized Crime, in: P. Evans et al. (eds) *Bringing the State Back in*. Cambridge: Cambridge University Press.

Tilly, C. and C. Tilly (1995) Capitalist Work and Labor Markets, in: N.J. Smelser and R. Swedberg (eds) *The Handbook of Economic Sociology*. Princeton: Princeton University Press.

Tokatlian. J. (1990) La Política Exterior de Colombia hacia Estados Unidos 1978-1990, in: C. Arrieta et al. *Narcotráfico en Colombia: dimensiones políticas, económicas, jurídicas e internacionales*. Bogotá: Tercer Mundo Editores.

Tokatlian, J. (1995) *Drogas, Dilemas y Dogmas. Estados Unidos y la narcocriminalidad organizada en Colombia*. Bogotá: Tercer Mundo Editores.

Tokatlian, J. (2000) *Globalización, Narcotráfico y Violencia. Siete ensayos sobre Colombia*. Buenos Aires: Grupo Editorial Norma.

Tovar Pinzón, H. (1994) La economía de la coca en América Latina. El paradigma colombiano, in: *Revista Nueva Sociedad*, 130, pp. 86-111.

Umaña Luna, O. Fals Borda and G. Guzmán (1962) *La Violencia en Colombia*, vol. I Bogotá: Ediciones Tercer Mundo.

UNDCP (1997) *World Drug Report 1997*. Vienna: UNDCP.

UNDCP (2001) *World Drug Report 2000*. Vienna: UNDCP

Uprimny, R. (1994a) Narcotráfico, régimen político, violencias y derechos humanos en Colombia, in: R. Vargas Meza (ed.) *Drogas, Poder y Región en Colombia*, 1. Bogotá: Cinep.

Uprimny, R. (1994b) Notas sobre el fenómeno del narcotráfico en Colombia y las reacciones a su control, in: Comisión Andina de Juristas (1994) *Drogas y Control Penal en los Andes*. Lima: CAJ.

Uribe, S. (1997) Los cultivos ilícitos en Colombia, in: F. Thoumi et al. *Drogas ilícitas en Colombia. Su impacto económico, político y social*. Bogotá: Ariel - UNDP - DNE.

Urrea Giraldo, F. (1993) Principales tendencias de los procesos migratorios en Colombia y la internacionalización de la economía, in: *Estudios Migratorios Latinoamericanos*, 8, 23, pp. 5-17.

Urrutia, M (1990) Análisis Costo-Beneficio del Tráfico de Drogas para la Economía Colombiana, in: *Coyuntura Económica*, 20, October.

US Census Bureau (1997) *March 1997 Current Population Survey (CPS)*.

Vargas Meza, R. (1999a) *Fumigación y Conflicto: Políticas antidrogas y deslegitimación del estado en Colombia*. Bogotá: Tercer Mundo Editores, TNI and Acción Andina.

Vargas Meza, R. (1999b) *Drogas, mascaras y juegos. Narcotráfico y conflicto armado en Colombia*. Bogotá: Tercer Mundo Editores, TNI and Acción Andina.

Verbraeck, H. (1985) *Junkies, een etnografie over oude heroïnegebruikers in Utrecht*. Utrecht: WGU.

Villamarin Pulido, L.A. (1996) *El Cartel de las Farc*. Bogotá: El Faraón.

Wagstaff, A. (1989) Economic aspects of the illicit drug market and drug enforcement policies, in: *British Journal of Addiction*, 84, 10, October, pp. 1173-1182.

Waldinger, R. (1995) The 'other side' of embeddedness: a case-study of the interplay of economy and ethnicity, in: *Ethnic and Racial Studies*, 18, 3, pp. 555-580.

Waldorf, D. et al. (1991) *Cocaine Changes. The experience of using and quitting*. Philadelphia: Temple University Press.

Wasserman, S. and K. Faust (1994) *Social Network Analysis: Methods and Applications*. Cambridge: Cambridge University Press.

Weppner, R. (1977) Street Ethnography: Problems and Prospects, in: Weppner, R. (ed.) *Street Ethnography: Selected Studies of Crime and Drug Use in a Natural Setting*. Beverly Hills: Sage.

Whynes D. (1992) The Colombian Cocaine Trade and the "War on Drugs", in: A. Cohen et al. (eds) *The Colombian Economy: Issues of Trade and Development*. Boulder: Westview Press.

Whyte, W.F. (1943) *Street Corner Society. The Social Structure of an Italian Slum*. Chicago: The University of Chicago Press.

Williams, T. (1990) *The Cocaine Kids, the Inside Story of a Teenage Drug Ring*. London: Bloomsbury.

Williams, T. et al. (1992) Personal Safety in Dangerous Places, in: *Journal of Contemporary Ethnography*, vol. 21, 3, October, pp. 343-374.

Williams, P. (1995) The New Threat: Transnational Criminal Organizations and International Security, in: *Criminal Organizations*, 9, 3/4, pp. 3-20.

Williams, P. ed. (1997) *Russian Organized Crime. The New Threat?* London: Frank Cass.

Wilson S. and M. Zambrano (1994) Cocaine, Comodity Chains and Drug Politics: A Transnational Approach, in: G. Gereffi and M. Korzeniewicz (eds) *Commodity Chains and Global Capitalism*. Wesport: Praeger.

Wilson, K. and A. Portes (1980) Immigrant Enclaves: an analysis of the labor market experiences of Cubans in Miami, in: *American Journal of Sociology*, 86, pp. 295-319.

Wilson, K. and W. Martin (1982) Ethnic Enclaves: A Comparision of the Cuban and Black Economies in Miami, in: *American Journal of Sociology*, 88, pp. 135-160.

Wood, S. (ed.) (1989) *The Transformation of Work?* London: Unwin Hyman Ltd.

Yeşilgöz, Y. et al. (1996) Georganiseerde misdaad als buurtprobleem, in: *De Gids*, July-August, pp. 644-654.

Yeşilgöz, Y. et al. (1997) *Het Arnhemse Spijkerkwartier*. Utrecht: IRT and Willem Pompe Instituut

Young, J. (1971) *The Drugtakers. The social meaning of drug use*. London: Paladin.

Young, J. (1999) *The Exclusive Society*. London: Sage

Zabludoff, S. (1997) Colombian Narcotics Organizations as Business Enterprises, in: *Transnational Organized Crime*, vol.3, 2, Summer, pp.20-49.

Zaitch, D. (1997) Colombianos en el mercado de la cocaína en Holanda, in: R. del Olmo (ed.) *Drogas. El conflicto de fin de siglo*. (Cuadernos de Nueva Sociedad 1). Caracas: Editorial Nueva Sociedad.

Zaitch, D. and J. Janssen (1996) Kroniek van een aangekondigde verwarring, in: *Tijdschrift voor Criminologie*, jrg 38, 2, pp. 167-183.

Lightning Source UK Ltd.
Milton Keynes UK
UKOW03f2352210114

224958UK00005B/1247/A

…ITIES AT MEDWAY LIBRARY

9 789041 118844